G000127455

The Company desktop guide

4th edition

David M Martin

THOROGOOD

First published 1998, 2nd edition 2004,
3rd edition 2006

Thorogood Publishing Ltd
10-12 Rivington Street
London EC2A 3DU

Telephone: 020 7749 4748 • Fax: 020 7729 6110
Email: info@thorogoodpublishing.co.uk
Web: www.thorogoodpublishing.co.uk

Special discounts for bulk
quantities of Thorogood books
are available to corporations,
institutions, associations and
other organisations. For more
information contact Thorogood
by telephone on 020 7749 4748, by
fax on 020 7729 6110, or email us:
info@thorogoodpublishing.co.uk

A CIP catalogue record for this book is
available from the British Library.

ISBN PB: 1 85418 604 3
        978-185418604-1

Printed in the UK by Ashford Colour Press.

Designed and typeset in the UK by Driftdesign.

About the author

David M Martin, FCIS, FCIPD, FIoD

David is a Fellow of the Chartered Institute of Secretaries, the Chartered Institute of Personnel and Development and the Institute of Directors.

He held senior positions with Xerox (USA) and SGB Group plc, and was Director/Company Secretary of Maynards plc where as well as the full range of the usual corporate duties he designed one of the first employee share ownership schemes, implemented a Group wide system of Consultative Committees and compiled several employee reports, annual reports and employee newsletters, all of which won national awards.

Since 1985 when Maynards was taken over, he has run his own business consultancy – Buddenbrook – carrying out various projects including corporate and internal communications, general administration and personnel documentation, etc., for a wide range of client companies including Filofax, British Aerospace, Safeway, Northern Foods, Boots, Trebor Bassett and others.

He is a regular seminar and conference speaker on company and employment law and personal skills, and has written over 40 business books. The 'clear communication' themes of many of his seminars are reflected in his books, many of which (including the international best-selling *Tough Talking, Tough Telephoning* and *Manipulating Meetings*) have been translated into several foreign languages as well as being available in all English speaking markets in the world. He is the series editor for ICSA's One Stop series for which he wrote the *Company Secretary, Personnel, Director, Customer Care, Property, Communication, Profit Management* and *Meetings* titles and co-wrote *Negotiation*.

He is the author/editor of Gee's looseleaf updating manuals *Employment Letters and Procedures* and *Employment Policies and Handbooks* and is consultant editor of Butterworth Tolley's *Company Secretary's Link*.

His latest books, *The A-Z of Facilities and Property Administration (2007)* and *The A-Z of Employment Practice – 2nd edition* (2006) are both published by Thorogood.

He is a CBI representative on the panel of Employment Tribunal members and is a member of the Registrar of Companies Wider Users committee.

Icons

Throughout the Desktop Guide series of books you will see references and symbols in the margins. These are designed for ease of use and quick reference directing you to key features of the text. The symbols used are:

case   Case study

g   Example

Practical pointers

Checklist

Please note

Throughout the text (other than where it is inappropriate), the masculine includes the feminine. In the interests of an holistic approach there is some deliberate repetition of certain items.

Company classification

'Small' company or Limited Liability Partnership (LLP) is defined as one to which two of the following apply:

- turnover £5.6 million or less

- balance sheet total £2.8 million or less

- average employees 50 or fewer

NOTE: A company with a turnover of less than £5.6million does not need to have its accounts audited.

'Medium' company or LLP – one to which two of the following apply:

- turnover £22.8 million or less

- balance sheet £11.4 or less

- average employees 250 or fewer

Group classification

'Small' group is defined as one to which two of the following apply:

- aggregate turnover £5.6 million net (£6.72 million gross) or less

- aggregate balance sheet total £2.8 million (£3.36 million gross) or less

- average employees 50 or fewer

NOTE:A company with a turnover of less than £5.6 million does not need to have its accounts audited.

'Medium' company or LLP – one to which two of the following apply:

- aggregate turnover £22.8 million (or £27.36 million gross) or less

- aggregate balance sheet £11.4 million (or £13.68 million gross) or less

- average employees 250 or fewer

Compensation and other annually reviewed figures

Many financial obligations in the employment field are reviewed annually. These are listed below and cross-referenced in the text:

- Unfair dismissal – maximum awards : basic £9,300, compensatory £60,600 (Feb 2007)

- Maximum weeks pay 'MWP' (used for redundancy calculation, compensation for failing to deal properly with flexible working request) – £310 (Feb 2007)

- Guarantee pay – £19.60 per day (Feb 2007)

- Statutory sick pay – £72.55 per week (April 2007)

- Statutory Paternity Pay, Statutory Adoption Pay – £112.75 (April 2007) or 90% of wage per week whichever is lower

- Statutory Maternity Pay (for women earning above Lower Earnings Level and with 40 weeks service before Expected Week of Childbirth) – 90% of pay (averaged over the 8 weeks commencing with the 23rd week before the EWC) for 6 weeks and lower of that figure or £112.75 (April 2007) for 33 weeks. A woman not so entitled may be able to claim Statutory Maternity Allowance from the State.

- 'Small employer' limit for reclamation of SSP, SMP, SPP, SAP – (total NI contributions of the previous year were less than) £45,000 (April 2005)

- National Minimum Wage:
    - Full rate £5.52 from (October 2007)
    - Reduced rate £4.60 (October 2007)
    - Youth rate £3.40 p.h. (October 2007)

- Lower Earnings Level (LEL) – £87 p.w. (April 2007)

- Graduate loan repayment threshold: £15,000 (April 2005)

- Inheritance Tax threshold: £300,000 April 2007, £312,000 (April 2008, £325,000 April 2009, £350,000 April 2010)

Statistics

EU classification of employers (with approx. numbers employed in UK)

- Micro enterprise: up to 9 employees (3.7 million)

- Small enterprise: 10 – 49 employees (.3 million)

- Medium enterprise: 50 – 249 employees (5.6 million)

- Large: 250 and over employees – including public service (12.4 million)

- Self-employed: 3.7 million

Proportion of types of employment contracts (approx)

- Full time 57%

- Part time 25%

- Fixed term 6.2%

- Self employed 11.8%

Contents

7

A meeting's two key players – The Chairman and Secretary — 155

8

Board without boredom — 173

9

An inspector calls — 189

17

18

Introduction

Background

Widespread lack of awareness

Personal liability

Practical help

Background

There are now over 2.5 million companies registered at Companies House and the same source indicates there are around 5.5 million names registered as directors and secretaries (of current, dormant or past companies). During my seminars throughout the UK each year I am able to speak directly to over 1,000 of those holding such offices. The impression continues to be that relatively few of them are fully aware of the obligations, responsibilities and liabilities placed upon them under Company Law and which they accept with the appointment as Director and/or Company Secretary. This situation can only worsen as the amount and complexity of legislation increases. The maxim 'ignorance is no excuse' may be valid but with the weight of legislation placed on companies it is difficult to see how many smaller organisations – and even some larger entities – can hope to remain within the law. Indeed it might be argued that that maxim can no longer apply – although to be safe it might be better to let someone else be the first to make that point in court – never be a test case!

Widespread lack of awareness

Assuming those attending such seminars are likely to be some of those most aware of the need to keep up-to-date one can only wonder at the lack of awareness of the others. These impressions were shown in an Institute of Directors' survey which indicated that 58 per cent of those asked were not aware of the Company Directors Disqualification Act 1986. If that were not bad enough, of the 42 per cent who stated they were aware of it, no less than 63 per cent felt it was not relevant to their business and 90 per cent thought it was not relevant to them personally! That Act, like all other company law, affects all Directors – and currently the law makes no distinction between a person who is a Director of a husband and wife company, which employs only the owners, and the massive listed PLC internationally based and employing hundreds of thousands.

Whilst many would welcome the right to be able to contract out of legislation (particularly given the current level of enactment), this is not feasible!

Personal liability

Limited liability companies have, since the mid-1850s, operated under a system of law which has developed piecemeal and in response to scandals of the guilty few, whose actions thus visit additional requirements on the innocent and hardworking vast majority. The liability which is limited in companies is that of the shareholders – not of the Directors whose personal exposure seems to grow daily. Since the passing of the Insolvency Act 1986 (another Act which experience indicates few Directors know about) Directors can be made personally liable to contribute to the assets available to creditors should their company fail and they be held to have traded wrongfully – an area where there are an increasing number of Court actions.

In addition, under employment, health and safety and environmental law, Directors can nowadays be made personally liable. This worrying trend within an increasingly litigious nation shows no sign of abating. Very often such personal liabilities are not insurable.

The increased rate of legislative enactments currently being loaded on to companies and their directors and managers, particularly since 1997, is very worrying. The Institute of Management Development recorded that the UK fell 13 places in the international competitiveness league between 1997 and 2004, whilst the World Economic Forum recorded a similar but not quite as severe drop from 4th to 11th place. It may come as a surprise to politicians, most of whom seem to know little of wealth-creation on which the economic future of the nation depends, that legislation is not the answer to every problem – neither is throwing money at a problem; management is needed. During the last 10 years the EU (particularly) has imposed a constant stream of regulations many of which when domestically implemented have had the effect of hindering the UK's former flexible and responsive economy. The UK Government's own Regulation Task Force estimates compliance costs industry £100 billion each year which is a full 10% of the UK's gross domestic product. However Ruth Lea, Director of Centre for Policy Studies, estimates only around 40% of the regulations visited on UK employers emanate from Brussels. The UK government initiates the majority of legislative requirements and rarely 'contracts out' smaller businesses from any EU initiatives (as some EU member countries do) – indeed very often the domestic legislative equivalent requirements are more restrictive than the original intent. UK legislators tend to enhance the restrictiveness of, or 'gold plate', the EU requirements. Greater legislation may be the Government's instinctive reaction to every problem – it is however unlikely to be the best answer. Ironically, directors are not only expected to ensure compliance with legislation but also to take risks – with the legislation ready to apply sanctions should their decisions be incorrect!

Practical help

Within a year of this edition being published, the Companies Act 2006 will be fully in force. In view of this the decision has been taken with this revised text to assume that Act has been fully introduced and produce a user-friendly and practically orientated handbook aimed at the layman Director. In addition in Appendix III we have set out the implementation schedule demonstrating when various parts of the Act have been, or are to be, implemented.

Thus this desktop guide is for the vast majority of directors who:

- have no legal training (thus although it refers in passing to the law it is not a legal treatise)

- need to know what they have to do (thus it is presented in an essentially practical format with checklists and hints and warnings)

- are pressed for time by virtue of their other priorities (thus it concentrates on the essentials which should enable the Director to 'get by' without breaking company law)

- are concerned about their liabilities (thus it not only outlines how these can arise but also provides practical guidance on minimising the effects of these liabilities)

It would be presumptuous to seek in this book to tell the reader how to run his or her company – although there are brief sections on planning and on leadership of employees which are requirements of Directors which are often overlooked. Nevertheless the book tries to guide those running companies so that they can be assured they will:

- comply with legislation

- ensure their companies are similarly compliant and

- minimise their exposure to personal liability.

Inevitably, it is impossible to explore all ramifications and obligations and thus these contents should be regarded as an essential foundation – a base for further knowledge. This law is complex and this book seeks only to act as a guide through the maze – quite properly in many instances suggesting that readers should take legal advice, however, it should provide the basic knowledge that will at least enable those seeking further knowledge to ask informed questions!

David M Martin

NOTE: This book assumes full implementation of the Companies Act 2006 (CA06), the final tranche of which does not come into effect until 1st October 2008.

Chapter one

The nature of the beast

'Defining the nature of Directors and their role'

Defining the term

How did we get here?

What is a company

Appointment

Appraisal

Joining the throng

What is a 'Director'

A Director's exposure

Aims and purpose

Rolling the message out

Duties

Summary checklist

Defining the term

> **Memo**
>
> To: A newly appointed Director
>
> From: The author
>
> Subject: Your Board appointment
>
> Congratulations on your appointment. May I wish you every success in your new role. However, may I also sound a note of caution – and suggest that you make yourself fully aware of all the responsibilities which you have acquired and the liabilities to which you are now exposed. You may be somewhat taken aback at the breadth of the latter – and even more so at the fact that there is very little you may be able to do about it in terms of personal protection. May I suggest you read on…

> **Memo**
>
> To: An experienced Director
>
> From: The author
>
> Subject: Survival – yours
>
> As a Director of some standing I expect that you are aware of the range of responsibilities and liabilities for which you carry responsibility. I hope you are up-to-date, although since you are also responsible for running your company the time you may have available for keeping up-to-date on current laws, requirements and changes may be limited. Beware – many of these changes are fundamental and, increasingly, the move is to action being taken against the individual rather than the corporate body. In the interests of self-protection, if nothing else, may I suggest you read on…

How did we get here?

Until 1856 unless their company was created by an Act of Parliament and became a 'statute' company entrepreneurs (risk takers who wished to float and operate companies) were responsible for the debts of those companies should they fail. As the British Empire flourished and companies grew to take advantage of the opportunities presented by the expanding trade, so do did the potential liabilities of these entrepreneurial shareholders. Pressure grew to protect the assets of the risk takers and the results were the Companies Acts of 1856 and 1862.

These Acts (a worldwide first, the principles of which have been copied in most countries) created a 'legal persona' – the limited liability company – with virtually the same rights as real or natural persons. However unlike real persons, the shareholding owners of such a company had their liability limited to the total value of the shares they had invested. Once they had paid that, unless they had acted fraudulently, they had no liability to creditors of their companies should these fail. The limited liability company was born.

It is fair to say that within a short time of this introduction of 'limited liability for shareholders', it was hailed as a 'rogues' charter'. The development was accused of being merely 'a means of devising the encouragement of speculation, overtrading and swindling'. These very real concerns were that some directors of such companies (who very often were the shareholders) could run the company into the ground knowing that they could walk away from a failed company with no liability to the unpaid creditors. Such observers were of course proved right and in a number of instances this is exactly what happened.

In addition in some instances it was clear that although the directors' names were known, in fact the companies were being 'directed' by persons whose presence was not acknowledged or disclosed. Thus the directors' actions were being manipulated by a kind of 'eminence gris' or 'shadowy' persona who actually had control of the company.

The price of limited liability protection is disclosure of information. Limited liability companies are required to 'disclose' information by lodging their details in the public arena. In 1844 the Registrar of Companies office was set up as a repository of information concerning companies, their ownership and control and direction and to provide a source of such information to which the public had access.

Information about limited liability companies was thus made available mainly to protect the creditors since they could inspect the financial results of the companies to which they were advancing credit.

Amongst other data, directors' details had to be lodged – but obviously the details of those pulling the strings of the board were not. The numbers of companies were quite small – under 100,000 at 1900 and under 500,000 by 1985. The explosion of numbers of companies has occurred since 1985 so that there are now 2.5 million.

The continuing legislative movement

As is customary, once it is known there are legislative loopholes, subsequent legislation is introduced to attempt to plug the gaps. Since the mid-nineteenth century every 15/20 years new company legislation has performed this function as well as adding considerably to the regulatory requirements placed on limited liability companies – and their officers.

From time to time – e.g. in 1948 and 1985 – there have been major rewrites of company legislation consolidating previous primary and secondary legislation. The 1985 Act was notable since not only did it consolidate all the legislation since the 1948 Act but in addition for the first time defined the 'shadowy persons' not acknowledged as directors at Companies House referred to above. Section 741 of that Act states a 'shadow director' means '*a person in accordance with whose directions or instructions the directors of the company are accustomed to act*'.

The Insolvency Act 1986

Linking with the 1985 Act and close on its heels, the Insolvency Act for the first time since 1855 placed liability on those actually running companies. The twin offences of 'wrongful' and 'fraudulent' trading were created. These require that directors (and others) who continue to run their companies when they knew or (the serious obligation) should have known that their companies were taking on credit which might not be paid on the due date – or within a reasonable time of that date – can be required to contribute personally to the creditors if their companies fail.

It must be said that there have not been that many prosecutions of culpable directors mainly since the Department of Trade and Industry's attitude is that unless there is a very good chance of success that it would not be appropriate to spend public money in such circumstances. (One is then tempted to wonder 'why bother to pass the legislation?') However the responsibility for initiating proceeding and gaining potential recovery from wealthy directors who have broken the law in this way has now been passed to Forensic Investigation and Recovery Services (FIRS) who may generate more cases.

Fraudulent trading is proscribed anew in the Companies Act 2006. S993 states that any person who carries on the business of a company with intent to defraud the creditors (or anyone else) is guilty of an offence for which the sanctions are potentially imprisonment for up to 10 years or a fine (or both) as well as personal liability for the debts.

The new Act

The above brought us to the mid 1990s. On 1st April 1997, Margaret Beckett, then the President of the Board of Trade, launched a consultation process that would eventually result, nine years later in a completely new Companies Act 'fit for the 21st Century'. The Companies Act 2006 received Royal Assent in November 2006 and will be fully in force by October 2008. The following text assumes its introduction, which is entirely logical since all parts (other than sections repealed which are detailed herein) of the 1985 Companies Act now appear in the new Act. (See Appendix III.)

What is a company

As set out above a company is a legal person – created by and operating under Company Law. It has an existence which is separate from its owners (shareholders, guarantors etc.) and separate from its officers (directors, company secretary and managers). A company is brought into being via a process laid down under the Companies Act – and it can be wound up under the same Act. Unlike real persons however, a company, as a legal person, can not only 'die' but by decision of the Court can be brought back to life in order to face a liability claim.

The Companies Act does not permit shareholders to run companies – they appoint directors to do that. In essence shareholders' rights are restricted to appointing directors and, if they do not like the way their company is being run, removing them. Recently in the UK there have been examples of shareholder power in the agreement of who should be (or continue to be) directors. A shareholder who does interfere with the running of a company runs the risk of becoming a 'shadow director' (see Chapter 2) with potential liability as such.

A company as a legal person must comply with its legal obligations – not only company law, but all laws. If it breaks those laws, then the company can be made subject to the sanctions set out in those laws. However, in most cases the company acts via its agents – the officers – who can also be held personally liable for such actions. If the actions are very serious then imprisonment may be the sanction. A company cannot be imprisoned – but the officers can.

Checklist: There are several types of companies

a) Private LTD, shareholder-owned companies. A company can have just one share owned by one shareholder (that is a 'Single Member Company') but many have more than one share and multiple shareholders. Private LTD companies constitute the vast majority of the 2.5 million listed at Companies House indeed over 90% of the companies listed there have fewer than 5 shareholders. An LTD is referred to as a 'private company' since the directors have the right in the Articles to restrict who owns the shares since they can block a share transfer if they do not want the proposed purchaser as a shareholder.

b) Companies Limited by Guarantee. Often used by charities and associations, clubs, Chambers of Commerce etc, these companies usually have no shareholders (although some older Guarantee companies do have shareholders) but simply a number of people who guarantee should the company become insolvent that they will contribute to the extent of their guarantee to the assets to pay off any creditors. Since there are no shareholders no dividends can be paid.

c) Unlimited companies do not seek to limit the liability of their shareholders who thus have unlimited liability for the debts should the company fail. These companies are mainly used to gain tax advantages. Since the shareholders have unlimited liability these companies (unless members of a group etc.) normally do not have to file their accounts at Companies House.

d) Public Limited Companies (PLCs) of which confusingly there are two types:

    i) Unlisted or unquoted PLCs must not place any restriction on who owns their shares and thus any Article restricting this must be removed. In addition, such companies must have a minimum share capital of £50,000 of which 25% or more must be paid up.

    ii) Listed or quoted PLCs which tend to be the largest companies and who have applied for a 'listing' on the London Stock Exchange. Due to listing requirements they must have made a minimum of 30% of their shares available to the public. Their share capital tends to be considerable.

e) Statute companies. Until the mid-1850s the only way in which share-holders could obtain the protection of limited liability was to have a company formed under an Act of Parliament.

f) Royal Charter companies. Some companies (particularly those used by professional bodies) can be formed under a charter signed by the monarch.

g) Partnership 'entities'. For some time partnerships have been able to become Limited Liability Partnerships (LLP) granting the principle of limited liability to their partners who otherwise have unlimited personal liability. An LLP is a hybrid – it is neither a partnership nor a company.

h) Oversea company

A subsidiary of overseas owners – e.g. a branch – is classified under the Companies Act as an 'oversea company'. Within one month of a company incorporated outside Great Britain establishing a place of business here it must send certain information to Companies House:

- the charter or articles

- names of the directors and secretary

- list of persons in the UK authorised to accept service of notice on behalf of the company etc.

i) Dormant

Just over 300,000 companies registered at Companies House are not trading – they are dormant (sleeping and inactive). They are required to submit an Annual Return each year and accounts (although instead of an actual set of accounts – which might be fairly skeletal – they can submit form DCA). At any time the company can be re-activated.

NOTE: It is widely thought that keeping such a named company dormant protects the name. Whilst it may stop another company with an identical name being registered (although even this is not impossible), it may not stop another trader using the name (without 'Ltd' at the end). The rule is that if a company has been placed on the register with a name which a previous company feels is too like its own name the original company has only one year to object. If an objection is raised, this will generate an investigation and if the complaint is upheld the new company will be required to change its name. However, if a year or more has expired there is nothing that can be done.

The protection given to companies whereby another company cannot have the same name is somewhat limited even within the UK. A company registered in the Isle of Man or Jersey, Guernsey etc. could have the same name as a company registered at Companies House. The mainland Registrar is unable to prevent this, if it does not establish a place of business here (in which case it would be required to comply with the Companies Act provisions regarding an oversea company) but merely operates via third parties (solicitors, agents etc).

j) Joint Venture companies

To develop a new product or concept two or more bodies (not necessarily companies) may agree to set up and operate a jointly owned subsidiary. In addition to framing the Articles of Association they will normally enter into a shareholders agreement to set out their relationship and the relationship they may have with those nominated to serve on the board. Most Joint Venture companies are LTDs although there is nothing to stop them being PLCs.

k) Societas Europaea (SE)

Since October 2004 it has been possible to form an SE which is a European Public Limited Liability company formed under the European Company Statute (ECS).The ECS contains a regulation allowing the formation of such a company under core company law provisions which apply throughout the European Union. An SE must have a minimum share capital of 120,000 Euros and is available to commercial bodies with interests in more than one European country. An SE allows UK companies to engage in cross border mergers with companies from other EU member states.Thus, rather than taking over a company in another member state a UK company can agree with the other company the formation of a jointly owned SE subsidiary or holding company.

l)   Community Interest Companies (CIC)

Enacted on 1st July 2005, this new type of company could be of use (to companies limited by shares – private or public – or guarantee) where the aim is:

–   a purpose that a reasonable person would think was beneficial to the public interest or community

–   to make its services/goods available widely and not to 'an unduly restricted group'.

The assets of the company are subject to a legal 'lock' in that they can only be used for public benefit purposes – although a CIC can pay its directors. A CIC could be used for the benefit of the employees of a single body provided its activities are not conducted for private gain.

A CIC limited by shares can either stipulate that no dividend will be paid on the shares or that only a limited dividend will be paid (the amount of the limit will be fixed by the State e.g. by reference to the Bank of England's base rate, and may be subject to periodic change). However where a dividend is to be paid to another CIC, the limit may be waived.

The existing control available to directors of LTD companies (i.e. that they can prevent the transfer of shares to anyone of whom they do not approve) is also available to boards of CICs.

(**NOTE**:A CIC cannot be a charity and its profits must be used for the public interest.)

Appointment

An appointment to the Board is a matter of achievement and praise but it is far, far more than that and those that feel that they have 'made it' when they hear those magic (and often long-awaited) words 'we'd like you to join the Board' owe it to themselves and their dependents to consider fully all the implications in at least as much detail as the perks and rewards that are now their entitlement. Indeed, so onerous are the existing and new obligations now placed on Directors and so swiftly are the occasions being extended where the Director may find him or herself personally liable, that appointees might be forgiven for feeling that the elevation may more closely resemble a poisoned chalice than a well-deserved promotion. This is not to say that any such appointment should be rejected but simply to advise that before making the jump from manager to director, the full implications of this quantum leap should be researched, understood and appreciated – which is the intent of this substantially revised edition of this Desktop Guide.

There is an assumption that directors understand their companies and their parameters and the environment within which they operate. Like many assumptions this may be false. Companies should discover the range of knowledge of their directors – and supply means by which any gaps are filled.

Many forward thinking companies ensure that their recruits are made to feel at home by being introduced to new colleagues and surroundings, and given an outline of the administration applicable to their new position and grounding in what is required of them in their job. Although this undertaking is widely referred to as 'induction' it may be better described as 'familiarisation'.

'Familiarisation' should have three distinct sections. Some items may appear in more than one section, since repetition is a fundamental way of ensuring we retain information – particularly when there is so much that is new to be assimilated. The three sections could be termed as 'introduction', 'induction' and 'instruction'.

- Introduction covers the application process, the interview(s), offer of employment and first day of work when many personal introductions will have to be made.

- Induction is the more formalized process of working through a checklist of items that a newcomer needs to know in order that they can start to contribute to the work of the organisation. Many of these will be fairly mundane (and thus tend to be taken for granted – and possibly overlooked – by 'old hands') but are nevertheless important to a newcomer.

- Instruction is the process by which there is reinforcement of knowledge provided during the earlier sections, but detailed and specific coaching in performing the job and moving to a level of required competence in that job.

So how does this apply to directors?

To some extent this is a non-question. Why should there be any difference in terms of approach between the most senior persons in the organisation – and the most junior? Even the most senior persons will require basic information about the organisation particularly if it is new to them, and the procedures etc. Operating at a senior level may well enable the routine aspects of the process to be speeded up but the organisation still needs to be able to satisfy itself that the requirements of the director are themselves satisfied. If there is a detailed familiarization process for (say) a senior management appointment, that could be used as a base however there are additional items that directors need to be made aware of.

Directors have a potential and personal legal liability for the activities of their companies, not shared with most other employees. 'The buck stops in the boardroom' and thus the boardroom needs to know for what they have responsibility. If the answers to the following are 'no' – coaching and/or reading may be necessary. Almost certainly this will be on-going since many aspects are constantly changing – it might be helpful for a brief précis of legislative and other changes to be presented at each Board meeting.

Checklist: Directors training/knowledge

Legal obligations

Does the director understand the legislative environment under which the company operates e.g.

- the basis and outline of company law?

- the latest commercial legislation including competition law?

- outline requirements of employment law?

- general requirements of other legislation affecting the company?

- the internal operating rules of the company (e.g. the Articles of Association)?

- has the Chairman checked the scope of such knowledge?

- and that the Board are responsible for the information required to be regularly filed at Companies House?

Finance

Does the director understand:

- the management and published accounts and ancillary data?

- that he has personal responsibility for the figures?

- the method by which queries should be raised?

- that since he must always be confident of the future solvency of the company he should not allow credit to be taken on when it might not be paid on the due date or within a reasonable time thereof?

- that commitment to expenditure on behalf of the company should only be in accordance with the regularly reviewed authority / risk chart?

Board work

Does the director realize

- that for the company's success, its aims and the means to attain those aims must be delineated (and updated regularly)

- that he has an obligation to attend Board meetings – and to contribute to the discussion (which infers that he is satisfactorily briefed on all matters)?

- that he should always declare an interest in any third party with which the company is dealing?

- that he should always exercise his decision-making process independently of other directors (even if this means he is in a minority of one)?

- that minutes should be read and agreed (or objected to and corrected) and not passed without consideration?

- his role is proactive not reactive – he must make things happen?

- that the performance of every board member should be regularly and formally assessed?

- that he should insist that at least two working days are allowed between the receipt of items (other than routine matters) and a decision time?

- that he should insist decisions are properly minuted and that any required dissent notes are included?

- that if there are matters of which he is unaware (both in and outside the Board room) that this should be made clear and he must take steps to obtain the information?

Morality

Has the director:

- been given a copy of the Code of Ethics, Corporate Governance and/or any other similar requirements?

- shown that he is he content that his knowledge of such items is adequate?

- been told that bribes inducements etc must not be offered or made by any person on behalf of the company?

- been told that, if he becomes aware of wrongdoing, he should take immediate steps to ensure it ceases and the errors are, if at all possible, rectified?

Accountability

Does the director realise:

- that he is answerable to the shareholders for the activities of the company and its results

- that he is expected to take risks but only after a proper assessment of those risks and their potential outcome

- that contingency and disaster recovery plans should be prepared and updated covering all major eventualities

- that he is answerable to the various regulatory authorities for the activities of the company and its employees

Employees

Does the director appreciate:

- that the true value and worth of employees can only be gained if they are properly and continuously trained and/or coached in their work and any changes?

- that the Board should regularly audit personnel practice and inter-facing – to generate real communication between the parties?

NOTE: This checklist draws attention to some of the main areas that need to be addressed. It needs to be customized to fit individual companies. Working through the headings will almost certainly generate other areas needing attention. With relatively little re-arranging the checklist could be used as a performance review basis since ideally directors should be assessed and their attention drawn to areas capable of improvement.

Appraisal

In addition to the above familiarisation concept (which listed or quoted PLCs are obliged under the Stock Exchange listing agreement to use) those companies are also obliged to ensure the performance of Board members is appraised each year. The following checklist may serve as a basis for such a process.

In the past year has the director:

a) accepted and worked towards the decisions arrived at by the Board?

b) contributed effectively to the corporate strategy decision making?

c) formulated the current and immediate future aims and purposes of the company and worked to the implementation of these?

d) ensured tactical decisions and actions have taken the same general direction as the strategy of the company (i.e. ensured that short term decisions have not been made which impede the progress to the long term strategy)?

e) helped formulate/update, promulgate and ensured adherence to an internal code of ethics?

f) ensured the company complies with its own constitution (i.e. the Memorandum and Articles) and, if a public listed company, the listing agreement, and custom and practice for the industry?

g) acted effectively as company spokesperson, promoting the corporate entity and its products/services at all times?

h) kept up to date his/her skills and knowledge and made it available at board level (and through board members and management at all levels)?

i) ensured his/her own staff are motivated to perform well, and warned and disciplined (in accordance with pre-set rules) when performance or actions have not been in accordance with requirements?

j) complied with controls over the commitment of the company to contracts, etc., and adequate authority control over all purchases and ensured those under his/her control have also complied?

k) displayed understanding of the financial records and reports of the company?

l) worked towards ensuring the products and services of the company are developed so that continuity of earning power of the organisation is continued and continual?

m) assisted effectively in the expansion of the company based on well-researched, well-prepared, and well-considered, plans?

n) updated or initiated contingency plans to protect its earning capacity in the event of a downturn or change in demand, and the effects of possible disasters affecting operations?

o) helped protect the corporate entity and the products/services from criticism, attack and loss as far as possible?

p) displayed comprehension of all new legislative enactments affecting the organisation?

q)   attended formal and informal meetings of the board and made effective contributions?

r)   performed in a proactive manner to the challenges affecting the company and/or his/her department?

s)   taken a properly independent attitude to Board decisions?

and so on.

NOTE: This seeks to identify the areas that could be addressed. A simple 'yes' may not be sufficient however and it may be better to require justification of the answer!

Joining the throng

In the United Kingdom there are over 2,500,000 companies registered at the three Companies Houses (Cardiff for England and Wales, Edinburgh for Scotland and Belfast for Northern Ireland). Every company must have a Director – and many have more than one. Many holders of the office have several directorships, and there are around 5.5 million directors names registered at Cardiff alone. This is roughly 9 per cent of the whole population, which is a sizable proportion of the total, bearing in mind that more than a few of these will be wealthy and powerful individuals able to wield a disproportionate amount of influence. Because such influence and power can be exercised for bad as well as good the parameters under which Directors are required to operate are increasingly defined – and constrained. Nowadays, society is becoming aware that power is moving away from politicians (who, whatever their faults are, at least in theory, subject to the electorate's choice) and towards corporations. As a result of amalgamations and takeovers, evident particularly since the globalisation of capital markets, the move is towards internationally based corporations becoming ever larger and more powerful. Over 50 per cent of the 100 largest entities in the world (that is including countries) are corporations. General Motors sales are 'bigger' than Denmark or Thailand, Ford Motor Co sales are 'bigger' than Turkey and WalMart sales (even before they took over Asda) were 'bigger' than Greece. These companies and corporations are controlled in theory by their shareholders but in practice by their Directors. To some people this is a subject of some concern which has been evidenced in recent years by pressure to enact ever tighter controls to try to ensure compliance and responsible corporate governance. There is no doubt that this move will continue and that every Director will be required to comply with a larger range of laws, practices and requirements backed by increasingly severe fines and penalties, and an extension of their personal liability.

What is a 'Director'

Most people will understand or assume, that a Director 'directs' in the same way that a manager 'manages' and a supervisor 'supervises', even though they might then be hard put to actually define the verbs used to 'define' the nouns. It seems logical to require a definition of the word 'director' and even more logical, since it is company law with which directors must comply, to refer to the latest Act to find a definition. Immediately, however, we strike a problem since nowhere in company law is the term 'Director' properly defined – even though the numerous obligations and requirements placed upon such persons and the penalties for their non-observance are dealt with at length. Indeed it may come as some surprise, since most companies are controlled by 'Boards of Directors', to realise that the legislation does not require companies to have a Board either – and neither does it stipulate that, if there is a Board, that it should meet (although how directors who do not meet would be able to demonstrate the exercise of their required 'duty of care', if challenged, is questionable). The situation is further confused by Section 161 of the Companies Act 2006 referring to 'the acts of a director' being valid notwithstanding any defect in his appointment. By using the word 'manager' with that of 'director' the Act apparently equates the role of the direction of the company with that of managing it. (One assumes the inference is that the 'manager' would be a 'general manager' rather than a departmental manager.) Even more confusion may be caused by the legislation referring to a company's 'officers' – the 'officers' being 'the directors, the company secretary and managers'.

Case study: Disclosing own breach

In *Tesco Stores Ltd v Pook*, a senior manager fraudulently arranged for payments on false invoices and received a bribe from the 'supplier'. Directors and senior managers not only owe their employers a fiduciary duty they also have an obligation to disclose their breach to the employer and advise their employer of any secret profits. Pook was held to be in breach of this fiduciary duty, and was required to pass the bribe to Tesco. In addition, the fraudulent receipts had to be repaid.

S 250 of the Companies Act 2006 repeats an earlier legal 'definition' stating:

'director' includes any person occupying the position of director, by whatever name called' which although it may be a warning to those acting as Directors without being properly appointed that they might become personally liable, is of little assistance in terms of a definition of what a director actually does. It may help if we suggest that a director is someone who:

- takes complete (but possibly shared) legal responsibility for all the actions and activities of a company and those working for it;

- determines the aims of the company and decides lawful and safe methods and procedures whereby such aims are attained; and

- plans the activities of and leads those working for the company to achieve such plans.

This may not be an ideal definition (and of course it has no legal standing) but at least it may serve to underline several important issues, particularly to those taking on the duties for the first time. These duties include the items listed in the checklist [overleaf/below] (which itself is illustrative rather than exhaustive).

A Director's exposure

1. Complete range of legal obligations and responsibilities. It is after all not only company law obligations that Directors assume but also those arising from the laws on employment, commerce, competition, environment, health and safety and so forth (all of which are ever-increasing in breadth and depth);

2. Responsibility for the actions of those employed by the company and its agents. There is an obligation to ensure, as far as possible, that they all act within the law, which in turn entails an obligation to set down and police adequate procedures and controls;

3. Acting as a Board, to lead the team that works for them in order to achieve the aims they have set the company; and

4. To determine the aims of and for the company, and generate plans to achieve such aims. Failure to attain such aims (or at least to preserve the status quo) could lead Directors into direct conflict with the shareholders who appointed them as their 'stewards' to operate their company.

Aims and purpose

Since 1855 companies have been required to have two constitutional documents:

*   a Memorandum of Association which states the date of incorporation, name and number, registered office, share capital, initial subscribers, and the objects or aims of the company

*   a set of Articles of Association which set out the internal rules by which the company would be operated by the directors.

(If a company did not adopt Articles then the pro forma set in Table A of the relevant Companies Act applied. Most companies adopted much of Table A with deletions and additions to customise it to suit their particular needs.)

The new Act effectively abolishes the main content of the Memorandum – the objects clause – 'what the company exists to do'.

The company's objects clause (which tend to be very lengthy attempting to allow all the things companies could possibly wish to do) was formerly a guide (and limitation) for the directors. If they allowed the company to do something not covered by its objects clause then they were stated to be acting 'ultra vires' – that is, beyond its, and their powers.

'Ultra vires' was effectively abolished by the 1989 Companies Act as far as the company and third parties were concerned – that is the contract would be binding whether it was allowed by the objects clause or not. The danger for the directors was that in allowing the company to trade outside its objects clause they could be held liable and the shareholders could hold them liable. The shareholder could subsequently ratify the matter (thereby effectively changing the objects clause – a change which needed to be filed at Companies House).

In addition the directors were best advised to obtain from the shareholders confirmation that they would not be held liable for any loss occasioned by entering into a contract outside that allowed by the objects clause.

The 1989 Act permitted companies to adopt as their objects clauses *'the company will be a general commercial company'*. This dilution of the restrictiveness of the objects clause was not taken up in many cases since banks asked to advance money to the company disliked such unrestrictive clauses.

The new Act overcomes such opposition by removing all the 'restrictions' of the objects clause (other than for companies that are charities). This may pose a problem for directors seeking to borrow money on behalf of the company since banks may well ask directors to personally guarantee the loans they advance, or possibly to give an undertaking for what purpose the money will be used (with personal liability if the funds are used for other purposes).

The detailed objects clauses in existing companies' Memorandums will now be deemed to be part of the Articles of those companies. For new companies the Memorandum will simply deal with the date of incorporation, company name and number, and the names of the initial subscribers.

The objects clause is effectively abolished in that a company's objects will be unrestricted unless the Articles restrict them (**s 31**). If the company alters the position regarding the objects under the Articles then this must be advised to Companies House (CH) and the change will not be effective until CH register the change. The Registrar will be able to force a company to file an updated set of Articles.

In fact even the detailed objects clauses usually give only the most general description of the aims of the company and one of the prime considerations of every Board should be to determine its operational aims, not just for its own use as a guide in planning for and directing the company, but also as a criteria for motivating and managing those who work for it. Increasingly companies are adopting aims, visions or corporate missions in order to identify objectives and to act as criteria for action.

Rolling the message out

In his book '*Making it happen*', former Chief Executive of ICI and star of the BBC TV series '*Troubleshooter*', Sir John Harvey Jones states 'with the best will in the world and the best Board in the world, and the best strategic direction in the world, nothing will happen unless everyone down the line understands what they are trying to achieve and gives of their best'. Unless the Company knows where it is going it can have no firm purpose. Aims are for Directors to develop (ideally with the active involvement of their employees – see Chapter 11) and codify, but they need to be regularly updated – and of course to be promulgated and achieved by a process of detailed planning, revision and execution of the acts entailed. Perhaps this epitomises the main role of a Director which we can summarise as:

'knowing where he wants to take whatever it is that he has control of, and ensuring that the company is constantly moved towards those goals'.

Lacking codified and promulgated aims and the plans that support them there is a danger that the company may drift into activities rather than be directed to purposeful ends – which may not be in the interests of the shareholders who appoint the Directors as their stewards. The aims also provide the shareholders with a criterion against which the performance of the Directors can be measured.

Duties

Having attempted to define the term 'Director' and demonstrated the need to delineate the aims of the company, it may also be helpful to list the various duties a Director would be expected to perform and the manner in which they are to perform them. Taking the latter aspects first, the manner in which a Director and the Board are to act will be found in the Articles which should be regarded as the 'the **Director's rule book**' and their contents known, if not by heart, at least in terms of a working knowledge. Like the Memorandum, the Articles are approved by the shareholders and can only be altered by the shareholders. To assist companies in drafting their Articles, each Companies Act (other than amending legislation such as the Companies Act 1989) includes a specimen set of Articles. Two draft sets of Articles (one for PLCs and one for LTDs) were drafted to accompany the Companies Act 2006. Companies are at liberty to use either of the drafts (or parts of them) as their Articles – or to 'mix and match' some of the suggested clauses with their own substitutions (or to devise their own Articles in addition or entirety). From whatever source they are drawn, the Articles belong to and emanate from the shareholders and are binding on the Directors.

NOTE: The draft Articles for both PLCs and LTDs can be downloaded from the DTI website. In Appendix IV are some suggested headings for Articles that could be added to the LTD draft.

With a group of companies (e.g. a holding company and several subsidiaries) it may be convenient to arrange (or alter) the Articles of the subsidiaries so that they all have a standard format (or are even identical) to avoid needing to remember which Articles apply to which company.

Directors could be said to have two sets of duties – those placed upon them by membership of the Board and those placed on them individually. Board membership embraces the doctrine of collective responsibility – the Board takes policy decisions as an entity rather than by individual Directors (although they may also take individual decisions) and is accountable to the shareholders. It has been proposed under current draft European Company Law that the Directors of a Board could be made personally liable for the actions of each of their colleagues. Because Boards make decisions as entities it is essential that there are properly taken and approved minutes of their meetings and decisions (see Chapter 8) and that these are adequately protected for posterity and are available for reference – not only in the normal course of the Company's activities but also in Court if there is a challenge.

As far as personal responsibilities are concerned, inevitably this will vary from Director to Director and indeed from company to company and the following checklist should be customised for both company and individual. Further, in the same way that the aims need to be updated from time to time to reflect changing circumstances, so too does any list of duties. Companies do not stand still – they either expand and survive, or contract and ultimately go out of business. Further the environment, both commercial and legal, within which they operate is also constantly changing and the aims and the list of duties need to reflect such changes.

NOTE: Since the rules laid down by the shareholders (the 'Articles') are binding on the directors, they should be known by the directors. Failing to comply with the Articles could mean personal liability on the part of the directors responsible; such a failure being actionable by the shareholders. Thus, particularly where there are shareholders who are not also directors, compliance with the Articles is vital.

Duties checklist:

The Companies Act 2006 for the first time legally introduces duties with which directors are expected to comply, namely:

1. To act within their powers (S171)

Few directors seem to read their company's Articles which set out the rules under which the shareholders are expecting them to run their company. Directors of LTDs that decide to operate without a Company Secretary would need to ensure one of their number – if not all – know the contents of the Articles and tries to ensure they do not act in excess of those powers. Directors who act in breach of the requirements of the Articles are said to act *ultra vires* – beyond their powers and are liable to the shareholders as such.

2. To promote the success of the company (S172)

The section states that directors must act in good faith and in the interests of the members whilst taking into account the interests of employees, customers, the environment and suppliers; and being aware of the long term consequences of decisions and the desirability of the company maintaining a reputation for high standards of business conduct. This of course may be easier said than done bearing in mind some of the above interests could be diametrically opposed. Minutes of Board meetings might have to be drafted carefully.

3. To exercise independent judgement (S173)

In the case of *Gwyer & Associates and anor. v. London Wharf (Limehouse) Ltd & ors*, a director made no effort to ascertain what were the interests of his company before voting on a Board resolution. The Court held he was not only negligent but also in breach of his fiduciary duty to exercise his discretion independently and bona fides in the interests of the company. In other words, directors should be prepared to be a minority of one. (If they are it might be advisable for them to require that the fact is noted in the Minutes.)

4. To exercise reasonable care skill and diligence (S174)

The test here is that the director should act with the degree of care skill and diligence that would be exercised by a diligent person with the general knowledge skill and experience reasonably expected of a person carrying out the functions for which they are responsible (wording taken virtually verbatim from the judgement in the *D'Jan* case).

5. To avoid conflicts of interest (S175)

A director will not breach this requirement if:

a)   the conflict has been authorised by the directors or

b)   for an LTD it is not specifically prohibited by the Articles, or

c)   for a PLC the directors are given specific power to allow it.

6. Not to accept benefits from third parties (S176)

However, if the benefit cannot reasonably be regarded as giving rise to a conflict of interests, the benefit can be allowed to subsist. In addition the section permits a director to seek authorization from the Board to exploit personally some property or opportunity even though there is a conflict between his interests and those of the company. In an LTD this can be done provided there is nothing in its Constitution banning it. However directors of PLCs can only do this if there is specific authorization in their company's Constitution that allows it.

7. To declare any interest in proposed transactions with the company (S177)

Such a declaration can be either a specific (**S184**) or general (**S185**) notice but a director does not have to make a declaration if the interest cannot reasonably be regarded as likely to give rise to a conflict.

Case study: Fraudulent concealment

In *Item Software (UK) Ltd v Fassihi & Ors*, a Director sabotaged negotiations between the Company (of which he was a Director) and a third party, so that he could divert the contract (and business) to himself. The Director was held to have breached his duties by:

a) sabotaging the negotiations which was a breach; and

b) failing to tell the company of that breach.

The Court agreed that this was fraudulent concealment and stated that if a Director appropriates business for himself then he has a duty to account to the company for any profit. The Director was ordered to pay damages for his failure to disclose the breach.

It may be helpful to clothe the bare bones of the legislation by identifying more detailed and comprehensive duties as follows:

- To ensure the strategy of the company is formulated, known widely and adhered to.

- To formulate the aims and purposes of the company and ensure that these are both known and borne in mind internally at all times, and that at appropriate times they are promulgated, with the strategic direction of the company, externally (e.g. to the media, shareholders, advisers, etc.).

- To formulate, promulgate and ensure adherence to internal procedures, codes of ethics and required behaviour.

- To ensure the company acts in accordance with the requirements of company statutes, Stock Exchange listing agreement (if a public listed company) and custom and practice for the industry.

- To ensure the company acts in accordance with the requirements of all other statutes – employment law, commercial law, environment law, competition law, health and safety law, road traffic law etc.

  NOTE: The Accounting Practices Board recently suggested that Boards should compile a register of all the laws and regulations with which their companies are required to comply. Compiling such a register is of course merely an administrative act – the underlying purpose of the suggestion is for a complete set of the company's obligations to be generated thus encouraging compliance – and policing. Indeed many companies would find the 'simple' act of recording the Acts is virtually impractical since currently the UK Government is passing over 4000 new laws each year and few are repealed.

- To ensure there are adequate controls over the commitment of the company to contracts, etc., and adequate authority control over all purchases (see Chapter 9), a requirement that will be increasingly required by Auditors.

- To ensure the financial records and reports of the company are prepared in accordance with legal and other accounting requirements, and that such reports are filed with the requisite authorities within the required time limits and that the Auditors are given every assistance to ensure proper accounting records are being kept and procedures adhered to, etc.

- To ensure the products and services of the company are developed so that continuity of earning power of the organisation is maintained.

- To expand the company based on well-researched, well-prepared, well-considered, and well-implemented plans.

- To ensure the continued composition of the Board with the blend of skills and expertise appropriate to the requirements of the company and its future development.

NOTE:With the obligation for directors to comply with the new legal expectations, a challenge may be to be able to prove that they did take account of these statutory duties when taking decisions. It may be that (perhaps at the first Board meeting after the start of every financial year – and the first meeting after a new appointment to the Board) there is a minute to the effect:

'The Board reminded themselves of the seven duties of directors set out in the Companies Act 2006 and confirmed that in taking all decisions they would continue to take account of these duties and bear in mind the disparate interests of the company's stakeholders.'

Individual duties

- To carry out the wishes/instructions of the Board.

- To ensure all tactical decisions and actions take the same general direction as the strategy of the company (i.e. ensuring that short term decisions do not hamper or impede the progress towards the long term strategy).

- To ensure the Board always know the state of solvency of the company(therefore the Board should consider regular cash forecasts and funds flow statements with notes of all outstanding commitments).

- To exercise care in all activities.

- To act honestly and provide a good example (particularly when acting as company spokesperson) promoting the corporate entity and its products/services at all times.

- To ensure the appropriate blend of skills is available at Board level and (through board members and management) at all other levels, that all employees know what is expected of them, are motivated to perform well, and treated with respect and fairly at all times, and warned and disciplined (in accordance with pre-set rules) when performance or actions are not in accordance with requirements.

- To ensure the company has formulated contingency plans to protect its earning capacity in the event of a downturn or change in demand, and the effects of possible disasters affecting operations.

- To protect the corporate entity and the products/services from criticism and attack as far as possible.

Warning – 'read before signing'

Directors are constantly required to sign a variety of documents in their official capacities. As a general rule they should always check what they are signing and ensure their signature is described as 'Director, XYZ Ltd' or 'or behalf of XYZ Ltd', particularly when signing cheques, to avoid any possibility, should the company not be able to provide funds to meet the cheque, that they personally may be liable.

Case study

Under company legislation, a director-signatory to a company cheque which does not bear the name of the company can be held personally liable for the cheque should it not be met. In *Fiorentino Comm Guiseppe Srl v Farnest and anor (Directors of Portofino Collections (London) Ltd)* it was held that because three cheques signed on behalf of their company by directors did not bear the word or abbreviation 'Ltd' the directors were liable to make payments in respect of all three cheques even though two of the cheques were not presented (the first having been presented and not been paid due to insufficient funds).

Directors should also take care that they do at least understand the outline of documents they are asked to sign unless, for example, it is a document prepared by the company's solicitors where it should be reasonable for the Director to be able to rely on their expertise. If unable (for example because of time pressures) to read all documents, it might be prudent to request that those requiring documents to be signed should make and submit a brief precis of their content.

Summary checklist

Directors should:

- Understand the range of their general duties and responsibilities, and their personal liabilities.

- Be required to update their knowledge and expertise in corporate matters as well as their line responsibility area.

- Be conversant with the content of the Memorandum and Articles (the Company's 'constitution').

- Devise (and update) detailed aims and plans for the company.

- Compose detailed checklist of duties of Board and of individual Directors – and ensure compliance.

- Arrange for preparation (and regular updating) of list of all Acts and Regulations with which the company is required to comply. List the implications and arrange compliance.

- Require preparation of precis or explanation of all items directors are required to sign.

Chapter two

A rose by any other name

The variety of types of Directors – and their responsibilities

A director is a director

Descriptions

Courtesy titles

Directors' expectations

Summary checklist

A director is
a director

Under company law there is only one 'category' of Director, although everyone who takes part in the senior management of a company could be held to be directing its activities and thus could be regarded as an 'officer'. In addition anyone (by whatever name called) who acts in a way so that the Board are accustomed to act in accordance with his wishes or instructions may become a 'shadow director' (see below). The report of the Cadbury Committee on Corporate Governance, (the main thrust of whose deliberations are aimed at listed PLCs now subsumed into the combined code of Corporate Governance) suggests that there are three main 'types' of Directors:

• Those who have executive responsibilities in the company;

• Those who are appointed to the board but have no executive responsibilities (non-executive Directors); and

• Non-executive Directors who are free from any connection (i.e. with the company and/or executive Directors) which might condition their opinions and behaviour. These are referred to as 'independent Directors' (an entirely novel concept) and the Cadbury Committee suggests the reason for considering their appointment as follows:

'An essential quality which non-executive Directors should bring to the Board's deliberations is that of independence of judgement. We recommend that the majority of non-executives on a Board should be independent of the company. This means that apart from their Directors' fees and (any) shareholdings, they should be independent of management and free from any business or other relationship which could materially interfere with the exercise of their independent judgement.'

Following the collapse of large companies and/or scandals connected with them there is increasing pressure currently on listed PLCs to:

• Retain truly independent non-executive Directors.

• For such Directors to exercise their duties in a pro-active manner.

• For those acting as non-executive Directors to have a limited number of such appointments so that they can give sufficient time to their duties. The concept and benefit of wholly independent non-executive Directors is obviously one which fits the requirements of large and/or listed PLCs better than the majority of companies but many companies of all sizes will certainly be familiar with the split between executive and non-executive directors. It is perhaps worth noting that:

a) much that is contained in the reports of the Cadbury Committee and its successors the Greenbury and Hampel committees (now subsumed into the general code of Corporate Governance) have been replicated in company law (some of the thrust of the Greenbury Committee recommendations re Directors pay were effectively implemented in 2003)

b) Draft Company Law from the European Union suggests that there should be a majority of non-executive Directors on boards of listed PLCs. This could be a trend which will ultimately spread to, initially at least, the largest private companies.

c) the report of the Cadbury committee refers to there being a 'lead' independent Director ('a recognised senior member') and the Hampel committee report, defending this concept, insists this would not be a divisive appointment (i.e. such recognition would not conflict with the position of the Chairman).

Descriptions

It may be helpful to review the descriptions commonly given to Directors as a means of identifying the responsibilities that attach to them and any individual considerations that may also apply. Despite there being several names and descriptions in common use it must be stressed that in law there is only one 'type' of Director and, regardless of name, duties etc., all using the title (or performing a directors' duties whether they use the title 'director' or not) can be held liable.

1. Executive

This is a Director who in addition to, or because of, his membership of the Board is authorised to carry out certain day-to-day functions including entering into contracts and managing employees and assets (that is 'executes' the decisions arrived at collectively by the Board). This type of Director is the most numerous and perhaps the one envisaged by the parliamentary draftsmen when formulating most Company Law. Because executive Directors have a managerial role in addition to their

Board responsibilities it can be difficult for some to separate their two roles and to contribute to the making of a Board decision which may adversely affect their own department or its work. Yet the need to view company problems from a holistic rather than a functional viewpoint is an essential concomitant of Board responsibilities.

2. Non-executive

The concept of the widespread appointment of non-executive Directors is relatively recent. Most company Boards consist predominately of full-time executives. Since it may be difficult for such executives to retain an overall and objective view of the company that their duties as Directors require, it has become increasingly common to appoint non-executive Directors. Drawn from senior management (and often from the ranks of retired former Directors) from other (or even the same) industries, these Directors have no executive responsibilities, but (at least in theory) provide executive Directors with advice and input based on their experience and views unfettered by a commitment to the company. Since they do not depend for their living on the salary drawn from so acting, they can be far more objective regarding the progress (or lack of progress) of the company, and, in essence, require answers to questions the executive Directors may least want asked. It should also be easier for such a Director to question the legality or appropriateness of certain actions. For example, in the Guinness affair the 'wrongdoing' of certain of the executive directors, was eventually challenged by the non-executive Directors. Should actions complained of continue, at least in theory, the non-executive Directors should find it easier than executive Directors to resign in protest, the potential attendant publicity (the so-called 'noisy exit') perhaps being their greatest weapon to try to effect changes. Of course in accepting a position as a non-executive director, the individual takes on all the duties, obligations and liabilities of an executive director. The terms 'executive' and 'non-executive' are descriptive of internal duties, but not restrictive of their liability. Company law on the other hand is prescriptive of everyone acting as a director.

Case study: 'Qui s'excuse, s'accuse'

The imminent collapse of hotel group Queens Moat Houses was avoided by the creditor banks providing ongoing essential financial support to avoid liquidation mainly since they could not let the company fail (as the massive bad debts would have affected their own balance sheets).

As a result of the subsequent investigation, members of the Board (which included three qualified accountants) were disqualified as directors for a variety of periods – 10, 8 and 7 years – whilst the former Deputy Chairman, Martin Marcus was also fined £250,000. Finally the Chairman, John Bairstow, who founded the company and built it into a major hotel chain, was disqualified for 6 years.

The judge stated 'had Mr Bairstow performed his duty as director and chairman of QMH properly he would have been aware from the information available to him that the profits figures given to the banks were seriously unrealistic'.

John Bairstow commented 'It seems that all directors, including non-executives, are deemed liable for any accounts whether they had any involvement or not.'

Well, yes Mr B, that is the effect of the law under which QMH operated. It would seem reasonable for investors and creditors to expect that to be known to the Chairman of a listed PLC.

Of course, it is not only wrongdoing that a non-executive should be able to question. It is all too easy for executive Directors – particularly Chairmen and Managing Directors – since they operate in a rarefied world of power to develop an over-confidence and belief that everything they do and feel is right. Unless such Directors (as do a number of Directors in household-name companies) 'walk the floor' and talk to and above all listen to people at the 'sharp end' of the business they run the risk of relying on information and opinions provided by subordinates who may report things in the way they think the Board may wish to hear news rather than the way they actually are (see Chapter 11). It may be – and on occasions does no harm and could save the shareholders considerable value – that a preferred course of action is at least questioned by an impartial observer. Nowhere is this more nec-

essary than when a takeover is under consideration – a process hitherto much beloved of a number of Boards as a way of 'growing the
Company' swiftly and without the level of commitment and investment
(and delay) associated with 'organic growth'. Research indicates that
shareholders in acquisitive companies rarely benefit from takeovers.

**'There have now been a series of academic studies done in both
the USA and Britain which show a remarkably similar pattern.
By and large the shareholders of the target DO receive more
money for their shares than they paid for them. But what is truly
astonishing is that the shareholders of the pursuing corporations rarely see any gain in their share prices as a result of a
takeover** (*from 'Takeovers'*).

A truly independent view from a non-executive may at least encourage the executive Directors to pause and reconsider. Non-executive
Directors rank equally with (and have the same potential liabilities and
actual responsibilities as) other directors in all respects. The Institute
of Directors and the Stock Exchange are very much in favour of the
extension of the non-executive Director concept not least as it may
be a means by which a repetition of some of the recent scandals associated with failed companies might be avoided. Retaining non-executives
may also encourage an awareness of the fact that responsibilities borne
by Directors should outweigh personal considerations.

Case study: Objectivity v subjectivity

The company had been formed to produce pine furniture just before
the onset of the UK recession. To provide working capital, the three
executive Directors mortgaged their homes to the bank. A year after
commencement of business two non-executive Directors were
appointed. They introduced some much-needed new capital but it swiftly
became apparent that a major injection of capital was needed if the
company was to survive in intensely difficult trading conditions. This
proved impossible to source and, after several months attempting to
refinance and/or attract new capital, during which further losses were
incurred, the non-executive Directors felt that the only course of action
in order to protect the creditors was to ask the bank (which had a charge
over the assets) to appoint an administrative receiver. The executive

Directors, who understandably feared losing their homes, resisted this suggestion until one of them, realising the deepening crisis and the potential liability for wrongful trading (see Chapter 3) voted with the non-executives. It was later discovered that the opinion of the Receivers was that when the company was put into receivership it had already passed the point when it was trading wrongfully. Had it not been for the objective viewpoint of the non-executives, the losses suffered by the creditors could have been worse and all the Directors could have been held personally liable for far more than the value of the executive Directors' homes.

Any marked extension of the numbers of non-executive directors (as required by proposed new EU directives and envisaged by the corporate governance movement) seems unlikely in the light of recent cases attempting to make non-executive directors liable for actions or inactions of the Board. For example, the former non-executive directors of Equitable Life (who were being paid on average less than £20,000 a year) were sued for £3.2 billion, the action alleging that they failed to exercise due care concerning the granting of guarantees to policy holders. Eventually the action was discontinued.

Few may be willing to risk personal liability for such relatively low rewards – particularly as a non-executive director is likely to know far less of the detail of what is going on in the company than their executive colleagues.

3. Chairman

As previously noted there is no legal requirement for companies to have a Board and many, particularly smaller companies, operate virtually without one – or at least without one operating with a degree of formality. There is no obligation on Directors to hold a Board Meeting in order to conduct the company's business – it can be conducted at any time – provided, however, all directors are present or at least are aware of the need to hold such a meeting.

Case studies: No notice = no meeting

3 (of 4) Directors met and decided a course of action which could have been legitimately passed at a properly convened and constituted Board meeting. The 4th Director objected to the decision (even though he would have been outvoted at a properly convened Board meeting) and the court held the original decision was invalid since it had not been taken at a Board meeting to which all Directors had a right of notice and at which they all had a right to attend.

In *Smith v Henniker-Major* a director 'convened' a board meeting without informing the other directors, and 'passed' a resolution although the company Articles stipulated that the quorum for valid Board meetings was two directors. The Court held that the resolution was a 'worthless piece of paper'.

Obviously many Boards operate informally, but if important decisions are taken in such a way, it might be wise to confirm such actions at a subsequent meeting and have the decision confirmed by the whole Board (and evidenced by being minuted) bearing in mind the doctrine of collective responsibility – and the duty of care placed on every Director. It is unlikely that a Board can operate at its greatest effectiveness unless one member acts as Chairman. Thus the Chairman will usually be a member, executive or non-executive, of the Board elected to chair the meetings of the Directors by the members of the Board. Increasingly, as companies are featured on the news (rather than financial) pages of national press and other media, such Chairmen can attain a high profile and tend to be referred to as 'Company chairman'. This is a misnomer as no such position exists. Further although Chairmen tend to remain in such a 'position' for some time they are usually elected by their peers 'for the time being' and there may be nothing to stop different Directors taking the chair at each meeting of the Board.

4. Managing

This position is sometimes alternatively known as Chief Executive or Chief Executive Officer – terms imported from the USA – although neither of these descriptions are currently recognised by UK company law and the Articles should be referred to for any titles required to be used. In many organisations the functions of Chairman and Managing Director are vested in one person. There has been considerable criticism of this practice in the past, critics alleging that the concentration of power in one person's hands can be detrimental to the overall control of the company and can lead to nepotism. However, research seems to suggest that the retention of the twin powers in the hands of one person tends to improve the company' performance more swiftly, compared with those where the functions are split.

Where there is a separate Managing Director function, the Chairman may be non-Executive, retaining a policy control function, leaving the Managing Director to ensure all remaining duties and responsibilities of the Board are effected. Thus the Chairman could be said to be looking outwards, interfacing with external parties, leaving the Managing Director to ensure other board members and management who report to him carry out the requirements of the Board and their own responsibilities – that is essentially an internal role. However, companies tend to operate in different ways – even, in some, letting the Managing Director assume a greater external role, whilst the Chairman adopts a lower profile. To a certain extent this is inevitable since the personalities and talents of the persons themselves may well affect the interpretation and scope of the roles. The rights and duties of the Managing Director will normally be set out in the Articles and may be different from those of every other Director. Further, provision relating to his re-election should be checked carefully. For example under some Articles, a proportion (often a third) of the Directors are required to retire at each Annual General Meeting of the shareholders and (if entitled) are able to seek re-election by the shareholders at that meeting. A Managing Director, however, is usually excluded from this requirement although he may be counted for the purposes of deciding the number of Directors who need to retire by rotation.

5. Alternates

Such appointees act as a full representative for their principal for whom they are the alternate and have right to receive all matters sent to their principal. Alternates can only be appointed if the Company's Articles allow. If an alternate's principal attends a meeting then the alternate cannot also attend, but they can attend (usually the main purpose of the arrangement) if the principal cannot. The appointment and recording and filing of details is identical for both alternate and principal – as are their rights and duties.

Historically there have been few alternate directors. This situation could change quite dramatically as a result of the recent extension of maternity leave to 52 weeks. If during a director's maternity leave, she is not present in the workplace, does not attend Board meetings etc., she could be accused of abrogating her 'duty of care' as a director. It may be inappropriate for her to resign and better for her to appoint an alternate to act on her behalf during her maternity leave. If the Articles do not allow for the appointment of alternate directors, these will have to be altered. Under the latest revision to maternity benefits, a new mother is permitted to work for (and be paid by) her employer for up to 10 'in touch' days during her maternity leave. This could be a suitable way of ensuring a female director continues to meet the requirements of her 'duty of care'.

6. Nominees

These are sometimes appointed by (for example) a major shareholder who wishes to exercise some control over the Board and company. (In fact care should be taken if exercising control in this way as it can have the effect of making the shareholder a shadow director – see below.) Nominee Directors owe obligations to two separate bodies and may need to take care to avoid conflicts of interests – the prime duty of a nominee is to the Company of which he is a Director. A nominee Director may have enhanced voting rights (e.g. a vote exercised by one or more nominee(s) may rank greater than the combined votes of all other members) particularly in joint venture companies. If the nominee is appointed by another company (e.g. one of the two or more owners of a joint venture company) and has enhanced (i.e. controlling) voting rights, then the company may be regarded as being a subsidiary of the appointing company, with all the implications (accounting and taxation etc.) that such a relationship entails.

NOTE: In many Joint Venture companies (and in some other companies) there are not only Articles but also shareholders agreements. Whereas the Articles must be filed at Companies House, thus becoming subject to public scrutiny, a shareholders agreement does not have

to be filed and its content can thus be kept private. However it is important to ensure that the requirements of both are not in conflict.

7. 'De facto'

Persons who exercise the powers of Directors but do not use the title
may still be regarded as Directors – with all the obligations, liabilities
and responsibilities that a Director has (that is 'the fact of the matter'
is they are acting as a Director).

NOTE: I have always been wary of boards insisting they consist entirely
of non-executive directors – arguing that it is an impossible situation
since surely at least one must be executive. If not, then someone else,
not on the board, must be a 'de facto' director. Indeed, one could argue
where all the directors are non-executive that other person may have
considerable power and might even become a 'shadow' director (see
below). Recently the Association of Chief Executives of Voluntary Organisations (ACEVO) have sought legal advice regarding their status vis-à-vis
their directorates where, very often, all directors are non-executive. An
ACEVO working group is reviewing the matter and considering whether
charity boards should include executive directors.

Case study: Disqualification bites non-'directors'

In *Secretary of State for Trade & Industry v Holler*, the company had
become insolvent and the husband/father (a director) had been disqualified. However, his wife and son acted as if they were directors,
taking decisions and requiring actions of others as directors. They were
found to be de facto directors and both were disqualified. A second
son also acted for the company but was not found to have been part
of its corporate governance and therefore was not a de facto director
– and hence could not be disqualified.

The judge offered some guidance to determining whether a person was
a de facto director:

a) Was the person part of the corporate governing structure?

b) A distinction must be made between someone who participates in
    collective decision making at Board level and someone who par-
    ticipates in management.

c) The decision is to be determined objectively on the basis of all relevant facts. A person may be a de facto director even though there is no day-to-day control of the company's affairs and/or is involved in only part of its activities.

d) Factors such a family relationship may be relevant.

8. Sole

Until the enactment of the 1989 Companies Act all companies had to have two shareholders. Since the passing of that Act there is nothing to stop a company issuing just one share. Limited companies need have only one Director (although that person cannot also be the Company Secretary). This has resulted in many sole traders forming limited companies with the same person as sole shareholder and sole director. Whilst perfectly legal (and currently tax advantageous) this has an inherent risk since if the individual can no longer operate (e.g. he dies) there is no one to run the Company – and no-one, until a Will or Letters of Administration are proven, to appoint a replacement Director. It would be wiser to issue 100 shares and allot 10 to someone other than the sole Director so that that shareholder (in the scenario set out above) could appoint a replacement Director. Advancing credit to such a Company may also be risky. Who can authorise payment for goods/services supplied but not paid for prior to the Shareholder/Director's demise?

9. Shadow

The legal concept of a person exercising control over a board as a kind of '*eminence grise*' or shadowy manipulator was introduced by the Companies Act 1985 (although examples of such persons had existed since the first Limited Liability Act). The Companies Act 2006 states that all persons 'in accordance with whose instructions or wishes the directors of the company are accustomed to act' are shadow Directors. Thus a major shareholder, or a creditor owed a considerable sum, who regularly gives instructions to the Board (or even 'suggests' courses of actions) with which the Board comply, could become a shadow director. Similarly representatives of the management of a parent company who regularly instruct Boards of Directors of their subsidiaries in such a way, so that the subsidiary Board follows their instructions, could also be regarded as shadow directors. The danger for shadow Directors is that, should the company fail and be held to have traded wrongfully, they could be required to contribute from their personal assets for the benefit of the creditors – just as can the other Directors. To protect parent company executives in such a situation, the parent company itself could be made a Director of the subsidiary. In that event the executives simply act on behalf of the parent company as director. Of course if the company fails and is held to have traded wrongfully the parent might then be required to contribute to the creditors' losses. The possibility of the subsidiary company failing might have been the whole reason for forming it as a subsidiary (i.e. if it fails only the assets held within the subsidiary are lost) in the first place and this process would then negate the aim of the parent company not being responsible for losses incurred by their subsidiaries. 'Shadow Directors' are legally directors and their details should be retained by the company and filed with the Registrar (when obviously they cease to be 'shadows'). The problem the person responsible for filing may experience in trying to file details of a shadow Director is the latter's refusal to sign the 'consent to act' undertaking on the form because they do not want their 'shadowy' status to gain such recognition. In such a case legal advice should be taken, as the Registrar will not accept a notification of a Director's appointment unless the person signs the 'consent to act' section on the form sent to Companies House.

NOTE: If there is legal action regarding the alleged operation of a shadow Director, the Court will look at the reality of the situation and may go 'behind the words' used in the Act and in the Minutes etc.

Case study: Riding roughshod

In *Re Mea Corporation, Secretary of State for Trade & Industry v Aviss*, A was director and sole shareholder of a parent with two subsidiaries. B was not a director of any company (since he had already been disqualified).

A and B required all monies received from any of the three companies to be placed in a central fund from which B would determine payments. Large payments were made from this fund to companies (in which A had a substantial interest) outside the group. Directors of the subsidiaries protested at this but A and B overrode their objections.

The Court decided that A was a shadow director of the subsidiaries and that B was a shadow director of all three companies. In the application of trading income and the payment of creditors both A and B failed to respect the 'separate legal identity' of all three companies, and this led to a substantial increase in the deficiency of all three companies to the detriment of the creditors.

A was disqualified for 7 years and B for 11 years (a longer term since he was acting whilst disqualified. Acting as a director whilst disqualified renders the person to unlimited personal liability for such acts.)

Courtesy titles

a) Associate, local, divisional etc., directors

Many companies (whether permitted by their Articles or not) grant to employees the title of 'Director' qualified by descriptions such as those set out above to indicate that the person has been granted authority at such a level. Such appointees are rarely Directors in the legal sense (i.e. recognised under Company Law) and they should not use the title in such a way that suggests that they are. If they do, they may be regarded as having 'held themselves out to be' (that is '*de facto*') Directors and thus may have personal liability as if they were Directors even though it is unlikely they will have all the information available to the real Directors. This is particularly important if such a person takes on credit on behalf of the company. All Directors are presumed always to know the state of solvency of the Company and should not take on credit knowing that the invoice might not be paid. If they do that is the offence of 'wrongful trading' (see Chapter 4)) and they may have personal liability for the debts so incurred.

Case study: Penalty for deceit

In *Contex Drouzhba Ltd v Wiseman and anor*. Wiseman caused the company of which he was a director to enter into an arrangement with a creditor whereby the company would pay the creditor within 30 days of invoice.

However the company's financial position was so poor that the director knew there was no way in which the requirements of the arrangement could be met.

The Judge held that there had been deceit on the part of the director and that it was 'inconceivable' that the status of director should protect him from personal liability. Accordingly the director was held personally liable for the invoice.

b) Titles such as 'Director of... '

Although some companies use such a description for executive Directors, this style may also be used to grant a level of authority to a person who is not a Board member and, indeed, may not even be an employee. There is a danger (similar to that set out immediately above) for the person using such a description since, again, they could be deemed to be holding themselves out as a Director and thus may share in the responsibilities and liabilities of a Director without necessarily having any say in the Board decisions concerning such responsibilities. Should the company fail, and the Directors be held to have traded wrongfully, they could also be liable to contribute to the assets available to the creditors.

Directors' expectations

In the following examples we have used extracts from comments made in the judgements of cases brought against several directors to demonstrate how the Courts interpret legislation and expect directors to perform their duties. These cases were brought under existing legislation. However, certain key words and phrases (set in italics below) uttered by the Judges in those cases now form part of the Companies Act 2006.

1. A director must be *diligent*

Case studies: Signed without reading

In the *D'Jan* case, where a director signed an insurance proposal form that contained an erroneous statement the Court stated that directors must be 'diligent person(s) having the general knowledge, skill and experience that may reasonably be expected of a person carrying out the same functions as are carried out by that director in relation to the company.'

In the case of *Continental Assurance* company, a 'corporate financier' was found to be unable to understand the statutory accounts of the company of which he was a director – a task most people would expect to be basic for a corporate financier. He was found unfit to be a director and disqualified under the Company Directors Disqualification Act.

2. A director must not be *reckless*

Case study: Voted without reading

In *Gwyer & Associates and anor. v London Wharf (Limehouse) Ltd & ors*, a director made no effort to ascertain what were the interests of his company before voting on a Board resolution. The Court held he was not only negligent but also in breach of his fiduciary duty to exercise his discretion independently and bona fides in the interests of the company. It went on to state that where a company was on the brink of insolvency the directors owed a duty 'to consider as paramount' the interests of the creditors. The director was found to be in breach of his fiduciary duties. Because the director acted in breach of his fiduciary duty, the resolution (of the London Wharf board) was void.

3. A director must *maintain his knowledge* of the business

Case study: Ongoing knowledge required

In the investigation following the collapse of *Barings Bank* after the devastating losses caused by *Leeson's* illegal trading in its Singapore office, the Court stated that:

'directors, collectively and individually (have) a duty to acquire and maintain a sufficient knowledge of the company's business to enable them to discharge their responsibilities'.

Under both Company and Insolvency law a responsibility is placed on Directors that at all times they will be aware of the state of solvency of their companies.

If this is not so and they continue to trade and to take on credit when there is no reasonable prospect of the creditors being paid on or within a reasonable time of the due date for payment of their debt, then directors can become personally liable to contribute to the shortfall to reimburse the creditors of a failed company.

4. A director has a *duty of care*

Case study: Liable even though 'asleep'

In *Dorchester Finance Co Ltd & anor. v Stebbing and ors*, there were three Directors of the company of whom two, X and Y, were effectively non-executive and left the running of the company to Z. X and Y often signed blank cheques for use by Z, and made no enquiry of how funds were obtained or used. The Company failed owing creditors considerable sums. The court found that both X and Y had failed to apply the necessary skill and care in the performance of their duties (and indeed that they had failed to perform any duties in their positions as directors). In addition, Z (who, like X was a qualified accountant) had failed to exercise any skill or care as a director and had misapplied the assets. All three directors were held to be liable for damages.

In the judgement the court ruled:

- Each Director must exercise in his duties the degree of skill that may reasonably be expected from a person of his knowledge and experience. (Thus, in considering liability in wrongful trading (see Chapter 4) a court might consider a Director who is a qualified accountant to be more culpable than a (say) personnel Director, because of the former's professional training and expected knowledge in the corporate field.)

- A Director must in the exercise of his duties take such care that a man might be expected to take on his own account. The question that could be asked is 'Would I be so cavalier concerning these funds, was this my own cash/orders rather than it being within my company?'

- A Director must exercise the powers granted to him in good faith and in the interests of the company of which he is a Director.

WARNING: This ruling also clearly demonstrates yet again that in terms of liability there is no distinction between non-executive and executive Directors' responsibilities. (See also QMH case study above).

5. A director should *promote the company* (and must not act against its interests)

Case study: Overriding duty to company

In *British Midland Tools v Midland International Tooling* four directors decided to leave their company and set up another in competition. Whilst three remained in office, their colleague resigned and commenced enticing employees to join the new company and poaching customers. The Court held that the three directors who remained in office had a duty to the original company to stop the enticement and poaching and were thus liable for not taking such action.

Perhaps the most well-known breach of this guideline was that made by Gerald Ratner when in a presentation to the Institute of Directors (and as a joke to enliven the session) he compared some of the products his company sold in its shops to human waste and having a value not much in excess of 'a Marks and Spencer sandwich'. In the aftermath he had to resign as Chairman and then as a director, the company had to sell nearly 200 shops and nearly failed whilst the share price plummeted.

6. A director must *act within his powers*

The powers of the company are set out in the Memorandum and the powers of the Directors (the rules under which they are required to act) in the Articles. Directors have an obligation to ensure their company does not exceed such powers (Lord Denning referred to the directors being the 'mind' directing the 'body' that is the company.) In fact, as noted in Chapter 1, since the passing of the Companies Act 1989, it is now possible, should a company exceed powers set out in its Memorandum (i.e. it is acting *ultra vires* or beyond its powers), for it to obtain retrospective approval for the act from the shareholders. In such circumstances, not only should the shareholders be asked to ratify the act that was '*ultra vires*' they should also be asked to absolve the Directors for liability resulting from the breach. If the shareholders do not absolve the Directors then the latter can be held personally liable for the breach. The powers of the Directors are set out in the Articles and, should a Director act in breach of the requirements then he could be held personally liable for the breach. Once again the shareholders could be asked to ratify the breach. In each case, should the shareholders ratify the exceeding of powers either in the Memorandum or Articles, the resolution approving this must be filed with the Registrar as the effect is to alter these documents of record.

Case study: Expensive short cut

In *UK Safety Group v Hearne*, a Managing Director 'appointed' a Sales 'Director' without gaining the consent of the rest of the Board. The parties signed a contract including a non-competition clause operative should the sales 'Director' leave. When he left, the Company was unable to rely on the clause since the Court held that he had not been properly appointed.

NOTE: In such a case the Managing Director was acting *ultra vires* his authority and the shareholders would have a right to sue him for any losses suffered by the Company as a result of such actions. The Law Commissions of England and Scotland recently stated that it should be made easier for shareholders to sue Directors who do not act in their best interests – this is now enshrined in legislation under the Companies Act 2006. This means it will be possible for a shareholder who believes that the company has suffered loss because of the activity(ies) (defined as *'an actual or proposed act or omission involving negligence, default, breach of duty or breach of trust'*) of a director to initiate legal action (a 'derivative' claim) against the director on the company's behalf. If the claim is successful it will be the company (not the shareholder initiating the action) that will benefit.

This is a worrying development since it changes the existing situation that a director cannot be liable for making a 'wrong' decision provided it was made in good faith, to one where the director could be held liable for an act (or omission) even if it was made in good faith and the person taking the decision does not benefit from that decision (i.e. there was no vested interest).

7. A director must ensure the company *files information*

Regardless of the nomenclature of those appointed by the shareholders (or by the Board subject to shareholder ratification at the following AGM) or of those acting as Directors (i.e. any persons holding themselves out to be Directors), all have a full legal responsibility for the company as a legal person, all its actions and those of its employees etc. To take up the appointment, personal details of each Director must be provided to the company which must record it and file it with the Registrar of Companies. This is just a small part of the information that limited companies are required to file with the Registrar and one of the legal obligations placed on Directors is to ensure that such information is filed within the required time limits which are increasingly backed by the imposition of fines and late filing penalties. Each year the Directors are obliged to ensure that the company files:

•   The report of the directors

•   The accounts for the latest financial period

•   A balance sheet as at the end of the financial period

•   An annual return confirming details of the directors, share capital and shareholders.

This obligation to disclose and file information can be regarded as the 'price of limited liability protection'. With their limited liability protection the shareholders can never be asked to contribute more than the amount they paid for their shares to satisfy the debts due to the company's creditors. In order that the latter know – at least in theory – the state of the liquidity of the company with whom they are dealing, or are contemplating dealing, the Company must file this information which is then regarded, since it is filed with and can be provided to everyone by Companies House, as being in the public domain. This is an ongoing liability and although it is usually delegated to the Company Secretary, it remains the Directors' responsibility to ensure filing takes place. **Indeed a repeated filing breach can entail disqualification from acting as a Director.**

8. A director must ensure the company is *compliant with legislation*

The maxim 'ignorance of the law is no defence' poses a considerable challenge to directors, particularly in the current legalistic environment where it seems the Government's answer to virtually all difficulties is to introduce another legislative requirement. Such mountain of laws is not of course restricted to Company Law but also to Employment, Health and Safety, Commercial, Environment and many other areas. This is a major problem for the board possibly requiring considerable investment of resources, not only to 'keep the company legal' and avoid its resources being consumed as a result of liability claims, but also to protect their personal position. Increasingly directors can be held personally liable. Often prosecutions (for example for a safety breach) may be linked to the Company Directors Disqualification Act where, if found guilty, the director can be disqualified from acting as a director for up to 15 years.

9. A director has a duty to disclose his own misconduct

Where a director has breached his fiduciary duty he has a duty to report himself for such breach to his company – since Directors have a higher duty to their employer than the duty of an employee.

Case study: Breach of duty

In *Item Software (UK) Ltd v Fassihi* a sales and marketing director set up his own company and by his actions forced a major customer of the original company to terminate its contract in favour of his own company. He was dismissed by the other directors. The Court of Appeal held that he was in breach not only of his fiduciary duty as a director (which was fraudulent concealment), but also of not advising the company of his breach since as an officer he was responsible for the success of the company.

10. A director must take action if he perceives (or should perceive) that the company is approaching insolvency.

This requirement (failure to observe which could lead to substantial personal liability), is considered in detail in Chapter 4.

Summary checklist

Directors should:

*   Be and remain aware of general developments in Company Law and corporate governance requirements.

*   Be appointed to the positions/descriptions in accordance with the requirements laid down in the Articles.

*   Comply with the various types of duty expected of them as set-out in new legislation.

*   Be aware of detailed expectations (i.e. guidance being given by decisions) in court cases.

*   Ensure filing with Registrar is kept up to date.

Chapter three

Scaling the peak

Appointment and status

Eligibility for appointment

Appointment of a Director

Notification of interests

Status – officer or officer and employee?

The service contract

The twin relationship

Summary checklist

Eligibility for appointment

Whilst most Director appointees will be perfectly entitled to take up their post certain people cannot be Directors (see checklist below) and, should such an appointment be attempted, can be disqualified from acting.

Persons unable to act as Directors checklist

- Those who have not attained the age of 16 (although the Secretary of State is permitted to make exceptions).

- Those who are or become bankrupt. This does not constitute a complete bar as the approval of the court can be sought to the appointment, which, if forthcoming, can validate it.

  NOTE: Under the Enterprise Act 2002 those who are deemed (by the court) not to have been culpable for their own bankruptcy can retain some funds and resume the position of Director in up to 12 months (rather than 3 years). (Conversely those who are proved to have been cavalier or to have deliberately brought about their bankruptcy may not be discharged from it for up to 15 years.)

- Those who are or become insane.

- Any person who has been convicted of wrongful or fraudulent trading or who has been convicted under the Insolvency or Company Directors Disqualification Acts.

- Any person who has been responsible for the persistent late filing of documents with Companies House and the Court has made a disqualification order.

NOTE: Directors can be disqualified from acting under the Company Directors Disqualification Act 1986 for anything up to 15 years if guilty of a number of offences and if their actions are 'deemed to be unfit to run a company'.

Case studies: Expensive disqualifications

Acting in breach of a disqualification order renders the person subject to unlimited liabilities and fines. In *R v Owide*, the director was disqualified for 7 years in 2000. However, he continued to run a number of businesses. In January 2004 he was disqualified for a further 5 years and fined £200,000. Unless the fine was paid within 18 months he faced an 18 month prison sentence.

In *R v Akrill* (re Portasun & ors) the defendant was the director of a number of failed companies in and around Hull, even though he was an undischarged bankrupt. He was given a 12 month jail sentence (suspended for two years) and fined £35,000.

Where Directors are barred from acting by legislation the Court will normally specify a disqualification period. A register of disqualified persons is maintained by, and can be inspected at, the offices of the Registrar of Companies (or via the Companies House website – www.companieshouse.gov.uk). This register shows the names and dates of birth of disqualified Directors, the Court which made the order and the date of the order's expiry.

Appointment of a Director

Those who are eligible for appointment are usually appointed by the Board (i.e. effectively co-opted by what may be regarded as a self-perpetuating body). However all Director appointments are subject to shareholder approval so that a new Director only holds office until the next following general meeting at which the shareholders must be asked for their approval of the appointment. All Directors hold their authority and position by virtue of the power of the shareholders and the principles and procedure by which this power is exercised and the Directors can act is set out in the Articles which will also govern the size of the Board. Provided they do not infringe any 'maximum number' set out in the Articles, the Directors can co-opt and appoint as many new Directors as they wish. Usually the re-election of a Director (either retiring because of recent appointment or by rotation) will be a formality but it is possible that the shareholders could vote against the re-election. The appointment of a Director is effected as set out in the checklist.

WARNING: Many board appointments take place on a relatively informal basis – that is, the new prospective director is known to and 'spoken for' by an existing director – and the vast majority of these work successfully. Nevertheless the normal recruitment procedures should not be subject to a short cut. Even high ranking directors and managers lie on their C.V.s as the recent case of the chief executive of InterContinental Hotel Group's Asia Pacific region demonstrates. Patrick Imbardelli was forced to resign just before he was due to be promoted to the Group's Main Board because it was discovered that three University degrees he claimed were false.

The basis of the employer:employee relationship is mutual trust and confidence. It hardly meets this requirement if applicants (regardless of their level of seniority) make false claims of matters material to the job. In addition, employers could incur costs if employment has to be terminated and another recruit found after all induction, training etc has taken place. Such wasted costs are likely to increase the more senior the appointment.

Using an application form (even in addition to a C.V.) should be regarded as essential – indeed when interviewing several applicants this may be helpful since using one's own form ensures all the information is presented in the same order. In addition, application forms should always be signed as confirmation of the content. Adding wording such as the following might at least make applicants think about the contents of the form:

'All claims and/or statements of skills, experience and employment will be checked. In the event of false claims being made, any offer of employment will be terminated. The [organisation] reserves the right to recover from the applicant any costs incurred as the result of the employment of an applicant who has submitted an application form containing false claims.'

One can only wonder whether Barings Bank would have employed Nick Leeson (the man who eventually destroyed them) as a trader had they checked his background. None of the county court judgements against him were disclosed in his application.

Appointment procedure checklist

a) (Subject to any requirements in the Articles) the Board resolve to appoint X with effect from a stated date.

b) This decision should be recorded clearly and comprehensively in the Minutes.

c) The Director is invited to accept the appointment and, assuming he does, must provide personal details of himself.

d) These personal details which comprise name (and any former names), private address, date of birth, occupation, details of other directorships held in the past 5 years and the date of appointment, must be recorded in the company's Register of Directors and Secretaries and also on which must be completed and sent to the Registrar of Companies.

NOTE: Whilst he continues to be a Director, any changes to this information must also be advised to the Registrar. From 1st October 2008 every director may request that his or her private address should not be made public. Both company and Registrar must still be told the private address however.

e) in addition to the data set out in d) above, the appointment form contains a statement that the appointee consents to act as a director which must be signed by the Director himself.

f) the form must be signed by a serving Director or the Company Secretary and filed with the Registrar within 14 days of the appointment. As with all filing it is prudent to obtain a receipt from the Registrar.

g) the Director must notify the company of any shares he owns in the company and of all changes to any shareholding. These details must also be recorded by the company. (Under CA06 required for PLCs only.)

h) the Director must also notify (and constantly update) the company of any interest he may have in any business conducted by the company and this must be recorded (as must any later changes – see notification of interests below).

i) at the next following General Meeting the Director must retire and, assuming he so wishes, offer himself for re-election by the shareholders.

Notification of interests

All newly appointed Directors must declare any interests in parties with whom the company does business and/or through which they might benefit personally. Thus if as well as being a Director of the subject company the appointee is also a Director or material shareholder of (say) a supplier to the company he must declare that interest. The Director should then refer to the Articles to check the position regarding his interest. The requirements laid down by the Articles can vary from company to company. Thus there could be any of the following:

i) A complete bar on the interest which must then be terminated (one would hope this would have been considered prior to the appointment to avoid embarrassment).

ii) A ban on the Director profiting from the interest (in that case he would need to pass any profits to the company).

iii) Permission for the interest to continue but the Director is prohibited from speaking and/or voting during any discussion of the matter at a Board meeting.

iv) The interest is allowed to continue and, subject to reminding the members of the Board before making any comment, the Director may be allowed to speak and/or vote on it.

v) The interest is allowed to continue without restriction.

Corporate fraud is on the increase. It has been stated that 60% of all UK companies are losing 5% of their turnover to fraud and theft. The impact is of course felt directly on the bottom line. For a company earning 10% profit on its turnover, sales of ten times any amount lost to thieves will have to be generated simply in order to 'mark time' (i.e. regain the pre-theft 'profit-position'). Fraud is specifically outlawed (oddly for the first time in English law) under the Fraud Act. There are 3 means of committing the new offence of fraud:

• by false representation

• by failing to disclose information where there is a legal duty to do so, and

• by abuse of position.

Since a director must by virtue of his position safeguard and protect the shareholders' assets, any dereliction of this duty means he commits fraud. Similarly if he abuses his position or makes a gain by abusing his position (or causes the company loss by so doing) that is also fraudulent.

The Companies Act 2006, S176 allows a director to seek authorization from the Board to exploit personally some property or opportunity even though there is a conflict between his interests and those of the company. In an LTD this can be done provided there is nothing in the

Constitution banning it. However directors of PLCs may only do this if there is specific authorization in the Constitution that allows it.

1. It is most important that the requirements of the Articles are known and strictly adhered to. Failure to declare an interest can render the Director liable to substantial fines.

2. Whether a Director who has an interest is allowed to form part of the quorum for the effecting of that item of Board business needs to be checked. If the Articles state that the Director cannot be counted as part of the quorum and the quorum exceeds the number of other Directors present this can invalidate any decision.

Personal interest

The foregoing sets out the obligations that the Director has to the company. However such an appointment is a two way process and the appointee needs to make certain checks on the company for which he is now taking personal (if shared) responsibility. The following checklist highlights various areas and aspects concerning which the new or prospective Director requires information – preferably before he agrees to the appointment.

Appointee's personal checklist

a) Obtain complete delineation of terms of appointment, service agreement, duties, reporting structure, etc. Check appointment has been made correctly and evidenced in Minutes.

b) Check how payments of fees, expenses, salary etc., are to be made (See below re question of relationship between the Director and the company. He is an 'officer of the company' but is he also an 'employee'?).

c) Obtain a copy of the latest accounts and management accounts (and any supplementary information) to enable an appointee to consider the financial state of the company (although of course any prospective appointee would be well advised to check the financial state of the company prior to agreeing to join the Board).

d) Obtain a copy of the Articles of Association to determine the powers (and restriction of powers) of the Directors and officers, and a copy of the minutes of Board for the previous year and of the company for the previous five years to check a) compliance and b) alterations to Articles.

NOTE: this check may also provide valuable background information on the tactics and strategy adopted by the Board, and disclose any authorities granted by the Board on an individual or committee basis, which may require further information, etc.

e) Check the statutory file regarding the submission of documentation to the Registrar of Companies – inspect the last Annual Return. Provide the statutorily required information for filing a record of your own appointment if not already done.

f) Check the statutory books for up-to-date entries.

g) Obtain a copy of the Directors and officers liability insurance policy and a copy of the renewal.

NOTE: Check the exact wording and cover (see Chapter 4).

h) Check the situation regarding the application and policing of internal procedures to minimise liability (see Chapter 5).

i) Obtain a copy of all loan notes, guarantees, charges, etc.

j) Check any requirement for qualification shareholding, and, if there is, acquire such shares.

NOTE: If there is a requirement that the Director holds a set number of shares and these are not subscribed for, not only does the appointment not become effective until such shares have been acquired, but also a Director who fails to take up such a share 'qualification' for more than 2 months, becomes personally liable for his acts as a Director.

k) Prepare a list of companies and/or matters in which the appointee has an interest, and with which the company may be trading or negotiating. These potential conflicts of interest must be disclosed within five days of appointment (and subsequently when they arise). Whether they are allowed to subsist, and/or the Director can vote on any such matter, and/or take any profit made from such interests must be checked with the Articles (see above).

l) Check other Board members' interests are noted and what they are.

m) Check such details are recorded in the various registers etc.

n) Check whether any directors are nominees of corporate shareholders and have any enhanced voting rights at Board meetings.

o) Request a copy of any code of ethics or equivalent, confidentiality undertaking etc., applicable to directors and/or senior members of the management of the company (see Chapter 10).

p) Request a schedule of Board meetings and arrangements for obtaining information for discussion/decision at such meetings.

Status – officer or officer and employee?

As previously noted, under Company Law a Director is an officer of the company. Once again although a term is used its meaning is unclear. The origins of directorships lie in the days of 'joint ventures' before the creation of the limited liability company. In those days the role of the entrepreneur (the equivalent of the shareholder) and that of the director tended to be blurred – often one person was both. Those that worked for the organisation were the equivalent of modern day employees (then regarded as 'servants') but entrepreneurs could not be similarly regarded. With the advent of limited liability companies, directors tended to be wealthy individuals who had no need of a salary but were content to take their reward by sharing in the profits, i.e. as dividends. Again they were not employees.

However most modern day Directors are not in the same position as either their shareholders or their employees – although their positions may contain elements of both interests. They will normally regard their work as a Director in the same way, albeit at a more senior level, as that of a manager. The question of a Director being an employee as well as an 'officer' therefore needs to be addressed. This problem has come before the courts on a number of occasions and a summary of recent decisions is set out in the following checklist.

Employment status of directors

i) In *McLean v Secretary of State for Employment*, a managing director (and major shareholder) had no written contract with the company for which he had raised money by mortgaging his house.

He was salaried – like his employees – and paid PAYE and Class 1 NI contributions. The company became insolvent. When the employer has no money to pay amounts due to employees, they can apply to an Employment Tribunal and if the case is proven, the State pays the amounts due. Mr McLean applied to be paid redundancy pay as had his employees. The Employment Appeal Tribunal (EAT) held that he was not an employee and could not claim a redundancy payment.

ii) In the cases of *Buchan v Secretary of State for Employment and Ivey v Secretary of State for Employment*, the EAT held that a controlling Director could not be an 'employee' for the purposes of employment legislation and thus in neither case could the Directors claim redundancy payments from the State when their companies became insolvent. Further in the case of *Heffer v Secretary of State for Trade and Industry* the EAT held that an individual with a 70 per cent shareholding in a company was not an employee. In making the decisions in the first two cases the EAT made the following findings:

- a limited company is a distinct legal entity from its shareholders and directors

- a director of a limited company may enter into and work under a contract of employment with that company

- a shareholder of a limited company may enter into and work under a contract of employment with that company.

However the EAT went on to point out that a controlling shareholder is able to prevent his or her own dismissal from the company and thus that person falls outside the class of persons who are intended to be protected by the arrangements for guaranteeing redundancy payments in the event of employer insolvency.

iii) In the case of *BMK Holdings Ltd v Logue*, the EAT held that when Mr Logue was dismissed by the shareholders as both chairman and chief executive, all his duties being bound up with his appointment as a director, this effectively terminated his employment as well as the office. The EAT went on to comment that there was no absolute rule as to whether a director was an employee – the facts of each case needed to be examined.

NOTE:These findings, whilst they demonstrate that the exact facts of the situation need to be examined (and will be examined by the courts), have to a great extent been overturned by the decisions in the cases of:

a) *Fleming v Secretary of State for Trade & Industry* where the Court of Session held that there is no rule of law that states that a majority shareholder cannot also be an 'employee' ,and

b) *Secretary of State for Trade & Industry v Bottrill* where the Court held that the fact that someone has a majority shareholding is only one relevant factor in determining whether they also have employment status and there was nothing to stop a person who was a controlling shareholder also being a director and an employee.

The service contract

Accordingly there is nothing to stop a Director even if he is also a shareholder (and possibly even a majority shareholder) being an employee in addition to being an officer and assuming he works full time for the company it would seem to be appropriate for the company to 'employ' him as both Director and employee.There is a legal maxim which states that in litigation the person with the best paperwork stands a better chance of winning.Taking this maxim to heart it would seem to be appropriate to suggest that if a company wishes its executive Directors also to be regarded as employees (which should be in their interests as they will gain employment protection rights) then it is logical and advisable for the appointment to be evidenced by a service contract which addresses both aspects of the relationship.

Service/employment contract

The usual service agreement/contract negotiated between a Director and a company specifies the salient details of the relationship. In many instances these items will be identical to that found in the average employment contract – pay, holiday, title and duties, sickness benefit, notice and termination and so on.The contract will often contain restrictions on the work that can be undertaken immediately after its termination which may make it somewhat more restrictive than those for an ordinary employee. Caution is needed in trying to incorporate restrictions on Directors (or other senior personnel) regarding leaving to work for competitors etc. Any clauses regarded as penalty clauses will probably prove to be enforceable. Thus whilst a company may be able to require repayment of (for example) the cost of bought-in training since that could be argued to be an identifiable loss, they would not be able to insert a clause requiring the Director to repay (for example) three months pay should he not give the required notice, since it is unlikely (although not impossible) that they could prove that level of loss.

In addition, any clause which could be regarded as a restraint of trade clause may prove to be ineffective. As a rule of thumb a prohibition in time of around 3/6 months before working for a competitor is probably the maximum enforceable. During such a period of 'garden leave', the company would be responsible for paying the Director the salary agreed under the contract. Bans on soliciting custom, staff etc., may also be best limited to 3/6 months.

Devising effective clauses that can protect the company from the loss of confidential material, competitive trading etc., can be extremely difficult. A contract which is fair to both parties can be difficult to draft, and legal advice may be best taken. The Courts have been involved repeatedly in this area. (See Chapter 10.)

Case study: Limitations

In the case of *Dentmaster (UK) Ltd v Kent*, the Court of Appeal held that a clause prohibiting (for 6 months after he left), an employee from soliciting any of those who had been customers during the 6 months prior to the termination of his employment and any of those customers with whom he had dealt during the whole of his employment was enforceable.

The twin relationship

Reflecting the twin (that is one person being both director and employee), or triple relationship (i.e. being shareholder, director and employee) relationship referred to above, ideally such a joint 'service/ employment' contract should specify:

- That the subject is an employee as well as a Director, and

- That it is the 'principal statement' required under the Employment Rights Act 1996 as well as being a service contract. Some companies not only address the twin relationship in one contract but also insert a clause which, in the event of termination of the contract, grants to the company a power of attorney giving it the right to act as if it were the Director. Thus the company would then be able to sign a resignation letter and any other documents which, in the event of a dispute, the Director could no doubt refuse to sign in order to retain a bargaining power. Granting such power would not restrict the right of the Director to take action under the service contract. (Several companies require their Directors to sign undated letters of resignation on appointment – a move which hardly generates confidence at such a time!)

Case Study: Danger of joint termination clause

In the case of *Cobley v Forward Technology Industries plc*, the Court of Appeal held that where a 'one termination generates the other' clause formed part of a contract, when the Managing Director ceased to be a director as a result of a takeover, he could not succeed with a claim for unfair dismissal. One way of avoiding this might be to incorporate a clause which excludes one termination automatically leading to another where a directorship ceases as a result of a hostile takeover.

Specimen service/employment contract

In the following checklist is a draft service/employment contract for a Director. Obviously the detailed requirements and terms to be included vary according to individual companies and legal advice should be taken.

Directors service/employment contract checklist

This Agreement is made this day of _____2_____, between [the company] of [address] (the company) and _____ (the executive).

It is hereby agreed that:

1. The company shall employ the executive as [title, list of duties, etc.] and the executive shall serve the company commencing the day of _____ 2_____ (the commencement date) for a rolling period of a maximum of three years so that (unless either party shall have given written notice of termination of this contract) the period shall be extended by a further one year on each anniversary of the commencement date. The appointment of the executive as Director and employment of the executive shall otherwise continue until the occurrence of:

   a) the last day of the month in which falls the executive's [age]th birthday, or

   NOTE: The imposition of a fixed retirement age may become difficult to enforce following the introduction of anti-age discrimination legislation from October 2006 (see Chapter 16).

   b) three months from the date on which either party shall give to the other three months notice of the termination in writing of both relationships with the company. For the purposes of employment legislation the date continuous employment commenced was [date], or

   c) the passing by the shareholders of a resolution removing the executive as a Director

   d) summary dismissal as a result of gross misconduct committed either as a Director or as an employee. The executive hereby grants a power of attorney in favour of the company authorising them to sign the required forms evidencing such removal as resignation from the post of Director, and all ancillary matters, notwithstanding any rights the Director may have under this agreement.

2. The executive shall during the continuance of this agreement well and faithfully serve the company and use his/her utmost endeavours to promote the interests of the company and its shareholders, giving it at all times the full benefit of his/her knowledge, skill and ingenuity, and shall perform all his/her duties as may from time to time be assigned or vested in him/her by the Board of Directors of the Company (the Board).

3. The executive shall during the continuance of this agreement devote the whole of his/her time and attention to the duties of the appointment (unless prevented from so doing by illness).

   He/she shall not, and shall cause his/her spouse/partner and immediate family not to, directly or indirectly enter into, or be concerned in any manner (other than with the consent in writing of the Board or as a minority shareholder in a company quoted on a public stock exchange or bourse) with any company or organisation deemed to be (at the discretion of the Board) a competitor of the company.

4. The duties covered by this agreement shall be mainly carried out at the head office for the time being of the company, but the Director will be expected to travel to all company locations and elsewhere on company business and may be required to relocate within a [250 mile] radius of [London].

5. During the continuance of this agreement the company shall pay the executive (monthly) at the rate of £_____ per annum or such other rate as may from time to time be agreed by the Board and will provide (at the cost of the company) a private motor car to the equivalent of _____ . [Exact terms of allocation and use of car are usually inserted here.]

6. In addition to remuneration, the executive will be entitled to reimbursement of all travelling, hotel and other expenses properly and reasonably incurred in the exercise of these duties and supported, as far as possible, by VAT receipts and invoices in the company name.

   NOTE: Following a successful action by the European Commission against the Dutch government, the UK may face a similar challenge the effect of which will prevent employers reclaiming VAT on expenses incurred by their employees on company business unless the receipt bears the name of the employer.

7. The executive will be entitled to [_____] days holiday in each year (exclusive of public or Bank holidays) at such times as may be agreed by the Board.

8. In the event of the executive falling sick and being unable to perform the duties, the company will continue to pay the normal salary (for the time being) for a maximum of [_____] days in any one year.

Should incapacity exceed such a period, further payment(s) will be at the discretion of the Board.

9. Should the executive become unable (by reason of ill-health, imprisonment) to adequately perform the duties, or fail or neglect to perform the duties, or breach any of the provisions of this Agreement, then the company may forthwith determine this Agreement as previously stipulated.

10. The executive shall not, without the consent in writing of the company, divulge to any other person, firm or company, and shall use his/her best endeavours to prevent the publication to any other person, firm or company of any information concerning the business or its finances or any of the secrets, dealings, transactions or affairs of or relating to the company.

11. The executive acknowledges receipt of the company's Code of Ethics and undertakes to abide by the requirements thereof.

12. The executive acknowledges receipt of the company's Stock Exchange listing agreement and undertakes to abide by the requirements thereof.]

13. The whole interest of the executive in any inventions emanating as a result of his/her employment by the company shall become the absolute property of the company without any payment being due to the executive.

14. Upon the termination of this Agreement (whether by effluxion of time or otherwise) the executive shall not (without the express written permission of the company) for a period of 6 months thereafter be connected with, or take part in the management of, or advise or direct, another business whose activities could conflict with the activities of the company. In addition the executive will not for a period of 6 months from such termination, solicit or take away any staff, custom, or business under the control of the company at the time of the termination.

15. If the executive resigns in order to join a competitor (or to set up in competition with the company, the company requires that for a period of 6 months from the date of such resignation the executive will not work for that competitor and will remain on 'garden leave'.

For the purposes of clarity it is stipulated that the principle behind this clause is to provide protection for the company in respect of up-to-date knowledge gained by the executive during employment. As such the company requires that, should a period of 'garden leave' be implemented it is expressly understood that during such leave, the executive will:

- take any accrued holiday to which they are entitled

- have no right to carry out any work for the company

and will not, without the express written permission of [the Chairman] of the company:

- approach or enter the premises of the company

- contact any employee, supplier or customer of the company

- represent him/herself to any third party as being or still being an employee/director of the company.

The provisions of the Contracts (Rights of Third Parties) Act 1999 are specifically excluded from this contract.

16. Any notice or other document required to be given under this agreement shall be deemed to be served if it is sent by recorded delivery:

- by the company to the executive at his/her last recorded home address, or

- by the executive to the company via the chairman or company secretary at their last recorded home address.

Signatures of parties _____

Witness _____

NOTES:

1. It is usual for such a document to be treated as a deed and sealed on behalf of the company rather than simply signed. Companies are now allowed to dispense with the seal and instead to have such documents 'signed as a deed' (which wording should appear somewhere on the document) by two Directors or by a Director and the company secretary, or in Scotland (only) by a Director and a counter signatory. It may be preferable if the subject of the service agreement is not one of the company signatories.

2. Termination of such an agreement may give rise to compensation, which unlike that paid to other employees must be approved by shareholders and noted in the company's Report & Accounts.

3. Often service agreements will require the subject not to work for a competitor for a set period after termination of employment which may mean the company has to continue payment (and to provide all benefits due under the contract) for the term of this so-called 'garden leave' period.

4. All service contracts with Directors must be made available for inspection by the shareholders for 2 hours every business day.

Summary checklist

•   Every appointment of a Director needs complete and comprehensive attention.

•   All Directors must notify potential and actual conflicts of interests existing at time of appointment and thereafter notify all changes.

•   New or prospective directors should complete a checklist ensuring they have sufficient information regarding the appointment.

•   Determine the employment status of directors and reflect all items in a single (or combined if appropriate) contract.

•   The Board should consider inserting protective clauses into contracts covering those (both at Board level and below) who leave to join competitors – or to set up in competition.

Chapter four

Board members – and others – beware

Liabilities and protections

Our litigious society

Personal liability for statements

Safety obligations

Employment obligations

Commercial requirements

The Enterprise Act 2002

The Insolvency Act

Operating in – and saving – the environment

Summary checklist

Our litigious society

In the UK we live – and members of Boards must direct and operate their companies – in an increasingly litigious society, one which seems to be reflecting a trend in the USA where there are more lawyers per head of population than anywhere else in the world. Similarly those responsible for the wealth-creating entities of our society are being made more accountable for their actions – and liable for non-compliance. As companies grow in size and power, governments are seeking to impose more controls on them and their activities – and on the activities and scope of control of those that direct them. Whereas once a Director needed only to have knowledge of and to consider the implications of Company Law to check his responsibilities to the corporate body and its owners, nowadays he needs to appreciate the implications of:

- A vastly increased (and increasing) number of commercial laws not least those protecting consumers and customers

- The whole panoply of employment law (which itself is increasing and developing and in the event creating situations where what is required is actually unclear) including all the anti-discriminatory legislation

- Prohibitions on arrangements which some might regard as legitimate business arrangements to maximise profit under Competition Law

- Environmental considerations, which are also likely to expand swiftly

- Health and safety law (undergoing considerable expansion at present)

    and so on.

A Director's task is not made any easier by the fact that some Company Law obligations do not appear in company legislation but are included in Acts related to general matters. Despite their best endeavours, it is difficult to imagine that there are many companies which act legally throughout their life – or that there are many Directors who always comply with the law. In late 2002 the London School of Economics released the results of a survey it commissioned which illustrated that around 33 per cent of company Directors are unaware of circumstances in their companies that could lead to regulatory intervention. Despite nearly all Directors recognising the rate of increase of the introduction of additional regulations etc. governing their companies less than 20 per cent said they were 'very confident' of the risk management in their companies. Few Directors seemed to realise how aggressive is the terminology of much of the new regulatory requirements. The fact that very often such breaches will be related more to ignorance than intent is, ignorance of the law being no defence, of little comfort since the breach could still render individuals liable.

Personal liability for statements

Directors can be held liable for the effect of statements they make and/or sign and thus should take care to read or have knowledge of the contents of documents they are asked to sign. See the *D'Jan* case in Chapter 1, and the *Gwyer & Associates and anor. v London Wharf (Limehouse) Ltd & ors* and the *Dorchester Finance Co Ltd & Anor v Stebbing and ors* cases in Chapter 2.

Safety obligations

1. Motor accident

A coroner held that a company's management was grossly negligent in allowing a lorry to operate even though none of its brakes were working. The lorry ran out of control and killed six people. Two directors of the company faced charges related to unlawful killing under the Road Traffic Act. Eventually the company that operated the lorry was fined £5,000. Personal charges against the Managing Director and transport manager were brought, although these were withdrawn once the company pleaded guilty.

2. Accident at sea

In the Lyme Bay canoe tragedy case (where several young people taking part in an open sea canoeing experience drowned) both company and director were found guilty of manslaughter – the director was jailed for 3 years whilst the company was fined £60,000.

3. Building site accident

In Germany, an English property developer was prosecuted following the death of a bricklayer who fell from a building. The developer was given a 5 month prison sentence (suspended), fined £6,500 in respect of negligent manslaughter and ordered to pay the bricklayer's widow a further £4,500.

4. Illegal employment of children

In a case brought by the Health and Safety Executive, a company was fined £2,000, a Director £4,500 and a manager £7,500 for employing under-age children for long hours.

Employment obligations

1. Employees discriminating against another employee

If employees (including Directors) discriminate against or harass or victimise other employees in a situation where the company has laid down rules regarding acceptable behaviour and has drawn the rules to the attention of the employee to and regularly polices such rules, the employees may find that they are either joined in an action with their employer or action is taken against them individually. If the company fails to lay down rules, or having laid them down fails to police them, or 'turns a blind eye' when advised of the matter, then it could find it is liable even though the act was committed by an employee. The adoption of guidelines can prevent liability, however.

Case study: Procedures provide sound defence

In the case of *Haringey Council v Al-Azzawi*, Mr Al-Azzawi claimed racial discrimination against his employer because a colleague referred to him as a 'bloody Arab'. The employer disciplined the person responsible and made him apologise. The Employment Appeal Tribunal threw the case out because the employer had a racial awareness policy, trained employees on what was acceptable (and not-acceptable) and disciplined offenders. Thus the employer had taken all reasonable steps to prevent discrimination occurring.

2. Costly careless words

In the *Bryans v Northumberland College of Arts & Technology* case a total of £29,900 was awarded to Mr Bryans whom, amongst other things, had been called 'an Irish prat'. Of the total, although the College (his employer) had to pay £13,000, his line manager had to pay £6,500, the curriculum director £1,500 and the colleague who actually said the words £5,000. The last three awards were required to be paid by the individuals themselves.

In the *Enterprise Glass Co Ltd v Miles* case, the Employment Appeals Tribunal ordered a male employee who had sexually harassed a female employee to pay her £750 compensation. It also ordered the company to pay her £1,000, the company having been held not to have provided a working environment in which the employee could work at ease.

In the *Yeboah v Hackney Borough Council* case, the Council had to pay their former employee £380,000 but in addition the person responsible for the acts of racial discrimination had personally to pay a total of £59,000 (slightly reduced on appeal).

4. Bullying and harassment

In the *Jones v Tower Boot* case the Court of Appeal held that the company was responsible for employees who branded, taunted and severely harassed a young black employee, even though as the Company claimed the employees were not 'acting in the course of their employment.

Under the Criminal Justice Act 1994, harassment is a criminal offence punishable by a fine of up to £5,000 and/or imprisonment of up to 6 months. Under the Protection from Harassment Act 1997 aggravated harassment is subject to up to 5 years imprisonment and/or an unlimited fine. It might be worth referring to this in internal guidance documents.

Commercial requirements

1. Water pollution

In the *National Rivers Authority v Alfred McAlpine Homes East Ltd* case a company was held liable for pollution caused by subcontractors washing cement into a stream. The court regarded the people responsible for directly causing the pollution as acting within the course and scope of their work and thus held the employer responsible.

2. Breach of price fixing regulations

In a long-running court case regarding the supply of ready mixed concrete a company stated that it tried to ensure at all times that their employees complied with the law and with trading guidelines. Whilst the Court of Appeal held that the company could not be liable for the action of its employees when they wilfully broke such rules and regulations and disobeyed instructions, this ruling was overturned by the House of Lords which held that a company WAS liable for the acts of its employees (even though the company had forbidden such acts and could prove in Court that it had done so). The House of Lords also commented that the original fines imposed (of £25,000) were too low and imposed fines totalling in excess of £8million.

3. Cartels and non-competitive tendering

The price-fixing punished as noted in item 2 above pre-dated the Competition Act 1998. Had it not done so the fines imposed could have been considerably more. The UK Competition Act 1998 reflects the EU's commitment to the eradication of:

- all anti-competitive practices
- any abuse of a dominant market position, and
- any agreements which provide no benefit to consumers.

Thus price-fixing (as well as market sharing, customer allocating, bid rigging and collusive tendering) either independently or in concert with others usually operating in the same trade, etc., which act to the detriment of the consumer:

- are subject to increased penalties.

The Office of Fair Trading (OFT) can identify and investigate those operating cartels and such practices – and impose fines. The OFT can (if there is reasonable suspicion of an infringement):

- require the production of documents (and take copies) from any person whether currently or previously employed

- subject to giving one day's notice, authorise premises to be entered.

(An investigating officer can require the production of documents (and take copies), require data stored in a computer to be downloaded and demand an explanation of any documents.)

If such authorised entry is denied (or the OFT suspects documents may be destroyed or concealed if access is sought) a High Court judge can issue a warrant to enter the premises without notice (a so-called 'dawn raid'). Failure to comply with a request to produce a document or permit entry and/or the provision of incorrect information is a criminal offence and can be punishable by up to 2 years imprisonment.

If the OFT considers there has been price fixing, monopolistic behaviour, anti-competitive measures etc., directions to cease such action(s) can be issued and fines imposed.

Those interviewed in the furtherance of OFT enquiries cannot remain silent – they must answer the questions posed or this will be regarded as obstruction and they can be charged with a criminal offence.

NOTE: There is a right against self-incrimination in the Act. Oral questions (usually posed during a 'dawn raid') will relate to enquiries about the documents. It is more usual to ask material questions in written form and via a 'section 2.6' notice.)

If required to attend an interview, a battery powered tape recorder should be taken so that there is some personal evidence of the interview. Batteries – with spares – should be used as those interviewed may not be allowed to use the mains supply.

Investigators have the right to seize documents and records that they feel may be needed as part of their investigation. There is no right of the subject organisation to take copies first – or even to know what has been seized – although OFT investigators will generally permit this. Legal advice is essential. The OFT has issued a draft 'Guidance to the appropriate amount of a penalty' (contact www.oft.gov.uk or OFT, Field House, 15-25 Breams Buildings, London EC4a 1PR). The maximum penalty is 10 per cent of the UK annual turnover (adjusted by the duration of the infringement – maximum 3 years, the gain as a result, and any aggravating or mitigating factors). Those who have suffered as a result of the infringement of prohibitions have the right to sue for damages in the courts (i.e. similar rights to the US anti-trust litigation) – a right which the new Act makes it easier to exercise.

Case studies

1. Napp Pharmaceuticals Ltd

Napp were the first company to be fined under the Act. For alleged abuse of market power (i.e. supplying community patients with a drug at excessively high prices whilst supplying hospitals with the same drug at discount levels that excluded competitors from the market) they were fined £3.21 million (reduced by £1 million on appeal).

2. Xco Ltd

Meetings held under the cover of a trade association were bugged to provide evidence of a cartel operated by the directors of Xco Ltd. All three directors of the company were disqualified for the maximum of 15 years and given 10 year prison sentences.

3. Nintendo

The UK competition law emanates from Europe. The EU is on record as stating that it intends to achieve a 'level playing field' and protection of consumers interests by stamping hard on any such practices. In 2002, acting under the instructions of EU Competition Commissioner, Mario Monti, it prosecuted the makers of Nintendo Computer Games (ironically one of the famous of which features Mario the New York plumber) and imposed a fine of just over £100 million. The offence was preventing UK distributors supplying European outlets where the prices charged were around two-thirds higher than in the UK.

4. Hasbro

Hasbro Toys (whose sales are about 20 per cent of all UK toy sales) were fined nearly £5 million for forcing their distributors to fix UK toy prices at a higher level than the distributors wished to charge. The UK distributors, had they connived in the artificial price-fixing, could also have been fined. However they escaped penalty since Hasbro threatened them with de-listing it they did not adhere to the prices Hasbro wanted charged.

Hasbro co-operated fully with the investigation by the OFT, and because it did so, the original fine of £9 million was reduced by nearly 50 per cent.

5. Hasbro (2)

In a second case involving Hasbro, the company dictated the price the game of Monopoly could be sold by Argos and Index (Littlewood's catalogue operation). Under cartel rules whoever 'blows the whistle' gains immunity and Hasbro did and escaped fine. Whilst Hasbro escaped a penalty which would have totalled over £15 million, Argos and Index were fined £17 and £5 million respectively.

6. Genzyme

Genzyme Ltd was fined £6.8 million for a range of anti-competitive and exclusionary pricing practices relating to the supply of the drug Cerezyme. It was stated that the company's abuse of its dominant market position (which prevented other providers entering the market) prohibited viable competition.

NOTES:

1. The second case above pre-dated the Competition Act but illustrates the extent to which investigators of anti-competitive actions will go in their determination to carry out the Treasury's aim of a world-class competition regime with productivity, innovation and low prices. As seen in the Xco case, they use the latest technology (video surveillance and electronic bugging).

2. The EU rules outlawing anti-competitive practices are increasingly being used. In the past two years:

    •   30 copper fittings manufacturers operating a cartel were collectively fined over £200 million.

- Microsoft was fined an additional £191 million for defying an earlier EU finding (and fine of £338 million) that it had abused its dominant market position vis-à-vis its Windows operating system.

- 11 power equipment companies producing electrical switchgear who were operating a cartel were fined collectively £493 million of which Siemens, the German electronics group proportion was £260 million. (One of the companies complicit in the cartel, ABB, a Swiss company, escaped any fine since it 'blew the whistle' on the cartels' activities.)

- In 2006 two British Airways executives were forced to resign following an investigation that the company had been involved in fixing the price of fuel price supplements.

Since the EU's own accounts have not been signed off by its auditors for many years due to the unacceptable level of fraud within its own organisation, one wonders what happens to the money generated by these massive fines. It is argued that anti-competitive activity can add as much as 10% to product cost. Similarly however the cost of the EU must add to the cost borne by its member states – and thus their citizens, i.e. consumers. A recent report indicated that the EU is being defrauded of £2 million each day.

The Enterprise Act 2002

This Act enhances the Competition Act. It extends the prohibitions on anti-competitive practices in a number of ways not least by allowing consumer groups to request the OFT to investigate companies or organisations that they claim are acting in concert and/or to the detriment of the interests of consumers. In detail the Act:

a) creates criminal sanctions against Directors, Company Secretaries and others that act dishonestly and engage in 'hard core' cartels and otherwise breach the Act. For operating a cartel, the maximum penalty is 5 years imprisonment, whilst Directors whose companies have infringed the Act can be disqualified for up to 15 years. (US research indicates that price-fixing increases the prices of affected goods and services by an average 10 per cent.)

b) provides opportunities to assist those affected detrimentally by such price-fixing to claim compensation. Consumer bodies will be able to bring claims for damages.

c) allows for increased support of the OFT's operation via additional staff (which they have been recruiting for some time)

d) permits an increased number of 'dawn raids' to be effected – the OFT wants to operate at a rate of at least 'two dawn raids a month'.

NOTE: The whole thrust of this legislation is to protect the consumer thus any arrangement whereby a price to the consumer is held by agreement with another supplier, and no matter how informal and unrecorded an agreement this is, will breach the Act and those found guilty will be subject to penalty. A cartel will be held to exist if one party dishonestly agrees with one or more other parties not to undercut or to 'fix' mutually agreed prices. A cartel will exist even if those who are parties to it do not have authority from their principals. Thus a manager operating in breach of a company rule not to price fix could result in the company as well as the manager being charged. In addition price-fixing, market-sharing, customer allocations and bid- and tendering-rigging are similarly outlawed and subject to increased penalties.

The UK Competition Commissioner stated in late 2006 that 'for two years' they would not seek imprisonment as a sanction for those found guilty of anti-competitive practices. No doubt this is a tactic to encourage members of cartels (or their employees) to whistleblow on others in the cartel – and thus escape personal penalty.

The Insolvency Act

In 1855 when limited liability protection was introduced it was ridiculed as a 'rogues' charter' and suggestions were made that the development was 'a means of devising the encouragement of speculation, overtrading and swindling', as many felt that the shareholders (i.e. the real risk takers) were being unfairly protected at the expense of the creditors. This was to some extent true since in the event that the company failed although the shareholders would lose their stake, their losses were likely to be smaller than the losses incurred by the creditors. Companies were required to file their accounts and also to indicate whether the assets referred to in such accounts were available generally to the creditors. However, this 'protection' of the disclosure of information was thought to be of little value – after all by the time the figures are filed they are badly out of date.

Nevertheless the intention was that creditors could inspect the accounts and would be able to form an opinion regarding the value of the assets available to finance their debts. However very often in order to finance its operations a company will borrow from (say) a bank, who will require it to provide security for the loan. The lender can create a charge over certain assets. Then, should the company fail the assets over which a charge has been created cannot be used to satisfy debts other than those owed to the lender taking the charge. This has the effect of reducing the value of the assets available to the other creditors. Accordingly all such transactions must also be notified to the Registrar of Companies and placed on public display. Under the Companies Act 1989 changes were proposed to the method of registering such charges but to date these changes have not been implemented despite two rounds of consultations. However such information is only of value if it is filed properly and within the required time which, in some cases, proved not to be the case. Thus, to some extent, the mid 19th Century critics were correct – if only because the attitude to filing information was low key and there were until very recently very few sanctions for those companies and directors who ignored the legal obligations – or filed so late that the information was useless for control purposes.

The Insolvency Act 1986 was passed in an effort to rectify the position by attaching considerable and personal penalties to those directors who abused the limited liability status at the expense of their creditors. The Act created two offences – Wrongful Trading and Fraudulent Trading.

Wrongful trading occurs when Directors continue to allow the company to trade when there seems no possibility of it being able to settle its creditors' accounts within a reasonable time of them becoming due. In such circumstances the Directors are taking on credit with the perception of or in the knowledge that they may not be able to pay for it. This is tantamount to fraud. At the very least this means that they are misleading their creditors since the latter have no means of knowing the true financial position of the company (even if accounts have been filed they are probably so far out of date as to be meaningless). If the company then fails and the Receivers or Liquidators feel that the Directors had traded wrongfully then, as part of the report to the Department of Trade and Industry that they are obliged to make, they are required to state this. The DTI can then decide whether to take action against the directors. If action is taken and the Court agrees then those Directors held to be responsible may be required to contribute personally to the assets available to a Receiver or Liquidator to attempt to satisfy the creditors. The moment when a company started trading wrongfully may be easier to assess with hindsight than at the time it occurs, particularly as the Directors may at that time have their attention on attempts to save the company. It seems likely that it is possible to start to trade wrongfully almost by default although in such a case it may be that the Directors would not be found culpable. If a company is getting into financial difficulties it is essential that the Directors take actions (such as those set out in the checklist [below]) since inaction (which could be regarded as negligence) could attract liability for wrongful trading.

Case studies: Costly ignorance

- Two directors continued to trade for 10 months after their company's auditors had warned them they were trading wrongfully. They were each required to contribute £75,000 to pay the creditors.

- David and Karen Gibbon were directors of DKG Contractors who continued to run their company even though it was insolvent – even paying themselves in preference to the creditors. They were jointly required to contribute £417,000 to pay the creditors.

- In *Smith & Williamson (Liquidators) (reVKVintners) v Dhiren Doshi*, the latter, a director of the company, was required to pay more than £2,000,000 after allowing the company to trade wrongfully. He was also disqualified from acting as a director for 12 years.

The number of such cases is likely to increase since the Official Receiver (who acts where there is a creditors compulsory winding up) now passes to Forensic Insolvency Recovery Service (FIRS) – a private recovery team – details of personally wealthy directors of failed companies. Hitherto, since a recovery prosecution has had to be funded by the unpaid creditors, there have been few actions since most creditors feel (probably correctly) that the risks and costs will outweigh the potential returns.

Protecting one's position checklist

1. Take advice – and act upon it – from auditors etc.

2. Cease trading and call a creditors meeting (whilst the immediate reaction may be horror at letting creditors know that they might not be paid, in fact the creditors are probably the last people who want the company to fail and usually are prepared to assist to try to rescue something from the situation). This echoes the old story 'if you owe the bank £5,000 and have no money – you have a problem; if you owe the bank £5,000,000 and have no money – the bank has a problem'. In recent months there have been a few high profile arrangements successfully concluded where the effect has been that the creditors exchanged their debts for equity in order to help keep the company afloat – often resulting in the former creditors holding the majority of the shares, as occurred in the Marconi case in 2003 where the former creditors now hold over 99% of the shares.

3. Appoint an Administrative Receiver (This option usually belongs to a Bank which has taken a charge over the company's assets and under the Enterprise Act 2002 is being phased out in favour of Administration orders).

4. Petition the Court for the appointment of an Administrator (this is only likely to be an option if there are funds available that might enable the company to attempt to trade out of the situation).

5. Raise loans, source additional capital, merge with another organisation, amalgamate, seek a new owner (the purpose of all of these is to enable the company to have access to additional working capital).

6. Throughout all activity, make a dated note of everything done so that should action be taken, the Directors can show that they were being proactive in their efforts to save the company. Receivers and Liquidators are required to report to the DTI on every company failure and depending on their findings the DTI may take action against Directors. Having available a log of all activity (composed at the time – not later) could be a valuable piece of evidence of the efforts that were being made to protect the interest of the creditors.

Case study: Duty to creditors

In *Gwyer & Associates and anor. v London Wharf (Limehouse) Ltd & ors*, a director made no effort to ascertain what were the interests of his company before voting on a Board resolution. The Court held he was not only negligent but also in breach of his fiduciary duty to exercise his discretion independently and bona fides in the interests of the company. It went on to state that where a company was on the brink of insolvency the directors owed a duty 'to consider as paramount' the interests of the creditors. The director was found to be in breach of his fiduciary duties. Because the director acted in breach of his fiduciary duty, the resolution (of the London Wharf board) was void.

Fraudulent trading occurs when a company fails following deliberate action to defraud the creditors. In this case unlimited fines and imprisonment can be imposed on the Directors responsible.

Case study

In *R v Ian Leaf*, Leaf bought companies that owed substantial sums to the Inland Revenue but had cash to pay what they owed. He then wrote off the tax debt against fictional losses in other companies by creating documents purporting to show that they owed millions to a fictional Nauru registered company. He swindled the Inland Revenue out of around £54 million but was found guilty on 13 charges of fraudulent trading and sentenced to 12½ years imprisonment. A further 'confiscation hearing' is to decide how much he must pay back – failing to do so will lead to an additional imprisonment term.

Holding the culpable liable

Many readers will be familiar with – and some of their companies possibly have lost money as a result of – the activities of those running phoenix companies. The mythical phoenix was supposed to emerge from the funeral ashes of its own cremation. There are many instances of those promoting companies, allowing them to fail leaving many unpaid creditors and yet the 'business' continues in different premises, even using a similar name etc. It is not always realized that unpaid creditors of the failed company can sue the directors concerned with such failure on a personal basis under section 216 of the Insolvency Act 1986.

Obviously the 'guilty' directors may have transferred their assets to others to reduce the pool of assets available to their creditors. In that case section 423 of the same Act (which is not subject to a time limit) can be used by the Courts to 'adjust' the transfer to render the assets available to the creditors. The DTI and Official Receiver whose duty it is to pursue such Directors where there is evidence of negligence, wrongful trading or worse, have until now rarely brought prosecutions against such persons, not least since the Government view is that they should not waste public money on such actions. Now however, the Forensic Insolvency Recovery Services (FIRS) operates in this area, often on a 'no win no fee' basis to both pursue rogue directors and to endeavour to recover funds to pay off (or part pay off) the unsatisfied creditors. In an article in *The Times* it was stated that in current cases under FIRS control it has been advised it has a better than 75 per cent chance of success in the proceedings.

Case study: Who is liable?

1. A company has been trading for some time but sales are not buoyant. Two new shareholders acting on financial figures provided for them, subscribe for a few shares and take up non-executive Directorships.

2. The two non-executives start questioning the figures presented stating that the accounts pages provided are inadequate to gain an impression of the company's progress or financial state.

3. The Chairman dismisses their concerns and heads off all these enquiries but the non-executive Directors persist and the Finance Director agrees to produce more extensive results next Board meeting. The non-executives press for earlier distribution but the Chairman says the next Board meeting (a month later) will do.

4. At the next meeting although the accounts are presented in a far more comprehensive format, the non-executive Directors feel that they still do not show the true picture, and question the Finance Director closely until the Chairman insists the meeting moves on.

5. At the next meeting the same thing happens except that the non-executives are assured by the remaining executive Directors that they have investigated the position and all is reasonably well.

6. Two weeks later the company collapses.

Task: Rank the order of culpability? (The suggested answer is in Appendix II).

Operating in – and saving – the environment

All companies operate within the environment in which they exist. Until, say, 40 years ago, relatively few organisations were bothered about the effect their processes might have on the environment unless these created pollution or could be injurious, and/or were subject to a relatively small number of legal obligations.

Increasingly, since those innocent days, society – indeed a world-wide movement – has been and is attempting to force all users of resources and energy to consider more carefully that use, and to minimize the effect on the environment. Under the Companies Act 2006, boards of directors, in running their businesses and taking decisions, are specifically required to take into account the interests of the environment which, with the employees, creditors and shareholders are now regarded collectively as 'stakeholders' in the business.

Supporters of the 'Gaia Capitalism' movement contend that the planet is an entity and all aspects of life and existence interrelate. Hence careless treatment of the environment can have not only a domino effect – but one that increases exponentially. For some time scientists and others have warned of 'climate change'. Whether this results from human beings and their activities generating too much CO_2 thereby creating 'the greenhouse effect' or because the temperature of the Sun itself has risen (which might explain the rise in the surface temperature of Mars which has no CO_2 generators), it seems certain that climate change is upon us and activities of commercial organisations have an effect on this – and thus a part to play in minimising any negative contribution. The Gaia (from the Greek for the Earth goddess – Ge or Gaia) capitalism movement seeks to enlighten everyone:

- to the dangers of climate change (regardless of source);

- of the need to take positive (and urgent) steps to reduce harmful emissions and pollution (and/or to replace the sources of such effects with non-harmful alternatives); and

- that everyone and every organisation has a part to play and that small savings by a large number of people mean a very large contribution in global terms.

This is too wide a subject to deal with in any detail here and it may be more appropriate given the environment of the topic to highlight some obvious areas of attention and some practical and relatively unsophisticated means whereby even very small organisations could play a part in this world-wide movement. Increasingly companies will be required to report on the steps they are taking. Thus, a board would be prudent to commence consideration of the impact of their company's activities so that they can report positively – as well as helping the planet.

For example:

a) Until the mid 1950s most UK organisations were virtually self-sufficient. That is they tended to make most (some as much as 90%) of what they needed to create their end product. Nowadays such self-sufficiency is a thing of the past and most of such internal self-generation has been 'out-sourced' or bought in. With the virtual disappearance of the UK manufacturing industry – many of these items are now sourced overseas, meaning that they have to be shipped in from China or India etc. In turn this has led to an explosion of demand in China which is now opening two power stations every week and shipping its products across the world – all of which play a part in raising the Earth's temperature (not least since the coal used by the power stations and the diesel used by shipping creates far more global warming than the fuel used by aircraft on which much media attention seems to be focused).

b) Until the same period, the UK created relatively little waste since most surplus materials were re-used or recycled (either automatically or as a result of government initiatives). Nowadays a great deal of waste is created and only a small (although increasing) percentage is recycled.

The UK Government has published strategies to reduce the production of waste and the risk of pollu-tion or harm to human health from waste disposal or recovery, with the twin aims of encouraging everyone to generate less waste and recycle more. The Secretary of State is also empowered to make regulations concerning 'producer responsibility' in order to increase the re-use, recovery and/or recycling of products or material for which initiatives there is increasing pressure from the European Commun-ity. A considerable amount of waste is created by packaging and in this respect the EU's Packaging (Essential Requirements) Regulations 2003 will increasingly bite.

The DTI's note on these regulations stipulates that packaging shall be manufactured so that:

- the packaging volume and weight are limited to the minimum adequate amount to maintain the necessary level of safety, hygiene and acceptance for the packed product and for the consumer;

- the presence of noxious and other hazardous substances and materials… is minimized with regard to their presence in emissions, ash or leachate when packaging or residues from management operations or packaging waste are incinerated or landfilled; and

- it shall be designed, produced and commercialised in such a way as to permit its recovery, including recycling, and to minimize its impact on the environment when packaging waste or residues from packaging waste management operations are disposed of.

Companies with over 200 employees are to be required to publish environmental policies covering waste, and to devise and implement systems to give effect to them. The Business Resource Efficiency & Waste (BREW) programme was launched in April 2005 and has available £284 million to assist businesses in:

- minimising waste;

- diverting waste from landfill; and

- improving resource efficiency.

Targets for recovered or recycled paper packaging are to increase by 1% per year from 65% in 2004 to 70% by 2008. Not all waste may need to be disposed of however – some may have a potential for re-use.

Case studies: Waste into energy

1. A pine furniture producing company had high wastage. Whilst steps were taken to reduce the wastage itself (by designing products which could utilise offcuts), it was realised that the surplus could be utilised as fuel. A wood-burning boiler was commissioned and the costs of heating the factory and ancillary offices were reduced by around 20%. This also enabled the relatively costly procedure for bagging and transporting away substantial quantities of waste wood to be avoided.

2. A similar approach was adopted by Swinton Park – an ancestral home – which switched its heating source to a woodchip burning boiler using the fallen wood and surplus timber from its 20,000 acres of woodlands. The annual saving was £18,000.

3. The Bank of England printing works in Essex constantly withdraws old and damaged notes from circulation. These are burnt (for under-standable reasons) in their own incinerators which are linked to the printing works' internal heating system.

c) Energy usage. Waste is endemic in what has become a 'throwaway' society. Yet everything that is thrown away had to be produced and almost certainly in that production emissions were created – and energy was used.

Many businesses are capable of saving between 4% and 5% of their turnover by employing waste-minimisation techniques – which, in some cases, would mean they could double their profits. However, that reflects an acceptance of waste-creation, whereas ideally it should be prevented. It has been estimated that implementing cost-effective energy efficiency measures, could save UK industry as a whole, nearly £2 billion a year. Energy costs will inevitably rise – worldwide demand alone is expected to double or triple by 2050. Energy demands from China and India (whose economies are expected to overtake the existing top 5 in the immediate future) are rapidly increasing. Greater demand will inevitably lead to greater cost.

The Carbon Trust (an independent organisation established by the UK Government with the task of cutting carbon emissions which are partly responsible for damage to the environment, global warming etc.) estimates that most organisations fritter away 20% and some waste as much as 50% of the energy they use. As the need to reduce energy consumption becomes more widely understood, those perceived to be economical energy users may be able to steal a march on their competitors – not least in recruiting the most responsible employees.

Example – Waste reduction

1 Boards should commission an annual report of the costs of all energy being used, reflecting not only the current years cost but also comparative costs over the previous five years. Expressing these costs as a percentage of the sale price of goods or services may help concentrate attention on the need and advantages of cutting waste.

2 Such a report might also focus on any progress to self-sufficiency and for outsourced items, their country of origin and the environmental cost of transportation.

3 All bills and readings should be checked for accuracy. Charges should be compartmentalised, so that the cost to each department/ process can be identified. Communicate the results to those using the energy. It might even be feasible to share any savings achieved with the employee users.

4 Many employees leave computers on stand-by believing there is no cost. All electrical items left on stand-by use electricity and the slight extra cost of starting up will usually be more than saved by switching off. Some computers now have energy-saving devices.

5 Leaving a photocopier on overnight means using energy sufficient to generate 1500 copies – often more than a day's use. Since copiers create heat, if they are sited in a separate office there may not be a need to heat it. Alternatively siting equipment within a general office might help reduce the cost of heating that area.

6 Implement a process whereby each time electric bulbs, strip lights and appliances need to be changed, consumption figures are considered so that low use replacements are installed. It is claimed that although energy-saving light bulbs are slightly more expensive than standard bulbs, they consume over 70% less electricity and last up to 10 times as long. Modern slimline fluorescent tubes are not only cheaper than thicker tubes, they also consume 10% less power.

7 Photoelectric cells can be used to ensure appliances are only activated when needed (for example, lights in toilets, cloakrooms, hardly-used passageways etc). Similar cells can be used for toilet hand-driers – and for the use of water in the urinals.

8 When refitting large offices or other areas, consider installing separate switching systems to break the overall area into smaller sections so that not all lights have to be on simultaneously.

9 Check heating/air conditioning systems. The situation where the central heating is on fully, the radiators are hot and immediately above them are open windows is very common. Reducing the level of the thermostat on a heating system by 1 degree centigrade can save around 8% of the cost. Alternatively the effectiveness of radiators is often impaired by placing desks, cupboards etc against them.

10 Water may be heated to too high a temperature. It is common to find that the water supplied must be cooled before it can be used (e.g. for washing hands). If so, this is (unless there are hygiene requirements) extremely wasteful – apart from being dangerous to the unwary.

11 Motors use energy, and a badly adjusted motor uses it inefficiently. Variable Speed Drives fitted to pumps to reduce speed of operation (if this is not essential) can considerably reduce running costs. All equipment regardless of energy source should be checked for efficiency.

12 Compressed air facilities are often subject to leakages which means the compressor is working inefficiently.

13 Do we really need to heat the whole facility? Remove heating from areas where employees do not work – or provide localised heating only where necessary. Providing materials stored in such areas will not deteriorate if cold, why heat such areas?

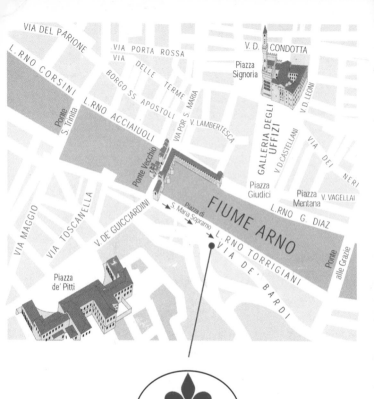

Osteria Vasari

Ubicato a 200 mt. dal Ponte Vecchio
Located at 200 mt from the Ponte Vecchio

Stampa: Color Print - Firenze

Locale caratteristico Fiorentino

Osteria Vasari

Cucina Tipica Toscana
Specialità di fattoria e selvaggina
con vini selezionati

Pranzo
Lunch
12,00 - 15,00
a partire da
start from
€ 12,90

Un primo a scelta +
un secondo a scelta +
un contorno

Optional fist and
second course with
side dish

Cena
Dinner
dalle 19,00
a partire da
start from
€ 18,90

b
e
v
a
n
d
e

e

s
e
r
v
i
z
i
o

e
s
c
l
u
s
i

DIFFIDATE DALLE
IMITAZIONI

Via de Bardi, 25 rosso - Tel. e Fax 055.2346435
www.osteriavasari.it - info@osteriavasari.it

Case study: Only heat the real work-place

The Zodiac toy chain acquired a new purpose-built warehouse in Bedford. At 40,000 sq ft and with an eaves height of 22 ft, the projected cost of heating was considerable. Since most product was not temperature-sensitive, rather than the whole area being heated, picking areas surrounded by plastic sheeting were created. Those (mainly using fork lift trucks) required to visit the unheated areas were issued with appropriate clothing – and high quality vending machines were on hand, so hot drinks were always available.

14 Warehouses need to open their main doors for deliveries and issues. The cost of opening main doors as well as the loss of heat whilst open can be considerable. Using plastic strip curtains can insulate the interior whilst still providing access to the exterior – particularly if a double 'air-lock' system is used.

15 For added security many organisations use exterior lighting, although much of the time it is simply consuming power. Increasingly powerful solar-powered lights are available. Most operate on an 'activity' generated basis – that is they light up when there is any activity – and thus their effect on security may be minimal. However, if half the lights could be supplied on a traditional basis with the other half powered by the sun – considerable savings can be made.

16 Solar panels can also be installed in roofs to generate an additional energy source – mainly as a supplement to traditional sources but every supplement may reduce costs.

17 Check with suppliers regarding their own commitment to energy and environment saving concepts.

18 Involve employees in energy-saving and environment-saving ideas, providing prizes to motivate innovation.

19 Encourage homeworking – not only does productivity tend to rise but also occupation costs as well as energy consumption tend to fall.

20 Report the results of all the initiatives in the Annual Report to shareholders.

d) The Sunday Times/Business in the Community 'Companies that Count' initiative seeks to highlight companies that have and are seizing the initiative to help reduce global warming, cut wasteful use of resources and to have a true sense of corporate responsibility. The citations for the top 100 companies in the survey provide a fruitful source of suggestions for those who have not already accepted this challenge.

e) Simply not taking what has always been done, as cast in stone for the future; challenging sacred cows is essential. The 21st Century is and will be a very different century from the 20th – flexibility of approach is essential. Boards need to question 'why' to existing processes and procedures – a commitment formerly called 'process re-engineering'.

Case study: Why?

The newcomer, soon after his appointment, was bemused on entering a factory office to see a bucket hanging from an overhead pipe. From the base of the bucket a length of hosepipe led to a broken window through which the end of the hosepipe was poking and discharging a fluid onto the waste ground outside. A cold draught was blowing through the broken window so the radiator was on full.

On questioning this bizarre set up, the newcomer was told that there was a leak in the process being conducted on the next floor up so the bucket had been installed to catch the leak. Since the bucket swiftly filled, the hose had been installed in the bucket to prevent it overflowing – and the window had been broken so that the contents of the hose didn't need to be constantly emptied.

The immediate question 'why not mend the leak on the upper floor' did not really elicit a proper answer.

Ironically one of the major sources of CO_2 (and thus many argue, global warming) is vehicle exhaust fumes generated by the consumption of fossil fuels, yet neither Ford nor Diesel, two of the great motor car inventors originally meant them to use such fuels. In a 1925 interview with the New York Times, Henry Ford stated that he thought the 'fuel of the future is going to come from fruit like apples [as well as] weeds and sawdust'. Ironically 80 years later fossil fuels are slowly being replaced by fuel derived exactly from those sources. Indeed, Ford's first car ran on fuel made from hemp. (See *'Screw it, let's do it'* Branson.)

f) Some activities are legally prohibited and could lead to prosecution – and cost the instigator severely.'

Officers of companies are personally liable (fines of up to £20,000) for damage to the ozone layer caused by harmful emissions into the atmosphere generated by their companies' activities.

Case study: Safety not first nor second

In the case of *Pharmacos*, a breach of safety led to the Managing Director being disqualified from acting as a director for 4 years and fined £2,500. The company was not fined since it went into liquidation.

Because the company did not have the raw materials to enable it to repackage chemicals, the Managing Director instructed two chemists to use a more hazardous process. As a result poisonous gas escaped into the atmosphere and mercury into the River Thames. He ordered the process repeated with greater controls and again poisonous gas escaped. The two chemists were then dismissed and they reported the matter to the HSE.

Where an organisation creates waste or emissions which create a risk to the environment they must apply to the local Inspectorate of Pollution or Local Authority Environment Health Officer. Disposing of waste in other ways will generate fines.

Case study: Expensive squib

Trojan Developments, a building company, disposed of 300 tonnes of controlled waste including toxic chemicals by building a 20 ft bonfire which they set alight on a couple of days after Guy Fawkes day 2003. They were fined £5,000 plus £1995 costs.

Summary checklist

- Require preparation and regular updating of all legislation affecting the Company and its operation

- Determine the range of liabilities of Directors and develop principles to minimise such exposure

- Require employees to abide by liability minimising rules

- Ensure all officers understand their personal obligations under the Insolvency, Competition and Enterprise Acts

- If in danger of trading wrongfully, keep detailed log of all actions taken to rectify position

- Consider the effect of the company's operations on the environment and attempt to minimise harmful emissions. Reduce waste.

Chapter five

The risk business

The requirement to take risk

As was recounted in Chapter 1, if the Company fails, in an insolvent manner, the shareholders lose the value of their shares, but cannot be asked to contribute more capital to pay off the debts. Limited liability thus protects the shareholders. The fundamental principle of Company Law, however, is that shareholders must not run companies. Shareholders own the company but appoint Directors to run their company. By owning shares in a limited liability company the shareholders liability is protected but the liability of the Directors is not – and as we saw in Chapter 4 in certain circumstances (if the Company trades wrongfully or fraudulently) the Directors can be required to contribute to the assets available to pay off the creditors. This situation is enhanced by the obligation placed on Directors to take risks on behalf of the shareholders in order to drive the Company forward, maximise returns on the shareholders investment and increase the value of the shareholders funds – and their dividends. In this the Directors may regard themselves as akin to the position of the Roman God Janus, that is with two faces trying to look in two directions simultaneously – taking risks and yet ultimately in certain circumstances, being personally liable for so doing – if the risk turns sour.

Such a dichotomy contains a further dimension. Inherent in running operations such as those normally undertaken by a Company, entails risk and the shareholders have the right to expect the Directors they appoint to take steps to ensure that such risks are identified and suitable precautions taken to minimise the effect on shareholders funds. Indeed if Directors do not undertake such action the shareholders could argue they have failed to act in their best interests and thus could take action against them.

Case study: Costly 'appointment'

It was noted in the case study in Chapter 2 that where a Managing Director, acting beyond his powers set out in the Articles, improperly 'appointed' a Director and because of the invalidity of the appointment was unable to rely on an anti-competition clause in the contract signed by the new 'Director' and that resulted in a loss to the Company, then the shareholders could have sued him for the loss sustained by their funds.

One of the prime duties of Directors should therefore be to identify risk and take suitable protective action to minimise its effect.

As noted above, under Companies Act 2006, it is possible for a shareholder who believes that the company has suffered loss because of the activity(ies) (defined as *'an actual or proposed act or omission involving negligence, default, breach of duty or breach of trust'*) of a director to initiate legal action (a 'derivative' claim) against the director on the company's behalf. If the claim is successful it will be the company (not the shareholder initiating the action) that will benefit.

Under the Companies (Audit, Investigations and Community Enterprise) Act 2004, companies are now able to indemnify their directors against proceedings brought by third parties. However such indemnity is limited to the legal and financial costs of a judgement and cannot, understandably, cover the cost of an unsuccessful defence of any criminal proceedings or of penalties imposed by regulatory bodies. In addition, companies can fund the costs of directors' legal expenses as these are incurred. If a director is found guilty they would need to repay the company unless a legally enacted indemnity has previously been given.

Contingency planning

Accountants Deloitte and Touche found that 30 per cent of UK companies had no formal disaster plan, which given by how much businesses can be adversely affected by events outside their control, is very surprising. Addressing the future for unfavourable developments should be a fundamental part of the duties of a Director and/or the Board as a whole.

The latest section of the examination of Corporate Governance was conducted by the Turnbull Committee whose recommendations, although covering listed PLCs, contain sound advice for all Companies and all Directors. Under the Turnbull recommendations now subsumed into the Combined Code of Corporate Governance, Directors of companies are specifically required to address risks. The process of risk identification and contingency planning entails an examination of every aspect of the business which could well be instrumental, even if the plan itself never needs to be implemented, in providing management with a great deal about what is going on in the business. Specifically Turnbull states:

• Internal risk control should be embedded in the company processes. It should not be seen as a separate exercise and for this reason the Board should regularly review contingency and disaster plans.

• Risk control should be responsive to changing circumstances in particular related to new risk areas.

• Companies should customise their own plans (and regularly update them) which could be summarised in the following procedure:

1. Allocate the responsibility to a board member.

2. Give the requirement a priority.

3. Involve management at all levels.

4. Identify clear objectives and satisfy them.

5. Identify all risk areas and prioritise the risks so identified.

6. Establish risk management, reduction programmes and procedures.

7. Regularly update the detail (considering as part of this process all new risks and threats).

In early 2003 Nigel Turnbull, speaking at the launch of the Risk Management Survey 2002, stated "Boards should review risk management processes on a monthly process". According to the 2002 survey (conducted by the Institute of Chartered Accountants in England & Wales) only 47 per cent of Boards actually do so whilst most Boards look at the issue once every 4 or 6 months, and 10 per cent consider it once a year. The top 3 risks identified by finance directors are:

• Reputation

• Operations and Markets, and

• Strategic challenges

whilst the bottom 3 are:

• Terrorism

• Accounting, and

• Non-compliance with rules and regulations.

This research underlines the danger to directors. Rating non-compliance with regulations the 'least risk' echoes the research from the London School of Economics that about a third of directors are unaware of circumstances that could lead to regulatory intervention. Ignorance in this area is anything but bliss!

Risk prevention planning

The aim of planning in contemplation of the unlikely but potentially disastrous is to identify:

- all possible areas where problems can occur

- all alternative reactions given such circumstances

- the ongoing effects of the problem and alternative reactions

- a senior manager (plus a team) capable of dealing with all aspects of the crisis – and its implications and to develop plans to cope with alternative scenarios

- a procedure by which unaffected parts of the business continue to work either as normal, or should there be potential profit downside as a result of the disaster, to an increased output plan to compensate.

As a basic precaution the following might be developed:

i) Prepare a list of contact numbers for all relevant employees and professional advisers

ii) Ensure evacuation procedures are extended to cover or prompt other action which may follow as a consequence of the incident. Thus the fire emergency procedure could be extended to form the basis of a contingency plan as follows:

   a) Sound alarm and evacuate

   b) Check attendance register against evacuees

   c) Advise firefighters of dangerous materials location

   d) Shut off services

   e) Information to neighbours, customers, media, etc.

   f) Postpone deliveries

g) Lay off (if allowed under their contracts) or find other work for, employees retaining key skills

h) Seek alternative premises (in accordance with requirements)

i) Cover production hiatus with temporary arrangements (these will need to be identified)

j) Utilise back up services

k) Interface with media, industry body, trades unions, customers, suppliers, etc.

l) Liaise with landlords, planners, architects, builders, etc., and so on.

iii) Train media spokesperson

iv) Set up a 24 hour a day telephone hotline

v) Retain skilled personnel – to counsel and console those suffering from any trauma

vi) Train personnel to deal patiently with those making enquiries regarding information.

vii) Provide a contact list for all services identified as being needed

viii) Give details of officials with whom the business may need to interface (e.g. investigation and governmental agencies)

ix) Source alternative sites for administration and/or production

x) Develop management succession plans showing who could take over in an emergency

xi) Set out recall procedures for faulty or contaminated product

Side benefits

Contingency planning needs the commitment of a perceptive and innovative senior manager who has sufficient time to develop thoughts and alternative choices to be considered in the event of a disaster. Having such choices (and their repercussions) immediately available, can help minimise the time taken to recover since the 'best route' may have been thought out in advance. Such planning can also disclose required improvements in the business administration to be implemented regardless of disaster. Planning is not a once and for all task – it needs updating and revising – as all businesses change constantly. Contingency planning is the classic example of the adoption of what seems to be the most beneficial solution, only after the sourcing of all required information, assessment of alternatives, and acceptance of the likely impact of each. An example of the process may assist.

Contingency plan

The problem

You are administrator of a company producing widgets. Widgets are a high value product which need careful handling and storage and have a relatively short shelf life. They are sold throughout the UK and there is a growing export market to immediately adjacent European countries. The company occupies three factories (two freehold and one leasehold; one large, two small) as well as a main warehouse (leasehold) plus a number of satellite warehouses supplying retail customers within 24 hours of order.

The production process is partly mechanised but entails a certain amount of manual work, which, since it requires dexterity, means a large proportion of the workforce is female. A shrinking product market has led to a lengthening list of debtors despite constant chasing by the credit control department. Meanwhile there has been a constant rise in raw material costs and difficulty in passing these on in the form of price increases to the customer. Formerly a small amount of raw material was derived as a by-product of animal experimentation, but this has not been the case for several years.

Certain anonymous terrorist threats have been made against the company and a number of small incendiary devices have been received via the post at both head office, factory and warehouse.

The Board is concerned that its operations could become a target for some serious (i.e. large scale) terrorist activity and has asked you to prepare a report highlighting areas of weakness and vulnerability, suggesting initiatives that could be taken to defuse the situation and, should such activity occur, to recover the status quo.

Suggested areas
of attention

Having identified an number of problems the task for the administrator is to consider how each can be eradicated – or at least minimised. The following suggestions are not exhaustive but provided as an example of areas to be considered:

Worst case scenario

In this case the worst case that could occur would be for all productive units to be wiped out simultaneously. This may be regarded as so unlikely that it can be safely ignored although animal activists have recently been able to incapacitate several facilities simultaneously so perhaps increased security at each should be considered. The next worst case could envisage the main factory being wiped out, followed possibly by the Head Office going and so on. In addition such activists may not stop at action against the premises but may also (by searching Companies House records discover the private addresses of the Directors and Company Secretary (and even the shareholders) – as happened in the action against the Huntingdon Life Sciences operation.

Action: Research enemy

Trying to establish who is likely to be the enemy (whether animate – the activists, or inanimate in terms of a fire, etc.) and what they need and what are their aims will help establish ways of dealing. For example if the Animal Liberation Front were suspected in this example, it might be possible to contact them to explain the cessation of the work which seems to be the source of their complaints. If fire is thought to be a serious hazard it must be realised that fire needs three factors before if can cause damage – a source, raw material and time. If any of these are absent, there can be little threat from such a source.

Protect privacy

As a result of terrorists finding the address of the Managing Director of Huntingdon Life Sciences from the company records filed at Companies House, they were able to attack him in the drive of his house. Legislation was introduced allowing directors subject to real or perceived threats to conceal their private addresses from public inspection. Initially this required confirmation from the Police that the person/ company was or could be a potential target, but under the latest Companies Act, all directors can 'hide' their private addresses. The company and the Registrar must still be told a director's private address as well as a 'service' address, but only the latter is to be made publicly available.

Consider advantages

The way this particular group is geographically spread provides an advantage. It has a number of sites and it is extremely unlikely, though not impossible, that all could be hit simultaneously. Assuming it is wished to retain such a multiplicity of sites, the development of flexibility of roles could be addressed, so that if one site is disabled another can cover, at least temporarily. Conversely, any inter-dependability of sites could be reduced.

Take advice

No-one can be expert in all areas. There are experts specialising in this field and their input could be sought. Even though the plan developed may never be used, the examination of procedures and practices may almost amount to a minor process re-engineering survey generating benefits of immediate use and value.

Examine vulnerability (examples only)

a) Post – institute controls and examination. Arrange for delivery elsewhere than own premises – passing to premises only when opened safely.

b) Access – examine security generally (entrances and exits, control, etc.)

c) Deliveries – institute letters of authority to ensure access provided only to genuine suppliers

d) Publicity – promote 'clean hands' image, termination of links with animal experimentation

e) Screen employees – check references, institute right of search, control internal access to sensitive areas, maintain records of unsatisfactory employees. (Of course it is not impossible for a representative of a pressure group to apply for and be given a job – and then act as a 'mole' for that group. This would almost certainly be a breach of their obligations as an employee – but this consideration is hardly likely to worry them.)

f) Increase internal security precautions – fire, explosion, etc. (creation of 'safe' areas)

g) Increase anonymity of units

Consider means of recovery

a) Relocation of workforce – difficult in view of nature of employment – consider 'bussing' people in to work

b) Possibility of production at warehouses

c) Need to check/circumvent lease restrictions

d) Keep watch on local property market for knowledge of what is available

e) Buy in product/assembly

f) Consider homeworking (check security and quality control) (see Chapter 16)

g) Prepare media messages and spokesperson

h) Attempt parallel working particularly of computer system (credit control seems especially vulnerable) and so on

Other risks

Included in the risk scenario are a number of other potential risks which could also be addressed:

a) With a largely female workforce the impact of the requirements under the 'family friendly' employment regime could create challenges regarding flexibility of working hours etc. Regardless of their attitude to such legislation, employers must work within the law and there may be an opportunity to gain from taking the initiative in such areas particularly where there are a number of people doing similar tasks.

b) There is a suggestion in the scenario that cash flow may be a problem. At times when trade is not buoyant again it may be advisable to be proactive in this area and ensure that the systems being used are providing a suitable base for the effective collection of cash owed to the business and so on.

Credit risk

The last item identified in the above example is common to many companies yet a large proportion are reactive to the challenge (i .e. chasing the debtors when the payment is already late) rather than being proactive and ensuring everything possible is effected in advance.

Case study: Training debtors

Maynards PLC had nearly 100 leased properties, rent being payable quarterly by a variety of types of tenants. Payments – needing several reminders – were received haphazardly. A pre-printed rent demand form was introduced and sent out 14 days BEFORE the due date. This form bore the words 'Please note that this payment is due on the date stated and should be received by that date. No reminder of payment will be sent and, should the amount not be received, the matter will be placed in the hands of our solicitors immediately. Costs related to any such action will also be recovered. Failure to pay by the due date is a breach of a lease covenant.'

Within a year of the introduction of the system all tenants were paying their rent within 14 days of the quarter day. As new leases were set up, a clause allowing the company to charge interest at 4 per cent over base rate in respect of any late payment, was introduced.

Being pro-active can create a climate where late payment is the exception rather than as happened at Maynards formerly almost the rule. Similar controls need to be placed over the taking of sales orders. Whilst this is a Sales Department responsibility, input from Finance is essential as they will be responsible for collection.

a) Effective order taking checklist

1. Delineate terms and bring these to the attention of the customer before the order is placed.

2. Review terms regularly – all businesses change, and terms need updating to reflect such changes.

3. Bring changes of terms to the attention of customers, either prior to the effective date or on the first placing of an order thereafter.

4. Show terms and payment basis on order and invoice

5. Check customers' credit worthiness, take references, check other suppliers records, if a company – search Companies House records (and be very wary if the purchaser is a 'sole director/sole shareholder' company – see Chapter 2)

6. Restrict size of orders until completion of [defined period] satisfactory trading/payment at lower levels. Consider use of pro-forma invoicing.

7. If credit is suspect obtain payment guarantees from a director/owner.

8. Ensure payment terms are adhered to (and that customers know extensions of credit are not permitted).

9. If reciprocal trading takes place, stipulate that any debt owing by the business to the customer, will be offset against any monies owed to the business by the customer

10. Encourage use of bankers drafts

11. Charge interest on late payment

12. Reinvoice any charges levied by bankers for dealing with late payment and 'bounced cheques'

13. Reserve the right in the terms to repossess the goods if payment in full has not been made by the due date (i.e. a retention of title clause)

14. Ensure credit control staff and/or sales force visit customers in payment default

15. Develop strict procedures for guidance of credit control personnel and ensure these are adhered to.

16. Give credit control authority to threaten sanction where necessary

17. If it appears that insisting on payment in full would bring about customer's bankruptcy or liquidation review the possibility of part payment, part reclamation of goods as security, pending payment – virtually encouraging a barter system.

18. Consider the possibility of acquisition of a non-paying customer's business

19. Ensure collection staff are trained to negotiate – and to bargain. (Liquidation can be used as a threat with a business whilst it retains its profitability and/or has assets that would be available to the cred-

itors. If such assets are not available, then liquidation is unlikely to be in anyone's interests, and negotiating a position where the debtor might be able to trade out of its cash crisis may be preferable.)

20. Set up a procedure (i.e. briefing solicitors) to action claims (i.e. via County Court etc.) or to initiate a winding up order against a company.

b) Effective Invoicing and credit control

1. Invoices will be sent at the same time as delivery of goods/services or completion of orders.

2. Second class post will be used. (As the invoice will not be paid for over a month there seems no point in paying for 'first class'.)

3. Payment terms are end of month following invoice date (every effort should be made to despatch orders with invoices before the end of each month)

4. Payment terms can be extended by prior written authority of the Board only

5. Seven days before the due date, a statement will be sent referring to the invoice and requesting prompt payment to avoid further action being taken

6. Two days after the due date, if settlement has not been forthcoming, finance/credit control will check by phone the reason for delay. If acceptable reason given set further time for chasing.

7. If an unacceptable reason is given for non-payment, chasing letter (first class or faxed) sent stating that unless payment is made by return, matter will be passed to Solicitors and costs will be charged.

8. Two days later, if settlement has not been forthcoming, request solicitors to start debt reclamation procedure.

9. The claim should include the original debt, costs of collection, including solicitors costs, plus interest on the amount due for the time overdue (which should be made clear in the terms)

NOTE: A free credit management advisory service has been made available by Better Payment Practice Group as part of its initiative to generate prompt payment – 'Collect the cash'. Information and advice via www.payontime.co.uk or telephone 020 7369 9333.

Liability protection

With this array of potential liabilities an understandable question from concerned Directors may be 'how can I eradicate my exposure?' and the only truthful answer is that you probably can't!

However it may be possible to at least minimise it as the above examples seek to demonstrate. There may be additional methods not least having procedures for dealing with the various aspects of business that could give rise to claims.

Principles for internal procedures checklist

Procedures must:

1. Address the particular problems which could create liability claims

2. Be regularly updated to reflect changes in law and the attitudes to laws (for example: the impact of Tribunal decisions in employment law matters can have the effect of changing, if not the law, at least its previously understood implications or interpretations

3. Be phrased in user-friendly language in order that comprehension by all is attained

4. Be promulgated comprehensively with everyone reminded of the implications and requirements (and particularly of any changes thereto)

5. Be policed rigorously and regularly so that everyone understands that the required code of conduct must be adhered to at all times.

In particular Boards should ensure that employees are aware of the requirements placed upon them to comply with procedures etc. Procedures on paper are helpful but it is only when they are promulgated, policed and sanctions applied if breached, that the Company and the Directors may have a defence. Thus, taking the rapidly increasing incidence of discrimination claims as an example, if there is a Dignity at Work or Equal Opportunities policy which, inter alia, requires all employees to treat others with respect and this policy is regularly brought to everyone's notice, and breaches are dealt with promptly and with appropriate severity, then it may be possible for the company and/or its officers to be absolved from liability in the event of an employee breaching the policy (see the *Haringey v Al-Azzawi* case set out in Chapter 3).

Conversely the absence of such a policy will place the employer at an immediate disadvantage. The development of policies such as is suggested here is not simply a question of prudent defence against liability claims, as shareholders, who ultimately bear the cost of such claims by diminution of their funds could argue that failure to devise and implement such policies is a breach of a Director's duties.

Safety

Increasingly Companies and Directors are being held liable for the effects of accidents at work. Once again being proactive may be a defence.

Case study: Risk assessment needed

In the *Rhone Poulenc Rorer* case an engineer went onto a fragile roof. At the entrance to the roof was a sign warning that it was fragile and that 'crawling boards should be used'. He ignored the notice, stepped on the roof, fell through and was killed. His widow sued the Company whose defence was that 'surely he was master of his own situation' and they could rely on the warning. The Court held the Company liable stating that it could not rely on a notice – there had to be practical preventative measures.

Some may feel that the court was being unreasonable but to put this in context the court is not saying 'we expect 100 per cent safety', it is reiterating an expectation that there should be practical preventative measures – reasonable in the circumstances. Companies should conduct a risk assessment (required in any event under Health & Safety law) and along the lines of the following stages:

1. Ensuring that those undertaking the work are assessed for competency

2. Stating that access to the roof was only allowed via possession of a key, only available from (say) a manager (not allowed to part with the key)

3. Instructing the manager to accompany the person to the roof to provide access (i.e. not loaning the key)

4. Before opening the door, the manager stating that access would only be granted on condition that the crawling boards provided would be used

   NOTE: the company would need to be able to show that these were in good condition and fit for their purpose to avoid liability.

5. The manager might instruct the person to put on a harness which if he did fall through would prevent him hitting the ground

6. The person might even be required before stepping on the roof to sign a statement that all the foregoing had been explained to him

7. Whilst the roof door was open the manager remaining there in order to ensure no-one else (unless under the same requirements as set out above) went onto the roof and so on.

Obviously the manager would not be able to force the employee once on the roof to wear the harness (or to stop him removing it if donned prior to access) but should an accident occur in those circumstances it seems likely that the Court would feel that the employer had done as much as they could to protect the person and thus liability might be avoided – or at the very least minimised.

NOTE: The above is for example only and it must not be assumed it would be comprehensive and/or suitable in such circumstances. A detailed risk assessment is required.

Fire

The Regulatory Reform (Fire Safety) Order 2005 simplifies fire safety law for non-domestic occupiers. It restates or initiates measures to:

- reduce the risk of fire – and risk of fire-spread
- ensure means of escape ('moe') and that these can be safely and effectively used
- fight fire
- ensure fire detection and warnings are provided
- provide instruction and training on fire
- mitigate the effects of fire.

The 2005 Regulations revoke the previous regulations but most of those requirements are restated with the very important change that no longer will Fire Certificates be issued. Thus the previous requirement to react to the advice of the fire officer, and obtaining guidance and clearance by the issue of such a certificate has now been replaced by a requirement to be completely proactive particularly regarding the preparation of (and regularly updating of) risk assessments. Such assessments must be carried out by a 'responsible person' (RP), If the workplace is under the control of the employer the RP is the employer; but if the workplace is under another person's control, the RP could be the owner. Thus where a property is in multi-occupation, in each of the 'suites' or areas occupied by individual employers, they are the RP for their own area. However the RP for 'common areas' would probably be the landlord.

Checklist: Fire safety duties

An RP should:

- take general fire precautions in respect of their employees (and others lawfully present) on the premises or in its immediate vicinity

- make assessment of all risks to which those present may be subject – with special attention paid where those persons are aged 18 or under. It might be best if these were in writing and dated, made available to all involved and regularly updated. Everyone should be encouraged to report hazards.

- ensure no new work activity involving a risk commences unless a risk assessment has been made and measures have been implemented

- implement the preventative and protective measures set out in the 1997 regulations

- eliminate (where it is reasonable to do so) or reduce the risks from dangerous substances

- ensure there is fire fighting equipment, detectors and alarms

- comply with emergency routes and exit provisions

- follow procedures for serious and imminent danger

- ensure there is a suitable system of maintenance of premises and safety equipment

- appoint competent persons to assist in conducting these preventative and protective measures

- provide information and training to employees (and others present)

- co-operate with other RPs (in neighbouring premises etc)

Enforcement is normally carried out by Fire Safety Inspectors (appointed by the local fire and rescue authority) although in some circumstances (e.g. where the subject location is a construction site) enforcement will be under the control of the Health & Safety Executive, or (where the location is a sports centre) the local authority. Failure to comply with requirements issued by an enforcement authority could lead to a fine of £20,000 or, on conviction, to an unlimited fine and/or two years imprisonment.

Pro-activity

Fire certificates issued under the previous legislation specified the means of escape and fire fighting appliances required, including that:

- appliances must be supplied with adequate notices and appropriate markings of fire escape routes etc.

- fire fighting appliances and equipment must be regularly maintained.

and so on. Most of the requirements are little more than common sense – regular safety checks to ensure escape routes are kept clear, there is no obstruction of fire exits, or of safety signs, or any reduction in the effectiveness of (for example) sprinkler systems and so on.

These obligations are now placed on the RP who needs to be pro-active – possibly needing to take advice from experts etc., – and to communicate (and update) and advise those affected.

Fire safety checklist

Inspection carried out on.........................by.....................................

In each case if answer is no – indicate when corrective action required to take place.

Paperwork

1. Do all notice boards bear an updated fire evacuation procedure?

2. Have all hazards reported since last inspection been dealt with?

3. Have all defect reports issued after last inspection been properly dealt with?

Monitoring

1. Are there fire marshals and deputies for all areas?

2. Have all marshals and deputies been trained?

3. Have changes in layout and/or procedures been brought to the attention of the marshals?

4. Have supervisors and/or marshals made all newcomers familiar with action required in the event of a fire?

Escape routes

1. Are all fire doors and exits etc checked each morning?

2. Are all escape routes clear with no goods, furniture etc obstructing such routes?

3. Are all escape routes well signposted?

4. Are directions to all escape routes clear from all departments?

5. Do all exit doors open easily?

6. Are all exit signs visible and legible?

7. Are fire resisting doors operative and undamaged?

8. Do fire resisting doors shut properly?

Equipment

1. Are all extinguishers, hoses etc., in place?

2. Is all such equipment within its time limit for checking?

3. Are all fire alarm call points in good condition?

4. Are all fire alarm call points clearly marked and not obstructed?

5. If smoking is allowed on the premises, are all departments supplied with well-maintained metal waste containers?

6. Is emergency lighting operative?

Assembly areas

1. Are all assembly areas clear and well signposted/identifiable?

2. Is protective clothing available? *

Action as a result of such checks should be initiated by written Defect Report with an action date. Checking to ensure that Defects noted at the previous inspection then themselves (as shown above) form part of the checklist at the next following Fire safety check.

* This may not be essential for all organisations. However I was impressed by preparedness of the Hilton Hotel at Edinburgh Airport when there was a fire evacuation at 1.30 a.m. one cold Thursday morning in December. Many guests had not stopped to grab a coat and the Hotel staff were issuing the foil wraps used by mountain rescue teams and given to runners at the end of marathons to retain body heat of those who had evacuated only in their night garments.

(From the author's *A-Z of Facility and Property Administration*).

Note: This is not exhaustive and is meant only as an example of an approach.

Road safety

It has also been suggested by the Health and Safety Commission that employers, which could include Directors personally, could in certain circumstances be held jointly liable with their employee drivers for accidents caused by the latter. It is estimated by the Police that 20 per cent of road accidents are caused by tiredness – the driver being at the wheel without a break for too long a period. Around two-thirds of vehicles on the road are company owned and thus a high proportion of 'tiredness induced' accidents are caused by drivers undertaking work-related journeys. Where it can be shown that an accident resulted from tiredness which resulted from the employer 'conditioning' the driver to undertake a long drive without a break, the proposal is that the employer should be prosecuted as well as the driver. To protect this situation it may be advisable for the employer to adopt a wording in employee-drivers' contracts such as:

Driving safety – and safely

1. In driving as a result of the requirements of the job, you must at all times comply with every law affecting such driving and road use. Failing to observe this requirement could result in a loss of insurance cover and your being made personally liable for loss caused. If driving your own car you must be able to prove you are insured for such business use and be able to demonstrate that it is properly maintained and roadworthy.

2. Tiredness is stated to cause 20 per cent of road accidents and when driving in excess of [100] miles during a working day you should ensure you take a break of at least 15 minutes and light refreshments. The cost of the latter will be borne by [the employer] to a maximum of [£x].

3. Mobile phones may only be used in a vehicle via a hands free system. Even with such a system it is preferable to stop to take a call.

   [OR, preferably to be prudent, 'Drivers on their employer's business should ensure their mobile phones are switched off whilst driving. They should also stop regularly (as referred to above) and during such stops could use the time to check and reply to messages left on the phone.]

4. In the event that in addition to the normal working day you are also required to drive in excess of [3 hours] you should plan the day so that suitable time for rest is made available – and take a break of at least 20 minutes during the drive.

5. If the requirements of the job are such that you finish working and are in excess of [100 miles or X hours] from home, you should book into a convenient Hotel for the night. The charge for this can include a light meal and/or breakfast and should not exceed [£x]. To ensure compliance with this clause every attempt should be made to pre-book such accommodation.

6. Medical advice should be taken when medication which causes drowsiness is prescribed.

7. You must present a valid driving licence before you drive on the company's behalf and confirm it is your only UK driving licence. Such licence must be presented for inspection annually. If you lose your licence as a result of prosecution etc. you must immediately notify the Company. Failure to do so is regarded as a dismissable offence.

8. When driving or travelling in a company vehicle, smoking is not permitted.

Notes

1. Since drink and drug taking also account for a substantial proportion of road accidents, employers should also consider how best to prohibit driving in such circumstances (e.g. by carrying out spot checks etc.)

2. In the event that the employer discovers that the employee has breached the clause action would be essential if their own position is to be protected.

3. A similar procedure should be adopted for any other persons (e.g. spouses or partners) who drive a company vehicle, and/or for those who drive their own vehicles on company business – although here there should be a check made to ensure the driver's own insurance cover extends to such 'business use'.

Case study: Good rules = sound defence

Unless an employer stipulates that employees should not use a phone (even hands free) whilst driving, should an employee have an accident which can be shown to be a result of a distraction caused by the use of the phone, the employer may also be found guilty. Employers should not only stipulate that phones should not be used whilst driving but should also be able to show that this was clearly laid down with individual employees – ideally by employees signing their acknowledgement of the rules. (If an employee refuses to sign then a 'witness' should be called to evidence that the employee was given the handbook – and could understand it).

Alan Millbanke was employed by a delivery organisation who had not only stipulated that employees should not use a mobile phone whilst driving but also put this in their handbook and required employees to sign their acknowledgement of receipt of the handbook. Millbanke caused a fatal accident whilst using a mobile phone when driving and has been found guilty – which carries a life imprisonment sentence. However, the employer was not prosecuted.

Stress

Background

Work related stress is the biggest occupational cause of absence from work (average 29 days per case), costing £3.7 billion per year.

It is not unknown for those under investigation on either a disciplinary basis or a financial irregularities investigation to state they are subject to 'stress'. The 'stress claim bandwagon' has gathered momentum in recent years and although no doubt some claims were genuine others seemed decidedly suspect.

Until 2002 there were an increasingly number of nationally reported cases, virtually all settled out of Court, where employees won substantial sums for stress brought on by workplace activities and because their employers failed to take action. For example, a warden at a travellers' accommodation site won record £203,000 damages from his employers, Worcestershire County Council, in an out of court settlement where the employer admitted liability. His employers failed to support him when the residents at the site subjected him to violent and abusive behaviour. He was the third warden at the site to suffer a stress-related illness.

The most common causes of stress are:

a) long working hours

b) work overload

c) job characteristics (e.g. dealing with the public)

d) lack of management support

e) lengthy and/or wearying travelling

f) bullying and harassment

and most are to a greater or lesser extent the responsibility of the employer.

Research

A survey carried out by independent think tank, Demos, concluded

a) 44% of the workforce return home exhausted

b) 60% of men and 45% of women work on Saturday (usually or some-
    times)

c) 28% of men work more than 48 hours each week (but 70% of those
    working more than 40 hours want to work less). It is claimed that
    UK employees work longer than employees in any other EU country.

d) 25% of managers take home work each week

e) 86% of women state they never have enough time to get things done

f) 33% of men work a 6/7 day week

g) The average lunch 'hour' lasts 30 minutes.

Of itself each factor may not have a harmfully stressful result – after
all some claim they work best when under pressure. Indeed those
working long hours might reduce their 'working stress' with shorter
hours but if wages are reduced in proportion (as would normally be
expected) their 'economic stress' trying to survive on a lower income
might be well increase.

However the overall picture suggests that people need to work longer
and harder to generate the income they feel they need to exist within
society, or because they feel insecure – or both. If it is perceived that
employers can be sued for 'causing' stress or its results, this could result
in an increased number of such claims – a trend which those that spe-
cialise in personal injury claims are now reporting. It would be prudent
for employers to be prepared.

Three enduring principles

For an employee to be able to successfully claim compensation for stress
in the workplace, three principles must be present. There must be

a) a breach of the employer's common law duty to provide all employ-
    ees with a safe working environment AND

b) medical evidence demonstrating that the condition was stress-related
    and that this was linked to the working environment AND

c) proof that the employer was in some way negligent in that the condition was foreseeable and yet the employer did nothing about it (or that the condition was reported to the employer and the employer then did nothing about it).

The Court's view

In a ground-breaking decision the Court of Appeal (Times 12.2.02) reversed this bias in favour of employees who claim to be suffering from work-induced stress. Overturning 3 stress awards (and only confirming a 4th with 'some hesitation') the Court's issued 12 points of guidance including:

a) employers are entitled to take at face value what they are told by their employees and do not need to make searching enquiries.

(Presumably therefore if the employer suspected an employee was under stress but the employee stated they were not, the employer would be able to accept that answer without further enquiry – although even then it might be advisable to take medical advice on the matter.)

b) employers are entitled to assume that an employee will be able to withstand the normal pressures of the job UNLESS they know of a particular problem.

(Again it would be advisable to investigate further, with medical advice if appropriate, if there is any suspicion that the employee is under stress.)

c) any employer who offers a confidential counselling service with access to treatment is unlikely to be held liable in the event of a stress claim.

(There are an increasing number of these agencies springing up and it may be economically effective (as well as providing an additional employee benefit) to retain their services and let all employees know of the facility.)

BUT

One of the cases that the Court rejected was *Barber v Somerset County Council*, which was then further appealed to the House of Lords. The HoL overturned the Court of Appeal's decision stating that the 'overall test is still the conduct of the reasonable and prudent employer, taking positive thought for his workers in the light of what he knows or ought to know.'

Although the Court of Appeal's advice that 'an employer is entitled to assume that his employee is up to the normal pressures of the job' was sound, it had to be read as that and not having statutory force. Every case would depend on its own facts.

Employer's requirement to be proactive

Inactivity on the part of employers would seem to be inadvisable, and a checklist such as the following may be an appropriate start point

1. Do we have knowledge of a past history of any employee having a risk to their health (either in our employ or that of a previous employer)?

2. Has the employee (e.g. on an application form or during an Appraisal interview) made it known that they have a problem?

3. Do we have such a check question on the Appraisal form – if not was the matter raised at interview?

4. Is the employees workload out of proportion to a 'normal' workload?

5. Is there managerial support for employees in potentially stressful positions?

6. Is the work particularly demanding, or subject to aggravation (e.g. working with angry consumers or members of the public) or emotionally demanding?

7. Is there a history of problems with other employees doing this job?

8. Is there a record of absence/sickness for those doing this job or the subject employee?

9. Does the employee have a history of 'stress' related disorders?

10. Has the subject used the employer's Employee Counselling service?

Employee Assistance Programmes (EAPs)

The last item in the checklist (and the third of the Court of Appeal's advice quoted above) would be covered by the employer offering an EAP. There has been a considerable rise in the number of employers providing EAPs in recent years.

Generally these are confidential services provided to enable employees to source advice and coun-selling regarding problems often, but not exclusively, related to the work environment and relationships. Making arrangements so that any employee feeling stressed should contact such a service for advice should help an employer defend a subsequent claim. Some private medical cover insurers provide stress counselling services – as increasingly do employer liability insurers. Making free access to such facilities would seem to be a suitable means of protecting against potential stress claims at least until new legislation is introduced.

In the *Best* case, Mr Best, following a breakdown took retirement from his employer – a University. Although there was a record of complaints from him about his excessive workload the Court of Appeal found that there had not been sufficient indication of impending harm to him. In addition the fact that there was a counselling service available which he had not used was a factor in rejecting his claim.

Current developments

The Health and Safety Executive (HSE) has adopted its Management Standards for Stress developed after a consultation process with public and private sector organisations. There are 6 main areas of investigation and it has been stated that an employer should be able to resist a stress claim if 85% or more employees state the Demands, Control and Support criteria are met, and 65% or more state the Relationships, Role and Change criteria are met.

Demands: Employees should be given adequate and achievable demands related to hours worked. Skills and abilities should be matched to job demands and the later should be within an employee's capability.

Control: Employees should be permitted control over their pace of work and when they can take breaks. Employers should encourage employees to develop their skills and to undertake new challenges. Employees should be consulted concerning working patterns.

Support: There should be clear policies and procedures to support employees adequately. Managers must support their team members and every employee should support each of their colleagues. Employers should know what support is available and how to access it.

Role: Employers should provide employees with clear information so that they can understand their role and responsibilities. There should be systems allowing employees to raise concerns about uncertainties and conflicts.

Relationships: Positive behaviour should be promoted in the working environment to avoid conflict and ensure fairness. There should be procedures to outlaw and prevent unacceptable behaviour. Employees should be encouraged to share information about their work.

Change: The employer should provide information to employees concerning all changes likely to affect them. There should be adequate consultation and a process whereby employees can influence proposals. Timetables for changes should be published and employees should have access to support during the change process.

The HSE believes that employers should adopt a standard that ensures:

a) employees indicate that they are able to cope with the demands of their jobs and

b) systems are in place locally to respond to any individual concerns.

Employers should use the 6 criteria as a risk assessment and follow a five stage approach. The HSE website (www.hse.gov.uk/stress/standards) states (with suggestions of action and explanations):

1. Identify the hazards that could generate stress. (Easy to state but not so easy to do since stress is essentially a personal problem – what one person might find stressful another would be able to handle with ease.)

2. Decide who may be harmed and how – using a survey (which might generate more problems than answers)

3. Evaluate the risk – essentially discussing problems with employees

4. Recording the findings and developing an action plan

5. Monitoring and reviewing.

Conclusion

This is not an area for the application of a 'one size fits all' procedure. Stress being essentially a one-off problem (that is a situation that one person finds acceptable could well be stressful to another) the arithmetical aspect of the above is not so much the test as to demonstrate (if the levels are not met) that the culture of the organisation creates a potentially stress-ful environment which could be dangerous for some.

Note

1. Under the Health & Safety (Directors Duties) Act, Directors are required to take reasonable steps to ensure that their company is complying with health and safety law and appoint one of their number as a 'Safety Director'. It is partly for this reason that Safety is shown as a regular item on the Board Agenda (see Chapter Six)

2. The Chartered Institute of Personnel and Development has produced a guide showing how to support, rehabilitate and retain employ-ees suffering from stress and other mental problems.

(Contact:

www.cipd.co.uk/subjects/health/mentalhlth/recrehabretent.htm)

Risk transference

Risk transference entails an acceptance that there may be risks but that the person at risk should be protected in some way – and/or that someone else should bear the cost. Whilst in some cases this may be possible there are several important principles to bear in mind which are set out in the following checklist

Limiting protections checklist

a) A company can include in its Articles a clause seeking to indem-nify its officers and employees from liability incurred in exercising their responsibilities.

Further, a company cannot alter its Articles or include in them or in any Director's contract a clause which seeks to absolve or indem-nify him from liability for dishonesty, negligence, breach of duty or trust, etc.

b) Many of the instances where a breach of law incurs liability now entail a criminal as well as a civil penalty but it is impossible to insure against such actions (since it is against the public interest to insure against a criminal act) – and would be improper (and almost certainly ultra vires its Memorandum) for a company to grant such an indemnity in such circumstances. For example in an action for Wrongful Trading, a Director found guilty would almost certainly be found to have acted dishonestly so no claim would be entertained by the insurer.

c) A Director can only commission actions allowed under the Articles. If a Director acts outside the requirements of its Articles (i.e. he acts *ultra vires* but not illegally in any way) the company could not, without the shareholders' Agreement, indemnify such acts. However the Companies Act 1989 amended the Companies Act 1985 by granting companies the right to effect Directors and Officers Liability Insurance cover – a right repeated in the Companies Act 2006 S 233. Further, provided the cost is declared in the Directors' Report in the Annual Report, then the cost of the premiums in respect of such a policy can be met by the company. Recent amendments to Finance Acts have also prevented the Inland Revenue from regarding the premiums paid as a benefit in kind for those directors and others covered by it. Some authorities have queried whether, since such a policy is to cover the directors, they can approve such a benefit as each will have an interest in the item of business and thus there may not be a disinterested quorum present at the meeting.

In case this is arguable it may be preferable either to amend the Articles to grant the Board the right to take out such a policy or to effect, say, two policies – each covering some of the Board and authorised by those not covered. It has been reported that several companies have changed their Memorandums to allow the companies to effect such a policy.

The exact cover of such a policy should be examined. It will usually exclude dishonesty, fraud, slander, libel, pollution and any actions resulting from a Director seeking to benefit personally. As indicated above if a Director was found to be guilty of wrongful trading that would probably be classed as dishonesty and no claim could be made. On the other hand if a Director was accused of Wrongful Trading but acquitted then the legal costs etc. associated with the case and borne by him would normally be claimable – the exact wording of such policies should be examined.

Summary checklist

- Directors in taking risks need to identify protections and minimise undue risk

- Contingency planning can assist risk identification and reduction as well as normal management control

- Procedures and rules need to be devised, promulgated to all concerned and policed (with sanctions applied for those responsible for breach)

- Insurance can be effected within limits – the wording of policies should be carefully scrutinised

Chapter six

'Ill met' – without method

Procedures for effective
Board Meetings

Determining the aims of Board Meetings

Agendas

Dynamic Agendas

Timetable

Aims

Interested parties

The effective meeting

Summary checklist

Determining the aims of Board Meetings

Open for business

Company law places no obligation on Directors to meet as a Board, or even for regular informal meetings of the Directors to be held. Perhaps more correctly it could be said that it carries no explicit requirements in this regard, although there are certainly implicit requirements that the Directors will meet and make decisions whether formally or informally, since should they fail to control the operation of the company they could be held to be in breach of their duty as Directors (see the *Dorchester Finance Co v Stebbing* case in Chapter 2). In addition the Directors must approve the accounts, balance sheet and report of Directors for submission to the shareholders. This lack of explicit requirement to hold Board meetings can lull members into a false sense of security. However a moments thought regarding the Director's duty of care will generate the question 'if we don't meet and decide formally – with a record made of the meeting – how would I be able to prove I exercised my duty of care if ever this was challenged?'

Extension of the powers of the Competition Commissioner and Office of Fair Trading is envisaged in new guidelines recently issued. Where one or some members of a Board have been involved in anti-competitive activities ALL members could find themselves disqualified even though some could legitimately claim that they knew nothing of such activities. This thus extends to anti-competitive activities the 'ought to have known' test set out in the Insolvency Act related to wrongful trading. Margaret Bloom, the then director of Competition Policy stated that there was no intent to implement 'witch hunts' but that the new powers will be a 'very valuable deterrent against anti-competitive behaviour [which will be] used very carefully'.

The taking and recording of minutes of Board meetings will become an even more necessary defence for the innocent – for example at the very least, non-executive Directors (and executive Directors in some cases) might want written and constantly updated assurances that everyone in involved in buying and selling is familiar with the requirements of, and is compliant with the Competition and Enterprise Acts. It might be advisable to set up a process of spot checking with suppliers and customers prices and terms quoted to them and (perhaps covertly) discovering the prices quoted by competitors to try to ensure there is no possibility or practice of 'price-fixing'.

Realistically most Directors will meet and discuss the conduct of the company with their colleagues and in most companies of any size or where there are more than (say) three Directors, this control is best exercised by holding regular meetings. Indeed in most companies a considerable amount of the work of most Directors revolves around meetings of the Board, of committees appointed by the Board and/or to discuss their own operational responsibilities. Irrespective of their level, all meetings should consider data, discuss proposals, contentions or conclusions arising from the data and make decisions. There is a saying that 'meetings take minutes and waste hours' – if so it is because three key aspects of successful (i.e. effective) meeting administration have not been given due regard. Specifically:

- The aims of the meeting need to be clearly defined

- The chairman needs to keep the attention of the meeting to the aims determined, and

- The secretary needs to ensure the meeting flows smoothly with everyone advised of all details regarding business previously noted for discussion (for example, by the provision of a dynamic Agenda – see below).

In addition the ethos of the organisation needs to be tuned to the accomplishment of business via meetings. This may be easier said than done since in some organisation's meetings seem to be held for 'meeting's sake' and in fact far from stimulating and generating swift decisions, they may be used as a means for delaying decisions and ensuring when taken that no one individual can be held responsible for their effect. This may be acceptable for some 'junior' meetings but it is unlikely to be acceptable for Board meetings.

Agendas

Every meeting should have an aim – if only 'to review progress since the previous meeting and consider how this impacts the attainment of short and long term aims'. To ensure the meeting adheres to its aim it may be advisable to state it at the commencement of the Agenda and to compose the Agenda in such a way that it delineates the business requiring decisions which meet the aim. Too often the composition of an agenda is given insufficient attention and serves as little more than a notification, to those required to attend, of the date and time of the meeting rather than creating an awareness of subject matter that need research, deliberation and decision. Inevitably the construction of an Agenda will depend very much on the type of meeting required – but equally the efficiency of the meeting can depend how constructively the Agenda is compiled. If it is a regular monitoring meeting it could comprise items drawn from the sources set out in the following checklist.

Sources for agenda items checklist

a) an annual list of items to be considered at set times (e.g. the dividend, preliminary announcement)

b) items to be considered or reconsidered requested from the previous or earlier meetings

c) new business arising since the previous meeting out of the operation of the organisation

d) items requested to be considered by members (individual house rules may apply to these items – e.g. they may be required to be approved by the Chairman prior to inclusion)

e) regular reports (accounts, cash forecast, contracts, etc.)

f) market, economic or legal changes affecting the business

g) statutorily (or similarly) required items (e.g. approval of the Report of the Directors and annual accounts for submission to the AGM, dividend recommendation, etc.).

h) original material, possibly generated by the Chairman as a result of his responsibility for driving the meeting and the company forward.

Alternatively a meeting may be required to consider a particular subject. In this case there is greater scope for determining the extent of the deliberations, the aim and even the duration of the meeting by generating what can be termed a 'dynamic Agenda'.

Dynamic Agendas

a) One-off meeting

AGENDA

For an [informal executive] meeting to be held on [date one week ahead] in the Company Boardroom at 2.p.m. prompt

Subject: Employee absenteeism

Aim of meeting

To devise and implement [up to five] tactics or initiatives for immediate implementation which will have the effect of reducing absenteeism to near or below the industry average.

Items for discussion

1. To consider monthly reports of staff absenteeism over past 12 months (See analysis attached).

2. To compare such reports with analyses of absenteeism throughout the industry (See report from [Industry] Trade Association attached).

3. To consider whether there are special reasons for this company's poor performance, and if so what can be changed/improved to ensure a reduction.

4. To determine [five or more] methods to ensure such a reduction. Members will be expected to attend with ideas for consideration at the meeting, such ideas must be capable of implementation within 14 days.

Administration

The meeting duration will be 2 hours. No interruptions or messages.

Attendance

Group Finance Director (Chairman), Personnel Director, Company Nurse, Company Secretary, Works Manager.

Notes

a) Setting the meeting a week ahead should allow ample thinking time

b) Providing internal statistics with external comparisons sets the problem in context with the delay before the meeting allowing time for assimilation of the data

c) Requesting members ideas should assist accountability

d) Stating that there must be no interruptions not only allows meeting members to brief their staff accordingly but also underlines the importance attached to the subject by the Chairman. It is not unknown for some meeting attenders to arrange for deliberate interruptions to meetings either to enable them to 'escape' some agenda items or simply to try to bolster their own importance

e) the tone and structure of the agenda itself seeks to demonstrate that action is required. It implies an urgency reflecting that of the Board regarding the subject matter.

b) Regular Board meeting

ANY COMPANY LIMITED   **AGENDA**

For a Board Meeting on 30th March 2xxx in the Boardroom at 10.00 a.m.

Apologies for absence

1. MINUTES of the Board Meeting held on 29th February (Copy attached)

2. SHARES

    i) Resolution to approve share transfers in favour of PQR

    ii) Consider recommendation that share registration work of the company be placed with Share Registrars Ltd. (Report and contract attached)

3. FINANCE

   i) Consider Management accounts to 29th February 2XXX. (Complete set to be distributed by Finance Dept by 25th March)

   ii) Consider recommended change to calculation of depreciation charge. (See report from Finance Dept on effect attached)

   iii) Capital expenditure.

      a) Proposed purchase of (units)

      b) Capex project 13/2XXX

   iv) Cash flow. (Projection for remainder of 2XXX attached)

   v) Bank Mandate. (New format in terms of attached draft is required to be adopted.)

   vi) Borrowings. (The Secretary to table a report concerning negotiations with the bankers regarding sourcing additional borrowing.)

   Draft resolution:THAT the Chairman and the Company Secretary be and they hereby are empowered to sign such documents and take such actions to provide the company's bankers with the documentation they required in order to facilitate the advance of the additional borrowing requirement.

4. CURRENT TRADING

   Managing Directors report (see enclosed confidential report)

5. PERSONNEL

   i) Wage negotiations for review 1st July 2XXX (see report from Divisional Director (Personnel) attached)

   ii) Impact of recent anti-discrimination legislation (Secretary to report at meeting with recommendations to be tabled.)

6. PROPERTY

   i) Board approval required for items X, XX, XXX in attached report.

   ii) Progress on sale (facility)

7. SAFETY MATTERS

   i) General report

   ii) Advice regarding [new project] implementation

8. SEALING

Approval required for items 345 to 361

9. BOARD MEETINGS IN 2XXX

Consider additional dates as follows 28th April, 30th May, 30th June, 28th July, 31st August, 29th September, 25th October, 23rd November, and 21st December.

NOTE: This is the Agenda which convened the meeting the suggested Minutes of which are set out in Chapter 8.

The advantages of a detailed Agenda include:

a)   a guide to the Chairman in defining decisions that need to be made

b)   a guide to members of the business that must be decided

c)   for the Secretary, an invaluable first draft of the Minutes of the meeting!

With regular meetings (e.g. board meetings), an Agenda should always follow a set format and order, whilst the grouping of like items under general headings may assist the logical 'flow' of the business of the meeting. Setting out under each item the aim of the business (for example a draft resolution) should help concentrate the mind on what needs to be addressed.

Timetable

Certain business needs to be transacted at set times of the year and the timing of these requirements should be reflected in the list of meeting dates which should be prepared for at least a year ahead. This could include firm dates for (say) nine months, with suggested dates for later meetings which would be confirmed by an updated timetable issued on (say) a rolling six month basis. This list should incorporate reference to such business, e.g. dividend payment, preliminary announcement and report publication dates etc. Ideally meeting dates should not be altered to avoid:

a) Members finding that although they could have attended on the original date they cannot make the amended date and

b) Those required to originate and submit items and reports for the Board to alter what can be complex reporting procedures. Ideally Board meetings should not be cancelled although a short postponement may be inevitable on occasion. In most companies there is routine business which needs to be authorised or considered and cancellation may mean that required authority is not obtained, either leading to delay or possibly commitment without authorisation.

Timing and despatch of Agenda

There is no currently legal requirement to generate an Agenda for Board meetings or any prescription regarding its contents – although the EU is drafting a directive which would require Boards of listed PLCs to meet at least 4 times a year and may set out certain business which needs to be reviewed. Commercial pressures (apart from the need already highlighted to be able to demonstrate to shareholders and others that proper control of the company is being undertaken – that is that the Directors are exercising and can be shown to be exercising their duty of care) however will usually dictate that Board Meetings should be properly convened. The simplest way of effecting this is by sending a properly composed and issued Agenda with back up data to every member in good time, so that Directors are:

a) Able to exercise the required control

b) Able to make informed judgements on the matters requiring decisions, and

c) Have information of the current company strategy and tactics (drawn from interfacing with their colleagues) to apply to their own direct responsibilities.

All Directors must be sent notice of the meeting (usually included as above as part of an Agenda) and supporting documentation. This should apply even when a Director has indicated that he will be unable to attend and/or will be out of the country (when company law states that there is no obligation to send him notice of a Board meeting). In this way the Director will receive not only the agenda but also the supporting documentation. Since most Boards operate under a kind of 'continuum', with policy developing in reaction to events, by reading the documentation and the minutes, even Directors who were unable to be present at a meeting should remain comprehensively briefed and updated. Ideally an agenda should be despatched at least 7 working days prior to the meeting and be accompanied by all relevant documents. Unless this occurs many members will attend not having read the papers, leading in turn either:

- To decisions being taken based on incomplete knowledge, or

- Using valuable meeting time whilst individuals check points in documents only received just before or even at the meeting. Where papers do need to be given to members late a summary, of the salient points should be requested as a covering sheet.

There have been instances where data relating to contentious matters have been deliberately held back and tabled at the meeting so that the sponsor can try to gain acceptance without proper discussion. This kind of approach should be stopped by the Chairman since it is a denial of the right of Directors to be informed on matters on which they must make decisions. Indeed if they take a decision on a complex matter which is tabled rather than subject to normal notice, it could be argued that they are not exercising their duty of care. It also acts against the principle of the Board working collectively as a team.

Aims

Meetings exist to take decisions. The Chairman/meeting should establish what decisions are required and by when. These should be stated when the body is set up (e.g. as its terms of reference) and possibly repeated at the commencement of the meeting to encourage focussing of attention. Where use is made of a dynamic Agenda this principle can be reflected within the Agenda itself. Much of the Board's work will be a consideration of routine business – nevertheless this is still an aim forming part of the overall duty to drive the business forward (i.e. taking relatively low key decisions to improve performance etc.).

Composition and cost

Only those required to attend should be present since a meeting's length tends to be proportionate to the number present. Obviously all Directors, unless unavoidably absent, should attend, but often a Board's numbers may be swelled by requesting the attendance of advisors – both internal and external (e.g. auditors etc.). Whilst the attendance of such persons may be essential for the proper consideration of individual items, they should be encouraged to attend only for the discussion of that item. If the Board is attended by persons whose contribution is unnecessary or irrelevant, the effectiveness of those required to be present and of the meeting as a whole will be diluted. Unfortunately attendance at a meeting can sometimes be regarded as an indication of importance which can then become an enticement to attend even when there is no point or requirement.

Calculating the cost per minute of those present at the meeting (based on annual salary plus on costs) may encourage a crude cost-benefit analysis of the value of the decisions reached. Consideration of such cost may concentrate the mind on the meeting's composition. All members should be encouraged to make effective contributions that are concise yet comprehensive. The rationale of a meeting is for its members to take decisions, and whilst some dialogue is necessary to explore all the ramifications of each item of business, allowing such dissection of data to become general discussions may be counter productive. Against this, 'brainstorming' should not be undervalued. However if this is required (e.g. to determine new products, direction, strategy etc. or simply to help formulate the latest business plan) it should be on a properly structured basis – at a meeting (perhaps off premises) deliberately convened for the purpose.

Data

Reports, analyses and all other data required for consideration by the meeting should accompany the Agenda (and be presented in Agenda order) or a note regarding late submission be appended thereto (see checklist below). Tabling a bulky or complex report should be avoided as decision-taking on its contents is likely to be uninformed. Where such data comprises bulky or complex reports, an accompanying precis of findings and/or recommendations may be useful. A rule that all reports should contain brief and prioritised recommendations and incorporate a requirement to analysis the effect of NOT proceeding in the way suggested, may encourage effective analysis and action. Whilst the aim of this is to ensure that the meeting has available the information required in order to make most appropriate decisions, the requirement to prepare a synopsis and recommendations and to consider a 'no progress' alternative can focus the mind and may even suggest further alternatives – that is to achieve a dynamism of its own.

Procedure at meetings

Although the level of formality of the meeting will differ widely according to individual company preferences and custom, it is usual for all members to sign a book of attendance, and to address and speak through the Chairman, and for the Chairman to summarise considered suggestions(s), before taking the 'sense' or decision of the meeting – usually by consensus, but occasionally by vote. Summarising the decision should aid the accurate recording of the decision in the minutes. In a Board meeting each person (since they are obliged to be present) has a right to be heard on each subject, not least since the authority for the decisions depends on the collective responsibility of the Board as an entity.

Apologies for absence

Even though there is no explicit obligation on Boards to hold Board Meetings, Directors are obliged to attend Meetings if they are held. Indeed in the draft Articles for an LTD accompanying the 2006 Companies Act, Regulation 18(d) allows the directors to terminate a director's appointment if 'that person [has] repeatedly and without reasonable excuse failed to participate in processes by which majority decisions may be taken'. Equally Directors are under pressure (if only to be able to demonstrate that they are exercising the required control over the company and thus fulfilling their duty) to attend Board meetings unless such absence is unavoidable. Failure to attend without good reason could lead to accusations of dereliction of the duties Directors were appointed to undertake (apart from rendering them liable for personal penalties should the company find itself in difficulties). Thus it is important to record both who is present and who is absent. Some companies require their Directors to sign an Attendance Book for each meeting. In addition should they need to leave the meeting prior to its conclusion this fact should be noted in the minutes – as should late arrival. If an Attendance Book is not used (and even if it is) the names of those attending the Board should be noted in the Minutes of the meeting.

Quorum

If a quorum is required under the Articles (or is set by the Directors as is allowed in the Articles accompanying Companies Act 2006), the Secretary should ensure these requirements can be met. If difficulty is regularly experienced obtaining a quorum (for example the number of Directors is four and there is no wish to increase the size of the Board since it operates well, but the quorum is also four), the requirement in the Articles should be considered for review. One alternative to this would be to allow a non-quorate meeting to take place with all decisions arrived at being made 'subject to full Board ratification'. At the next following meeting at which a quorum is present all the acts and decisions arrived at by the non-quorate body can then be ratified. The problem with such a device is that if there is any appreciable time delay between meetings of the non-quorate body and the Board with a proper quorum any decisions may be held to be *ultra vires*. Legal advice should be taken. Whether Directors with interests in the subject matter can be counted as part of the quorum should also be checked to avoid the situation where decisions are made by a non-quorate Board with potential implications for those responsible.

Where the number of Directors is relatively low and the quorum required relatively high, care should be taken that a meeting which starts quorate does not become 'non-quorate' because a Director has to leave before its conclusion. Subject to authority in the Articles of course the Directors could appoint alternates to act if their principal is absent.

Where a Board is larger and requires specific matters to be considered by sub-committees, each of them should be given terms of reference including a quorum requirement. If a Board fails to observe quorum requirements then any decision can be put aside.

Case study: A singular problem

In *Smith v Henniker-Major* a director acting on his own purported to pass a Board resolution. The Articles stated that the quorum for valid Board meetings was two directors. The court stated that the resolution was a worthless piece of paper.

All directors (unless they are outside the UK) have a right to notice of a meeting and thus the director in this case was also in breach of this requirement.

Further, if, as a result of his illegal action, the company was subject to loss, presumably the shareholders could take action against him for acting 'ultra vires' the Articles and against their best interests.

Written Board resolutions

Although the concept should ideally be covered in the Articles, there is little to stop a Board passing resolutions regarding its business by means of written resolutions. To effect this, a copy of the resolution required to be passed should be sent to each member and if they agree they should be invited to sign their copy and return it. Ideally such a process would require unanimity but in theory at least there is little to stop a majority decision being binding provided all have had a chance to consider and vote on the matter (which is the process they would have gone through had they actually met).

Voting

Experience indicates that most business at Board meetings is agreed by consensus. Given that, to be effective, the Board must act as a team and despite sometimes divergent views share a common aim, this may not be surprising. However there may be occasions when consensus is not possible and a formal vote needs to be taken. The voting power of individual members needs to be checked against the terms of reference/appointment – for example:

a) The chairman may be granted a second or casting vote in the event of an equality of votes

b) In some instances the chairman only has a vote where there is an equality of votes

c) Where a Director(s) is/are 'nominee(s)', for example of a major corporate shareholder (or of the 'senior' partner in a joint venture company), they may have enhanced voting rights in particular circumstances and so on. Once again the Articles (or the contents of a Shareholders Agreement. Such an Agreement should be carefully checked to ensure that there is no conflict with the Company's Articles) need to be referred to, to ensure votes are properly exercised – and a record is taken and preserved.

Interested parties

Under Company Law on appointment, or on gaining the interest if later, a director must indicate all interests in third parties with which the company is trading. Failure to do so or to breach the requirements regarding conflicts of interest, are subject to a fine. Thereafter the internal rules regarding such conflicts should be found in the company's Articles. Many will state a director must not vote on a matter in which he had an interest. Some Articles go further and state (for example) that he may not even join in the discussion and/or that he cannot be counted in the quorum for the meeting, etc.

The effective meeting

Although the responsibility for the convening and running of Board Meetings lies predominately with, and should be delegated to the Company Secretary (reference should be made to Chapter 7 to review the secretary's responsibilities), ultimately Directors are responsible for all activities of the company. Few activities are more important than that of running Shareholder and Board meetings and every Director should be aware of the need to ensure that their meetings are effective, efficient and that all required business is reviewed and necessary decisions made. Board meetings should exist for one purpose only – to consider reports, data and business, thus enabling the Board to take decisions that will have the effect of driving the company forward to attain its aims. It should be obvious that to achieve this, those present need to be comprehensively briefed on the subject matters. This can be best achieved by ensuring that all reports, data and proposals are set before the members well in advance of the meeting so that they have time:

- To consider the content
- To think about it, and
- To make their own investigation or research on the subject, etc.

Inevitably there will be occasions when a report etc. has to be tabled – in such a case members should be required to present the report amplified by a brief summary of the findings and/or recommendations. The concept of providing a summary can be a valuable time-saver for other business – bearing in mind the responsibility placed on directors to be aware of the detail of items that they might be asked to sign. (See the *D'Jan* case in Chapter 1). For this reason a 'Data submission checklist' may be helpful.

Data submission requirements checklist

Timetable

1. A timetable for all required to attend and/or submit data to the meeting will be prepared on a rolling 6 month basis and issued by the Company Secretary.

2. Other than in the most exceptional instances, the timing of meetings will not be changed and any member unable to attend must let the Company Secretary know as soon as possible.

3. A member wishing to raise business at a Board Meeting must agree its inclusion with the Chairman 10 working days before the meeting and, providing the Chairman has approved its inclusion, advise the Company Secretary of the need to add it to the Agenda for the next meeting.

4. An agenda with supporting data should always be issued at least 7 working days prior to a meeting.

Data required

1. All information and reports should be made available to the Company Secretary at least 9 working days before the meeting.

2. All data should be submitted with the required number of copies. This number should be the number of persons entitled to receive the agenda plus any required to be sent out for information, plus, say, 2 spares.

a) Some companies distribute Board reports (even confidential material) to senior executives. An approved distribution list needs to be compiled.

b) Where it is usual for a number of documents to accompany the agenda, colour coding such documentation could be considered to aid swift reference during the meeting, although if the members keep their papers in 'Agenda order' this should not be a problem.

3. If data is not available to meet the submission deadline a written note of its availability date must be given, the Chairman must be informed and notes of the expected date of receipt/issue and source entered on the Agenda.

4. Those submitting data late must ensure it is conveyed directly to the meeting members prior to the meeting with the required number of spares given to the Company Secretary. Asking for data to be allowed to be tabled at the meeting, particularly if it consists of detailed, involved or lengthy reports may result in the item being 'left on the table' for consideration at a later meeting.

5. Documentation will always be presented in agenda order.

Presentation

1. Every item prepared for the [Board/committee] will be required to prepare a standard covering sheet (see below).

2. Subsequent sheets may be presented in the format most suitable for the subject matter.

3. The utmost brevity, commensurate with the subject matter, should be employed. Commentary (other than the minimum necessary to explain approach etc.) should be avoided and facts and suppositions, and opposing data, suitably differentiated must be presented clearly.

4. Source(s) of data should be referenced, and a summary used, rather than including such data as part of the submission.

5. The conclusions and recommendations that are required to be set out on the first page, must be clearly evidenced within the report.

6. Plain English should be used with jargon avoided. Where jargon is essential, a glossary accurately defining the terms used should be included.

7. A summary of the effect of NOT proceeding with the proposals should be provided.

Supporting commentary

1. At the meeting, the report's originator or person responsible for the subject matter should be prepared to speak to the report, to answer questions from other members and generally to assist the meeting to come to a suitable decision regarding its content.

2. Should the meeting require amplifying documentation this must be provided in the same format as that used in the original report and submitted for the next following meeting (or as agreed at the Meeting).

3. Proposers may be restricted to only one opportunity to support or promote the subject matter and should therefore cover all salient facts in their short presentation.

   NOTE: This will entail marshalling all facts, data, comments and so on, balancing brevity against comprehensiveness, highlighting only the most important aspects and avoiding repetition, other than when necessary as a result of other members' questions.

4. Other meeting members should similarly endeavour to speak only once, putting forward their objections or comments in the same manner as set out in 3 above.

5. After such proposal and counter-comments, if the subject is of such import the Chairman may wish to encourage a short general discussion on the subject, otherwise the next move will be to summarise the content and take the sense of the meeting.

Decisions

1. Decisions will be summarised in the Minutes of the meeting. A synopsis for non-Board members will be communicated by the Company Secretary and/or the sponsoring member.

2. If referred back for reconsideration the decision will be supported by a copy of and extract of the minutes dealing with the subject which will include any conditions, timing, capital expenditure, and so on.

Draft covering sheet for data submitted

Report title _____

Date of report_____

Author/sponsoring dept _____

Data to be considered by meeting _____

Subject matter (aims of report/submission/etc.)

_____

Recommendations   1 _____

　　　　　　　　　　2 _____etc.

Summary of facts/contentions supporting recommendations

_____

Summary of facts/contentions contesting recommendations

_____

Implications for organisation if not proceeded with

_____

Implications for organisation if not proceeded with NOW

_____

Capital expenditure implications

_____

Skill/personnel implications

_____

Timing required _____

Summary checklist

- Set up aims, purpose and ongoing future timetable for Board meetings

- Give the preparation of an agenda constructive attention to help the meeting reach suitable decisions

- Convene meetings with sufficient notice for consideration of the data for the business to be conducted

- Provide guidelines for the submission of data to be considered

- Delineate procedures re attendance and absence, quorum, voting etc.

Chapter seven

A meeting's two key players – The Chairman and Secretary

Key players

General responsibilities of the Chairman

Progressing the meeting

Controlling the members

Motivating members

The role of the Company Secretary

Responsibilities

Before and at Board Meetings

Summary checklist

Key players

Whilst every meeting is different and every requirement varies, there are two key players common to most meetings: a chairman and a secretary – someone to lead the discussion and ensure the meeting makes the required decisions, and someone to take notes of the decisions arrived at. Effective meetings need both and as key players their joint and separate impact on the meeting can be considerable.

General responsibilities of the Chairman

The position of the Chairman is pivotal in terms of the effectiveness of the meeting and its approach to and determination of its work. One of any Chairman's prime tasks should be to drive the company forward which may mean ensuring that the Board is posed with strategical challenges and a requirement to formulate at least medium term plans, rather than concentrating on results which are often 'past news' before they are considered. The meeting will normally reflect far more the character, drive and inspiration of the Chairman than any other factor or member. If this is not so then it may be that the meeting is being dominated by someone other than its Chairman. The Chairman should be able to lead by force of personality and respect.

Chairman's general responsibilities checklist

a) To ensure that each meeting is geared to moving the company forward to the aims set for it and to attain the plans set by the meeting itself

b) To take responsibility for pushing the meeting itself to consider all its business (including forward planning) and to attain its aims

c) To be conscious of what is trying to be achieved from each item of business and from the entire meeting

d) To ensure that not only is each item on the agenda dealt with comprehensively, but also that all members are heard on the subject, which may mean actively inviting members to contribute, rather than passively waiting for them to do so

e) To ensure that members act and deliberate as Directors for the whole company rather than as managers for their particular function

f) To bring the meeting back to the business in hand should it stray from such considerations

g) To close down members' arguments or contentions where these threaten to detract from proper consideration of the subject matter and are not progressing the discussion. This is particularly relevant if the meeting is subject to a time limit. The problem is that often the value of such contributions may be in inverse proportion to the amount of time spent propounding them. Moving the meeting on can then take a great deal of tact.

h) To ensure the decisions arrived at are recorded and promulgated and subsequent meetings are arranged only when business requires.

i) To lead the discussion and the meeting itself. A chairman is a leader and an effective leader is someone who makes things happen and achieves results through people. The required work of the chairman is thus to make things happen.

An effective Chairman will have determined the purpose of the meeting, and should wish to see the items of business considered by the meeting moved towards the attainment of the purpose. If he becomes aware of any possibility of this aim being frustrated, it is his responsibility to try to 'take out' or 'neutralise' the opposition. Since this may be difficult in the meeting itself, as it will gain attention and the opposition might gain support, it may be best for him to take the initiative in advance of the meeting.

Case study: Constructive diversion

The Chairman became aware that a board member intended raising the question of standards of on-site safety at the Board. He was also aware that the Director responsible was under great pressure and were such an emotive matter to be raised in public forum, a divisive argument was certain to develop. Accordingly he set up an informal discussion before the Board to consider how safety standards could be improved. In such a neutral atmosphere and under duress from the Chairman, a joint approach using the skills of both parties in harmony was developed. The Board simply received a brief verbal report of the initiative.

Key technique

In this instance the Chairman was made aware of the development by the Secretary who acted as his confidante and shop floor 'ears and eyes'. As an alternative the Chairman needs a high profile presence so that he becomes aware personally of the developments, or has sufficient perception to second guess them. However by virtue of his position it may be difficult for him to receive such messages – few may be prepared to reveal the true state of affairs.

Progressing the meeting

Chairmanship relies on a strong personality, to carry both business and members along, and in order to manipulate the meeting so that its aims are achieved. The chairman needs to have:

- Vision, to move the meeting towards the attainment of its aims

- Perception so that almost by instinct and certainly from a process of sound leadership and active listening (see Chapter 11) he is aware of the aspirations and preferences of each member

- Good communication skills so that this vision is easily communicated to the other meeting members

- Enthusiasm to motivate members so that they learn to believe in plans and in their own ability to perform and achieve them, and

- The ability to delegate, to force decision making and accountability down the chain of command, not so that someone at a low level can be left 'carrying the can' but to widen their horizons, make them aware of the issues and encourage them to make suggestions – an awareness that from time to time certain board members may need support and be prepared to provide this. Boards are at their most effective when they act as a team under a dynamic leader. Individual disagreements need to be sublimated in favour of a common concerted approach.

Case study: Laying it on the line

The chairman in his opening address to the new divisional Board, not only welcomed all members but stated that the Board would be run as informally as possible, but that this would be matched by a need for total accountability and commitment. He added that he only wanted members at the meeting who were prepared to operate under those guidelines and invited anyone not prepared to do so to leave the meeting. No-one moved.

Key technique

This public declaration acted as considerable peer pressure on all present.

Controlling the members

Effective meetings may require the Chairman to manipulate both meeting members and the meeting itself, which may not be as difficult or Machiavellian as it sounds, since if people can identify with a successful effort they tend to co-operate and work more effectively in most cases. If they have something of which they can be proud, and know that their contribution is important to the meeting and the organisation, they tend to commit to a far greater degree than is otherwise the case. In any event basic involvement tends to create an environment where individuals work willingly.

What is needed is for the Chairman to motivate the members, possibly by the judicious use of praise, as well as allowing them to bring to the meeting certain problems for discussion and assistance. Meetings can be used as sounding boards although they should not be allowed to operate as a means of gaining collective decision where such decision should have been taken individually. Even though such business may be outside the strict aims/business of the meeting, allowing discussion should engender a positive attitude. Within an established meeting consensus may often be achieved, although there may be instances when conflict will surface. Indeed it is arguable that a certain amount of constructive conflict can generate ideas and move the meeting towards its aims. If destructive conflict arises, the Chairman needs to be able to either remove it or direct it positively.

Motivating members

The role of Chairman combines that of 'first among equals' with that of leader, and this dual role should always be recognised. In the latter endeavour the Chairman should ensure the best of each member is brought out. Unfortunately it can be easy for a dominant person to take over the meeting and for less dominant members to be overshadowed to such an extent that they make little or no contribution. If this occurs then the Chairman's responsibility is to encourage the quieter members to make a contribution, even, if necessary, silencing others in order to allow them to do so. In this the Chairman may find it helpful to adopt the following guidelines.

Motivating members checklist

1. Ensure everyone knows why they are present. In this he may need to restate the meeting's objectives. He may also state the time within which he would like to see the business conducted. Such strictures must be promoted positively, the aim being to complete the business properly, recognising that time is scarce and valuable.

2. Treat every member as an individual with rights to make the points they wish. This may require the Chairman inviting a contribution by name from 'less forward' member(s).

3. Encourage every member to identify with the body as a whole and to relate to every other member. This will take time and, with some members, can be difficult.

4. Encourage a sense of pride in the meeting and its achievements. Without being excessive, the Chairman should praise achievements whether these be joint or individual. As a nation we in the UK tend to criticise too much and praise too little, even though praise (which costs nothing) can be the most powerful motivator and incentive. It is also helpful when trying to manipulate a meeting, since this 'feel good' effect can stifle or neutralise what could otherwise be objections. A survey conducted for Colette Harris Associates (CHA) disclosed that people had a 'surprising degree' of pride in their work and 60% believed their job was making a difference to the success

of their organisation. Pride in their job and in their employer's organisation can be an important factor in employee motivation. The CHA survey suggested that pride in the firm could be built by:

- being known for treating employees and customers well

- making a difference to people's lives and the community

- being successful and providing good products and services

- having respect for ethical behaviour and standards including to suppliers and the environment

- being innovative.

5. Ensure all members are treated fairly and given a chance both to explain their views and attitudes and to argue their cases. Obviously this in turn requires the opposition to have a chance to do the same. If members see that each is allowed his own turn to put forward arguments, the temptation to filibuster or use other means by which the arguments of others are not heard should be reduced.

6. Ensure members feel that business which they feel is important does receive the attention it deserves. This may be difficult in the early life of a meeting and the Chairman needs to be tactful in accepting or rejecting business requested by members. If it is entirely germane to the business in hand, it may be worth considering, even if that in turn means the meeting overruns its allotted time span. If it is not appropriate, a tactful suggestion 'perhaps we could have an initial chat about that after the meeting' might solve the problem without disincentivising the member.

Dealing with opposition

Whilst most business and most Boards operate with mutual respect and consensus, from time to time opposition may arise which despite prior attempted pre-emption may surface at a Board meeting. This will need careful handling by the Chairman although having some advance notice of a potential problem may assist. If determined opposition is expected then the meeting should be seated perhaps more informally than usual. Seating everyone in comfortable chairs may reduce the capacity for opposition (although it can also generate a relaxed approach which could impair efficiency) or ensuring that seating position is determined by the Chairman. This could provide an opportunity for the dispersal of those who are likely to oppose. This does not mean banishing them to the far corners of the discussion table as this may enable them to regroup and even solicit support from uncommitted members. If there are three people who seek to oppose, then at least one, preferably the leader, should be seated very near the chairman which may enable the latter to control him. If the meeting uses the principle of the House of Commons, where before speaking a member has to catch the Speaker's eye, so that to speak the chairman has to grant permission, even if only by the briefest of nods then the person located nearest the chairman will then have the greatest difficulty, by sheer juxtaposition, in catching his close neighbour's eye!

Other opposition members need to be spread amongst supporters of the Chairman. In this way, their apparent strength or weight will be marginalised, they will find it difficult to communicate between themselves, which may be necessary in order to re-group or seek an alternative tactic. In addition, if they are each seated next to a strong supporter of the business, the opposition may feel inhibited about making their protest at all, or continuing it in the face of experienced or heavy opposition. The layout, set out below, shows how opposition groups can be split and to some extent neutralised.

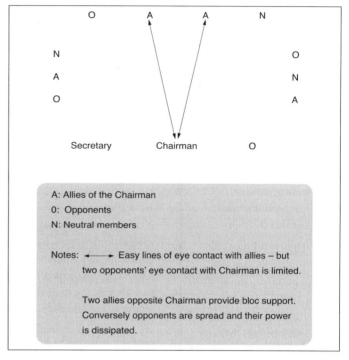

Seating plan negating opposition 'blocs'
(from 'One Stop Meetings', David Martin, ICSA Publishing)

The above (and following) comments are only intended for use when opposition is perceived as destructive. Obviously constructive opposition can be valuable and should be welcomed in the interests of exploring all aspects of a particular subject. In any event every board member is entitled to have their say and to adhere to a view which may not be shared by the majority.

Silencing the opposition

As well as physically splitting the opposition, the Chairman has power to downgrade their contribution by:

- 'Not seeing' that they wish to make a contribution and thus not inviting their input

- 'Cutting across' their contribution should they stray for one moment from the core of the subject

- Applying 'kangaroo' or 'closure' motions, (i.e. restricting comments and arguments and discussion of the whole to a short period).

In addition the Chairman can allow dissenters too much time so that they start repeating themselves. Allowing too much time can imply that what has been said has not been very telling and it is assumed that they have further points to make. If none can be made, the inference is then of an unfinished and possibly insufficiently supported case. Conversely, in allowing a right of reply, the Chairman may allow a supporter more time 'by mistake' to try and counter the case, although advance briefing of this possibility may be necessary.

Should the situation develop where a project thought to be essential for the business is likely to fail, due to the activities of the opposition despite all the steps taken to negate their impact, the Chairman may need to act swiftly to ensure its survival, if not at the current meeting, then at an adjournment or subsequent meeting. In such a situation, the Chairman, anticipating being outvoted and defeated may need either to withdraw the item, to propose that it 'be left on the table', (that is held over until the following meeting) or to adjourn the meeting itself. His powers to perform any or all of these acts will depend on the terms of reference of the meeting and the support of the members. It is essential that the Chairman knows his terms of reference, the delineation of all his powers and his likely support.

The role of the Company Secretary

Good secretaryship, like good administration, tends not to be seen but to play its part with quiet efficiency. The origin of the word is very old and means 'a person in someone else's confidence sharing secret or private matters with them'. It is derived from the Latin 'secretarius' meaning 'a confidential aide'. Being expected to be low key tends to underplay the importance of the role of the Company Secretary as:

- Guardian, ensuring fulfilment of the company's obligation to comply with legislation

- Facilitator, easing communication between the Board and management

- Confidante, supporting all members of the Board and particularly the Chairman and

- Chief administrative officer of the company (including being a legal 'officer' of the company with all the attendant responsibilities and liabilities that description entails – Section 744 Companies Act 1985).

In 1971 the then Master of the Rolls, Lord Denning defined the Secretary as 'the chief administrative officer of the company – he regularly makes representations on behalf of the company and enters into contracts on its behalf. He is entitled to sign contracts – all such matters come within the ostensible authority of the Company Secretary'. Since then the role has gained an increasing prominence – likely to be further enhanced by new initiatives in company compliance.

To a large extent the importance of the role is determined by the fact that unlike Directors, there are restrictions on those who are able to be appointed Company Secretary in the Companies Act 2006 – at least for PLCs. Effectively, unless there are very strong reasons for ignoring the requirements, a PLC company secretary must hold a professional qualification.

Writing in '*Chartered Secretary*' (the journal of the Chartered Institute of Secretaries) former Chief Executive of ICI, Sir John Harvey Jones commented 'the Company Secretary is an absolutely key appointment – more important than that of any Director' and went on to describe the role as 'creative'. In Sir John's view, 'the Company Secretary needs to be dynamic'.

In some companies, in his relationship with meetings, a good Secretary, like Victorian children, may be required to be seen and not heard, only supporting the meeting administratively. But this somewhat restricted view of the role, may be shortsighted as the Secretary will often have a more comprehensive view of the business under discussion than some members and certainly has an obligation to be fully aware of all legal obligations. To quote Sir John again 'I always work with a positive Board system, by which I mean I don't allow silence. After discussing each subject I ask each member of the Board what their opinion is and why – this includes the Company Secretary as I have always believed that his view should be heard'. The views of the Company Secretary may be more objective than that of Directors some of whom may, despite their Board responsibilities, be more interested in 'fighting the corner' for their own executive responsibilities. The Cadbury Committee on Corporate Governance recognised the unique position of the Company Secretary stating 'the Company Secretary has a key role to play in ensuring that the Board procedures are followed and regularly reviewed. The Chairman and the Board will look to the Company Secretary for guidance on what their responsibilities are'.

The Cadbury report also suggested that all Directors (and this would apply particularly to non-executive Directors which it regarded as having views that were independent from and potentially more objective than, executive directors) should always have access to the Company Secretary and that any suggestion of the dismissal or removal of the Company Secretary should be considered by the whole Board. It is one of the responsibilities of the Board to appoint a suitable and capable company secretary and to ensure that the appointee maintains these attributes. In many ways this is his most onerous task since the impact of legislation on companies from many areas is immense and continues to grow and a prime responsibility of the Company Secretary should be to 'keep the company legal.'

The paragraphs immediately above (indeed the whole content of this Guide) demonstrate the benefits – indeed virtual necessity – for the Board to have a Company Secretary on whom they can rely as 'the keeper of the company's conscience', or, (perhaps more pragmatically) to keep the members of the Board out of jail! Despite the essential nature of these points, whilst the Companies Act 2006 was making its way through Parliament, for a considerable proportion of its passage, it was suggested that the requirement for LTDs (i.e. the vast majority of all companies registered at Companies House) to have a Company Secretary should be abolished. Who was going to take responsibility for their company's legal compliance – other than the directors themselves – seemed to be ignored, despite remonstrations to this effect – a classic example of legislation being drafted by those who actually have little, if any, 'hands on' working knowledge of the subject. Such 'experts' dismissed the almost wholesale opposition to this proposal of those they consulted during the drafting of the legislation, sometimes describing such opposition as being as motivated by 'vested interests' (a suggestion which was as scandalous as it was insulting).

Fortunately at the last gasp, the proposal to 'abolish the LTDs' company secretaries' was itself abolished and instead LTDs have been given the option of having a company secretary. If one is appointed then details of the appointee must be filed at Companies House as hitherto has been the case since 1855.

Responsibilities

There are now over two million companies and no doubt over two million different job descriptions for their Company Secretaries. In the following checklist are set out the main responsibilities of most Company Secretaries but this needs to be individually customised. It is a prime responsibility of the Board to ensure these duties are carried out – if not by the Company Secretary then by someone else – ideally a director since the board have ultimate responsibility.

Main duties of the company secretary checklist

a) Understand and interpret the requirements and obligations contained in the Memorandum and Articles and guide the Board on these

b) Maintain statutory registers. This entails updating and keeping updated the various statutory books including the register of members which involves transferring shares, issuing new certificates etc. although many companies with large numbers of shareholders delegate such work to specialised divisions of, for example, the clearing banks

c) Update Registrar of Companies records. The Secretary is responsible for advising the Registrar promptly of all changes in directorate, of all charges over assets, of changes in shareholders at least once a year, etc. and other matters affecting the corporate nature of the company

d) Ensure compliance with company law. The Secretary must have a good working knowledge of the requirements placed upon the Directors under company law and ensure that the company complies with such requirements and all changes and innovations

e) Liaise with shareholders. The extent of this responsibility will depend on the individual companies – in some, the Directors take on this role, however in most the Secretary is responsible for at least the documentary contact with shareholders – i.e. notice of meeting, preparation of Annual Report etc.

f) Ensure legally required documentation is prepared. This is a very wide-ranging responsibility since much of what is required is derived from obligations under commercial, employment and other laws and as Secretary familiarity with such laws and obligations is essential

g) Convene company and Board meetings. The Secretary can only do this at the direction of the Board but to ensure the Board fulfils its own duties he needs to ensure that Board meetings are held regularly

h) Compile minutes of meetings and subcommittees. This is an onerous but essential part of his duties not simply to preserve the record of control, but also to have available documentary evidence which might be needed as a defence in any actions against Directors

i) File accounts and Annual return. Increasingly the obligation to file such items within specified time limits is being backed by rigorously enforced fines. Repeated failure to file on time can lead to disqualification from office

j) Carry out instructions of Board. As the chief administrative officer of the company the Secretary may have the prime role for interfacing with management. Alternatively executive Directors may take this role – whoever takes it needs to comply with the exact requirements of the Board

k) (For PLC only) Liaise with the Stock Exchange and ensure the requirements of the Listing Agreement are complied with.

l) Act as Board/Chairman's confidante. This is often one of the roles played by the secretary particularly where he is not also a Director as he can bring an objective view to the work of the Board. It is also often possible for the Secretary to be aware of internal developments of which Directors are not aware and thus provide a valuable communication conduit to the Chairman

m) Act as chief administrative officer. The scope for this responsibility will vary from company to company, nevertheless the Secretary is often the source from which management first learn of and are required to implement decisions

n) Protect the company's assets. It is the Secretary's duty to protect the statutory books and records of the company and the confidentiality of the Board's work. It may be logical to make him responsible for other aspects of corporate security.

o) Ensure all proper returns made (and in time). The officers of the company, of which the Secretary is one, have an obligation to comply with the filing regulations of company law. If these are not filed by the due date, fines can be levied, repetition of which could lead to disqualification

p) Oversee legal matters. Often the Secretary is legally qualified or will be the only executive with some experience of the law. Increasingly the law is intruding on company activities and someone must assume this responsibility

q) Oversee the arrangements to allow shareholders and others to inspect certain records of the company and to provide access to statutory and other bodies to inspect other records

r) Ensure compliance – with all:
   - contractual and commercial law
   - Health & Safety law:
   - Environmental law
   - Employment law

   and so on.

This is so vast an obligation it is difficult to visualise how a working Secretary with the usual range of additional duties can hope to provide advice and guidance on such matters.

As if the foregoing range of requirements were not wide itself many Company Secretaries also take responsibility for insurance, pensions, property, security and even employment and/or financial matters.

Before and at Board Meetings

Much of the Secretary's work will revolve around convening, servicing and administering Board meetings. His responsibilities in this work are summarised in the checklist below but inevitably particular companies will have different requirements. Directors have an obligation to ensure that this work is carried out appropriately bearing in mind that Board meetings and the minutes thereof provide evidence of the reasons for and the decisions taken by the Board.

The Secretary's responsibility for Board Meetings checklist

a) Generating an agenda in liaison with the Chairman (see Chapter 6 re the value of a dynamic agenda)

b) Ensuring all data for consideration by the Board accompanies the Agenda or there is a date by which it will be ready and distributed. Accompanying data should be presented in the order in which it will be considered on the Agenda

c) Convening the meeting in good time. There is no legal requirement regarding notice due to be given of a board meeting but for commercial reasons and to allow the Directors to be properly briefed at least 7 days notice with required data should be given. It would also be logical for the secretary to take responsibility for compiling and updating a timetable of future meetings

d) Ensuring, if a quorum is required to be present before the meeting can commence, that at least members satisfying that requirement are to be present to avoid wasting the time of others attending

e) Taking, reporting and recording any apologies for absence and noting any late arrivals or early departures so that it can be shown who was present when any decision was taken.

f) Having available any statutory and other registers that need to be inspected and/or signed (e.g. the Registers of seals, Director's interests, etc.)

g) Checking members have all the documents required but having available spare documents in case members have mislaid or forgotten them

h) Ensuring meeting's supports, provision of refreshments, note taking aids, protection against interruption, and so on, are in operation

i) Ensuring meeting adheres to and does not overlook any item on the agenda

j) Ensuring those who speak and vote are entitled to do so

k) Ensuring the meeting does take required decisions and that these are clear and clearly understood by all present

l) Noting the sense of the meeting in the minutes

m) Preparing minutes, having them approved in draft by the Chairman, distributed to the members and approved by them at their next following meeting

n) Keeping the minutes secure and available to members of the Board and the Auditors

o) ensuring action is effected as required by the meeting and reported on at the appropriate time

p) anticipating the level of support available, and any antipathy or opposition to, matters due to be considered by the board and briefing the chairman accordingly

q) being proactive in all respects and so on.

Summary checklist

- The duties and responsibilities of the Chairman in forcing the work of the Board should be delineated and promulgated to all

- The Chairman must take responsibility for pushing the meeting to achieve its purposes (and the company its aims)

- The Chairman must also take responsibility for controlling and motivating Board members and ensuring the positive outcome of Board business

- The Board must delineate the responsibilities of the Company Secretary and ensure these are carried out

- The Secretary must be proactive in ensuring legal compliance and internal administration as a result thereof.

Chapter eight

Board without boredom

Preparation for and administration of Board Meetings

General preparation

Preparing effective reports

Planning

Appointing subcommittees

Minutes – example and usage

Board Meeting Minutes

Summary checklist

General preparation

Experience indicates that some Directors attend meetings and, whilst they may have read the papers provided, have made little preparation for the decision-making task with which they are charged. Scant attention to meeting preparation is dangerous since not only is there incomplete understanding, but also this may be based on inaccurate data. Investigating the data enhances understanding as well as enabling checks on its credibility and accuracy to be made. A Board which has worked together for some time may be able to 'take data as read' since they will understand the way each member thinks and know they can rely on the data being provided. However even where such confidence exists it may be preferable for Board members to make their own investigations and even compile their own records simply since the process of making up one's own record tends to fix the facts in one's mind. In addition it is not unknown for some reports or proposals to provide a 'gloss' or 'spin' for a particular project which suppresses information which could contradict data put forward to support the contentions. Ideally members of a close working unit such as a Board should avoid such tactics but realistically one needs to be aware that such tactics can be adopted.

One reason for recommending that all data is sent to Board members at least 7 working days before the meeting is to enable members to study the proposals, to have the opportunity of asking the author for more information and to conduct their own independent investigations. The antithesis of this is the device already referred to where a bulky report is tabled and the Board is put under pressure to accept the recommendations without sufficient time to consider them or to make independent investigations. Whilst on occasions there may be no alternative the Chairman should insist that this is the exception to the rule – after all ultimately the Directors could be held personally responsible for their decisions and thus they need time to consider not just the recommendations put forward but also the 'knock-on' effects of such decisions.

WARNING: Failing to prepare adequately for a Board meeting and then making decisions without such preparation could mean that a director is acting 'recklessly'. (See the Gwyer case).

Preparing effective reports

The decision making process will be assisted immeasurably if the reports being presented to the Board are:

- Effective

- Short and explicit

- Presented in a common format.

Report-writing is an art which is often overlooked. The main problem is that those required to prepare a report often compose it from a particular angle – their own as the author. In doing so the essential purpose of a report – that is the requirements of the reader for a clear concise and easily understandable review of the matter – may be overlooked. Every written item exists for one purpose only – the interest of the reader. If the reader doesn't understand the report there is only one person who is responsible – the writer, who must compose their data in a way that is conducive to the reader's comprehension, ideally at a first reading (bearing in mind that the time available to most board members is limited). Reports should therefore be short, sharp and provoke attention, and following the layout suggested in the following checklist may be apposite.

Report composition guidelines checklist

1. Providing a title for the report can allow the reader to gain instant guidance to content

2. The author and date of the report should also be given to allow reporting back

3. The terms of reference or aim of the report should appear at the beginning of the report and it may assist if immediately under the aims or purpose the recommendations are also set out. This enables the reader to gain an immediate view of the opinion being adopted by the writer and places the content in perspective. It should also help the author to check that they are dealing with the exact subject matter and purpose of the report (that is that they have not deviated from the original point).

175

4. The main content of the report could comprise:
   - Background (i.e. the reason the report has been prepared)
   - History (i.e. the developments that have led to a situation where a report is necessary)
   - Methodology
   - Data and research on which the contentions or recommendations are drawn
   - Perspective data (i.e. it may assist consideration of a report on, say, a declining return on the company's capital investment, if the industry figures which either match or conflict with the company's own results are included)

5. The report should conclude with a repeat of the recommendations, amplified by reasons for putting them forward, and may also incorporate a timetable or list of steps to be taken. If the writer of the report is not to be present when the report is read or considered it may help the readers to explain the recommendations thus pre-empting some questions.

6. Whilst the content of a report is the most important consideration, its presentation is also important. A sound report can be damaged by poor presentation whereas a merely adequate report can look impressive providing it is well-presented.
   - Graphics (where these arise naturally from the text and can provide the reader with an instant view of the point being made) should be used – although not to excess.
   - Jargon, unless the writer is certain that every reader will know the meaning, should be avoided. (If the writer is unsure of this but wishes to use jargon it may be safest to include a glossary of terms used.) Ordinary everyday English is the best language to use although often one reads reports that seem to have adopted a 'reportese' language which does little to aid comprehension! (Inveterate jargon users might usefully be advised of the dictionary definition of 'jargon' – that is 'the meaningless babble of made by an infant (literal meaning 'without words') before it learns how to speak properly'!)

- The likelihood of instant comprehension of problems can be checked by submitting the report to a Fog Index – i.e. a check of the readability of the prose based on the length of sentences and complexity of the words used.

7. Where data has been drawn from sources which are themselves bulky it may be better simply to cross-reference to the source and to state where this can be found.

8. If the report consists of more than, say, six pages, it may help to include a list of contents. The effectiveness of a contents list (and of the report itself) can be aided by using key words or headlines throughout. Not only can this guide the reader to those parts of the report of most interest to them, it will also maintain interest which will also be stimulated by putting up slabs of text into 'digestible chunks'.

Planning

Most of the Board's responsibilities entail a requirement to look to the future even though much of the data on which such decisions are required to be taken may be historical. Planning involves the board in making reasoned guesses based on the information they have available to them as to likely events and situations and the company's possible reactions to those events. There are three essential needs in planning for future actions which are often overlooked:

a) The need to retain flexibility so that if what was anticipated does not develop in the way required an alternative approach is available

b) The need to take action quickly once it is obvious that things are not going the way they were planned and

c) The need to plan for things going wrong in the same way as planning in the expectation of things going well. Crisis or disaster planning (e.g. in the case of fire, loss of key person, adverse media attention, etc.) is increasingly being adopted by Boards so that there is at least a checklist of possible actions or activities which can be considered immediately rather alternative actions needing to be considered when time is likely to be at a premium following a disaster. Shareholders of companies appoint Directors to drive their companies forward. Inevitably most decisions taken are more akin to a 'touch on the tiller' which steers the company in the best direction. However at times major changes of direction may need to be taken to preserve the business of the company and/or to allow it to maximise its investment. Shareholders expect their Directors to take decisions and to plan for eventualities and it is at least arguable that the Board that does not make plans no matter how outline these may be, is failing in its duty to its shareholders.

Board alliances – and disputes

The most effective and successful companies are probably those where the Board, whilst they may have individual differences, act as a cohesive team with shared aspirations and plans. Inevitably from time to time differences may arise and the Director who wishes to gain approval for a pet project will be somewhat short-sighted if he does not attempt to gain support from colleagues in advance of consideration of the matter at a Board meeting. Seeking support, even if entails a 'quid pro quo' from the other party may be a sensible way of approaching the matter. Few people like losing out or ending up on the wrong side, particularly in a public forum, and such public defeat may be avoided by broaching the subject with colleagues in advance, gaining their reactions and either toning down or altering aspects of the suggestion or, if there seems to be little support or total animosity, dropping the idea altogether.

Such a strategy has a number of advantages

- It grants the member the reputation of being a good team player. Reputation and respect can help win arguments in meetings and dealing with a possibly controversial matter outside the meeting, particularly if it concerns or is raised with the Chairman, may well earn the instigator some prestige for future use, even though the actual subject matter gains no support on the present occasion

- It avoids embarrassing the person as it could were it to be raised in open meeting. The position of that person, particularly if he is the Chairman, is thus protected. He can explain opposition or reaction in private, and possibly even in confidence, to the instigator, without the pressure of the meeting

- It enables the instigator to gain some measure of the depth of feeling likely to be encountered were the matter to be raised in meeting. If the reaction is very hostile he can back off immediately.

- The concept itself is brought into the open. Whilst it may not gain support this time around, repeated references to the idea may ultimately win over those formerly antagonistic to it, particularly if later events are used to illustrate its advisability. Occasionally however, despite all endeavours, antipathy can surface at a Board meeting even leading to a situation where one Board member finds himself completely at odds with his colleagues. He may feel so strongly that he wishes his dissent to be noted in the minutes. Most chairman will try to avoid this, not least since it is breaking the cohesion of the Board team, but if the Director is adamant then a suitable minute should be included.

Appointing subcommittees

With a company of any size, requiring the Board to consider all the business can make the main Board meeting over-lengthy and inefficient. This can be avoided by appointing committees of the Board (usually with power to co-opt other members – not necessarily Board members) to consider certain aspects of the operations with reports of decisions only submitted to the Board for ratification.

Where such committees are appointed, their exact terms of reference, composition and quorum should be set out clearly. They should also be required to take accurate minutes and to submit those minutes to the Board so that any recommendations can be ratified or approved. Minute writing is an acquired art and if there is no person available to write up their minutes this may be best done by the Company Secretary at the direction of the chairman of the sub-committee. The Secretary should not object to writing such minutes (even if he was not present at the meeting) provided it is made clear who was there and that they subsequently approve the minutes as a true record.

Minutes – example and usage

Minute-taking is an art and, without practice few can compose reliable and accurate minutes, which normally comprise only a summary of the decisions taken. This however is for the meeting to decide and some Boards may find it preferable for the minutes to provide details of the main arguments as well as the decisions. This can however be dangerous since it can lead to dissent regarding the arguments put forward and generally the shorter and more succinct the minutes the better. Most minute takers tend to write notes at the time and then write the full minutes up from those notes.

Minutes should be approved at a subsequent meeting and ideally signed by the Chairman (indeed this may be a requirement set out in the Articles). Once the Minutes have been approved, the notes should be destroyed. In the event of a challenge to the Minutes it could be potentially damaging if the final version as approved is not in accord with the original notes. Once Directors have approved Minutes that should be the record (even if in redrafting etc. original decisions have been rethought). This may be reminiscent of last four lines of the 19th Century rhyme (*source unknown*):

'And so whilst the great ones repair to their dinner
The Secretary stays getting thinner and thinner
Racking his brains to record and report
What he thinks they will think that they ought to have thought'.

However once Minutes are approved normally they will be binding. In the case of *Municipal Mutual v Harrap*, Mr Harrap claimed that the Board had taken a decision – an assertion they denied. The Minutes were made subject to legal discovery and brought into court. Mr Harrap pointed to the decision in the Minutes which the Directors tried to pass off as a 'mistake'. The judge referred them to the next set of Minutes which started with the approval of the Minutes one of the items being the disputed decision.

To start the process of Minute-taking it may be helpful if a copy of the Agenda is word processed but double-spaced and with further spaces left after each item so that notes can be inserted. Secretaries with experience of the way their Board thinks and acts may be able to go one stage further and develop what can amount almost to a 'pro forma' copy of the Agenda which includes likely or drafts of resolutions and decisions. This all aids the Secretary in restricting the amount of writing and allowing more concentration on the business being transacted. Although this process can lead to accusations that the Secretary is writing the minutes before the meeting takes place, the advantage of having Agenda and outline minutes on one document sheet should not be underestimated. After all if care has been taken in the composition of the Agenda there should be a reasonably clear idea of the likely decisions that will be made and thus the composition of the minutes. The aim of such a gambit, is not so much to manipulate the meeting as to make sure it achieves effectiveness, – and, after all, a draft is simply that.

Minutes must be a true, fair and accurate record. This is particularly important if the organisation needs to produce a certified copy of a minute to a third party, e.g. to evidence a signatory's authority to sign a contract or to confirm the setting up, or variation of of a Bank Mandate.

Board Meeting Minutes

It is perhaps easier to consider the means of composing and advantages of having available well-written minutes by reviewing a set of minutes and highlighting particular aspects as is shown in the following checklist:

ANY COMPANY LIMITED   182(1)

MINUTES of a BOARD MEETING held on 30th November 2_____
at [address] at 10.00 a.m.

Present: XYZ (in the chair)
        ABC
        DEF
        GHI

In attendance: JKL (company secretary)

Mr. TSS, Auditor was in attendance for items
covered by Minute 2 i and ii)   (2)

An apology for absence due to illness was received from UVW.
Those present signed the attendance book.   (3)

The Board reminded themselves of the seven duties of directors set
out in the Companies Act 2006 and confirmed that in taking all decisions they would continue to take account of these duties and bear
in mind the disparate interests of the company's stakeholders.

1. Minutes

The Minutes of the Board Meeting held on 27th October 2_____
previously distributed were taken as read, approved and signed.   (4)

2. Shareholder matters

It was resolved that a share transfer covering 500 Ordinary shares in
the company from Mrs MNO to Mr PQR be and it hereby is approved
and that a share certificate in the name of Mr PQR be issued and the
required entries be made in the Register of Members. The Secretary
was asked to write personally to Mr PQR welcoming him as a shareholder.   **Action: JKL (5)**

A report from the company secretary recommending that responsibility for the share registration work of the company be placed with
Professional Share Registrars Ltd, from a date within the following three
months was accepted and the terms of the contract approved. The
company secretary was requested to make the necessary arrangements
in liaison with the Chairman.   **Action: JKL**

(Mr DEF, having previously notified the company that he had a consultancy agreement with Share Registrars Ltd did not take any part in
this discussion or vote on the proposal.)   (6)

3. Finance

i)   Management accounts.

     The full set of management accounts for the month of October and
     the cumulative 6 months were tabled and discussed in detail. The
     favourable comparison with budget was welcomed, as was the Man-
     aging Director's report of a favourable Autumn trading period for

which full comparative figures would be available shortly and his opinion that the trading and financial situation would continue to show improvement, both in real terms and against budget. It was noted that the situation regarding discounts and promotional payments was still being clarified and additional controls would be introduced from the start of the new financial year. A number of estimated provisions were listed for possible incorporation in the year end accounts.   **Action: ABC**

ii) Depreciation

It was agreed to change the company's accounting policies so that depreciation would be charged on vehicles, office equipment and computers @ 33.3 per cent p.a. straightline. It was noted that this change would have to be recorded in the Accounting Policies note to the next set of audited accounts.

iii) Capital expenditure

a) It was agreed that a further 5 product units at a cost of around £4000 each could be purchased on stages over the remainder of 2_____ and the first 6 months of 2_____ to allow the sale of [detail]. Mr UVW, whom failing the Company Secretary, would authorise each item bearing in mind the effect on cash flow.

Action: UVW/JKL (7)

b) The Chairman referred to Capital Expenditure Project form number 13/2_____ for the investment in [detail] which projected a first year return of 14 per cent rising to 17 per cent in year 2 on a fully absorbed basis. The project was approved for implementation no earlier than 31st January 2_____

Action: ABC

iv) Cash flow

The latest projection for the period ending 30th June 2_____ was tabled, discussed and approved

v) Investigations for the replacement of the company vehicles allocated to 6 area managers would be carried out. The guidance of the auditors as to the Company's and individual's tax situation would be sought   **Action: GHI**

vi) Bank Mandate

The Secretary reported that the company's bankers had requested that a new mandate on the main drawing account be completed. It was resolved that the company operate the No 1 Main Drawing account in its name with the Finance Bank Plc on the terms and subject to the restrictions set out in a new mandate a copy of which initialled by the Chairman for the purposes of identification is attached to these minutes, and that the Secretary be and he hereby is empowered to take such actions as might be necessary to give effect to this resolution **Action: JKL (8)**

vii) Borrowings

The Secretary reported that in the absence of Mr UVW he had negotiated an additional £100,000 overdraft facility with the Finance Bank on the same terms as the existing facility. This additional borrowing was available for the 5 months from 1st January until end May 2_____ . Although he had expected to receive documentation requiring Board approval to evidence this borrowing this had not arrived before the meeting.

It was resolved that the Chairman, ABC and UVW (whom failing the Company Secretary) be and they hereby are empowered to sign such documents and take such actions to provide the company's bankers with the documentation they required in order to facilitate the advance of this additional borrowing requirement. The Secretary was instructed to let each Board member have copies of the relevant items and documentation when these were to hand.

The Secretary confirmed that even with this additional borrowing the limits in the Articles had not been breached.

Action: XYZ, ABC, JKL (9)

4. Current trading

The Managing Director reported that [summary of report.........]. An analysis showing the deterioration over a five year period of sales of the main product was tabled and it was agreed that the deadline for delivery of supplies of Project X needed to be brought forward to compensate for the expected shortfall in sales in the latter part of the calendar year. **Action: ABC**

Mr DEF requested that his dissent from this course of action be noted in the minutes with the note that in his opinion not enough was being done to incentivise the sales force and he had serious doubts concerning the effectiveness of the recently appointed sales manager.   (10)

5. Personnel

i)   A report from the Divisional Director (Personnel) had been sent to all members and the contents were accepted. It was agreed that negotiations should commence with employee representatives to try to agree the wage increase with effect from 1st April 2_____ along the lines outlined in the report.

ii) The Secretary reported that he had investigated the requirements encapsulated in the most recent anti-discrimination legislation and tabled a brief summary of the additional action he felt it was necessary for the company to take in order to comply with the requirements. The Board requested him to obtain detailed cost estimates for the various requirements with, in each case, an indication of the proposed timetable for implementation of the recommendations.   **Action: JKL**

(At this point Mr DEF apologised and, with the Chairman's permission, left the meeting.)   (11)

6. Property

The following items were noted: (12)

a)   Little progress had been made on any of the pending rent reviews which would update the list accompanying the agenda for the meeting other than the following:

[Facility]: Approval was granted to a letter of response to the Landlords requesting that an extension to the user be agreed.

[Facility]: Evidence thought to be misleading had been submitted by the Landlord's agents and rejected

[Facility]: The Landlord's agents had reduced their figure for the reviewed rent to £13,500.

b)   The sale of [facility] was proceeding with exchange of contracts expected for mid-February and completion by 1st April. It was noted that receipt of the sale monies had not be built into the cash flow forecast and that it this sale completed as anticipated the additional overdraft facility would not be needed.

c) The possibility of selling the business and licensing or underletting the lease at [facility] was being pursued urgently.

d) Insurance:The Secretary would draft a letter to Landlords requesting that the interest of the company be noted on insurance policies to ensure any liability in the event of loss was minimised.

Action: JKL

7. Safety

a) The Board considered the report [dated] prepared by the Safety Director.Approval was granted to the expenditure of [£...] to improve safety rails etc.

b) [Project].Risk assessments regarding the implementation were tabled and the Safety Director was requested to reduce the risks identified in the [detail] and to seek advice regarding eradication of the risk identified at [detail].

Action: GHI

(13)

8. Sealing

The Secretary produced Register of Seals to the Board and approval was granted to the affixing of the company seal to items numbered 345 to 357 and 359 to 361, and approval granted to the signing as a deed of item 378.The Chairman was authorised to sign the register in evidence of this approval, and did so.

(14)

9. Board meeting timetable

The dates of the meetings of the Board for the second half of the following calendar year (dates for the first half remaining unchanged) were confirmed as 28th July, 24th August, 23rd September, 26th October, 23rd November, and 21st December.The Secretary was requested to inform Messrs UVW and DEF of these dates as soon as possible.

(15)

Chairman_____

23rd December 2_____

(16)

Notes:

1. Pages of Board meeting minutes should be consecutively numbered (particularly if a loose-leaf binder is used).The subject of each minute (where applicable) should be indexed and a degree of cross-referencing provided.

2. Stating the exact length of attendance of advisors, and even of members if they do not stay for the whole meeting, is advisable.

3. It is also advisable for Directors to sign an attendance book

4. Ideally the Chairman should initial each page of the minutes of each meeting except for the last which should be signed. See 16 below.

5. Placing the initials of the person due to deal with the item enables the minutes (already a document of record and reference) to act also as a means of encouraging action.

6. Depending upon the requirements of the Articles it is important that any Director with an interest in the subject matter declares that interest.

7. Framing a decision in this way leaves some leeway for delay should the circumstances at the time warrant such delay.

8. Where a lengthy document is required to be approved, rather than repeating the whole item in the minutes, copying it and attaching it to the minutes is advisable. It should then be numbered either consecutively after the last page number for that meeting, or take the number of the past page with a designatory letter added for each page of the item. Banks may wish to have a set form of resolution adopted for the approval of their mandate and similar business.

9. Reference should be made to the Articles to ensure the Board are acting in accordance with them.

10. In the event that any Director wishes his/her dissent to be recorded this must occur although often the Chairman will seek to avoid or minimise the inclusion of such a comment.

11. Ideally all Directors should be present for the whole meeting but if this is not possible, the time that a director arrived/left should be noted.

12. To save the time of the meeting, it may be possible to distribute a report (as here) with the Agenda and simply report on any update since the date of the Agenda.

13. The HSC has recommended that Boards should accept collective responsibility for the safety of their companies' operations. The regular inclusion of safety as an Agenda item and a consideration of reports and recommendations would seem to be prudent.

14. Although not a statutory requirement, the use of a Register of seals and subsequent approval of all entries provides Board authority for the items. It also enables details of items signed as deeds where the use of the seal has been dispensed with to be noted. The Chairman should sign under the last number authorised at the meeting and should add the date. Ideally the number of each seal entry in the Register should appear on the item sealed as a further cross-reference of authority.

15. When meetings are arranged in the absence of a colleague, these may clash with other commitments already entered into. Early advice of the dates is essential. Ideally the dates of Board meetings should be arranged on a rolling 18 month basis. With the immediate 6 months date firm, the following 6 months subject to some leeway and the third 6 months indicative only.

16. Inserting a place for the Chairman to sign and adding the date (of the next planned meeting) emphasises the importance of signing as well as making the minutes themselves appear better presented.

NOTE: Some companies number each minute consecutively, starting at 1 at the commencement of each financial or calendar year.

Summary checklist

- Board members must have sufficient time and data to prepare individually for meetings and to check data submitted

- Reports need to be prepared concisely and effectively and ideally in a standard format

- Where 'pet' business is to be transacted, principles of negotiation and/or powerplay with colleagues need to be addressed

- Business decisions need to be recorded accurately in Minutes which are not only vital records of business but also can be used to progress chase – and not least to demonstrate the exercise of the duty of care.

Chapter nine

An inspector calls

Access, Authorities and Auditors

General requirements to create and protect records

Protections and inspections

The officers of a company have a general duty to preserve and protect the statutory and other records of the company – not least the financial records and there are severe penalties for failing to do so. In addition, included in the duties of the Board in general and the Company Secretary in particular should be the obligation to arrange for the inspection of the company records by those entitled – an obligation often overlooked.

A short time ago a national newspaper bought a few shares in each of a number of leading listed PLCs and sought to exercise the right of inspection of the statutory books as a shareholder. It sent a representative to the registered offices, but the answers the enquirers received were many and varied and in several cases totally in breach of company law. One leading company refused to produce the Directors' service contracts, another tried to defer the inspection for a month whilst a Director of a third company commented 'I'm far too busy running the company to bother about things like that'. Whilst hard-pressed Directors and Secretaries may have some sympathy with the last comment it is still an illegal response and reflects poorly on the professionalism of the companies. Since each company was in the top 100 one would expect their officers to know the law and be the first to comply.

Access to and inspection of records can be regarded under the following two headings:

a) the rights of access of shareholders and others to inspect the statutory books of the company (see checklist) and

b) the rights of access and inspection of these and other records by a variety of other statutory bodies and those with whom the company has contractual relationships.

Statutory records inspection

Shareholders own the company and the records of the company technically and legally belong to them. The former wide-ranging rights of inspection of the statutory records of a company have been curtailed by the Companies Act 2006 in that those wishing to inspect the records are required to explain who they are and why they wish to see the records. If a company is not satisfied with the reason, an inspection can be refused. If the person persists in their application they will have to apply to Court.

Rights of access to statutory records checklist

The following have rights of access to the records stated

a) the company's creditors: free access to the Register of Charges and any Statutory declaration of payment out of capital for redemption or purchase of its own shares:

b) the public: to items under a) above (for which an access charge can be made) PLUS the Registers of Members, Overseas Branch, Directors & Secretary, Significant shareholdings (PLC only), and Debenture holders; reports on disclosure of holders under section 793.

c) the company shareholders: free access to items under a) and b) above plus Directors' service contracts.

Of course copies of some of these records are lodged with Companies House and it is now possible for those wishing to inspect to do so electronically – and without the company knowing of the inspection, or the person wishing to view, leaving their desk- via the Companies House website.

NOTE: Under CA2006, these physical rights of inspection are substantially curtailed. Those, other than members, wishing to conduct an inspection will have to give notice and if the Board feel the inspection is not for a fit purpose they can resist the request.

External authorities

As well as the rights of access of shareholders, creditors and the public to the statutory records, a seemingly ever-increasing number of bodies also have rights of access to both the company premises as well as its records and, again, if the company is not to be seen as acting unprofessionally as well as illegally Directors should make arrangements for, and brief their staff in the administration of such visits.

Rights of access of authorities and parties to contracts checklist

Policy

1. Representatives of the following organisations have a right of access to company premises, have rights (brief details as shown below for each) to inspect records and interview employees and may also have a right to remove records, data and registers etc.

2. The receptionist/gate keeper on duty should establish the agency the visitor(s) represent and inspect their credentials to ensure their bona fides. (S)he should conduct them to the waiting room and contact the company representative stated who will be responsible for dealing with the enquiry.

3. Agencies with right of access, company contact and initial action:

    a) Department of Trade and Industry (DTI), Financial Services Authority (FSA), Serious Fraud Office (SFO), Competition Commissioner/Office of Fair Trading (CC), European Union (EU) Inspectorate.

        Contact: Company Secretary (whom failing Assistant Company Secretary, whom failing Chief Accountant).

        Action: telephone corporate lawyers to interface, telephone public relations firm to brief them in case media require information and/or to prepare a press statement, advise Chairman and Board. Meet representatives and endeavour to ascertain requirements. Check requirements with corporate lawyers. Endeavour to assist investigators whilst indicating the potential damage to the company name and reputation. Write report of visit, requirements, action carried out, records inspected/ removed, and so on.

NOTE: Representatives of some of these organisations have a right of immediate access, to seize documents and to demand statements from personnel (who may not have, on pain of penalty, a right of silence) – immediate legal advice is essential. (See Chapter 4)

b) HM Revenue and Customs (the regulatory body formed as a result of the merger of the Inland Revenue, Dept. of Social Security and Customs and Excise), Occupational Pensions Regulator, Information Commissioner (formerly known as the Data Protection registrar), Rating authorities, The Home Office.

Contact: Chief Accountant (whom failing Finance Director, whom failing Company Secretary).

Action: meet representatives and establish nature of enquiry – provide information required. Advise Chairman and Board and corporate lawyers (via Company Secretary). Ensure, if errors are found that systems are changed to avoid a repetition. Discipline staff if procedures have not been followed correctly. Write report of visit, action required and effected, and so on.

c) Fire, Police, Factory Inspectorate, Gas, Water and Electricity utilities, Minimum wage inspectors.

Contact: Personnel Director (whom failing Company Secretary, whom failing Personnel Manager).

Action: meet the representative and establish problem. Rectify if required and possible. Update procedures if required. Write report of visit and action effected.

d) Environmental Health, Trading Standards.

Contact: Retail Director (whom failing Personnel Director, whom failing Company Secretary).

Action: Meet representative and establish problem. Rectify if required and possible. Update procedures if required. Write report of visit and action effected.

e) Department of Transport.

Contact: Transport Manager (whom failing Company Secretary)

Action: Be prepared to produce operators licence and back-up records (e.g. plating records etc.).

f) Landlord and agents.

Contact: Company Secretary (whom failing Assistant Company Secretary, whom failing Chief Accountant).

Action: Meet representatives – since most leases state that (say) 48 hours notice of such an inspection must be given there will be no need to allow immediate access unless it is an emergency. Good landlord/tenant relations may require a positive and helpful approach. Note requirements. If a dilapidations notice (a schedule of 'wants of repair' that have arisen because the repairing obligations of the lease have not been complied with, or complied with to the required level) is to be served, refer to the lease for the procedure to be followed.

Details of aims of and data likely to be required by bodies requiring access:

• DTI – to investigate company affairs, ownership, dealings in shares including insider dealing. Exact nature of investigation needs to be ascertained.

• FSA – has powers under the Financial Services Act and the Financial Services and Markets Act to investigate the affairs of their members.

• SFO – the Serious Fraud Office has powers, wider in many cases than those available to the police or SROs, to investigate matters of fraud likely to total in excess of £2 million and to be of public concern.

• CC/OFT – the Competition Commissioner with and via the Office of Fair Trading has an obligation to investigate whether supplies of goods or services breach the principles of the Fair Trading Act 1973 and/or the Competition Acts 1980 and 1998 and the Enterprise Act 2002 – i.e. whether there is control of a market which acts against the interests of the consumer, price-fixing, collusive tendering etc.

- HM Revenue and Customs. The IR & DSS powers of access tend to be exercised by their Audit Departments and Compliance units, charged with the duty of checking the validity of the way an employer has deducted tax and NI from his employees and paid it over to the Revenue. The Inland Revenue also oversees the assessment of properties for commercial rating purposes whilst the DSS also oversees the appropriate payment of the National Minimum Wage.

  The C&E – have wide powers of access in respect of their VAT collection duties which emanate from their old role as Excise officers. The penalties for, even totally accidental, errors, in VAT collection and payment are severe although currently under review.

- EU – inspectors have rights to enter the premises of organisations of member states under EU law although it has been stated that, in doing so they should try to act in accordance with the laws of the member state concerned (and via domestic authorities)

- Home Office – to check that those employed since 1.4.04 have the right to work in the UK.

- Pensions Regulator – has a right of access to inspect pension records under the Pensions Act 1995 and a right to apply for a warrant to search premises for purposes connected with compliance with the requirements. In addition officials can check whether a Stakeholder pension is required to be provided and deal with breaches of this legislation.

- Information Commissioner has a right of access under the 1998 revision/extension of Data Protection legislation.

- Fire – the local Fire Officer has a right of access to premises mainly for the purposes of checking compliance with Fire regulations matters, and requirements regarding fire safety previously made by him – or required under statute to be carried out by the occupier and/or owner. The Fire Officer effectively becomes a regulatory inspector checking compliance. For this reason it is suggested that the Responsible Person for each location (required under the Fire Safety Regulations) should regularly complete and retain for such inspection a checklist (a draft of which appears in Chapter 5).

- Police – unless in the belief, or in connection with such belief, that a crime is about to, or is being committed, or in 'hot pursuit' of a suspected person, or to prevent a breach of the peace, the Police have no immediate right of access to premises other than with the permission of the owner.

- Health and Safety Executive, Environmental Health Officers, Factory Inspectors – have a range of powers which vary from industry to industry. Operators of large (and potential hazardous) facilities are obliged (under the Control of Industrial Major Accident Regulations 1988) to file and keep up to date details of plans and emergency evacuations etc. which will require an interface with the appropriate department which may well wish to check the site.

- Dept of Transport – have rights to inspect transport operators licence and administration.

- Local Authorities – have an increasing range of obligations – particularly under the Food Safety and Environment Protection Acts

- Rating officers (a) and Trading Standards Officers (b) need access to check details of the establishment (a) for the purpose of assessment to the Uniform Business Rate, and (b) to ensure compliance with the relevant trading laws

- Gas, Water, Electricity utilities – access to read meters and, if leaks/ breaks are suspected or, in the event of emergencies, to rectify

- Landlord and agents – to inspect condition and use of premises, assess value for insurance, prepare dilapidations reports, erect letting signs at end of lease etc.

In addition to the above list, further bodies have powers of access for particular industries. These should be established and their details, sphere of authority and action required added to the list. For example interested parties (which could include members of the public) have a right to inspect Safety Plans drawn up in compliance with the Construction (Design and Management) Regulations 1994 relating to building works.

WARNING: It is important that the request for access is dealt with properly. Denying access can in some cases be a criminal offence.

Control

Another prime responsibility of the officers (not only to provide adequate financial controls but also to attempt to protect their own position and) is to ensure that:

a) Control for the acts of the company are taken in accordance with agreed procedures and

b) All commitments are entered into by (and only by) properly authorised persons. The company can be held liable for the acts of its employees who will often be deemed to be acting as its agents or in the course of their employment (even if such actions would not normally be considered as such or authorised by the Board – see summary of decisions of cases in Chapter 4). Directors should ensure that employees are aware of the manner and scope of their action – and that such rules are actively policed and breaches made subject to appropriate sanctions.

Minimising liability – a checklist for employers

Ensure that:

1. All rules regarding trading, outlawing price-fixing, safety, recruitment as well as attitudes and actions towards employees during employment regarding respect and fair treatment are clear and adhered to at all times

2. All employees have read and understood the rules and all procedures etc., are regularly checked and policed and always adhered to (without exception)

3. Immediate action is taken if there is any question of an accusation or suspicion that there is a breach of such rules and that sanctions are effected against those in breach

4. All safety rules are adhered to, specifications regarding maintenance are compiled with and inspections are carried out in accordance therewith

5. All reports of problems affecting or potentially affecting safety are dealt with immediately

6. All employees are advised of their responsibilities for their own, their colleagues', and their employers assets' safety.

7. Everyone is constantly reminded of the need to adhere to rules, procedures etc., to think before acting or speaking and to consider the implications of liability claims

8. The company rules and procedures are:

   - Codified

   - Regularly updated and promulgated

   - Always adhered to, and that

   - Employees can be shown to have knowledge of them.

Controlling exercise of authority

Commitment authority

It is essential for the proper control of the monetary and other assets of the company, that authority is granted at, and only at, the appropriate level in order to incur expenditure or approve the disposal of stocks (and any other assets) other than in the normal course of trade. Since the officers could be held to be liable to third parties when liabilities have been created due to approval being given at a level which had no authority to grant such approval, there is a strong incentive as well as a commercial validity in publishing, updating and ensuring adherence to a schedule of authority such as the draft set out in the following example. Most auditors will welcome the use of such a schedule as it should assist them in checking that approval was given at an appropriate level and by an authorised person to all transactions. Further the development and policing of authorities' control can be an effective means of minimising fraud. As a result of the requirements of the Companies (Audit, Investigations etc) Act 2005, increasingly one would expect Auditors to ask to see, and request directors to ensure adherence to, an Authority chart.

g

Authority chart

Business name	**Authority levels**

Business name

Philosophy

It is essential for the proper control of the company that approval is granted to contracts by suitably appointed personnel, and for the allocation and disposal of money and stock assets of the organisation that authority is granted at an appropriate level.

Contracts

All contracts between the company and third parties, other than those covered by items specifically set out below, must be channelled through the Company Secretary's office, to ensure correct status (i.e. whether it is to be regarded as a Deed or not) and approval.

For a document to be sealed or signed as a deed at least two weeks notice of the effective date of approval should be given and, should it consist of more than [say, 5 pages] a synopsis should be provided.

The Company Secretary will arrange the passing of suitable Board resolutions granting approval to specified person(s) to sign on behalf of the company. It should be noted that sufficient time (specify requirement) to obtain such a resolution should be allowed.

Contracts of employment for those earning in excess of [sum] must be signed on behalf of the company by [name]. Contracts for those earning less than this sum must be signed by [name].

Authority levels

Business name **Cash Commitment**	**Authority levels**
Capital projects	
Authority for all projects (note: no minimum threshold)	Board
(All items must be supported by a Capital Expenditure (Capex) Form	
Repairs and renewals, purchase of furniture and fittings (All items must be supported by a Capex form)	
• Up to £1000	Manager – level
• Over £1000 and up to £5000	Director
• Over £5000	Board
Vehicles	
(Supported by Capex form, for new allocations, or Replacement form (for write-offs and replacements)	Board
All purchases to be in accordance with Policy	
Expense items	
• Up to £500	Manager – level
• Over £500 and up to £1000	Senior manager
• Over £1000 and up to £5000	Director
• Over £5000	Board
Committed expenditure	
Rent, rates, utility costs – where no change or increase is less than rate of inflation	Manager – level
Where change has taken place	Director

Business name	Authority levels
Bought ledger	
Raw materials, services etc., in accordance with budgeted level of production	Purchasing manager
Not in accordance with level of production	Director
Personnel	
Wage adjustments	
Annual review	Board
Other than annual review, or for new staff, or replacement at other than at old rate	
• Salary up to £15,000 p.a.	Manager – level
• Salary over £15,000 p.a.	Board
Discipline	
Warnings (verbal)	
Warnings (written – grades [x] to [y])	
(written – other grades)	Manager – level
Dismissal	Director
Hearings that may result in the issue of a formal warning or more severe sanction (including dismissal) must only take place if a Complaint form has been issued to the employee concerned in good time before the time set for the hearing. The right of appeal must be made clear to the employee. (See Chapter 17 for rationale.)	

Business name	Authority levels
Sundry transactions Credits (cash or stock), samples, etc.	
• In accordance with policy and less than £1000	Manager – level
• Over £1000	Director
Gifts, donations (cash or stock) In accordance with policy and budget	Personnel Manager
Stock write-off and/or authority to dispose in stated area(e.g. to market trader, staff shop, by gift, etc.)	
• Up to £1000	Sales Manager
• Over £1000	Sales Director in liaison with Finance Director
Expenses Personal expenses (inc. telephone bills etc.)	By level above level submitting the expense claim
• Up to £500 (i.e. using the required company form)	
• Over £500 (All VATable expenses to be supported by a VAT receipt in the Company name.)	By level two above person submitting expense claim
Removal expenses In accordance with range of reimbursement agreed at time may only be authorised by a Board member. All invoices should be submitted in the name of the company to allow recovery of VAT.	

Business name	Authority levels
Loans	
Loans to assist a new employee during the first weeks of his/her employment (i.e. during the working of the 'week in hand' arrangements)	Personnel Manager
All other loans	Board
Tips and inducements:	
Other than normal business entertaining and acknowledging special service, the provision of inducements bribes etc in the name of the organisation is expressly forbidden being a criminal offence. Any instance where this is expected or required should be referred to [name] for guidance.	
Price fixing	
It is illegal for any organisation to conspire with another to fix the price of any product or service – indeed even discussing prices might infringe the rules. Sanctions include imprisonment. On no account is any employee permitted to discuss prices with a competitor or to enter into any arrangement regarding prices no matter how informal. Any instance where this is expected or required should be referred to [name] for guidance. Breach of this rule is gross misconduct.	
Issued by Finance Director on (date). Next update due [date].	To be updated 6 monthly.

Notes

1. The reference to outlawing tips and inducements is partly included because the Anti-Terrorism, Crime & Security Act 2001, part 12 has the effect of strengthening the existing laws on bribery and corruption. As a result any bribery or corruption conducted by UK companies overseas is now subject to the same restrictions and penalties that would be applied if such acts were committed within the UK.

   The Government has stated that it would not prosecute for minor infringements of this new law – e.g. a small gratuity to facilitate the issue of a visa. Whilst this appears sensible some may be excused for thinking this undermines the whole point of the Act.

   Since the Government seems inclined to ignore its own legislation where UK jobs could be imperiled as a result of the protestations of friendly overseas powers (e.g. the BAE Systems and Saudi Arabia contract), one must wonder at the point of the whole legislation. The reality of life is that in some countries one does not obtain any business without some tip or inducement being paid. To believe this can be eradicated by the UK acting alone (since most of our competitor countries ignore the reality of this situation) and that this will in some way counter terrorism seems dangerously naive. Indeed the wider concept that everything can be answered by legislation is similarly naïve. In addition, it is claimed by the Foreign Affairs Committee on Human Rights that the backlash from the decision to stop the investigation into the BAE Systems bribery case has caused considerable damage to the UK's international reputation for fairness and probity – and also to its fight against corruption. In addition, at time of writing, both Switzerland and the USA wish to carry out investigations of their own. The USA had already protested to the UK government at the cessation of the domestic investigation. Since the USA is a major customer for BAE Systems products this story could have considerable implications.

2. Price-fixing, collusive tendering, operating a cartel and any other restrictive practice which disadvantages the consumer is prohibited under the Competition Act 1998 as enhanced by the Enterprise Act 2002. Boards can be held liable for the acts of their employees – hence prohibiting such activities. (See Chapter 4.)

3. Whilst an authority chart such as the above may help minimize unauthorised commitment of the organisation's resources, cash spend may not necessarily be the best criteria in terms of risk to the organisation. For example two contracts might have the same cash value but one (if, for example, the specification is incorrect) could involve the organisation in substantial loss.

Example

Two identical value contracts are placed:

A. For the supply of office furniture. The risk here is virtually nil since if the items are wrong very often they can be replaced – probably without charge and certainly without any knock on effect.

B. For the supply of computer software to a specification generated by the organisation. If incorrect there could be serious financial and other consequences to the organisation.

It may therefore be advisable to incorporate an added dimension – 'risk to the organisation' – to the simple levels of authority, requiring the originator of the order to obtain higher level of authority where the perceived risk (for example) exceeds the value of the contract.

Theft's vicious circle

It has been suggested that in the average organisation if a circle represents the workforce, a quarter of the circle represents the 25 per cent of employees who are honest, another quarter represents the 25 per cent who are dishonest and the remaining half-circle represents half the workforce who are as honest or dishonest as the organisation's rules and procedures let them be. Devising controls such as the above can help not only control expenditure but also 'send the message' that there are strict controls thus possibly deterring potential thieves. Management is stated to commit the 'lion's share' of fraud and leading accountants, Ernst & Young, conducted a survey which determined that 85 per cent of managers who had ripped off their companies had been in position for under a year. Directors having a high visibility (that is being seen throughout the operation – unannounced – and taking note of the environment in the widest sense of the words) can also assist in reducing theft.

Boards cannot be complacent.

As noted in Chapter 3, corporate fraud is on the increase. Many companies, concerned at the rising cost of corporate fraud have not only tightened up reference-taking of applicants but are also checking existing staff – with alarming consequences. In one case a company checking how an accountant had defrauded it of £11M, found that his qualifications had been obtained whilst serving a prison sentence in Strangeways Prison – during a period shown as a gap in his employment record. Another woman claimed to have undertaken voluntary work in an old peoples home. In fact she had been dismissed from a previous job, convicted of fraud and as part of her sentence required to perform community service – in an old peoples home. It was claimed that more than 1 in 3 job applications contain lies and that in 1999, retailers recorded a 43 per cent rise in thefts by employees. It is prudent, at the very least, to incorporate a sentence on application forms stating (e.g.) 'All claims and/or statements of skills, experience and employment will be checked.' Employers could go further to state 'In the event of false claims being made, any offer of employment will be withdrawn, and any employment will be terminated' and 'The [employer] reserves the right to recover any costs incurred as a result of the employment of an applicant who has deliberately submitted an application form containing false claims etc.'

Case study: Watching and waiting

The Director was always perplexed by the apparent wealth of the transport manager who drove a Jaguar, smoked expensive looking cigars and was always well-dressed. Prompted by these signs of wealth the cost of which could not be financed from his salary alone, he kept a close eye on the transport department and one day when there on his own answered the phone. The caller was one of the dealers through which the company disposed of its surplus vehicles who wished to know whether the Transport Manager wanted cash or cigars this time as his 'commission' for putting the business 'their way'.

Being pro-active, implementing controls, being generally aware and checking items – such as is suggested in the following checklist – may assist to protect the organisation from theft.

Theft prevention guidelines checklist

- Round sum payments made to suppliers or unknowns

- Payments made without an invoice or order number

- Lifestyle of executive out of balance with salary

- Employee (all levels) who does not take holiday

- Regular discrepancies in takings, till-roll and other reconciliations

- CCTV monitoring (known to those affected)

- Control budgets and accounts by ratios (comparing data with industry and similar Operations – as well as with prior periods – may disclose variations which should be investigated)

- Explanation of all variations from budget or prior year etc.

- External stock checking

- Install a whistle blowing policy and protection for anyone reporting wrongdoing

- Sole authorisation of purchases or sales

- Restrict issue of order books

- Use termination interviews to encourage reporting of any unusual occurrences and so on

Directors' loans

The above authority chart allows an organisation to make loans to its employees. This is entirely a matter for commercial decision subject to Inland Revenue guidelines concerning any favourable rate of interest becoming a 'benefit'. Loans to Directors, however, are governed by Company Law. Making loans to Directors is anathema to many companies and this may be a prudent approach since in an age where considerable and adverse attention is given to the rewards that some companies provide for their Directors, such a policy can create an unfortunate impression to many outsiders (particularly creditors kept waiting for payment) and even some shareholders. Legally however companies are allowed to make loans to their Directors within the following broad limits.

In general, except where the loan is to enable the director:

- to carry out the work of the company and/or

- to incur costs in defending himself in civil or criminal proceedings or in an investigation re negligence etc (where if he is found guilty the loan must be repaid)

   (both of which loans are subject to a £50,000 limit)

a company is only allowed to make loans to its directors and/or connected persons up to the following limits (larger amounts need the permission of the members):

- a loan or quasi loan up to £10,000 (previously £5,000)

- a credit transaction £15,000 (previously £10,000)

- a loan in the ordinary course of the company's business (e.g. part of the company's business is to lend money to allow the purchase of an individual's main residence) – no limit (previously £100,000).

This is a very brief summary of the implications of sections 197-214 of the Companies Act 2006.

Auditors

The accounts of all companies (other than those that are dormant or exempted – as defined below), are required to be audited. If auditors are not appointed or replaced, the company must notify the Secretary of State for Trade, who has powers to make such an appointment. If in these circumstances, notice is not given to the Secretary of State, those responsible are liable to penalties. Auditors are appointed by and report to the members. In fact they are very often effectively Board nominees reporting to, working with and being guided by the Board – nevertheless it is the responsibility of the Directors to ensure accounts are prepared in accordance with the law, and it is the Directors who must answer criticisms regarding such accounts.

NOTE: Companies exempted from the requirement to have their accounts audited are those whose turnover does not exceed £5,600,000 (formerly £1,000,000) and:

- are not a PLC, bank, insurance company or broker, registered under the Financial Services Act 1986 or the Trade Union and Labour Relations (Consolidation) Act 1992

- do not have a balance sheet total in excess of £2.8 million and

- are not a charity with a gross income of more than £250,000.

Whilst the actions of some members of the audit profession have failed to enhance the reputation of that profession recently, the vast majority provide a decent service, try to ensure compliance, provide guidance to the directors and, by their actions, provide a degree of reassurance to interested parties that the published results are reasonably accurate – and can be relied upon.

Without this kind of 'audit brake' deviation from required practices can go unchecked – and potentially unnoticed – possibly until the company fails. Even where there is no dishonest intent genuine mistakes are unlikely to be corrected without an independent view. Further, the interests of a number of parties could be potentially prejudiced if a company's accounts are not audited:

a) Trade creditors. Accounts are published publicly to protect the interests of the creditors. Without any external checking of the directors' figures such protection disappears. The lack of audited accounts could also inhibit the subject company being able to take on future credit from prospective suppliers. Who is likely to advance credit to a company whose accounts have not been audited?

b) Shareholders (who are not directors) who will have to rely on the figures without the benefit of their appointees – the auditors – checking them. In addition they could be precluded from action (e.g. removing the directors) by the fact that a worsening situation has been concealed – until of course it is too late.

c) Banks and finance houses who have advanced credit to the subject company. They may well insist that an independent audit is conducted before continuing the credit (or advancing new credit) – at almost certainly a higher cost than the regular audit. Future borrowing may only be permitted if it is supported by directors' personal guarantees.

d) Non-executive directors could be at risk since they may lack intimate knowledge of internal developments yet have personal liability should the company trade wrongfully.

e) Employees whose reputation and future employment prospects are dependent on the existence of the company and on their employer's honesty (as the employees of the failed Bank of Credit and Commerce found to their cost).

Case study: Damaging employees' reputations

The Bank of Credit and Commerce International (BCCI) failed due to fraud at a senior level. After its failure, lower ranking employees (not involved in any fraudulent behaviour) found their reputation 'tainted' by having worked for BCCI and their future job prospects diminished. In a class action they recently won £30 million because of this damage.

f) Regulatory authorities who will not know whether the published results of companies with non-audited accounts have been prepared in accordance with the requirements. The attitude of Inland Revenue corporation tax collectors may be interesting and, of course, if the auditors are not available who is to calculate the tax liability (and to ensure the company gains all the exemptions and allowances to which it is entitled)?

g) Insurers. Credit insurance may be impossible to effect without audited accounts, as also might be employment risks insurance.

NOTE: A recent survey of companies who could now opt out of the need for an audit showed that more than 80% would not do so, which rather begs the question of why it was legislated for in the first place.

WARNING: Of course the directors themselves gain from an independent audit. Not only do they obtain specialist advice about the latest disclosure requirements, corporation tax allowances and calculations etc, but also it should provide some reassurance that procedures and practices have been reviewed – and that those that administer (and could thus breach those procedures) know there is to be an independent review of what they have done. With the growth of 'derivative claims' an audit may be regarded as essential to be able to mount a defence.

Qualification

An auditor must have a recognised accountancy qualification. The qualification of auditors is supervised by Recognised Qualifying Bodies (RQB) and their operation is regulated by Recognised Supervisory Bodies (RSB). To be able to operate as RSBs and RQBs (one body can act as both) organisations need to be approved by the Secretary of State for Trade. Only registered auditors are eligible to audit the accounts of companies. If accounts are audited by an unregistered auditor, the Registrar can reject the accounts and require the accounts to be properly audited. The cost of such work may be borne by the directors personally so it is important to ensure that the appointed auditors are registered.

Rights and tenure

By virtue of their appointment by the members, auditors are required to hold an independent view of the activities of the company and the Board and to report on it to the members. An auditor has a right to notice of, and to attend and to speak at a general meeting of the company. The first auditors are appointed by the Board of Directors at any time prior to the first Annual General meeting. At the first and subsequent AGMs auditors are appointed (or re-appointed) by the members. Under the elective regime, members can dispense with the annual re-election of the auditors at the AGM in which case they are automatically re-elected. They hold office from the conclusion of one AGM until the conclusion of the next. Auditors also have rights of access to all records of the company (including the minutes of Board Meetings) necessary for them to be able to complete their audit, and to require Directors and staff of the company to provide information for the same purpose.

Replacement

An auditor can resign during a term of office. In such an instance the Directors could appoint an auditor to fill such a casual vacancy. On occasion it may be administratively convenient for a company to appoint replacement auditors – e.g. when a parent acquires a new subsidiary, it may be logical for the parent company's auditors to become the new subsidiary company's auditors. When an auditor resigns he is required to lodge at the company's registered office a statement of any matters that he feels should be brought to the attention of the members and creditors. In addition, notice of the resignation must be given to the Registrar of Companies within 14 days.

If there are matters which the auditor feels should be brought to the attention of the members and creditors such a statement must be lodged with the company. The company then has 21 days to take the matter to court to gain authority to have such a statement suppressed, and, if it decides to do so must notify the Auditor that it has taken such action. If within 21 days of lodging the statement with the company, the Auditor has not received a statement that appeal has been made to the Court he must lodge his original statement with the Registrar. The Court has the authority either to suppress the statement or to require that copies be distributed to the members. To ensure that matters are brought to the attention of the members, a resigning auditor who feels that members should be aware of matters, can call upon the directors to convene an Extraordinary general meeting which must be convened within 21 days of the auditors request and be held within a further 28 days. The auditor also has the right to have a statement distributed to members attending such a meeting, and to be heard at the meeting, although no further action can be taken, unless a member(s) wishes to press the point.

Removal

A serving auditor can only be removed from office by resolution of the members in General meeting. Special Notice must be given of this Ordinary resolution. If the resolution is passed, the Registrar must be notified within 14 days. This procedure applies even if the change is made at the general meeting at which the auditors re-appointment would otherwise be proposed. If a member wishes to propose that the current Auditors not be re-appointed then he must give notice of this proposal (only once in each year) to the company at the Registered Office. The Directors must convene a general meeting (with 21 days notice since such a resolution requires 'special notice') to consider this proposal within 28 days of this notice being lodged. If the resolution is passed, then the Auditor's office terminates at the end of the current financial year. If, however, such a notice is lodged within 14 days of the accounts for the previous financial year being issued then the auditors' appointment may cease with effect from the end of the financial year being reported upon.

Payment

Fees paid to Auditors must be determined by the company in general meeting. It is usual, however, for the members to authorise the board to agree the amount of such fees which must be disclosed in the accounts (such amounts being split between charges for audit and any other work carried out for the company by the audit organisation, for example, taxation calculations, consultancy, etc.).

Administration

Auditors should be:

- Treated with respect by everyone in the company (who should also be briefed on their rights to ask questions of anyone),

- Accorded decent and secure working conditions and

- Provided with the data they require as swiftly as possible, the demands of the business permitting.

Their investigatory role means that auditors may need to act as a kind of 'critical friend' – appreciating the pressures placed on the board but ensuring that legal and normal commercial requirements are adhered to. Inevitably at times this means that they can come into conflict with the directors who may (legitimately or not) have other considerations which force them to a different conclusion or attitude. Such conflicts need to be resolved but if they cannot and they are of such severity it may be necessary for the Board to consider recommending that different auditors are appointed. Whilst there is nothing to stop shareholders and companies changing their auditors (as set out above) – and there has recently been a considerable increase in the number of companies doing so – not least because of the highly publicised scandals of inept or improper auditing and the failure of large corporations on both sides of the Atlantic) the effect can be potentially dangerous and/or damaging to the company's reputation, particularly if the auditors hold views which are supportable in legal and/or financial terms.

Enhanced penalties

The recently published review of the Macrory Committee concluded that in many cases the penalties for failure to comply are far too lenient leading to a virtual 'invitation to breach' on the basis that 'if you get caught the penalty is less than the cost of compliance' would have been. The review suggests:

- considerable increases in penalties for failure to comply

- use of criminal prosecution as a sanction

- restorative justice – those affected by the non-compliance being able to address the harm and prevent a recurrence

- profit orders, i.e. that, as well as any fine, the profit resulting from the non-compliance should be seized

- corporate rehabilitation orders

- penalty orders in addition to the basic fine etc.

- publication of those found guilty

NOTE: There is a consultation process in operation at present concerning the fines for late filing (e.g. Accounts) at Companies House. This could be introduced when the filing time limits are shortened.

Summary checklist

- Ensure all involved appreciate rights attaching to shareholders and others to inspect statutory records and set up appropriate procedures to deal with any such requests

- Ensure all involved appreciate rights of statutory and other authorities to have access to the company and its records and set up appropriate procedure for each with guidance as to individual scope

- Restrict ability to commit company and to grant authority to expenditure etc. to those authorities by means of (regularly updated) Authority Chart

- Loans to directors must only be made within legal parameters and be properly recorded and disclosed

- Auditors are the custodians of the interests of the shareholders who appoint them. Their legal rights should be known, protected and respected.

Chapter ten

Setting an example

Behaviour and approach

Required approach

Confidentiality undertaking

Non-competition clauses

Other security aspects

Electronic transmissions

Controlling other risks

Insider dealing rules

Share trading

Summary checklist

Required approach

As a result of the increasing general interest being shown by society in the activities of companies and those that run them, emanating not least from a number of scandals involving well-known companies, their Directors and their advisers, and more positively because generally it is seen to be an indication of sound corporate governance, a large number of leading companies now adopt codes of ethics giving guidance on the level and type of behaviour expected of directors and senior personnel. Similar codes are available from the Institute of Directors and other professional bodies. The advantage of adopting such codes is that they provide a criteria of expected conduct and in case of doubt can be referred to for guidance – however all codes are only as effective as those that comply with them and those that police them.

Dubious practices may not only be unacceptable in terms of the way the organisation wishes to operate they may also be tantamount to illegality. Included as part of the Anti-Terrorism, Crime & Security Act 2001 which was implemented on 14th February 2002, part 12 has the effect of strengthening the existing laws on bribery and corruption. As a result, any bribery or corruption conducted by UK companies overseas is now subject to the same restrictions and penalties that would be applied if such acts were committed within the UK. Ideally no responsible Director should condone bribery but it must be said that in some countries in the world, business is simply impossible without some form of local inducement.

The Government has stated that it would not prosecute for minor infringements of this new law – e.g. a small gratuity to facilitate the issue of a visa. Whilst this appears sensible, some may be excused for thinking that this undermines the whole point of the Act.

The Organisation for Economic Co-Operation and Development (OECD) is also committed to stamping out bribery and corruption in business. Countries are paired and carry out inspections on each other to try to combat national and international bribery, which it has been estimated totals one trillion dollars each year. The UK is paired with France and in July 2004 officials from France visited the UK as part of this initiative.

Code of Ethics/behaviour

1. This company operates under high quality standards – of products, or service and of customer care and requires these standards to be adhered to at all times in all its dealings.

2. No-one working for or employed by, or providing services for the company is to make, or encourage another to make any personal gain out of the activities of the company in any way whatsoever. Any person becoming aware of a personal gain being made so that it offends this clause is required to notify [name] of their suspicion. Provided there are reasonable grounds for such suspicion the position and identity of the person reporting the matter will be protected (see 13 below). Anyone placed in a position where they feel that they could make a personal gain should notify [name] and follow the procedure required.

3. Other than properly authorised trade and retail promotions, no inducement may be offered or given to any customer or outlet whereby they will be induced or encouraged to place an order for or take any product or service offered by the company.

4. Whilst it is acceptable to entertain a customer to lunch or dinner to discuss normal contractual matters, this must be at places and to the limits laid down in the company's entertainment/hospitality guide. On no account must the limits and guidelines included in that guide be breached.

5. In the event of any person considering that (s)he needs to entertain or provide a gift for a customer and that the limits are inappropriate (for example the matter concerns an attempt to compensate for previous poor service, quality etc.,) the written authority of a member of the Board should be obtained and referred to in the subsequent expenses claim.

6. Employees are allowed to accept hospitality from major customers and suppliers in terms of lunches and/or dinners or other similar value entertainment, to a maximum of [number of occasions] per year. In the event that the value obtained is in excess of that laid down in the company entertainment guide, this fact must be made known to a Board member as soon as possible. If the entertainment provided is considered to be in excess of that warranted by the circumstances, the director responsible may need to contact the third party to explain the policy.

7. Other than at Christmas [or other religious festival as appropriate], employees are not allowed to accept or retain gifts made by any customer or supplier or other third parties, generated because of the business relationship. In the event that such gifts are delivered and it seems potentially damaging to the relationship to return them, then, subject to the approval of [director] the gifts may be retained and will be handed to the Social Club for use as raffle prizes or disposed of in a similar way. The Director will contact the donor and explain what has occurred and why.

8. At Christmas, employees are allowed to accept the normal gifts to a maximum of [amount] per donor. If gifts above this level are received then, subject to the approval of the [director] they may be retained on the basis set out in 7 above.

9. If multiple gifts are received to mark good service received from a number of employees, these may be retained and divided amongst the employees concerned provided the value per employee does not exceed the guidance laid down in the entertainment/hospitality policy.

10. The attention of all employees is drawn to the danger of a customer or third party using the previous or anticipated delivery of such gifts as a bribe or to exert pressure to obtain concessions (e.g. orders, better terms, preferential treatment) or any other consideration, or using the threat of or actual publicity concerning the acceptance of a gift or lavish entertainment as pressure to obtain concessions etc. In all circumstances the comment 'I cannot comment further – I must contact [director] to discuss this matter' should be made.

11. Any suggestion of using facilities owned, occupied or available to a third party (for example a holiday villa or other property, concessionary travel, etc.) either on a free basis or for any consideration which seems or is less than the market price, should be communicated to the [Director] at whose discretion the matter can proceed or be concluded.

12. The company operates with the [specify] industry and is required to and wishes to comply with all laws, regulations and codes of practice etc. It seeks to trade legally, fairly, openly and honestly with all third parties and to give value for money in all its dealings. It requires and expects its employees to carry out their work and responsibil-

ities and to conduct their relationships and dealings with third parties in accordance with these precepts. All dealings must be conducted openly and fairly in such a way that should every aspect of the transaction become widely known (for example in the media) this would not cause any embarrassment, injury or damage to the reputation of the company whatever.

13. All employees at whatever level in the company are encouraged to report any activities which seem to them to be in breach of this code to [director]. Such a report will be treated as confidential and provided it is made in good faith and not be made with the aim of personal gain, the person making the report should not fear reprisals or detriment.

14. Act responsibly, decently and with due regard for the dignity and rights of others in both business and personal dealings. In many instances personnel (particularly senior personnel) will be seen as acting on behalf of, or by virtue of their position in the company, the reputation of which must be protected at all times.

NOTE: It is possible that there will be an increasing likelihood of 'whistle-blowing' by employees (and others) as a result of the implementation of the Public Interest Disclosure Act 1998. This legislation protects those who report illegal or unacceptable activities within an organisation. The Act enables any person who has suffered a detriment as a result of trying to rectify wrongdoing by reporting it externally (provided they had previously tried to rectify the position internally) to complain to an Employment Tribunal. There is no limit to any compensation awarded in respect of such a claim.

Case study: First whistle-blowing claim

Mr Fernandes was the Financial Controller of *Netcom* whose Managing Director on two occasions gave him petty cash slips, unsupported by receipts, totalling over £200,000. When he protested to the MD and then to the owners of the company that this was probably a fraud on the Inland Revenue (and others) he was told to 'keep your nose clean and pay it'. He refused and was told to resign. He refused and was dismissed. He was awarded £293,000 compensation.

Since the enactment of the Public Interest Disclosure Act in 1999 there have been over 1600 'whistle-blowing' cases – that is claims made by those who, having tried to have illegal practices eradicated by an internal complaint have failed, taken their complaint to an external authority and as a result suffered some detriment at work – e.g. being dismissed. There is no limit on compensation for unfair dismissal in such circumstances. The average payout is around £100,000, and the highest so far is £805,000.

Confidentiality undertaking

Where the business, products or plans of an organisation are confidential either on an ongoing basis or by virtue of developments that occur from time to time, it may be advisable to require those staff likely to be privy to such information to sign a confidentiality undertaking. For public companies subject to the rules regarding the non-disclosure of price-sensitive information this is essential. An assumption that those responsible for a breach would be aware of the rules is hardly likely to be an effective defence for any subsequent action. It is possible for there to be an accidental breach of a confidentiality rule and this needs to be addressed by the organisation. In some ways, acknowledging that accidental breaches can occur and they will be excluded from the requirements and sanctions set out in the following policy may provide an escape for those deliberately in breach – that is they can try to claim it to be accidental. On the other hand the point that even accidental breach can be subject to sanction helps underline the seriousness of the regard of the employer for the matter. Ideally the organisation should request the undertaking to be witnessed. This should avoid the possibility of an employee subject to sanction for breach of the undertaking trying to disclaim knowledge of it by stating that the signature is not theirs and they had not signed such an undertaking.

Draft confidentiality policy

1. The business of the [organisation] entails the development of plans and the production of figures, data and descriptions all of which are confidential to it and the leakage of which to other parties (or allowing others to become aware of in any way) whether by accident or design is potentially damaging.

2. All employees above [specify grade] are required to sign a confidentiality undertaking. [For public listed companies only: All staff of whatever grade who will be involved in the production and recording for publication of information likely to be price-sensitive must on no account divulge such information or give any hint or make any sign or take any action likely to indicate the detail, type or scale of figures or results to a party not privy to such information. Such employees should make themselves aware of the law which seeks to prohibit insider dealing.] *(See later)*.

3. Any member of staff refusing to sign such an undertaking, or proved to be knowingly in breach of such an undertaking having signed it, will be regarded as being guilty of serious misconduct and subject to sanctions including summary dismissal.

   NOTE: Although the seriousness of the situation must be emphasised, some leniency may be allowed where, say, a more junior employee, unwittingly disclosed price-sensitive information to someone not authorised to receive it.

4. The undertaking (senior employees)

   i) All information originated, amended or processed in any way for or from the Board, or any committee of senior management, or connected with the preparation of the Company's Annual and Interim reports is to be regarded as totally confidential.

   ii) All backup information, graphics, data, statistics etc., prepared for or as a result of such work is similarly totally confidential.

   iii) No information can be divulged to any person below the level of senior management without the previous written authority of the [Chairman].

   vi) Nothing covered by items in this Undertaking may be removed from the [organisation] premises without the prior written authority of the [Chairman]. No other information may be removed from [organisation] premises without the prior written (and express) authority of a [director].

   v) Infringements of this undertaking (which could in turn, and amongst other things) lead to the breaking of Stock Exchange rules and legislation) are regarded as a most serious breach of company rules which could lead to dismissal.

vi) No information which in any way could be regarded as price-sensitive may be divulged to anyone other than signatories to this Undertaking or to retained company advisors themselves working under a professional obligation to preserve confidentiality.

NOTE: It may be necessary to warn against persons claiming to be members of, say, the audit team, telephoning to 'discuss' the figures, hoping that the respondent will disclose information unwittingly. Where there is a possibility of such espionage, the use of alpha/numeric passwords may be necessary.

vii) Similar restrictions to the above apply to all [organisation] material, including (but not exclusively) product development work, research data, personnel information, etc.

viii) All those required to sign such an undertaking must do so in the presence of a witness able to verify their identity.

5. The undertaking (junior employees)

i) The work of the [organisation] which consists of [detail], must at all times, be treated as confidential and protected from disclosure. It is an express condition of employment that no employee may divulge to a person outside the [organisation] any such information, or aid the outward transmission of any such information or data.

ii) All backup information, graphics, data, statistics, reports, etc., prepared for or obtained as a result of such work and activity is similarly totally confidential to the [organisation] and must only be used for its purposes.

iii) No such information may be removed from the [organisation] premises (other than in the ordinary course of business) without the prior written (and express) authority of a [director].

iv) Any deliberate infringement of these rules will be regarded as a most serious breach of organisation rules and could lead to instant dismissal. Accidental breach, due to negligence, will also be regarded as a breach of rules and may be subject to disciplinary action.

v) All those required to sign such an undertaking must do so in the presence of a witness able to verify their identity.

Non-competition clauses

In a survey regarding breaches of company security, over 60% of employees admitted that they had stolen confidential documents, customer databases, details of contacts and/or potential sales leads from their employers. Of those who admitted it (how many had stolen such data but did not admit it?) half (i.e. 30% of those asked) said that they believed sales leads and business contacts belonged to them and not to the employer.

Data and Genetics International (DGI), which specializes in investigating data theft, states that in 70% of the cases in which they are involved, the guilty parties are company insiders. (A separate survey revealed that 33% of directors admitted stealing corporate information from their companies. Many such thefts involve using computer memory sticks since transferring the information to such a tiny device is so simple.)

With this level of claimed 'ignorance' and/or confusion regarding the ownership of such property, the onus is very much on employers to ensure that their employees do realise that disclosure or theft is unacceptable. Directors are not immune from temptation and there are innumerable instances of top people ripping off their companies not least since they have so many more opportunities for theft than their employees.

Directors however have an added responsibility in this regard. Each year they must give account of their stewardship to those that own their companies. If they have failed to protect adequately the assets under their control the shareholders can hold them responsible. Companies Act 2006 permits shareholders to take action ('derivative actions') against directors who have not acted in the best interests of the shareholders. Consideration should therefore be given to protective clauses in both directors and key employees' contracts.

Great care however needs to be taken in devising such contracts since Courts are always keen to ensure that there is no 'restraint' of an employee's ability to earn their living because an ex-employer has insisted they sign non-competition clauses – or clauses that retain the right of inventions etc., made by the employee during their employment.

Wording such as the following might be helpful:

'It is a fundamental term of this contract that all data, inventions, research, and/or customer contacts whether listed or not etc., is and

always remains the property of the employer. Any person, during or after employment, using for personal or another party's gain, or passing to another party any such details or data (without previous specific authority of the employer signed by at least two directors), commits a serious breach of this obligation and renders any such person (and any other party involved) liable to legal action.'

Case studies

In *Fox Gregory (FG) v Spinks and anor*, Spinks left FG to work for another firm of estate agents taking with her confidential information including a list of potential contacts. FG protested this was in breach of her contract but Spinks' new employer told her to ignore their protest. FG required the new employer to give an undertaking not to encourage Spinks in breaching her contract and when FG commenced injunction proceedings, the new employer gave the undertaking. (Obviously to be effective (and thus protective) immediate action is needed.) FG later won a case for their costs in the action.

In *Cureton v Mark Insulations Ltd*, an agent worked on behalf of an insulation company. The agent built up a customer database. The EU Database directive stipulates that whoever builds a database is the person who owns it. Since the agent built the database, he owned it and did not have to return it to the principal. (Of course had the contract stated any database had to be retained by the principal should the contract be terminated, the decision would have been reversed.)

In *Dunedin Independent plc v Welsh*, the Scottish Court of Session held that a former employee did not breach a restrictive covenant in his contract when he contacted customers or clients of his former employer. In the opinion of the judge, the clause as drafted did not stop an ex-employee simply contacting such clients to state that he was now running his own business.

Normally such clauses stipulate that a former employee should not solicit or canvas business from their clients. It may be wise to ensure that such wording is revised to (purely as an example) *'shall not solicit and/or contact…'*, so that the simple act of contacting a former client (even without any intent to solicit) would be covered by the prohibition.

In *Helmet Integrated Systems Ltd v Tunnard & ors* it was held that a salesman (i.e. not an employee responsible for product development) who had researched and developed a product similar to that sold by his employer did not breach his duty of fidelity to his employer. The activity the employer complained of related to 'preparatory competitor activity' during his employment whereas his contract referred to activity post termination. In any event the product on which he worked was not of current interest to his employer. Once again it demonstrates the need for the accurate drafting of the clause which is to be relied on.

Other security aspects

The development and reliance on computer systems and intranets whilst providing enhanced access to a mass of data entails both security and relationship problems highlighted in the following checklists:

Computer System protection checklist

The Computer Misuse Act 1990 makes offences of:

* Unauthorised access to computer material (i.e. both hacking and access by unauthorised users)

* Unauthorised change of computer material – e.g. the insertion of a time bomb (March 6th/Michelangelo bug) and the Friday 13th data destruction glitch, and

* Ulterior intent (i.e. unauthorised access for the purpose of committing a crime)

Penalties for unauthorised access (apart from those provided for under the Act which can be as much as 5 years imprisonment and/or an unlimited fine) can include dismissal for employees. Thus the Employment Appeal Tribunal (EAT) held in the Denco v Joinson case that an employee was fairly dismissed when he gained unauthorised access to his employer's computer system (including its payroll files) even though no purpose, other than curiosity, was the cause and no 'loss' (other than of the integrity of the system) occurred. The EAT commented that organisations should make it clear to their employees that unauthorised use of its computer system carries severe penalties – the following is suggested:

Access and use of computer and systems

1. Employees may only operate within the areas of their own departmental operations and service areas. Access to other areas is restricted to authorised personnel only. Access to the systems of the organisation, particularly, but not exclusively, the computer systems, is reserved to authorised personnel only.

2. Unauthorised access to, or in any way tampering with, any computer system or software, or computer installation (including but not restricted to the items in this rule) will be regarded as gross misconduct and will render the offender liable to dismissal.

3. All computer records will be backed up daily (or more often if required) with back up stored in (a remote location). Data files altered during daily working will also be backed up daily with back up disks stored in (a remote location)

4. In no instance should any computer owned or leased by the business be used for playing games or any purpose other than the legitimate work of the business.

5. No software and/or discs etc. other than those owned or leased by the business must be used in the business computers.

6. All software and discs must be purchased new from recognised and reputable suppliers, backed by a confirmation that all such items are free from viruses etc., and/or with a guarantee/liability acceptance in the event that virus(es) which have caused damage, were present on purchase.

7. Anti-virus programs should be used regularly (specify intervals) to check that all systems, software and discs etc. (including back up files) are virus free. Any item found to be infected must be immediately separated from any networking arrangement, and steps taken to eliminate the virus.

Electronic transmissions

The rapid development of electronic message transmission and data access (e-mail, intranets, the Internet etc.) has led to an over-casual use and abuse of systems such that some basic requirements – and a lack of respect and manners – have been ignored.

Problem areas

i. **Section 82 of the Companies Act 2006** authorises the Secretary of State to specify what data must be stated and where. Previous legislation required companies to state certain data (i.e. full name, registered country, number and office) on their notepaper etc. and failure to do so is punishable by fine. If a message is sent by e-mail it is considered to equate to a message sent on a letterhead (i.e. to be a business letter) and as such this required data must appear. Since January 2007 similar information (with the addition of the Company's VAT number) is required to be stated on any website operated by the company.

   NOTE: Computer programs should be altered so that this standard information always appears.

ii. **The ability to generate instant responses** rather than needing to wait for a letter to be typed has led to numerous instances where ill-considered, over hasty and even rude messages have been generated – and later regretted since they have led to confrontations which more thought and tact could have avoided.

iii. It is possible for one party to **create binding contract a** where this was not intended. It may be advisable to require all external correspondence to carry a disclaimer to attempt to indemnify the sponsoring company against improper use of electronic messages or to stipulate that a contractual relationship will only exist when confirmed in hardcopy.

iv. It is possible to **create libel** via e-mail which, once sent, is treated as a written document and can be used in court. If the message is defamatory, the persons responsible can be sued.

v. All e-mails can be reconstituted in hard copy for up to 2 years. Such messages can be made subject to **disclosure requirements** – thus a third party with whom the company is in dispute can require details of such messages. The commitment to sourcing the relevant information should not be under-estimated.

vi. **E-mail and intranets are used widely for the dissemination of personal material**. In addition third parties can 'dump' unwanted messages. As a result valuable messages may be buried in unwanted electronic communications resulting in considerable time being wasted in sorting the essential from the trivial.

NOTE: In the USA, the receipt of junk e-mail (or 'spam') has become so widespread (and costly in terms of reading the unwanted material) that some large organisations are banning external incoming e-mails having failed to adequately control it with internal shields.

vii. External e-mails can contain **viruses** capable of affecting the recipients computer systems. Suitable virus shields should be installed.

viii. In a number of instances companies' **websites have been either tampered with** or copied (albeit with unauthorised additions / deletions. The format of the website should if possible be protected by copyright whilst employees must be advised that such actions are gross misconduct.

ix. The EU carried out a survey recently and found that on average **employees use their employer's access to the Internet** for an hour each day for private purposes – often to source pornography. As a further development, in a number of instances such material has then been circulated via the employer's intranet leading to claims for harassment and discrimination referred to above.

x. The 'away from office' function (e.g. on holiday for two weeks) has been used by criminals who by cross-referencing that information with online directories have been able to discover personal information and even home addresses. They then know that it is likely the house will be empty for a period.

xi. E-mail **and intranets are increasingly being used for harassment, discrimination and bullying** which could mean potential liability for the company and possibly its officers as well as those generating such illegal acts. A recent survey indicated that 50 per cent of those questioned had received obscene, sexist or otherwise inappropriate e-mails within the previous year. In addition access to the Internet enables 'electronic stalking' to take place. This situation is becoming so serious that companies must at least consider implementing a policy/procedure such as the following example, outlawing abusive practices.

xii. **'Blogging'** – the term given to keeping a diary in the Internet (weB LOGGING) – is on the increase. Where such a diary is kept by employees (using their employees access to the Internet) and is accessible by others, some have taken the opportunity to insert caustic comments about their employer and other employees. Whilst many such comments may be regarded by the author as 'humourous' and harmless, the subject may find them to be not so innocent.

There have been a number of dismissals (so far mainly in the US) where the employer believed the comments 'damaged' their reputations. It may be advisable to include a prohibition on making such comments in disciplinary rules and to advise employees that they need to be careful when making comments which may be read publicly, not least since apart from disciplinary matters, it may give rise to an action for libel in which, (since the employer's access to the Internet was being used), the employer could be joined.

Electronic transmissions policy

1. E-mail should be used primarily to distribute/update information, confirm arrangements, confirm meetings etc. [It may not be used to distribute personal information.]

2. As an exception the system can be used to leave messages where the recipient is unavailable and the message awaits their return.

3. E-mail should not be used to substitute for face to face or telephone conversations since messages they convey lose much that is conveyed by body language. The medium is comparatively ineffective in this area. Research indicates that people reach the best decisions when they occupy adjacent physical space – using e-mail blanks off this advantage.

4. Unless video and audio links are available, electronic communications should not be used for meetings or managerial control. Research indicates that people reach the best decisions when they occupy adjacent physical space – using electronic communication blanks off this advantage.

5. Items for dissemination via e-mail should be checked after drafting for clarity, accuracy of message and absence of abusive, emotive,

etc. words. The language used must be consistent with conventional standards, decency and respect for others, and good manners.

6. Commenting on or about another person or body should be avoided but, if it is unavoidable (i.e. it is a necessary part of the information under consideration), should only be based on and backed up by facts (failure to have available a factual basis for such items could lead to a libel action). Employees must not by using electronic or other means publish derogatory remarks concerning the employer and/or other employees. Not only this is regarded as gross misconduct, but also if such comments are untrue, this could give rise to an action for libel.

7. On no account should the internal or external system be used for vindictive, harassing, discriminatory or abusive comment or criticism of anyone, whether this is the target, another employee or any third party. Further it must not be used for electronic stalking.

8. A person receiving an item which they feel should have been prohibited by item 7 above should notify [name].

9. Any person proved to have deliberately sent an item prohibited by item 7 above and/or item 13 below will be deemed guilty of gross misconduct and will be dealt with under the disciplinary procedure accordingly. Some of these offences also breach criminal law and can be made subject to sanctions including imprisonment.

10. All messages etc., should be clear and unambiguous and coded from 5 star to 0 star in order of priority (in accordance with the priorities of the recipient rather than those of the sender). Since clarity is preferable to brevity jargon should be avoided unless the sender is absolutely certain that the recipients will understand it.

11. An e-mail message should be treated as if it were a hard copy letter and drafted and checked in the same way. In law an e-mail message has the same value as a hard copy letter. All e-mails can be re-captured in hard copy.

12. No e-mail message or response to an e-mail message should ever be sent in haste, anger or hostility. Ideally a time for consideration should elapse between drafting and sending a reply.

13. No e-mail or other communication containing a virus or equivalent damaging content may be sent internally or externally. No electronic

device capable of receiving e-mails or other communication from external sources may be used without being virus protected.

14. Access to the Internet is for the purposes of the employer's business only and such access must not be used for an individual's requirements whether personal or on behalf of another. Failure to comply with this will be regarded as gross misconduct.

    [Alternatively: Access to the Internet for personal purposes is permitted only (for example, i.e. outside working hours) before 8.30 a.m. and after 5.30 p.m. On no account must any data or information so derived be used in or passed round the organisation in any way whatsoever without the written permission of [name].]

15. All communications including e-mail, faxes, telephone conversations etc. generated and/or received by employees may be monitored by the company as is allowed under the contract of employment. Where private business is to be transacted employees can use the payphones provided. These phones are not monitored.

16. Personal mobile phones may not be used at the workplace and must be switched off during working hours. They can be switched on and used during recognised breaks provided this can be effected without causing any dislocation to the computers and other property and procedures of the company. If incoming urgent messages are required to be made other than at times of breaks, these should be left with the switchboard operator who will pass messages to employees. Where the matter is urgent an employee may use their own phone or a payphone to return the call subject to gaining permission from their supervisor or manager to leave their place of work.

17. On no account may any organisation information stored in any electronic data or other system (including purely for example computer aided design work) be copied or removed (including by electronic transfer) from the premises of the organisation without prior written permission of [name].

18. The company websites are the sole property of the company and any unauthorised interference with, or copying and variation of such websites is not only gross misconduct but also can generate an action for damages.

19. On no account must an employee in receipt of a personal incoming e-mail distribute such material internally or externally without specific prior permission from (designated person).

20. For security reasons and to prevent fraud, covert monitoring may take place both on an off company premises.

21. Persons undertaking job-sharing will be allowed access to their partners electronic and other transmissions.

22. The 'away from office' function should be used with discretion. It may be preferable not to state dates of absence and to redirect messages to a colleague. On no account should personal details (address, telephone number etc.) be placed on such a function.

23. On every occasion, before using the system employees will be required to type 'YES' in answer to a screen prompt 'Are you aware of the [Organisation's] Electronic Transmissions policy and that breach of the requirements is gross misconduct' before they can proceed.

24. Breach of this policy is gross misconduct

Advising users that e-mails can be recovered in hard copy form for up to two years and can be made subject to legal disclosure rules may encourage users to think more carefully of the content of their messages, whilst if the employer wishes to be able to monitor all messages (e.g. telephonic, electronic and hard copy) a suitable clause such as the following must be inserted in the Contract of Employment so that the employee effectively 'grants permission' for such monitoring.

'Right to Eavesdrop' clause

'The employer provides electronic transmission systems for the purposes of its business during normal working hours only. Employees will be expected to operate such systems from time to time and it is a basic rule that in working hours such access must be only for the employer's business purposes. Monitoring devices are installed and e-mails, as well as faxes, letters and telephone calls may be checked to ensure that only the employer's business is being transacted and that this is being conducted in an acceptable way using reasonable language, etc. A pay phone is provided [specify] and communication via this phone are not monitored.

It is a contractual requirement that employees agree to such monitoring. As a concession (which the employer reserves the right to withdraw at any time and without notice) employees will be allowed access to the Internet for personal purposes outside normal working hours providing this is at no expense to the employer, that no embarrassment or damage would be caused to the employer should details of the material accessed be widely known, and that no material thereby derived is disseminated internally, or to any shareholder, customer, agent or supplier in any way whatsoever without prior written approval from [name]'.

As an alternative or addition to the above, some leading companies (e.g. LloydsTSB) completely ban private use of electronic communications including e-mail at the office and regard any breach as gross misconduct.

Controlling other risks

Using employees involves risks and these days should an employee suffer loss or damage as a result of their activity at work, they are more likely than hitherto to seek to hold their employer responsible and sue. Adequate health and safety precautions should not only be taken but also be clearly seen to have been taken – and, above all, to be regularly policed and updated. Most organisations may see this requirement as so obvious as for it to be unnecessary to be reminded, however there are areas where precautions could well be overlooked.

The requirement for some employees to travel on their employer's business is widespread and most such travel is on a national level. Even this involves danger. Precautions such as requiring employees not to both drive and work for periods materially longer than the normal working day should be obvious. However international travel is on the increase and inevitably some employees sent overseas find themselves in locations that can be described as 'high risk' or even downright dangerous and it is not impossible to imagine a scenario where directors of companies could be held liable should an employee suffer injury or worse as a result of being located in such areas.

It has been suggested that around a fifth of employees of many companies have been on trips to countries that are on the Foreign Office's list of 'don't go there' locations. Before allowing a person to go abroad it could be advisable to:

a)   request local information (from a reliable source) concerning the types of risks that the employee could face at the location

b)   prepare, brief and discuss with the employee a full risk assessment covering such risks

c)   consider ways in which the risks can be minimised (or, if possible, eradicated)

d)   locate appropriately-secure personal and business facilities for the employee

e)   address the risks inherent in moving between personal and business facilities (and recreational travel)

f)   consider whether bodyguards or equivalent should be provided

g)   prepare contingency plans in the event of kidnap (where the input of insurers may be necessary), injury or death.

Such data should be provided to the employee before they depart. In locations that are deemed to be high risk it may be preferable to use local agents rather than one's own employees.

An employer has no right to post an employee overseas unless the contract of employment contains such a clause. If not, the two parties need to negotiate a suitable variation to the original contract or to conclude a new one. This variation or new contract should address at least the following:

•   the period for which the employee is required to work overseas

•   the currency in which payment is to be made for the work done overseas

•   details of any additional incentives being offered and 'paid' to attract the employee to work overseas

•   repatriation terms (that is on what basis – and at what level in the organization is it intended that the employee return to the UK at the end of the overseas posting).

Under the Employment Rights Act, where an employee is to work overseas such a contract must be given to them no later than their date of departure for the overseas work destination (even if this is less than two months from them starting work).

Normally UK laws will govern the contract, and even if the rules of another jurisdiction are to apply, the employee cannot be deprived of the normal employment rights applicable to a UK employee. If the posting is within the EU, the protection of EU law is available but again the UK employment rights will normally apply. However this only extends to those who 'work within Great Britain' and those who work abroad temporarily. The situation regarding the rights of those UK nationals working elsewhere may be unclear and in fairness to both parties should be clarified before the employee departs.

Insider dealing rules

Included in the confidentially undertaking and related only to companies whose shares are listed on a Stock Exchange are concerns over a lack of discretion or deliberate leaking of information in a Director's possession which could be price-sensitive. The principle of the Stock Exchange is that all who deal in shares should have the same information available to them. Hence all information the company wishes to disclose must be made public simultaneously (most often by means of the publication of its Preliminary Announcement which gives a synopsis of the results for the latest financial year – see Chapter 14). Inevitably Directors (and other senior managers) will be privy to information at this and other times which if published might affect the share price. Such data is known as price sensitive information and it is inherent in the position of Director that it should not be disclosed other than where running the business so demands. If such data is disclosed other than at those times and to people (who have no business right to know) who then trade in the shares, that act and the act of providing the information is known as Insider Dealing.

The Criminal Justice Act 1993 lists three instances where insider dealing occurs:

1. If an individual who has inside information deals in securities using such inside information. Thus if you are the director of a public company and knowing that information to which you were a party would affect the price of the shares were it to be made public, and

you then traded in the shares, you could be held to be guilty of insider dealing.

2. If an individual who has inside information encourages another person to trade in the shares he may be guilty of insider dealing and if the person who is encouraged to deal knows that the data is 'inside information' because the informant is in a position to have access to such information then that person may also be guilty.

3. If a person discloses price sensitive information to another person other than in the proper performance of his duties. Thus, if a Director told his/her wife/husband who then traded in the shares on the basis of the information then she would be guilty. If the director's wife, husband or partner told a friend and that friend knows the Director's position in the company and thus that the source of the information is likely to be authoritative, then if they trade in the shares, they may also be guilty.

Thus a person in no way connected to the company (other than by knowing the data) can nevertheless be guilty. Similarly if a Director has a professional adviser – e.g. an accountant – looking after his interests and they learn the information and trade then they too will be guilty. For those found guilty – the penalties are severe – up to 7 years imprisonment and/or a fine. There are some defences including 'that the act of trading would have taken place whether the inside information had been known or not'. This should cover the situation where the person concerned needs to sell shares in order to raise money for a specific (and presumably time-related) purpose. In addition if a Director disclosed the information in the ordinary course of business not believing it would be used for the purposes covered by the Act then that should also be a good defence. There have been around 30 cases brought under the Insider Dealing regulations and at least two jail sentences imposed.

The whole aspect of the control and prevention of insider dealing has been given in creased impetus as a result of the passing of the Financial Services and Markets Act which created the Financial Services Authority as the single body with statutory power to regulate all financial business in the UK, and came into effect in December 2001.

The Act covers not only listed companies but also their Directors, their employees and advisers and private individuals. The thrust of the legislation is to try and enhance the principles of the Criminal Justice Act 1993 referred to above. Thus a listed PLC must:

- Comply with the updated listing rules of the Stock Exchange
- Abide by the requirements regarding the dissemination of 'price sensitive information' (PSI)
- Avoid breaching the principles of the 'market abuse' regime and
- Avoid breaching the wider financial promotion regime which now covers all corporate communications.

Market abuse

'Insider dealing' is replicated – but extended – in the new requirements. Thus market abuse occurs:

- If a person has information not available generally and that person deals or encourages another to deal. There is no requirement for profit to be made from the action or even for the information to have been price sensitive.

- If a person's behaviour will give a false or misleading impression of the price or value of shares. Thus a listed PLC could commit market abuse by failing to advise the market of material matters or giving misleading or false announcements.

- If a person's behaviour is likely to interfere with or distort the proper operation of market forces.

General compliance with the Listing Rules and Takeover Code then will probably be a sound defence as will be the case if the actions are not below the 'reasonably accepted standard' of behaviour.

Case study

In *R v Carl Rigby*, the former Chairman and Chief Executive Office of software firm AIT was sentenced to 3½ years imprisonment and disqualified from being a director for 6 years for criminal market abuse.

Intent

The offence of 'market abuse' does not require intent and thus if a person unknowingly breaks the new rules they could be held liable. Until there is some case history it is difficult to see how this will be regarded by the UK Courts (the Government resisted the efforts of the House of Lords to clarify this point). However of more concern may be the EU's proposed directive on market abuse (i.e. insider dealing and market manipulation) which does not require that the person intended to commit market abuse. As an example the EU state that if a person makes an untrue statement believing it to be true that is market abuse – and the offender is liable. So draconian are these rules that companies should ensure everyone affected knows the detailed requirements and the following checklist for action may be of assistance.

Internal action checklist

1. The existing requirements regarding 'insider dealing' should be revisited and revised.

2. All those involved in market operations need to understand the new requirements – particularly the question of lack of intent.

3. Checking advisers have installed more vigorous verification procedures regarding company announcements to ensure no breach occurs.

4. Ensuring all involved understand the requirements of the 'PSI' regime (see Financial Services Authority 'Code of Market Conduct' which gives examples of market abuse).

5. Checking all issued information (including any posted on the company's website) for compliance and accuracy

6. Re-issue internal guidance regarding directors and employees rights and actions vis-a-vis trading in the company's shares ensuring that full reference to the new rules is included in that guidance.

WARNING: The Financial Services Authority is attempting to clamp down on Insider Dealing and since 1st July 2005 has required all managers (in addition to their directors) of listed PLCs who have access to inside information to disclose publicly every time they trade in their employer's shares. To some extent this is required as a result of the requirement to implement the European Market Abuse Directive. Brokers and spread betting firms are required to advise the FSA if they suspect or consider there is insider dealing or market manipulation.

Share trading

Although the custom of requiring Directors to hold shares in companies to whose board they were appointed has tended to die out, recently, not least due to the suggestion made in the Cadbury report that this was advisable, there is a growing pressure to encourage Directors of PLCs to hold shares in their companies. This poses them a problem in terms of the timing of any purchases and/or sales since almost inevitably at every stage in their company's financial calendar they will have access to information which, if released, could have an effect on the share price. In recognition of this the Stock Exchange listing agreement suggests that Directors should observe a two-month 'dead period' before the publication of interim or preliminary announcements during which time Directors should not buy or sell any of their companies shares other than for the most urgent reasons. In addition, most companies now require their Directors to notify the Chairman every time they trade in shares or options. Some companies apply wider time limits than those suggested.

Summary checklist

- Generate, promulgate and police a code of ethics/behaviour

- Generate, promulgate and police a confidentiality undertaking (possibly devising two or more versions depending on seniority of signatories)

- Generate, promulgate and police electronic and other communication policies and procedures

- Brief all Directors and officers re insider dealing restrictions and any 'dead' periods for trading on an ongoing basis

Chapter eleven

'He who communicates leads'

Leadership and management

Distinguishing between leadership and management

Leadership qualities

Maximising the human resource

Communication principles

Briefings

Summary checklist

Distinguishing between leadership and management

Definition

The chapter title is derived from a saying of Jack Jones, the former general secretary of the Transport and General Workers Union. Another quotation, this time from Steven Covey, the American business author and leadership guru, may highlight the differences between these two types of control. Covey suggests that 'management without leadership is akin to arranging the deckchairs on the Titanic'. Circumscribed as it is by legislation there is a great danger in considering the work of the effective Director that we concentrate so much on 'doing things right' that we overlook the overriding need for the company – and particularly the Directors leading the company – to do the right things. In this context doing the right things involves planning and managing the company – or in the widest sense of the word, providing leadership to all who work for it. Thus as well as complying with all their legal obligations Directors must take the initiative in terms of 'leading' their companies and above all their employees. The concept of leadership should be obvious and yet experience suggests that perhaps because it is deemed to be so obvious it is taken for granted and thus is ignored in too many organisations. In too many instances Boards of Directors have become aloof and disconnected from the team they have a duty to lead. Such a situation can only operate to the detriment of the organisation – and thus render its performance far less effective than possible.

There are innumerable books about leadership and there is no doubt that good leadership can be improved by the guidance thus provided. Whilst this may be so it does seem that the best leaders tend to operate more by instinct for what is their view of the 'best' solution rather than as a result of learning what is a 'good practice'. Perhaps their guidance in making the 'right' decision and taking the 'right' approach is derived from the 'doasyouwouldbedoneby' dictum – i.e. 'if it were me that was affected by this decision, rather than me making it, how would I react?' – that is the doasyouwouldbedoneby principle. Appreciating how the other party to a decision will react is critical to good management or leadership. This does not mean that the decision should be altered but that if we appreciate likely reactions before acting we may be guided to modify our approach, which if we then receive a more positive reaction can mean we gain where a poorer, less perceptive approach may have generated a negative reaction.

Leadership qualities

In carrying out around 200 'Preparing for Management' sessions (as part of a personal skills course) throughout the UK over the past 15 years, I probed the question of leadership and what those being led wished to receive from their managers. The five most valued (and wanted) characteristics that the considerable majority of those questioned (a total of around 2500 supervisors) wished to obtain from their managers can be summarised and grouped into a useful mnemonic shown below:

A manager's most wanted qualities

The ability and preparedness to:

- Listen
- Encourage
- Advise
- Delegate
- Support

In other words in being a good manager, the person **LEADS**.

Listen

Sir John Harvey Jones suggests that 'the ability to listen is the rarest of all characteristics. Listening is all about what people don't say.' Perhaps it is unsurprising that real active listening is such a rare commodity considering that at school (and indeed before our formal schooling starts) we may be taught to talk, taught to look, taught to read but rarely these days taught to listen. Children are rightly taught to express themselves but without necessarily being taught to listen to others expressing themselves – the result leans towards a figurative Tower of Babel! The Victorian dictum 'children should be seen but not heard' may not have helped children express themselves as well as many can now do, but at least it encouraged the skill of listening which seems rare in these 'enlightened' times.

Similarly in later life Directors are subjected to a vast amount of data coming at them from all directions. In such a situation it can be very difficult to find time to listen to one's subordinates but it is only if such time is found (which may be where the fourth characteristic in the above figure is all-important) that mutual respect can be fostered and the Director will gain an insight into the true attitude and feelings of the subordinate. Too many Directors claim to 'know what my people are thinking' – which, even if they practise active listening, is likely to be nothing more nor less than a dangerous self-delusion and displays both a conceit and a breathtaking arrogance. Actively listening to members of one's team and observing their actions may give a more accurate guide to the way they are feeling.

Active listening takes time – time which preferably should not be interrupted by phones ringing, visitors or unwanted distractions. If any of the latter are present and are allowed to interrupt, then the message being conveyed to the other party is 'you are not as important as this item which has interrupted us' which is hardly guaranteed to impress, motivate or incentivise the other party – which should be one of the basic challenges for management. As an adage runs 'the purpose of management is to help people succeed'.

Requirements for active listening checklist

a) allow sufficient time for the interface

b) allow the other party to talk without interrupting (e.g. close down the computer!)

c) take the phone off the hook and close the door to visitors

d) pay attention to what is being said

e) try to determine – and probe to discover – what is not being said

f) demonstrate that you are concentrating on what is being said

g) ask questions (even if not essential to your understanding) to demonstrate that you are concentrating

h) watch the other party's body language to try to gauge whether or not they are being accurate and truthful

i) watch your own body language to ensure you are giving signals which indicate you are paying attention.

j) don't make snap decisions – ask for time to consider points or requests made

k) make notes – but don't doodle

l) don't interrupt except to ask for more clarification of a point made

m) don't dismiss points out of hand – if you don't agree prepare arguments which counter the points made

and so on

NOTES:

1. The essential ingredient is time. Even if the answer is no, if sufficient time has been allowed to the other party to put their viewpoint, they should feel that justice has been done.

2. The antithesis of this positive approach is never to listen but merely to make decisions from the manager's sole viewpoint. Sometimes the right decision will be made and respect may be gained – often it will not and respect will be nil. It is virtually impossible to lead those who have no respect.

Encourage

Few are able or chosen to be leaders. Most people – probably around 90 per cent – are content to be led – to follow the lead and participate as members of a team (remembering the adages 'Together Everyone Achieves More' and 'none of us is as good as all of us'). Most are also prepared to put up with strict regimes – provided they are fair. However what most followers need is to be encouraged and stimulated in their work. It is reckoned that a sizable proportion of people are capable of performing well at one level above that at which they currently perform. An effective manager will recognise this and by encouragement attempt to show team members how to take on more responsibility and to develop.

NOTE: The converse here is to insist people do as they are told and not to encourage them to make suggestions, ask for help etc. In such a situation it is hardly surprising if mistakes are made or there is no commitment to working together.

Advise

In most instances a manager should have a reasonable command of the rudiments of all the tasks being undertaken by his team, if not the actual detail. With this knowledge they should be able to provide advice if one of those team members requires assistance in carrying out their duties.

NOTE: Failing to provide advice (which entails a failure to listen actively) will demotivate the team member – who else can they turn to if not to their manager?

Delegate

Faced with the need to listen, to encourage and to advise and provide support to their team members many managers will retreat behind the age-old complaints (or excuses) 'insufficient time' or 'too busy on my own work'. It should be pointed out to such 'managers' that the main task of a manager is to 'manage' i.e. to direct and lead those who report to them and it is this that is their priority. The job of a manager is not to do the job themselves, even if they are able carry out the duties more accurately and swiftly than their subordinates, but to ensure that the latter carry out the duties providing assistance when necessary. Many of the more routine duties undertaken by managers could, with a little training and guidance be carried out by more junior employees which has the advantage of:

- Freeing the manager's time

- Making the subordinate's job more interesting

- Encouraging commitment from the team members by demonstrating faith and confidence in them.

Principles of effective delegation checklist

a) Assess (on an ongoing basis) the subordinate for capability and willingness to assume a greater workload

b) Establish precisely the duties, responsibilities AND authority that are to be delegated

c) Check whether subordinate can assume extra duties delineated immediately or needs training, or a delay before taking over such duties (and check regularly after delegation)

d) Delegate only to those able and WILLING to carry out the work

e) Brief and train the delegatee to carry out the work

f) Advise all involved of the delegation

g) Provide time, support and guidance for the delegatee (ongoing)

h) Avoid the destruction of confidence by undercutting the authority of delegatee

i) Regularly review progress and accomplishments

j) Constantly support and motivate – never denigrate

Support

If the manager is really leading and his subordinates are team members, there will be mutual support – although the team may only be as good as its leader, the leader will only be as good as his team. However by providing support and encouragement at the required times, good leaders can make members of a team perform above themselves. In truth the total performance can be greater than the sum of the parts – and in reality 'together everyone achieves more'. Many people lack self-confidence, but with the support of their manager or leader, often they can achieve at a level that they never thought possible.

Maximising the human resource

If Directors are responsible for maximising the value of the assets of their company (which they should be) and those that work for the company are the greatest assets of their company (which they usually are), then there is no more important task for the directors than obtaining the greatest output from the company's human assets. Whilst this can be done via positive leadership, it is unlikely to be achieved by issuing dictats from a position remote from such assets – yet this is how many Directors try to direct their employees. We could perhaps summarise this human asset management as shown in the following checklist.

Guidelines of good leadership/management checklist

a) Build a team and constantly work with it and as part of it to make it achieve its aims

b) Clearly define and set the task for the team (use unambiguous and clear language) and coach and support those required to achieve it

c) Manage (i.e. lead by listening, encouraging, advising and supporting) the team members

d) Talk to and actively listen to each member of the team – creating mutual respect

e) Delegate (or empower) to as great an extent as possible so that you can stand back, plan for the future and manage the team members

f) Discuss problems and use suggestions and ideas from those involved

g) Use organisation charts to demonstrate relationships without letting them become straitjackets

h) Outlaw demarcation disputes – resolve altercations via discussions

i) Draw solutions from those at the sharp end rather than imposing solutions on them

j) Be visible, approachable, and patient

NOTE: These guidelines are applicable to the teams led by Directors. However each Director needs to ensure that each management level in turn leads their team in the same way.

Additional guidelines

• Acknowledge achievement – praise is an extremely effective means of motivation (and it costs nothing!) – but to be really effective it must be genuine

• Monitor and demonstrate progress – if we praise progress, then when there is no progress or there are mistakes, the need for effort, objective criticism and correction is obvious and is more likely to be positively accepted.

• Share the preferred tasks – and the awkward tasks, so that all members of the team (including the leader) take their turn at both – example is a powerful motivator

• Encourage team members to discuss their concerns and problems – to think positively thereby helping create a better team spirit

Management is a continuing responsibility – everything about the role is ongoing – and no-one should be more aware of this than the Board of Directors whose view must always be partly focussed on the long term. Whilst setting up the principles and practice of good management/leadership is essential – so too is a commitment to continuing this approach which may be a harder task than actually starting.

When things are up and running, we need to continue to stimulate attention; good leaders understand the need for consistency of approach. The items set out in the following checklist may provide a reminder of what is required.

Ongoing requirements of leadership checklist

1. Give praise when merited

In the UK we tend to criticise too often and praise too little. Yet praise is incredibly cost-effective and usually very motivational. Most people want recognition and respond positively to it. If we give praise when things are done well then we will find it easier to achieve a positive response when we have to criticise.

2. Provide incentives and rewards

Simple praise may be a valuable motivational force but it needs to be substantiated by material recognition – money, vouchers, etc. which reflect the genuine appreciation of the organisation for good work etc. Peer recognition can be a valuable aid in motivation.

3. Training

Being prepared to invest in employees by means of funding (or even part funding) training for the mutual benefit of employee and employer can not only motivate employees but also retain the best performers. Research indicates that in some fast moving industries good calibre people tend to be attracted to employers who will provide career training.

As we shall see in a later chapter, there is a skill shortage in the UK – likely to worsen before it improves. The organisation that offers applicants the chance to improve their skills to mutual benefit is likely to be the one that manages to attract a better selection of recruits – or preferably a selection of better recruits. Research indicates that the organisations that offer training and a career path are those that tend to retain their employees. A well motivated and trained workforce is as much about retention of good calibre people as attracting them.

4. Counselling

From time to time most employees will encounter problems that can affect their performance. Encouraging them to use a confidential counselling service can not only assist solutions but also demonstrate the wish of the organisation to provide assistance. Stress is a major cause of poor performance and absenteeism. An employee under stress cannot perform to the best of their ability. Genuinely assisting or being prepared to assist the employee under stress (whether work or home-generated) should help relieve the stress and return full productivity. The benefits on the rest of the team should not be underestimated.

5. Flexibility of relationship

Flexibility of working, of attitudes, of rules, and so on, creates an ambience of a partnership between organisation and employee. Nowadays there is increasingly a recognition that there is a need to provide a balance between the demands of employees' own lives and their working lives. The relationship is moving to one between equal partners where 'give and take' is required from both, rather the blind obedience of the 'master and servant' relationship of the recent past. Unfortunately this has been misnamed as trying to create a 'work/life' balance which seems to infer that work is not part of life. 'Work/leisure' balance may be a more accurate term.

6. Flexibility of work

If there is a variety of relatively straightforward (even boring jobs) try to train personnel so that they can periodically have a change round. In this way, new relationships as well as new approaches may result. Indeed it may be that someone newly performing a task will see a way in which it could be improved.

7. Listening

Team briefing, quality circles, workplace forums, improvement groups, suggestion schemes may all play a part in encouraging thought about the jobs and the way they are performed – and in welding a team together. Often it is the simple fact of leader and team talking and discussing matters which is the conduit through which the results are achieved.

8. Delegate and empower

Responsibility should be pushed as far down as possible. This will leave time for man/woman management as well as making the delegatee's job more rewarding. Encouraging employees themselves to work in teams harnesses peer pressure, which should then tend to improve output and communication and generate a willingness to take on more responsibility and tasks.

9. Motivate

Demotivational forces such as unfairness, discrimination, harassment, favouritism, verbal and physical violence, bullying, and perceptions of worthlessness, must be outlawed. Ensure fairness at all times.

10. Create teams

Encouraging employees themselves to work in teams harnesses the pressure of the team members to make their team successful. This should improve output, communication and productivity. The phrase 'Together Everyone Achieves More' (TEAM) is a useful mnemonic to help put the concept across and to ensure it is memorised.

As five times gold medal winner Sir Stephen Redgrave and his rowing partner Matthew Pinsent state:

'For any team to reach its true potential it needs all of its individuals to communicate clearly and work together. It means understanding each other's talents and then using them to the full, and it means knowing when to bolster each other's performance to become closer, stronger and more flexible. What started as a group of individuals ends with relationships permanently strengthened by the experience.'

11. Extend employee ownership

This movement has been around for many years with tax incentives encouraging the spread of the process. Even Gordon Brown stated in 1999 that he wanted to encourage such ownership:

'Share ownership offers employees a real stake in their company .... I want targeted reform, to reward long-term commitment by employees. I want to encourage the new enterprise culture of teamwork in which everyone contributes and everyone benefits from success.'

Research in 2001 for the Chartered Institute of Personnel and Development by Professor Freeman (Harvard and London School of Economics) found that the increase in productivity from implementing an approved profit-sharing scheme was 17% whilst introducing a share option plan increased it by 12%.

12. Communicate, communicate, communicate

Unfortunately the word (and action) of providing 'information' is often confused with 'communication'. Information consists of giving people facts and data which they may or may not understand – it is essentially a sole directional process, does not require input from the target and does not generate any communicative process. Only if we encourage and generate feedback will we start a two-way process which, when both parties understand the viewpoint of the other, will become communication. True communication helps unleash employees' thoughts which may in turn provide a guide to leading/managing them.

In attempting to communicate we should always try and see the message through the eyes (or ears) of the recipient. If the reader doesn't understand the message, the only person responsible is the writer. We must construct messages in a way that our target audience can easily comprehend them. Our aim should be not so much as to make the message easy to understand, but to make it impossible to misunderstand.

(Internally it may be preferable to refer to the process as 'communicaction' – that is 'communication in action' to try to remind everyone that it is a dynamic not passive process. See below.)

NOTES:

1. A recent 3 year study of 40 major companies demonstrated that a key driver of company profitability was the commitment of the employees. The key factors behind such commitment were:

   - the leadership skills of managers
   - the opportunities of staff to develop their own skills and
   - the extent to which employees were empowered to discharge their responsibilities.

Generally UK employees rated their leaders less favourably than US employees and had lower levels of commitment. Profitability suffered as a consequence. The average UK leader was out-performed by their US counterpart and, in comparison with the worlds best-managed and most-profitable organisations, the majority of UK companies are even more poorly-led. (ISR Survey www.isrsurveys.com)

This may be as much a question of changing traditional priorities as of bad practice (although realistically it is probably as much one as the other). Traditionally directors have been required to prioritise their top three responsibilities as 1. Shareholders, 2. Customers and 3. Employees.

However to quote one person generally regarded as a good leader (and voted as 'the leader's leader' in a recent poll), Sir Richard Branson has other ideas: 'For us' he writes in *Losing my Virginity* 'our employees matter most. It seems common sense to me that if you start off with a happy, well-motivated workforce, you're far more likely to have happy customers – and in due course the resulting profits will make share-holders happy'. Such logic is difficult to shake – but it seems is followed rarely.

2. A survey of 100 chief executives of manufacturing companies conducted by Aston Business School concluded that 'Chief executive officers (CEOs) who are positive, optimistic and enthusiastic create a positive culture in their organisations and that in turn leads to better performance. People when they feel positive are more committed to the organisation.' Measured over a year it was evident that where CEOs displayed positive emotions, staff felt there was more concern for employees and the company had more clarity of direction. This in turn produced a higher company productivity.

Communication principles

The key to the whole question of management or leadership is communication (or more accurately 'communicaction' that is communication in action) – a concept which is widely misunderstood despite the millions of words written on the subject. Leading consultants McKinsey estimated that before the end of the first decade of the 21st Century, over 70 per cent of all European jobs would require professional skills (that is 'A' levels or higher). The Confederation of British Industry, commenting on this research stated that 'outstanding communication skills' will be needed by these employees. The problem is that the word 'communication' is often misused and those guilty of such misuse are often those at director level and include:

- Those who claim 'our communication is excellent' and in evidence produce handbooks, Annual Reports, procedure manuals, newsletters and so on. Such documentation may be excellent – and essential – but it is NOT communication.

- Those who state that their internal communication is first class because their chief executive regularly makes presentations to the employees. This admirable and valuable but it is NOT communication.

- Those who describe the provision of excellent product and service data to their customers as 'first class communication'. Again the documentation is of real value – but again it is NOT communication.

Information is NOT communication

That 'we have a communication problem' may be true – but in reality 'we' have three problems – of definition, of application and of interpretation.

1. The definition problem is simply stated, absolutely vital but often entirely overlooked. We tend to use the word 'communication' when actually we mean 'information'.

Case study: Information =/= communication

If A, a manager, tells B (a member of his staff) that there is a requirement for B to produce 1000 widgets by next Friday (or, worse, sends him an e-mail or memo), very often A will regard himself as having communicated with B. In fact all that has happened is that B is in receipt of an instruction or some information (which he may or may not understand). If B is in the situation that he has half his team away sick, there is an overtime ban preventing the remaining part of the team from working longer and there is a problem obtaining raw material from stores, there is little possibility of him complying with A's request. However only if B replies 'no chance' and explains his problems (i.e. provides feedback so that not only does A understand B's problems but also – on a far more fundamental level – he understands that B has understood the original message) does a communicative process start. The essential difference between the terms is that Information is one-way whereas Communication is two-way. Information requires no input from the recipient so how can they possibly be communicating?

2. **Application.** Echoing the end of a) above, 'communication' requires a dialogue – a meeting of minds between two or more parties. Where the parties are face to face it is possible that communication will ensue even if it was not intended. If the two are face to face, B's body language, even if he utters no words, may well provide a message to A (provided A is prepared to look for and appreciate such messages). It is said that, when face to face, words are only 7 per cent of the message – body language, tone, situation and so on provide 93 per cent.

    However face to face communication, invaluable although it is, is possible in only a minority of the instances when we wish to 'communicate' with our target audience or do we wish to communicate at all? Are we not in the position that all we want to do is to inform them? There is nothing wrong with informing – indeed it may be essential and, in some cases, even a legal requirement. The danger comes when:

    i) we assume that because we have told them, 'they' understand the message in the way that we intended – but how will we know?

    ii) we assume that this one way simple (easy to generate) provision of information is the same as a dynamic, two-way dialogue which is true communication. Assumptions are dangerous – it has been estimated that over 80 per cent are in some way false.

3. **Interpretation.** Because we learned to talk without formal teaching and others tend to reply when we use the skill, we assume that we know how to communicate and that others will always understand what we mean. However research indicates that this assumption is false.

Communication barriers checklist

*   If we read information (without making notes) on average we will retain around 10 per cent of the subject matter,

*   If we hear information (with no opportunity to ask questions or take notes) we will retain around 20 per cent

- If we see information (e.g. a video) we will retain about 30 per cent of the message (the reason that such a medium is more suitable for general messages than detail)

- If we see and hear information (for example at a presentation) we will retain about 50 per cent

- If we are involved in the information provision so that we have an input we will retain about 70 per cent

- If the information is provided in a learning situation (e.g. a trainee talks his/her way through a process) we will retain about 90 per cent

The golden rule to remember in seeking to start communicating is to frame the data with the interests of the target audience in mind – and to make sure we check they have understood the message in the way we intended. As a corollary it may be worth recording that when providing written information, if the reader doesn't understand it – it is the writer's responsibility. The challenge for the writer is to express him or herself in such a way that the target audience should understand most of the message.

Nowadays in addition to traditional means of conveying information there is a whole panoply of technological developments – faxes, voice-mail, e-mail, the internet, intranets and so on. In truth we have a magnificent range of excellent information transmission tools. Such developments are obviously welcome but we need to guard against assuming that in using them we are communicating (or, even worse, are improving communication) – we are not – all we have done is speed up the transmission and recording of information – nothing more. The barriers to communication set out in the above checklist remain.

Putting the requirement in perspective

The following quotations may place the challenge in perspective:

- As the late management guru, Peter Drucker, said 'the solutions to organisational problems frequently lie not in the executive suite but in the collective intelligence of the workforce.'

- The Chartered Institute of Personnel and Development report 'Impact of People Management Practices on Business Performance' concludes '...if managers wish to influence the performance of their companies the most important area they should emphasise is the management of people. This is ironic, given that our research has also demonstrated that emphasis on human resource management is one of the most neglected areas of managerial practice within organisations.'

- In reviewing worldwide communication research over the last 20 years, Dr Jon White of the City University Business School found a consistent correlation between high business performance and good organisational communication.

- Franklin D Roosevelt said 'The art of being a great leader is to get people to do what you want them to do because they want to do it.' If we seek to lead we need first to communicate. Those who communicate will lead – if it is not the Directors who communicate then whoever is will be 'doing the leading' – and leading those who follow in a direction possibly other than the one the Board wants.

Briefings

Inevitably time constraints will mean that even if we wish to interface individually this is impossible other than on isolated occasions (e.g. when conducting appraisal or performance review interviews which is one occasion when active listening is essential – and interruptions should be outlawed). Accordingly we may need to use other means to communicate, for example briefing either of the team interfacing with their immediate leader or by Directors interfacing with groups of employees. For many years the Work Foundation (formerly the Industrial Society) particularly when led by John Garnett (an inspirational speaker and leader) espoused the concept of 'cascade briefing' whereby Directors brief senior managers who brief middle managers who brief junior managers who brief supervisors who brief those at the sharp end – the information thus cascades down the chain of command. Whilst this process is better than nothing, it has limitations.

The concept suggests that information can automatically cascade through the organisation like water flowing downhill as in the following illustration (see over). The concept is fine in principle but it can founder if not introduced properly if a number of suppositions prove false. After all the process assumes that all those doing the briefing are:

1. all committed to the principle

2. able and willing to brief adequately

3. able to answer the questions that the briefing session will generate

4. prepared to remove all barriers to the disclosure of information.

In fact generally it is found that:

a) Some managers resent passing on information – regarding access to the knowledge almost as a 'perk' of management

b) Few people are natural communicators and messages can become distorted either if the speaker does not understand the matter fully or cannot deliver the message in a clear way – i.e. in terms capable of being easily understood by the audience.

c) Where the subject matter is particularly complex and not fully understood by the briefer it is very unlikely that they will be able to answer questions.

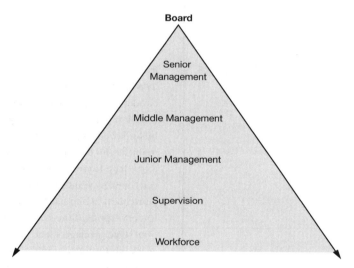

The cascade briefing model

The foregoing overlooks what is perhaps the most major problem of the whole process – the fact that messages can be misconstrued in repetition. Making oneself understood can be difficult at the best of times but when one's message needs to be passed through several intermediaries, almost inevitably they will be misinterpreted, misconstrued, and/or misunderstood.

It is generally accepted that each time a message is passed on between 15 per cent and 25 per cent of the true meaning will be lost. However what often occurs is that inaccurate or imprecise data and/or opinions is/are substituted for the 'missing message' passages in order to make up something similar to the original volume. If this were not serious enough at least it assumes that the parties who misconstrued the message genuinely wished to pass it on. In some cases those involved may deliberately (or accidentally) distort or suppress part or all of the message. Even with the utmost commitment to the truth it is difficult to repeat to another other than the simplest message in the way intended by the originator. This simple truth reflects the inherent danger of cascade briefing. However it can be made even worse since delegating communication empowers those down the line with the opportunity should they wish to filter and skew the messages. In addition any feedback or return messages also run the risk of being mangled in repetition, if not similarly filtered.

Each of the problems highlighted above can be overcome to a major extent by adequate training which itself underlines the necessity for any such procedure to be introduced only after all involved have received training in making presentations and dealing with questions outside their spheres of knowledge. This in turn however discloses another problem – that cascade briefing's greatest value (that of disseminating information to a large number of people in a short space of time by using the management chain of authority) can be also its greatest weakness since the process will inevitably generate questions. Unless such questions are answered there seems little point to the process. Thus, at very least, there needs to be a 'reverse cascade' by which such questions can 'flow up' to the Board and answers and further information can 'flow back'. Even where such a process is set up, some managers may 'filter out' questions which they feel may reflect badly on themselves or they concern matters they do not want discussed – or known at a more senior level.

It should be easy to get water to flow downhill – it is almost impossible to get it to flow uphill yet the whole point of briefing is to do just that. A one-way flow is not communication – it is merely information – and not necessarily accepted and/or understood in the way intended by the initiator. To generate communication (and thus encourage commitment and motivation) a two-way flow is needed such as is depicted in the illustration shown overleaf. Here the question are passed up to the Board and their answers are passed down.

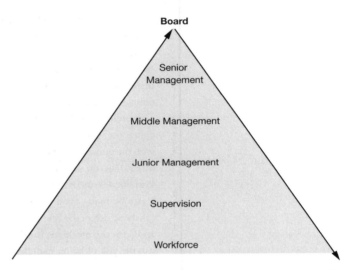

Encourage commitment and motivation – a two-way flow

This may work although part of the problem is that it can take so long for answers to come full circle, via the 'downhill' cascade, that the point of the questions may be lost. Indeed it may create so great a logistic problem that it may be preferable rather than using the cascade principle to appoint one senior manager to carry out all the briefings on a regular basis. If this is done, time-consuming although it may be, and questions are encouraged then true communication may be achieved. After all:

- The messages to all are likely to be the same

- Authoritative answers are likely to be given to employees asking for additional information/clarification and

- The true unfiltered views of the Board will be fed to the workforce and the true unfiltered reactions of the workforce will be fed directly to the Board.

Human capital management

Some time ago the UK government, through the Department for Trade and Industry, set up a Task Force to examine the manner in which UK employers could and should take a strategic approach to the development of their human assets in order to maximise their performance (and through their performance, their employer's performance) and ways in which this could be reported to their owners. Historically directors of companies have been required to report to their shareholders mainly on financial figures. However, that emphasis has been changing over the last decade.

'Although the reports of the directors are addressed to the shareholders, they are important to a wider audience, not least to employees whose interests boards have a statutory duty [under the Companies Act 1985] to take into account.'

(Cadbury Report on Corporate Governance)

'Effective employee dialogue can help staff feel more involved and valued by their employer, make them better aware of the business climate in which the organisation is operating, and help them to be more responsive to and better prepared for change. This in turn can benefit the business through better staff retention and lower absenteeism, increased innovation and adaptability to change. This should allow a greater ability to react to opportunities and threats, thereby ultimately enhancing a company's productivity.'

(Introduction to DTI's consultation document 'High Performance Workplaces: Informing and Consulting Employees' – the forerunner of UK legislation which will implement the EU Directive on Informing and Consulting and require UK employers to set up Works Councils – see Chapter 17.)

Nowhere in the world does there exist an organisation that can achieve even the simplest of its goals other than via the efforts and interactions of those that work for it. Whilst Boards of Directors have the ultimate responsibility to manage and direct, their aims can only ever be achieved via the actions of their employees. As former chief executive of ICI, Sir John Harvey Jones stated in 'Making it Happen' his best-selling management book:

'with the best will in the world and the best board in the world and the best strategic direction in the world nothing will happen unless everyone down the line understands what they are trying to achieve and gives of their best'.

The benefits that flow from employers:

- attempting where possible to deal with an organisation's human resources in a mature and adult way by a process of real and pro-active communication (the 'communicaction' principle)

- recognition that those employees have other strong pressures in our modern society which may require the employer's requirements to be sublimated at times (the flexibility principle – see Chapter 16)

- acceptance that most employees are rational thinking human beings with ideas and opinions of their own which can be of considerable mutual benefit to both employer and employee (the 'consultability' principle)

can be considerable.

During research for a study ('New community or new slavery? The emotional division of labour'), the Work Foundation (formerly the Industrial Society) found that one in three employees stated that work was the most important thing in their lives. For some employees, dismissal or being made redundant can equate to the trauma of divorce. For many home is a place of oppression whilst work is a place of liberation. Half those asked stated they liked their job and would carry on working even if they had enough money not to need to.

Those organisations who have actively involved their employees in more general terms to drive their businesses forward, report considerable and tangible benefits as the following selection of quotes and data indicates.

....

1   In an article in 'Involvement' the journal of The Involvement and Participation Association, Dr Jon White of the City Business School recorded that as a result of research carried on a worldwide basis over 20 years the conclusion was that:

    'there was a consistent correlation between high performance and good organisational communication. This data shows that businesses benefit dramatically from good communication management – but also that (in the UK particularly) this message has fallen on deaf ears'.

2   The Economist report on 'Corporate cultures for competitive edge' argued that *'strong business performance depends upon open and free communication between all levels of an organisation'.*

3   The Institute of Directors refers to research on employee commu-
    nication in its Guidelines for Board Practice. Of companies with
    employee communication policies, over 65% credited them with
    creating significant improvements in increased productivity.

4   MORI research disclosed that 1 in 3 employees felt that they could
    do more work without effort, but that 53% of those surveyed felt
    that management was more interested in giving its point of view than
    in listening to what employees had to say. In addition, previous research
    concluded that around 50% of employees were capable of perform-
    ing at a level one above that at which they were performing.

5   Towers Perrin, employee benefits consultants, report that in the US
    research on 135 highly performing companies indicates that the man-
    agement in all these companies constantly seek suggestions from
    front-line employees, delegate and maintain two-way communication.

6. In addition, giving employees a stake in their company can be a valu-
    able method of increasing productivity. This movement has been
    around for many years with tax incentives encouraging the spread
    of the process.

The Task Force recommendations

In the past it had been suggested that companies should 'account' for
their human assets by historic cost (the original cost of their recruitment and hiring), replacement cost (the projected cost of replacing
them by a person with the same level of skill and experience) or by
using discounted cash flows. Such suggestions have not been taken
up, mainly due to the deficiencies each has – the figures by themselves
are hardly meaningful, let alone the problems (and cost) created in calculating such figures.

It seems likely, even if the exact means cannot currently be defined,
that there will be some requirement in the near future to try and assess
the monetary value of these 'most valuable assets'. With such evidence
the perception of employees as an increasingly valuable and valued part
of the asset equation can only be strengthened. In addition, if such costs
are known, it may well result in even greater efforts being made to retain
good employees and help minimise the costs of their replacement.

However, the Task Force suggested that companies should provide detailed information on:

- the size and profile of the workforce;
- training and development;
- remuneration;
- career opportunities; and
- fair employment practices.

Best practice audit

Boards cannot afford to assume that the practices they wish their managers to adopt are being implemented and a regular check on how well the company is being lead may be advisable. The questions set out in the following checklist may provide a base. Ideally each answer should be 'yes'!

'How are we managing' checklist?

1. Have we devised plans and discussed their implementation with employees so that the employees themselves 'own' the plans to gain their active commitment to them?

2. Do we encourage employees to make suggestions and constructive criticism about the company, its products, procedures and endeavours?

3. Is there mutual respect between management and employees and are the pressures on employees in terms of working and private lives balanced?

4. Does management listen actively to employees and vice versa on every occasions so that the full facts and implications of all matters are exposed?

5. Are initiatives introduced via consultation and agreement thereby generating a 'yes' reaction and a genuine commitment?

6. Does everyone involved realise that as part of a single team their objective is to satisfy their customer in order to achieve the aims of the organisation?

7. Is training provided and are employees encouraged to develop their skills and talents at all times?

8. Do managers and employees work in job-related teams mutually helping solve problems, meeting output targets that they have agreed?

9. Is there an open culture whereby information flows both ways thus generating genuine two way communication – and is this situation confirmed by the employees?

10. Are employees proud to state that they work for the organisation?

It is worth repeating the results of the survey conducted for Colette Harris Associates (CHA): people had a 'surprising degree' of pride in their work. 60% believed their job was making a difference to the success of their organisation. Pride in their job and in their employer's organisation can be an important factor in employee motivation. The CHA survey suggested that pride in the firm could be built by:

• being known for treating employees and customers well

• making a difference to people's lives and the community

• being successful and providing good products and services

• having respect for ethical behaviour and standards including to suppliers and the environment

• being innovative.

Summary checklist

• Directors must provide leadership to ensure all those involved work towards the aims set for the company (if they don't who does?)

• Managers must also adopt leadership techniques – active listening, encouragement, advice provision, delegation and support to those they lead

• Directors need to ensure that quality communication exists within their companies remembering that information (a one-way flow) is not the same as communication (a two-way interaction)

• People respond to the provision of information and the opportunity to communicate and have a wealth of ideas which can be used for the positive benefit of the company – who knows how to do the job, and how to improve it better than the person doing it?

- Direct (that is:'Board to sharp end/sharp end to Board') interfacing should provide the best communication interface

- Regular audits of personnel practice and interfacing should be conducted.

Chapter twelve

Meeting the owners

Shareholders' Meetings

The Annual General Meeting

Briefing the Chairman

Minutes

Extraordinary General Meetings

Resolutions

Summary checklist

The Annual General Meeting

'The AGM is often the only opportunity for the small shareholder to be fully briefed on the company's activities and to question senior managers on both operation and governance matters.' – report of the Hampel Committee on Corporate Governance. Whilst the shareholders own the company – they must not run it. If they start to interfere in the actual direction of the company they run the risk of becoming shadow Directors. Thus, although the Directors report to the shareholders the control that shareholders exercise may be actually quite limited for the following reasons:

- Whilst they receive the Accounts and Report of the Directors they can do nothing with them. Even if they don't like the figures they cannot 'vote the accounts down'.

- They have no control over the dividend unless it is a final dividend and then can only approve, reject or reduce the figure recommended by the Directors.

Strictly speaking the control of the shareholders could be said to be limited to two actions – they appoint Directors and they can remove Directors. Since they are appointed by the shareholders, Directors are required by company law to report regularly to the shareholders and to give an account of their stewardship of the assets entrusted to them. Currently within 18 months of incorporation and thereafter at not more than 15 month intervals, a company must hold an Annual General Meeting (AGM). However LTD shareholders (provided they are completely unanimous -100 per cent approval is needed) can 'opt out' of the need to hold AGMs. The Companies Act 2006 stipulates that LTDs do not need to hold AGMs unless their shareholders wish to 'opt in' to the obligation. Whilst the concept of giving an account of their stewardship of the board may still be met by providing the shareholders with the Report and the accounts, the general move towards greater accountability – and also enhancing the power of shareholders – seems completely negated by this development.

It must be said that very often, because the shareholders powers are very limited (as referred to above) and the holding of the meeting and the business which must be transacted at such a meeting are both prescribed by law, many AGMs are formal, even legalistic, events at which there is often very little meaningful communication. Further although it is true that financial results are provided via the Annual report (in which very often the notice convening the AGM is contained) as we shall see in Chapter 14 the information given in many reports is couched in a format that most non-financially aware shareholders find unhelpful and uninformative. Unfortunately in some cases this is not only effect but also cause since such Boards really pay only lip service to the concept of their accountability to the shareholders and seem to minimise the amount of information they provide. As there is increased interest in the activities of wealth-creating companies and in their power and control changes may be forced on those adopting such attitudes. Indeed in the report of the Hampel Committee referred to above, it is suggested that at AGMs 'which are well attended', the Board should make a business presentation which could force greater disclosure of plans and aspirations. The words 'which are well attended' are apposite. It is perhaps understandable that if few shareholders attend (other than Board members and their families) it seems akin to being futile for the Board to spend considerable time preparing such a presentation. On the other hand, the fact that so few attend is probably a result of the general belief that AGMs are meaningless and shareholders learn next to nothing at them. However, this seems to be looking at the situation from the wrong angle – make the AGM a more meaningful exercise – for example with an obligation that a business presentation was to be made and this might actually encourage greater attendance and thus greater interest – in turn creating greater demand for increased transparency of activities and results, and for improved accountability – thus leading to greater interest and attendance. The Hampel report also suggests that where a shareholder raises a matter at the AGM which cannot be answered at the time, the Chairman should provide a written answer subsequently and the Board should be prepared to enter into a 'dialogue based on a mutual understanding of objectives.'

This echoes the moves being made by several leading institutional share investors to take a more active role by exercising their voting rights at general meetings. Some time ago the DTI issued a consultative document seeking views regarding increasing the rights of shareholders to ask questions at general meetings whilst Margaret Beckett, launching the review which led to the 2006 Companies Act referred to 'transparent stewardship' (of institutional investors exercising voting right on behalf of their investors) requiring 'positive use of voting rights'.

Generally AGMs of the future may be more informative and meaning-ful than many have been in the past. Whilst much of the thrust of the foregoing applies to listed PLCs rather to private LTDs, it may be the precursor of a general move towards greater accountability of all Boards to their shareholders.

Notice

The prescribed notice must be given of the AGM. Currently a PLC's AGM needs 21 (LTD: 14) days clear notice, with 'clear' meaning that neither the day the notice is posted nor the day of the meeting count towards the 21. In addition, care should be taken as notices posted by 1st class post are deemed to take 2 days to arrive whilst notice cannot be served on a non-business day. Thus a notice posted on (say) Thurs-day 21st May would not arrive until Saturday 23rd May but could not be deemed to be served until Tuesday 26th May (assuming 25th May is a Bank Holiday). 26th May would then count as day 1 of the 21 day period. Thus the earliest the meeting could be convened would be Tuesday 16th June (i.e. 27 days after posting).

NOTES:

a) Only 20 clear days notice is required for companies registered in Scotland.

b) If all the members entitled to be present so vote the requirement for notice can be dispensed with in whole or in part

c) The Hampel Committee endorsed the suggestion made by the Char-tered Institute of Secretaries that meetings should be convened giving at least 20 WORKING days notice and listed PLCs are now required by the Stock Exchange to give this amount of notice. (In the example given above of the notice being sent on 16th May this, if adopted generally, would mean the meeting could not be held until 23rd June – as all Bank Holidays and weekends must be excluded.).

Whilst the AGM of a 'director-owned' or 'family-owned' company may be little more than a formality, that of any company where there are shareholders outside the Board (and particularly if the company is Stock Exchange listed) is an occasion when the corporate entity is 'on display'. For that reason, the meeting needs careful planning to ensure that the company is seen in the best possible 'light' – not least since the media may be present (although they have no right of attendance) and will seize on anything out of the ordinary or 'bad news' on which to hang a story. Whether the meeting is to be such a promotional showcase, or is regarded more as an administrative chore, it still needs adequate preparation, and at least the items set out in the following checklist may need attention. The checklist included in Chapter 14 for the production of the Annual Report should be considered in conjunction with this list.

AGM Preparation checklist

1. Prepare list/timetable of all items needing to be addressed

2. Allocate items to named delegatees – as in following example:

Item	Responsibility
Decide date and time	Board
Visit venue, check facilities	Co.Sec/Board
Book venue (6/12 months ahead)	

Check
- Room and overflow facility
- Air conditioning/ventilation
- Acoustics/amplification
- Accommodation including catering/ toilet facilities
- Notice boards/room directions
- Tables for signing in

If product/services display required
- Display tables/pin or felt boards
- Computer graphics, etc.

Stipulate timetable for arrivals
- Serving tea/coffee)
- Lunch (if required)   indicate responsibility
- Likely departure   for all items

Delegate items to staff e.g.

- Greeting arrivals

- Ensuring arrivals sign in

- Ushering to seats

- Care of Registers & Proxies

- Act as teller (in event of Poll)

- Care of statutory & minute books, service contracts, etc.

- Liaison with catering

- Checking arrival of proposers/seconders (and arranging substitutions in event of absence)

- Display of products/tour of premises

- Preparation of chairman's crib (i.e. a script to cover each part of the meeting – see below).

- Preparation of and answers to awkward questions

- Preparation of Board presentation

- Briefing on preparations, likely problems etc. (i.e. a meeting scenario) for Board and advisers

- Liaison with Auditors, Solicitors, Brokers, Public Relations (and, through them, media representatives)

- Liaison with company registrar (including printing of tax voucher/ dividend warrant and arrangements for giving authority to post vouchers etc.)

- Transport arrangements (particularly for guests)

3. Ensure all delegatees understand requirements
   Newcomers to the task should be fully briefed in the requirements and their progress checked regularly. It may be helpful for those who have not attended an AGM previously, if they attend the AGMs of a few listed PLCs to gain an insight into procedure.

4. Recheck preparations one month prior to event
   The attention to detail is essential to ensure the public showing of the company is smooth and efficient. It will, after all be a reflection of how the company operates.

5. Consider style/content to be adopted with Chairman/Board
    Some companies are making their AGM less formal.

    Thus several companies send a 'personal' letter from the Chairman
    explaining the business which is to be transacted at the meeting with
    the formal notice. Some even advise that members of the Board will
    be available before or after the meeting for individual discussion. If
    the company adopts the Hampel recommendation of making a busi-
    ness presentation this could help comprehension of strategy (and
    even aid Board support in the event of a hostile takeover bid).

6. Coach spokespersons in handling the media particularly in dealing
    with hostile or critical questioning.

    Unless well-prepared and well-briefed for this type of examination,
    reputations (of both person and company) can be irreparably
    damaged and unnecessarily bad impressions provided.

7. Obtain advice on difficult questions which might be asked. Not only
    is it important to contact supportive shareholders to obtain proxy
    if not attending, and to arrange tame 'proposers' and 'seconders' to
    avoid silences at the meeting when the Chairman invites nomina-
    tions etc., it is also essential that if hostility is expected, then it is
    prepared for, as follows:

    •   Identify source and extent of support and of opposition

    •   Ensure 'hostiles' do have a right of attendance (if not exclude
        them)

    •   If time allows, consider possibility of a private meeting to avoid
        public confrontation

    •   Monitor arrivals – arrange for security forces to be nearby to
        deal with any physical disruption.

    •   Canvass proxies sufficient to ensure overcoming any potential
        opposition.

    •   Prepare a list of the questions least wished to be asked – and a
        crib of suitable answers.

    •   Brief the Directors concerned of the source of the problem and
        the steps taken to control/deal with it

    •   Brief media contacts and provide media trained spokesman to
        answer follow up queries

- If hostile shareholders wish to make a point they should be allowed such a courtesy, answering the points made as far as possible and offering subsequent discussions if this is feasible.

8. Prepare required documentation including:

   a) Letter of invitation

   b) Arrangements for Directors

   c) Attendance card

   d) Admission cards

   e) Proxy

   f) Mailing list application

   g) Change of address form

   h) Dividend mandate form

   i) Product discount details (if applicable)

   j) Dividend/share exchange data (if applicable)

   k) Annual Report (see Chapter 14)

9. Prepare draft press release to follow conclusion of meeting. Whereas this may be able to be produced in advance where it is known that certain statements will be made, should hostility be anticipated the production of any press statement may need to be left until after the meeting. If hostility has been experienced some statement rather than 'no comment' is advisable.

Briefing the Chairman

Running a General Meeting is not the same as running a Board meeting – particularly if the media and other outsiders are present. Those unfamiliar with or new to the process may find a brief or script of value. Rather than waiting for the meeting itself before using such a brief, it may be better to 'trial' it by suggesting the Chairman runs a dummy meeting using the script so that he/she is fully familiar with the process. The brief may then be used more as an aide memoire than script.

Script example for routine AGM

Chairman's crib for xxth Annual General Meeting to be held on (date):

- ACTION (A): At (time) call meeting to order

- SCRIPT (S): 'Ladies and Gentlemen I welcome you to the ___th AGM of [Company name] Ltd/plc. We will now deal with the formal proceedings, following which you will be able to meet members of the Board and other executives and chat informally over some refreshments. We have as you can see around you provided displays of our products and services.

  The Notice of this meeting was dispatched to all members of the Company on (date) and I will ask the Secretary to read the notice.'

A: Secretary reads notice

S: 'The first item on the Agenda concerns the consideration of the directors report with the report and accounts for the (twelve) months ended (date). Those accounts and the Balance Sheet as at that date have been audited by your auditor Messrs (Name) and I request Mr (name) a partner of that firm of registered auditors to deliver the Audit report.'

A: Auditor reads report

  NOTE: Neither the notice nor the report of the Auditors need to be read although it can be helpful to use this simply to cover the arrival of latecomers!

S: 'May I propose that the Report of the Directors, together with the annexed statement of the Company's accounts for the (twelve) months ended and the Balance Sheet as at that date duly audited be now received, [approved] and adopted.'

NOTE: Legally there is no need for these items to be approved by the shareholders but as many assume it is, it may be easier to take this route and only if there is opposition to make the point that approval is not required.

S: 'Has anyone any questions or comment?'

A: Pause – If questions are raised it will be necessary to deal with them or if they are of a technical/financial nature pass them to Finance Director to answer.

S: 'As part of that proposal may I also propose that a final dividend of (amount) per cent or (amount) pence per share on the Ordinary shares of the Company payable on (date) be now declared for the (twelve) months ended (date). I call upon (name) to second that proposal.'

A: Seconder speaks

S: 'All those in favour please raise your hands (pause) Anyone against (pause)'

A: Assess and declare result

NOTE: The Directors can pay an interim dividend without shareholder approval but need shareholder approval for a final dividend. The shareholders can either approve, reduce or reject a proposed final dividend – they cannot increase it. In the, perhaps unlikely, event that the Directors wish to ensure that the amount of the final dividend is paid (but suspect the shareholders might not approve it) it might be preferable to pay a 2nd interim dividend – which does not need shareholder approval – and not to ask for shareholder authority to pay a final dividend at all.

S: 'I therefore declare the motion carried.'

S: 'Item 2 concerns the re-election of the retiring director(s). The Director(s) retiring by rotation is/are and I have much pleasure in proposing that (name) be and he/she hereby is re-elected a Director of the Company. I will ask (name) to second that proposal.

A: Seconder speaks

S: 'All those in favour (pause) and against (pause) (Declare result) I declare Mr/Ms (name) duly re-elected a Director of the company.'

NOTE: If more than one Director retires by rotation separate proposals are required for each unless an additional proposal to deal
with all such re-elections as a single entity has first been passed.
There may also be needed proposals to re-elect Directors who have
been appointed since the previous AGM. Re-elected Directors may
wish to express their thanks to the meeting.

S: Item 3 concerns the re-election of Messrs (auditors) as Auditors of
the company and I call upon Mr (name) to propose that resolution
and Mr (name) to second it'

A: Proposer and seconder speak

S: 'All those in favour (pause) Anyone against (pause) (Declare result)'

S: 'Item 4 authorises the Directors to fix the remuneration of the Auditors and I will ask Mr (name) to propose that resolution and Mr
(name) to second it'

A: Proposer and seconder speak

S: 'All those in favour (pause) Anyone against (pause) (Declare result)'

S: 'Is there any other ordinary business for consideration?'

NOTE: Other than the proposal of a vote of thanks to the Chair-
man/Board it is unlikely that anything else can be discussed by the
meeting since notice of such business will not have been given
although of course if all shareholders are present notice could be
waived.

S: 'I therefore declare this xxth AGM closed. Thank you.'

Minutes

The following draft demonstrates how the minutes of a meeting such as the one for which the above Chairman's brief was prepared might appear. Such minutes should be prepared immediately after the conclusion of the meeting and approved as a true record by the Board at its next following Board meeting. There is no need to send the minutes to the shareholders or to have them available at the next following general meeting although shareholders have a right of inspection of the Minutes of their Meetings for 2 hours every business day and the Minutes must be held at the Registered Office for this purpose.

ANY OTHER COMPANY LTD   431(1)

MINUTES of the [x]th ANNUAL GENERAL MEETING
held on Thursday, 24th September 2_____ at [address] at 10.00 a.m.

Present: ABC (in the chair)
     EFG
     HIJ
     KLM
     NOP
     12 shareholders

Apologies for absence were received from QRS, TUV and WXY

In attendance: AAA (Secretary)
             BBB (Auditor)

1. Notice
The Secretary read the notice of the meeting   (2)

2. Directors Report
For the year ended 30th June 2_____ The Chairman referred members to the Report and Accounts for the year ended 30th June 2_____ and the Balance sheet as at that date. He requested Ms BBB (of accountants – name) to read the audit report which she did.   (3)

The Chairman proposed, NOP seconded and it was resolved unanimously that the report and accounts of the company for the year ended 30th June 2_____ and the Balance Sheet as at that date be and they are hereby approved.   (4)

3. Declaration of the dividend

The Chairman referred to the payment of an interim dividend in January 2____ and to the fact that the Board were recommending payment of a final dividend of 2p per ordinary shares. He proposed, KLM seconded and it was resolved unanimously that on 25th September 2____, the company should pay a final dividend in respect of the year ended 30th June 2____ of 2p per ordinary share (plus tax credit) to the holders of ordinary shares registered on the books as at 1st September 2____

(5)

4. Retirement of Directors

The Chairman stated that in accordance with the Articles of Association and as set out in the notice of the meeting, Mrs EFG and Mr KLM retired by rotation and each being eligible, put themselves forward for re-election. The Chairman proposed, Mr HIJ seconded and it was resolved unanimously that the re-election of both retiring Directors could be put to the meeting as one motion. (6)

The Chairman proposed, Mr K Jones, a shareholder seconded, and it was resolved unanimously that Mrs EFG and Mr KLM be and they hereby are re-elected Directors of the company.

5. Auditors

The Chairman referred to the need to re-elect Auditors of the company. It was proposed by Mrs EFG, seconded by the Chairman and resolved nemo contendare that Messrs [Name] be and they are hereby re-appointed auditors of the company until the conclusion of the next following AGM on terms to be agreed by the Directors. (7)

The meeting terminated at 10.25 a.m.

Chairman _____

26th October 2____ (8)

NOTES

1. Every page of Minutes should be numbered consecutively. Often minutes of general and board minutes of companies are kept in the same folder and numbered consecutively as one complete record. This can be difficult should a member wish to inspect the minutes, as members have a right to see the minutes of general meetings but not of Board meetings. Thus the minutes would have to be separated and the numbering would look somewhat odd unless General Meetings minutes use a different prefix to Board Minutes.

2. As noted above there is no need to read the notice of the meeting or for the Auditors to read the audit report (which they will already have had to sign) but again it does little harm and, at the very least, helps identify the auditor to the members.

4. Strictly speaking under common law, when the Chairman proposes a resolution, it is not necessary for him to have a seconder. However, since few members may know this it may be better to arrange seconders. In the interests of democracy it may be better to arrange for seconders to come from shareholders who are not Directors.

5. The members can either approve or reduce the dividend: they cannot increase it. Using a 'striking date' of some time before the meeting should enable all the calculations to be carried out and cheques drawn/credits arranged on the assumption that the dividend will be approved. Once this happens, the payments can be authorised so that members receive them on the due date. PLCs have also to notify the Stock Exchange once a dividend is approved (and indeed to give notice of a Board meeting at which consideration of a dividend will take place).

6. The re-election of Directors en masse can only take place if the meeting have previously approved (as here) that the re-election can take place in this way.

7. 'Nemo contendare' means that no one objected to the proposal. Thus, although everyone voted in favour of all the previous proposals, in this instance, whilst no-one voted against, one or more members abstained. (Latin tags are no longer supposed to be used – but some persist.)

Extraordinary General Meetings

All meetings of the shareholders other than AGMs are Extraordinary General Meetings (EGMs) which need 14 days notice (see above for guidance regarding the definition of days of notice). At the AGM envisaged above, only ordinary business was transacted. There is no reason why other business cannot be transacted at the AGM, although the notice would need to reflect such business. An EGM can be convened by:

- The Board

- Members themselves in accordance with the articles

- Those holding 10 per cent of the members' voting strength

- The auditors, should they resign and feel there are matters which should be brought to the attention of the members, and

- The court.

If the members request the Board to convene an EGM then the Board must do so within 28 days of receiving the members' request and the EGM itself must be convened for a date within a further 21 days (that is the meeting itself must be held within a total of 49 days from the date of the original request). This request would be the process used if, for example, the shareholders wished to remove a Director from office.

Under the Companies Act 2006 all resolutions (other than those requiring special notice) are subject to 14 days notice. Notice of an EGM can be waived with the support of 95% of those entitled to vote although this threshold can be varied by the members.

Resolutions

The business at a General Meeting is conducted by the shareholders passing (or refusing to pass) resolutions usually set out in full as proposals in the notice of the meeting. There are a number of different types of resolutions and they require different lengths of notice. This is somewhat confusing and the current proposals for new company law indicate the possible removal of Extraordinary resolutions and the streamlining of others. Currently however companies have available the range of resolutions set out in the following checklist.

Company resolutions checklist

a) Ordinary – used to obtain approval by members in general meeting by means of a simple majority of votes cast. Normally other than recording the decision in the minutes and implementing it, that is the end of the matter some ordinary resolutions must be filed with Registrar. These include those that:

   i.   Increase the authorised share capital

   ii.   Authorise the directors to allot shares

   iii.   Authorise a voluntarily winding up of the company, and

   iv.   Revoke an elective resolution (see below)

Special Notice. In addition to the above the following ordinary resolutions require SPECIAL NOTICE (i.e. at least 21 days):

   i.   any resolution relating to an auditor other than for the re-election of an auditor elected at the previous AGM or to settle his remuneration

   ii.   the forcible removal of a Director

b) Special resolutions are required to

   i.   Alter the objects clause of the memorandum

   ii.   Alter the Articles

   iii.   Change the name of the company

   iv.   Re-register a private company as a public company, an unlimited company as a limited company, or a public company as a private company

   v.   Disapply pre-emption rights of shareholders (i.e. the rights of shareholders to subscribe for any new shares in the proportion that their existing shareholding bears to the number of shares in issue)

   vi.   Reduce the company's share capital (which also needs the Court's approval)

   vii.   Authorise purchase of its own shares or provide assistance to allow purchase of its own shares

       NOTE: Special resolutions need the approval of 75 per cent of those members entitled to vote present in person or by proxy at a meeting of which 21 (14 under CA2006) days notice has been given.

c) Under previous legislation companies could use Extraordinary resolutions which would be ratified (with 14 days notice) if 75% of those
who voted supported the motions. Under the Companies Act 2006
there is no need to perpetrate this category of resolution, the subject
matter of which can be passed by means of a special resolution.

d) For PRIVATE COMPANIES only there are two relaxations to the above
rules:

- **Written resolutions**: If a majority of those entitled to vote
  members sign and return a copy of a resolution, then the resolution will be passed notwithstanding that the members have
  not gathered in one place. The effective date of the resolution
  is the date the last copy is signed and once signed it must be
  recorded in the Minute Book and filed with the Registrar within
  15 days. This written process cannot be used for resolutions
  removing Directors or Auditors.

- **Elective resolutions**: If having been given 21 days notice and
  ALL members entitled to attend and vote at a general meeting
  agree, then private companies can pass resolutions to:

  i.   give or renew Director's 5 year authority to allot shares

  ii. dispense with laying of accounts before a meeting (in this
       case the accounts must be sent to each member with the
       proposed elective resolution)

  iii. dispense with the holding of an AGM

  iv. reduce the percentage required for sanctioning short notice
       of meeting from 95 per cent to 90 per cent, and

  v.   dispense with annual re-appointment of Auditors (in which
       case the auditors are deemed to be automatically re-elected.

  All elective resolutions must be filed with the Registrar as must
  any resolution (ordinary) revoking them. Should a private
  company reregister as a public company all elective resolutions
  are automatically void (from the date of re-registration).

NOTE: Elective resolutions are effectively rendered obsolete by CA06.

Summary checklist

- The AGM is a public showing of the corporate body and needs to proceed smoothly and attention to detail is essential.

- Required notice must be given taking account of 'non service' days

- A timetable of items with those responsible should be compiled

- A brief should be provided for 'first time' Chairman to ensure the event goes smoothly

- Minutes must be prepared and made available at the Registered Office for inspection by shareholders

- The use of and requirements of support for the various types of shareholder resolutions need to be fully understood and the Articles referred to for any special requirements.

Chapter thirteen

Going public

Aspects of the PLC requirements

Corporate reregistration

Public flotation and the implications

Application for Stock Exchange listing

Notification of major interests

Corporate governance

Payment of Directors

Summary checklist

Corporate reregistration

Most companies start life as private companies – often with a tiny share capital (say £100 nominal) and only two shareholders (each holding one share) – or, under the authority of the 1989 Companies Act, with just one shareholder with one share. A company that trades success-fully, will accumulate assets, and, assuming the owners wish the company to continue to grow, part of these profits can be retained – possibly with additional shares issued in respect of the additional value created. Alternatively fresh capital may be introduced evidenced by addi-tional shares being issued. However the amount of capital that can be acquired either by the retention of profits and/or by introducing new capital from relatives and friends of the first directors and/or share-holders is usually limited. If substantial additional capital is required it may be necessary for the directors to consider a public flotation – i.e. offering shares on the capital market operated by the stock exchange either for public subscription or by subscription through contacts of a broker (a share placing, which has the advantage that to some extent, at least initially, the company will know its shareholders). Ignoring the mechanics of the share issue itself, for a private (LTD) company to become a public (PLC) the formalities set out in the following check-list must be observed.

Re-registration LTD to PLC checklist

a) The company needs to change its name to end in 'Public Limited Company' or 'PLC' (instead of Limited or LTD) by the passing of a special resolution) and to alter its Memorandum (i.e. to reflect the name change and any alteration regarding the amount of share capital)

b) The company may also need to change its Articles (again by reso-lution of the shareholders) to remove any restriction on number of members the company may have and the Directors rights to refuse a share transfer. (Many LTD companies restrict the total numbers of shareholders and give Directors considerable powers to refuse to register new shareholders.)

c) In accordance with S90-92 of the Companies Act 2006, the follow-ing must be filed with the Registrar of Companies:

    –   a statement from Auditors that the net assets of the company exceed the sum of the paid up share capital and undistributable reserves

       –   a balance sheet made up to a date not more than 7 months prior to the re-registration application with an unqualified auditors report, and

       –   a statutory declaration made by a Director or the Company Secretary

d)   The company must obtain a certificate of re-registration on change of name

e)   The company must ensure it meets the requirements regarding paid up share capital – it must have a share capital of at least £50,000 of which 25 per cent must be paid up and received – and this must be confirmed by the auditors to the Registrar. If the value of the shares is to be met by a consideration other than cash then 'receipt' of this value must be confirmed.

       Following the submission of the items referred to above, when the Registrar is satisfied, a certificate to commence trading will be issued. Until the receipt of this certificate the company must not trade as a PLC – if it does the Directors responsible are in breach of company law and liable to fine etc.

f)   If the LTD does not have a Company Secretary, one must be appointed.

NOTE: Any elective resolutions (e.g. not to hold an AGM – see Chapter 12 passed by the company when it was an LTD cease to be effective once it becomes a PLC.

WARNING: Providing it complies with the above requirements a Company can be a PLC without being listed or quoted on a Stock Exchange. There are around 19,000 unlisted PLCs – and just under 4,000 listed PLCs.

For the sake of completeness it may be appropriate at this point to record the requirements should a PLC wish to revert to being an LTD and these requirements are set out in the checklist below:

Re-registration PLC to LTD checklist

a) The company must change its name (by means of a special resolution) so that it ends in LIMITED or LTD and must alter its Memorandum to evidence the name change and must also resolve to re-register as an LTD company

b) The company may need to change its Articles

c) In accordance with S98-99 of the Companies Act 2006, an altered copy of Memorandum and Articles must be filed with the Registrar

Public flotation and the implications

As noted above in order to expand, businesses need capital, and LTDs traditionally source this from:

- The founders/owners
- Their family and personal contacts
- Banks and money lending organisations (e.g. factors, etc.)

But once these sources have been tapped additional capital may need to be accessed from the capital markets, including:

- Third party individual investors
- Institutional investors
- The international money market.

A public flotation has both advantages and disadvantages.

Flotation implications checklist

Advantages

1. A Stock Exchange listing grants a prestige to the company. In itself it may mean that Directors no longer need to give personal guarantees; the Company may gain an edge in negotiations, and there may be assistance in obtaining further finance, etc.

2. Subject to its trading performance, a listed company possesses a capacity to issue additional shares thereby generating more capital – on which, if it is equity capital, the return (i.e. dividends) can be restricted in poor years. In addition the company should have easier access to the non-equity capital market (i.e. fixed-interest bearing securities).

3. As far as the existing shareholders are concerned, the drawback of investing in a private company is removed as a market exists to encourage trading in the shares. Owners can time their withdrawal to match market buoyancy.

Adverse factors

1. Full disclosure of all the activities of the company (and its officers) must occur, particularly where the company has a high consumer profile. Because of the effect of loss of confidence on the share price, such disclosure needs to be handled very carefully.

2. It is not just the media and the analysts who will be aware of the company – so too will be the consumer. Adverse publicity can affect the attractiveness of the sector/company and thus the attractiveness of the shares.

3. Few companies exist without competition and thus attention to the sector may generate individual company attention, even though the comments may not apply to individual companies. Preparation to defend a position and promote awareness of it is essential.

4. Being in the public eye and being part of a sector, companies are judged by reference to their peer group (despite the obvious imperfections of this). In addition due to the pressure put on institutional investors pressure (both latent and actual) is brought to bear on public companies to perform. This may have the effect of forcing the creation of enhanced short term profits albeit at the expense of longer term development, training, experimentation etc.

5. The shares of public companies become commodities. Different view-points may emerge between those we can call share investors (principally institutions many of whom will seek shorter term gains from trading in the company's and other companies shares) and share-holders (predominantly private shareholders most of whom tend to hold the shares on a long term basis). The former may seek to make shorter term gains out of an investment which is really geared to long term holding. The latter tend to act as a homogeneous mass and may, if there is a hostile bid, tend to support the company – if only through inactivity.

6. The activities of the company, as well as its results, may become subject to strict attention the focus of which depends as much on social comment and pressure as on profitability.

Application for Stock Exchange listing

For the up-to-date detailed requirements for a public flotation, refer-ence should be made to the latest edition of the Stock Exchange's Admission of Securities to listing (a loose-leaf updated manual com-monly called the Yellow Book because of the colour of its folder) although the main principles are set out in the following checklist:

Application for listing requirements checklist

A company must:

- Be an established business with a 5 year record of trading with unqual-ified opinion on its results given by the reporting auditors

- Have adequate management skills and systems

- Be prepared to make a minimum of 25 per cent of its shares avail-able to the public

- Have an expected market capitalisation of £700,000

- Expect to achieve annual pre-tax profits of at least £1M

- Issue a prospectus

- Undertake to comply with the obligations contained in the Admis-sion of Securities to Listing book and the City Code on Takeovers (the blue book)

In addition listed companies are subject to a number of continuing requirements including:

- The provision of all information necessary to enable holders of the company's listed securities and the public to appraise the position of the company and to avoid the creation of a false market in the securities. The principle behind a listing is that all those dealing in the shares should have the same information.

- Application to list new shares of a class already listed must be made not more than a month before listing. All holders of the same shares must receive equal treatment with existing holders having rights of pre-emption.

  NOTE: Rights of pre-emption – i.e. that new shares must be offered to existing shareholders in the proportion their shares bear to the total in issue – are often voted away in general meeting.

- Companies wishing to raise money must find a sponsor – typically a merchant bank. Share issues of up to £25 million can be placed entirely with the clients of the sponsor. For issues over £25 million but under £50 million, shares can be sold partly by placing and partly by an offer for sale. Shares with a value of £50 million or more must be marketed to the public.

- The company must notify all information which would have a material effect on the price of its shares.

- The date of any board meeting at which a dividend may be decided, or at which profits(losses) for any period, are to be approved, must be notified by the company at least 10 days in advance. Any decision taken at the meeting must then be notified to the stock exchange immediately.

- Any board decision regarding a change of the capital structure or redemption of listed securities, or a change in the rights of any listed security of the company, must be notified immediately.

- Depending on the percentage of value of the assets being changed (e.g. disposed of) to the total assets, the company must provide a range of information concerning the contract

- All matters concerning the interests of Directors (including the interest of any spouse and/or infant children) in the securities of the company, must be notified immediately. Within 14 days of appointment Directors are required to submit formal statements of past and present business activities. A statement must be made of the possible liability should a Director's service contract be broken.

- Should the company wish to purchase its own shares and the Board wish to submit a resolution to this effect before a general meeting, then that decision, and the decision of the meeting, when held, must be notified immediately.

- Where a shareholder owns or acquires a holding of 3 per cent or more in the company securities, or changes such holding by 1 per cent or more, the company must be informed and it must notify the Stock Exchange forthwith. In addition, anyone who holds shares by means of what are called non-material holdings must also disclose their interest if the aggregate of such material and non-material interests reach or exceed 10 per cent.

- An annual report and accounts must be issued within 6 months of the end of the financial period. Such accounts are subject to detailed requirements, for example:

  a) If the company has subsidiaries consolidated group accounts must be published

  b) Any significant departure from standard accounting practices must be stated

  c) Results which differ materially from any published forecast made by the company must be explained

  d) A geographical analysis of turnover and profits of non-UK operations must be provided

  e) Details of each subsidiary in which the company has an interest of 20 per cent or more in the equity must be given

  f) A detailed analysis of borrowings in terms of amount due up to one year, one to two years, two to five years and five years or more must be provided

  g) The interests of the Directors (including spouses and infant children) in the shares (including options) of the company and any changes during the year must be given

h) The material interest of any shareholder holding in excess of 3 per cent of the equity capital and the non-material interest of any shareholder controlling in excess of 10 per cent, and any interest which in aggregate (material and non-material) exceeds 10 per cent must be stated.

i) Whether the company is a close company (i.e. all its shares are owned by the Directors, or of 5 or less members) must be stated

j) Any contract in which any Director is interested must be stated

k) Particulars of any contract between the company (or a subsidiary) and a substantial corporate shareholder must be given

l) Details of shareholders authority for the purchase by the company of its' own shares must be provided and

m) The identity of independent non-executive Directors with biographical notes on each must be given.

In addition to the above application and continuing obligations a listed company must also comply with a number of administrative requirements.

Stock Exchange administrative requirements checklist

A company must:

a) Have one (or more) brokers to represent the company

b) File 6 copies of every circular sent to shareholders with each Stock Exchange on which it is listed

c) Ensure its Directors comply with the model code, including not trading in the company's shares for two months prior to the announcement of any results or of the publication of information likely to affect the price of its shares. The aim of this restriction is to try to prevent abuse of knowledge – i.e. to restrict insider dealing.

d) Notify all changes in the directorate or changes in office

e) Make available copies of all Directors' service contracts of more than a year (or a written summary, if the contract is not in writing) for inspection at the registered office or transfer office during usual business hours between the date of the notice of the AGM and the date of the AGM, and for at least 15 minutes prior to the AGM. The potential liability should the contract be terminated must be stated

f) State that such contracts are available for inspection during that time in the notice of the meeting

g) Provide details, in the case of any Director whose re-election will be considered at the AGM, of the unexpired portion of such service contract in the Directors' Report.

Notification of major interests

Any shareholder who holds 3 per cent or more of the issued shares is required to advise the company of the fact. The company must then immediately notify the Exchange. In addition, each time the holding varies by 1 per cent (up or down) further notifications are required.

In addition those with a non-material interest (e.g. an interest as a Trustee for a beneficiary who is the ultimate holder) of 10 per cent or more (or who have material and non-material interests which in aggregate reach or exceed 10 per cent) must also notify the company and be notified to the Stock exchange.

Not all holders use their own names to control the shares, and to negate the effect of the shareholder trying to hide behind a false name, under Section 793 of the Companies Act, a company can require the shareholder to disclose the name of the holder. If the company serves such a notice the shareholder can be obliged to reply within two days. The identity of the actual shareholder(s) (i.e. not any nominee names) with 3 per cent of the shares or more must be stated in the Directors report in the Annual Report.

Draft Section 793 notice

(Request to be served on the shareholder notified, if the company suspects the name in which the shares are held is not the name of the real shareholder.)

To: Shareholders name and address

Subject: Interest in [company] shares

Pursuant to section 793 of the Companies Act 2006, we require you to provide us with the following information in writing (or by telex, fax or electronic transmission) within [number] days of the date of this letter (i.e. by [date])

a) The number of shares in which you have an interest in this company as at the date of your reply (your current interest) and the number of shares in which you have had an interest at any time in the last [up to 3 maximum] years preceding the date of this notice (your past interest)

b) The nature of your interest in the above shares

c) The date(s) when you acquired and/or disposed of the shares

d) The full name and address of each person who has an interest in those shares together with particulars of the interest and the number of shares in which each person had an interest

e) Details of any agreement or arrangement relating to the exercise of any voting or other rights applying to the shares in which you have or had an interest, together with the names and addresses of each party to any such agreement or arrangement

Yours etc.

NOTE: Should a shareholder not comply with the request for information then the company may disenfranchise the shares. Companies considering this action should discuss the proposals first with the Stock Exchange. The Exchange does not encourage disenfranchising shares since it can have the effect of shares with different rights being in circulation.

Corporate governance

A company listed on the Stock Exchange must sign a copy of the listing agreement which entails all Directors undertaking to comply with it. These listing agreement obligations have developed as a result of the deliberations of the Cadbury, Greenbury and Hampel committees on Corporate Governance (now subsumed in the Combined Code).

The Cadbury Code of best practice checklist

Board should:

- Meet regularly, control the company and monitor management

- Ensure a distinction between the roles of Chairman and Chief Executive to ensure a balance of power (if the roles are combined there should be a strong independent, and non-executive, presence on the Board)

- Appoint non-executive Directors capable of exerting power

- Prepare and adhere to a schedule of matters for consideration

- Arrange for Directors to take independent professional advice at the expense of the company and to have access to the Company Secretary

- Discuss as a body any question of the removal of the Company Secretary

Non-executive Directors should:

- Bring an independent judgement in board matters

- Include a majority who can act independently free from any relationship which might interfere with their judgement

- Be appointed for a set term without automatic reselection

- Be appointed formally by the whole Board

Executive Directors should:

- Not be granted service contracts in excess of 3 years duration without shareholders' approval (currently the pressure exists to limit service contracts to a duration of 1 year)

- Ensure their pay is subject to the deliberations of a remuneration committee comprised wholly or partly of non-executive Directors

- Disclose clearly and fully their total emoluments as well as the actual figures for the Chairman and highest paid Director providing separate figures for salary and performance related elements

NOTE: In 2003 new requirements regarding the approval and disclosure of Directors pay came into force. Details of the following must be published:

- Details of individual salaries

- The role of the remuneration committee

- The Company's remuneration policy

- The policy which links pay to performance

- Any payments made to Directors in charge of failed operations

- Details of performance requirements, monitoring etc.

In addition shareholder approval must be obtained to remuneration packages. Boards can proceed with proposals even if shareholders do not agree – although this could be unwise. Whilst there is no doubt that some Directors do abuse their positions it is doubtful if this is true, at least in material terms, of the majority. In arguing about the levels of Directors pay, and some are too high, it is however appropriate to remember the wide range of liabilities (which seem to be ever-increasing to which those in charge of Companies expose themselves and their personal assets. High risk and high reward are usually acceptable bedfellows.

Reporting:

- The Board must exercise its responsibility to present a balanced and understandable assessment of the company's position, utilising an objective and professional relationship with the Auditors and acknowledging this responsibility in a note in the Accounts adjacent to the audit report

- An audit committee (see below) should be established comprising mainly non-executive Directors

- The Board should report on the effectiveness of the company's system of control and on the basis of a going concern with supporting assumptions or qualifications as necessary.

An audit committee might examine the following:

- any change in accounting policies and the reasons for the change, and that such policies are most appropriate for the company

- any reservations indicated by the Auditors concerning the accounting policies or their implementation or interpretation

- issues raised in the audit management letter

- compliance by the accounts with latest standards

- material changes from estimates included in previous accounts or statements

- the effect of all known contingencies and material events being adequately reflected in the accounts

- that disclosures have been made of all relevant party transactions

- that the accounts disclose the effect of any and all acquisitions and disposals and any contingent liabilities including outstanding litigation

- that interim accounts have been prepared in accordance with similar processes and policies as used at the year end, updated as necessary

- compliance with changes in standards, law and/or Stock Exchange regulations

- relationship between the company and professional advisers

Obviously Directors and Secretaries of public companies need to be aware of the latest requirements in this area. This however may not absolve Directors of LTD companies from being similarly aware since it is possible that some of the requirements suggested by those committees may be replicated in a future Companies Act although it has been stated that this is not the current intention of the Government. In its document commencing the consultative process that will eventually lead to the creation of a new Companies Act the DTI refers to the deliberations of these committees and the creation of a supercode from them as being more appropriate to best practice rather than legislation. However the document goes on to state that '**there may however be a need for legislation in certain areas which are not covered by the new Code or where experience shows that some**

legal underpinning is needed' and suggests the following areas for further legislation:

- The duties of Directors where it is suggested that the Government should 'clarify Directors' duties to take a broader view of their responsibilities' which could include the interests of other parties such as employees, creditors, customers, the environment and the wider community (although as already noted there are already existing obligations on Directors to take account of most of these interests). As noted above, the new Companies Act sets out seven duties explicitly expected of directors.

- The conduct of General Meetings where changes might be aimed at enabling shareholders to play a more active role in their companies. As was set out in Chapter 12, currently shareholders actually have very little scope to play such a role – and indeed very little actual control. The new legislative stipulation that LTD companies will only need to hold AGMs if their shareholders specifically request them sits rather oddly with this intent.

- Shareholder control over Directors pay (as referred to in the initiative set out above).

(See combined code in Chapter 18)

Payment of Directors

Considerable attention has been focussed in recent years on the question of Directors pay not least since there are a number of well-recorded instances where Directors, particularly of former nationalised industries continuing to operate in a virtual monopolistic situation, have awarded themselves substantially increased salaries and benefits. It may of course have been the case that the previous levels of pay were inappropriate and the new levels are commensurate with changed responsibilities and liabilities but the fact remains that the increases have seldom been handled appropriately and with adequate explanation. In one case a massive increase for the Managing Director was announced at the same time as 2000 redundancies. Whilst both decisions may have been correct the juxtaposition of the announcements must call into question the quality of management (let alone leadership) of the company failing to anticipate the outcry that followed – and the demotivational force on the employees. Unfortunately we live in a society where relatively few 'performers' in the entertainment business (including the sporting field) can command very large payments even though they have relatively little responsibility. Compared with such earnings, the amount we pay most of those who control our wealth-creating companies and who carry considerable and far greater responsibilities as well as laying themselves open to the liabilities referred to earlier, may not be at all disproportionate.

Nevertheless in the UK there seems to be a far wider gap between the earnings of those who direct companies and those at the sharp end who carry out their instructions. It is not impossible to imagine a situation where a company could simply adopt a widely known multiplier which when applied to the earnings of the sharp end employee would generate the maximum payable to the Managing Director. Thus if the average salary of the shop floor operative was £15,000 and the multiplier was 20 the maximum salary of the MD would be £300,000. Inevitably as the 'worth' of those on the shop floor rose as a result of market pressures so to would that of the Managing Director. Such a concept need only be a guideline (and it is at least arguable that there should be some recognition of the potential liabilities that apply to Directors but not to the shop floor which could be 'added on') but divergence from such a norm would require explanation which itself would force objective justification of top people's pay.

In 'Having their Cake' (Young and Scott, Kogan Page, 2004) the authors record that the pay of the highest paid FTSE 100 companies directors is 68 times that of the average employee – a larger differential than any other developed company other than the USA. The authors argue that [public listed company] directors tend to be rewarded for creating a high share price not a good company. Since a company's share price is an amalgam of a number of factors there is an obvious fallacy in using share price as a criteria.

(**NOTE**: In 2005 it was reported that for some large UK companies, the actual multiple of 'shop floor pay' to top job, is in excess of 400. The same report demonstrated that a reducing share price did not necessarily mean a reduction – or even a reduction in the rate of increase – of top job pay. The Work Foundation's report 'The Risk Myth' comments that rapidly growing executive pay packets are unjustified because the stewarding job (e.g. of directors) is relatively low risk compared to the entrepreneurs of old. Similar concerns are emerging in the USA. James Webb, senator for Virginia recently lamented the growing social and economic inequalities in America stating:

'When I graduated from college, the average corporate CEO made 20 times what the average worker did; today it's nearly 400 times. In other words it takes the average worker more than a year to make the money that his or her boss makes in one day'.

Summary checklist

- The detailed requirements and implications of re-registration need to be assessed prior to taking such a step

- Full advice should be taken before considering a public flotation and the requirements of the listing agreement and the continuing obligations appreciated

- All major interests (i.e. of 3 per cent or any change resulting in a whole percentage figure alteration) in shares must be recorded and notified to the Stock Exchange on which the shares are quoted

- Public listed companies need to comply with the Combined Code of Corporate Governance or to state in their Annual Report with which items they have not complied.

- Rewards for Directors should be capable of being objectively justified – ideally with some link to the pay of those further down the chain of command.

Chapter fourteen

'Write a better book'

Shareholder communication

The Annual Report

'*If a man write a better book… the world will make a beaten path to his door*'. Ralph Waldo Emerson's 100 year old dictum might still be useful guidance to those responsible for modern corporate literature which often it must be said leaves a great deal to be desired in terms of clarity and a genuine wish to inform. Like many such wise words there tends to be an equally valid saying with an opposite meaning for example 'They say if you invent a better mousetrap the world will beat a path to your door – rubbish – it's marketing that makes the difference!' (with which sentiments many inventors and authors will ruefully agree). But perhaps the sentiment is not diametrically opposed to Emerson's view. Unless the document is well-marketed (e.g. well presented to its target audience in a format they can appreciate) it will not be read, no matter how good the content – and that is the Board's challenge.

Directors are required to give annual account of their stewardship of the assets placed under their control to their shareholders and specifically must provide them with:

- The company's financial results and accounts (and explanatory notes thereto) for the latest financial period

- A balance sheet as at the end of that financial period and

- A Report of the Directors on the financial period and any material facts since its close.

As well as reporting to the shareholders, such data must also be filed with the Registrar of Companies. The contents of these items are prescribed by law, and standards of accounting practice (which have the authority of law). Although the Directors are required to include in their report a summary of the company's activities in the period under review, for companies in the public eye, this tends to be supplemented by a far longer and more descriptive statement usually under the name of the chairman or chief executive. In fact there is no legal requirement for a company to publish a Chairman's statement but most listed public companies and many unlisted companies do publish this as part of the document that is usually known as an Annual Report. For most private companies the Annual Report will be a fairly simple document concentrating primarily on the financial results. However for listed companies the report is regarded not only as a document of record but also a chance to promote the corporate entity. As a result many such documents tend to resemble corporate brochures – but lacking the clarity of message that many of those expound. It has to be said that whilst many may find the illustrations of interest, the presentation of financial and other information leaves much to be desired. So complex have the reporting requirements become, that the interests of the average reader seem to be subsumed in a mass of data. As the Institute of Chartered Accountants Report on Summary Financial Statements (see below) comments:

'*we believe that the complexity of modern accounting disclosures militates against clarity of communication*', whilst in its book 'Making corporate reports valuable' the Institute of Chartered Accountants of Scotland commented '*present-day financial statements are often almost incomprehensible to anyone other than their preparers*'. Sadly such comments are borne out by surveys of report readers.

Shareholders views of the Annual Report checklist

In a recent survey of shareholders:

- 23 per cent stated they had not received their company's Annual Report (since Royal Mail state that less than 2 per cent of posted items 'go astray', one is tempted to wonder if so little did the report appeal to most of the 23 per cent that they could not remember having received it!)

- 18 per cent said they read none of it

- 24 per cent said they 'glanced through it'

- 15 per cent said they read 'some of it'

- 11 per cent said they read 'most of it' and

- only 9 per cent said they read 'all of it'.

Source: MORI

If a score of 20 per cent reading most or all of such reports were not low enough, a study of comprehension levels was carried out by the London Business School and Wolff Olins/Hall. The study revealed that 75 per cent of those who claimed to have read their company's reports stated that they understood them. However when they were tested, only a third displayed a 'reasonable grasp' of the contents. If only 20 per cent of the total audience actually read reports and of the 75 per cent of them who claimed to understand them only a third displayed a reasonable grasp this suggests that only around 5 per cent of the original audience actually understood the documents. Other comments made in the London Business School survey were that the reports were too 'stodgy and technical', whilst only 40 per cent of the audience identified any part of the report as being 'particularly informative'. If new company law is aimed at increasing shareholders interest in and control over the activities of their companies, it seems there is a urgent need to encourage more constructive and intelligible financial reporting – not least since if Emerson is correct, companies which produce a better 'corporate book' might find the world beating a path to their door – which is unlikely to be bad for business!

Determining the target audiences

In considering preparing the 'corporate book' the following provides an outline guide to the task, the first consideration being the identification of its target audiences.

Audience for Annual report checklist

1. Shareholders – private, institutional and prospective

2. Stock exchanges

3. Analysts

4. Mailing list

5. Advisers, brokers, media

6. Government agencies, local and national politicians

7. Accounting professions

8. Creditors, lenders, developers, customers, landlords etc.

9. Employees (current and retired)

10. Recruitment agencies, schools and universities

11. Trades unions

12. Pressure groups

13. Archivists and libraries

14. Competitors

NOTE: Whether intended for them or not competitors are likely to obtain a copy, so care needs to be exercised regarding confidentiality of products, processes etc.

Given the difficulties of communicating meaningfully to those that actually have money invested in the company, it may be impossible to satisfy all the audiences but at least identifying them may help consideration of the holistic nature of the document. It may also focus attention on the need to make the document more understandable to those who are not financially orientated.

Filing the document

All companies are required to file their results with the Registrar of Companies within a strict timetable – by the end of the 6th month after the year end for public companies, and by the end of the 9th for private companies. (Filing time limits are strictly applied and subject to fine if breached. An LTD filing one day late attracts a £100 fine – rising to £1,000 depending on the length of the delay. A PLC filing a day late attracts a £500 fine which can rise to £5,000. The level of these fines is currently being reviewed.)

Reporting results, however, is not simply a matter of complying with statutory requirements. Business is about confidence and, particularly for a public listed company, the reporting of results is an important facet of the building and sustaining of confidence. The tone, quality and presentation of the Annual Report says a great deal about the company and for this reason, amongst others, great care needs to be exercised when considering the timing and execution of statements concerning the company's achievements. It is for this reason that all those who may wish to see the report should be listed and their requirements considered. This does not mean the report must be all things to all men – the prime function is to report to the shareholders. However in preparing a report there is no reason why, if it is felt appropriate, the interests of other audiences should not also be addressed. In this the aim may be more corporate promotion than company reporting but there is no reason why Directors should not use one document to serve two purposes – indeed it may be cost-effective to do so. Why not encourage the use of the Annual Report as a means of corporate promotion – at least if it has this aim there will be more pressure on those who create such reports to make them readable and their content accessible?

Range of content

Companies are legally bound to include within their Annual Report a range of items including those set out below.

Required items to be included:

- Accounts and Balance Sheet plus explanatory notes as required under Company Law, required Statutory Standards of Accounting Practice (SSAPs) and (if applicable) the Stock Exchange listing agreement

- Auditors report

- Report of the Directors which in turn must include:
    - a statement of the principal activities of the company
    - a review of the development of the business in the period
    - details of developments since the year end and any anticipated developments
    - details of research and development
    - transfers to reserves
    - profit, and retained profit, after dividend payment
    - dividends paid and proposed
    - significant changes of assets
    - own share acquisition or disposal
    - details of persons who were Directors throughout the period
    - details of shareholdings totalling or exceeding 3 per cent (and non-material holdings totalling or exceeding 10 per cent in aggregate)
    - political and charitable donations

   –   information concerning the employment of disabled persons
       and of action taken to consult and involve employees (compa-
       nies whose workforces exceed 250)

   –   information concerning the arrangements re health, safety and
       welfare of employees and so on.

The Directors Report must be approved by the Board and signed on
its behalf by a Director or the Secretary. It must be laid before the company
in a general meeting and then filed with the Registrar with the accounts
and balance sheet, and within the specified time limits. Although many
companies require their shareholders to 'approve' the report and accounts
in fact there is no requirement to gain shareholder approval and even
if the shareholders reject the items, they are still the report and accounts
of the company for that period and as such can and must be filed with
the Registrar. A Directors Report is not required for a 'small' company.
The thresholds which determine such a company are regularly
reviewed.

Theme

Although the legally required items cannot be changed, the relative
importance of the aims and audiences of an individual report will vary
both from company to company and within the same company from
time to time. The aggressive conglomerate growing by acquisition may
normally wish to use a high profile image, although conversely at times
it may need to 'dampen things down' – perhaps whilst secretively stalking a particular prey. The High Street chain store may have (and wish
to sustain) a higher awareness profile than a similar-sized manufacturing company. The newer 'high-tech' industries tend to have a higher
profile than the older, more established companies, and so on. The relative importance of each aim needs to be assessed and built into a theme
to which constant reference should be made to ensure the impression
given by each item (particularly if these are written by several
authors) is consistent, and that illustrations and pictorial inserts similarly reflect the same 'message'.

Style

There are and can be no hard and fast rules concerning the design of corporate communications, other than the fact that the style of communication should reflect the style of each individual company at that particular stage of its development. Above all however a report should (and many fail) to seek to EXPLAIN the results and the strategy in simple everyday language – and this aim of explanation should be tested from time to time by surveying the audience. As noted above far too many corporate reports leave all but the qualified accountant numb with incomprehension and the private shareholder, perhaps understandably, somewhat annoyed that a considerable amount of company resources has been devoted to producing what they perceive to be a largely unintelligible document.

Research has suggested that many private shareholders gain most of their appreciation of the progress of their company and of the salient features of the results, by reading an Employee Report if one is produced (see below) rather than by studying the Annual Report. In preparing an Employee report, simplified in content for a non-financially aware audience, the editor is forced, if only by lack of space, to concentrate on the salient features and general trends rather than the mass of detail which can tend to obscure the important central messages in an Annual report. Writing with the awareness that the target audience may not be largely financially aware helps the best of such reports to achieve admirable clarity. However it is often overlooked that the overwhelming majority of number (if not of shareholding) of the target audience of most annual reports may be non-financially expert. Both in writing and in presentation clarity and lucidity should be watchwords.

A timetable for action

Planning

Whilst the following timetable attempts to address all situations, it is provided merely as a draft and needs to be customised to satisfy individual needs. In some companies the overall responsibility may be that of the Financial Director rather than, as envisaged here, that of the Company Secretary, either of whom may in turn delegate much of the detail to a designer. Whether the Chairman (and other executives) write their own statements or have them (or at least an initial draft) written by the Company Secretary or a professional ghostwriter also needs to be determined. Since the annual report of most public listed companies incorporates the Notice of the Annual General Meeting the Company Secretary will need to relate all requirements in that regard – booking the venue, arranging the event, ensuring the report is posted and gives sufficient notice, etc. – to this timetable.

Timetable for Annual Report production checklist

THE TIMETABLE   *(D = Despatch date)*

Item	Timing	Executive(s)
Prepare budget	D – 100	Comp. Sec./Fin. Dir.
Prepare timetable (in liaison with ghostwriter/designer/ typesetters/printers)	D – 90	Comp. Sec./Fin. Dir.
Rough mock-up of report	D – 80	Designer/Fin. Dir.
Board agree budget and mock up		Board
Chairman's statement 1st draft		Ghostwriter/Chairman
Executives' reports 1st draft		[Initials]
Proxy and other cards (e.g. AGM attendance and admittance cards) 1st draft		Comp. Sec.
Chairman's statement, etc. 2nd draft	D – 75	Ghostwriter/Chairman
Analyse numbers of report required	D – 70	Comp. Sec.
Advise printer so that paper can be ordered		Comp. Sec.
Photographer/illustrator commissioned and instructed		Designer/Comp. Sec.
Chairman's statement, final draft and copy to printers/ typesetters	D – 60	Ghostwriter/Chairman

Liaise with registrars and provide checklist	D – 50	Comp. Sec.
Liaise with corporate public relations		
Liaise with brokers		
First proof back, checked and returned to typesetters		Comp.Sec./Auditors
Second proof to company/ auditors	D – 40	Comp.Sec./Auditors
Photographs/illustrations reviewed and agreed		Chairman
Third proof (colour)	D – 30	Comp.Sec./Auditors
Preliminary announcement	D – 25	Comp.Sec.
Insert figures in third proof for typesetters		Comp.Sec.
Commission dividend warrants		Comp.Sec.
Final proof checked	D – 15	Chairman/Comp.Sec.
Print order given. Printers liaise with registrars to collect envelopes and despatch	D – 10	Printers/Comp.Sec.
Report despatched externally	D – 1	Despatch
Report distributed internally	D – day	Comp.Sec.

The Chairman's statement

In many respects the statement by the chairman or chief executive is the key item in the report and the main item of commentary and information for the owners of the business. There is currently no legal requirement to include such a statement although its omission from a listed company's report would generate adverse comments. Indeed given the fact that little of an Annual Report seems to be read and understood by 95 per cent of the target audience it would be regrettable if the one part of the report that is likely to be read was not available to put flesh on the 'bare bones' provided by the figures. In addition whereas the remainder of the report considers past events – some as much as 18 months old – such a statement is the one item that can, as well as explaining reasons, strategy, etc., actually look forward – a view likely to be of greater interest to most investors. However views of the future tend to be couched in generalistic and wide terms (see below).

Approach

The type of statement will very much depend on the personality of the Chairmen and on the 'attitude' adopted by the company at the time of writing.

Style and content for a Chairman's statement checklist

Style

- Establish impression to be given (e.g. forward looking, high quality performance, retrenching, expansionist, etc.)

- Adhere to a theme and (if supporting reports are written by a number of executives) ensure this theme is repeated in individual reports (which may require some editing of other's reports)

- Provide reassurance and confidence (but only if that view is supportable)

- Give an indication of progress (or explanation of reason for lack of progress)

- Endeavour to bolster prestige and reputation if applicable

Content

The statement should include:

- Brief summary of the salient financial data (sales, profit, dividend, amount reinvested) in each case possibly compared with the figures for the previous year.

- Commentary on trading (and sometimes general economic/political) conditions and how the company has reacted to them. This may be expanded either within the Chairman's statement itself so that each division within the organisation is featured (possibly even with individual results) or may form part of a separate 'divisional' review which may incorporate photos etc.

- Acquisitions and disposals (at least those of any significance)

- Explanation of exceptional items (i.e. those that are outside the normal business activities)

- Trade investments

- Adherence to (or deviation from) required corporate governance requirements

- Board changes, employee details, training etc.

- Product development and launches (where these can be discussed publicly)

- The political/economic climate and, if the company is a strong force within its sector, perhaps where it is ranked (and any change, and the reasons, for such change in position).

- The trading strategy for the immediate future (again where this can be discussed publicly)

WARNING: In fact any comments on this last subject are likely to be given only in general terms as most Chairmen will be wary about giving 'hostages to fortune' in their statements. For this reason this part of the statement tends to feature somewhat bland and generalised comments rather than being precise. Chairmen of PLCs particularly need to be careful not to include what could be construed as a 'profit forecast' and the advice of the auditors or legal advisers may need to be sought.

Checking history

When drafting a statement, care needs to be taken to check what is already on record as no Chairman will relish being 'caught out' (particularly when answering questions at the AGM and/or posed by the media) because something in a later report contradicts, without adequate explanation, a comment or policy previously on record. In preparing the statement, the comments need to be placed in context and the author (whether the Chairman or another internal or external ghostwriter) needs to refer to items such as those set out in the following checklist.

The existing record checklist

The content of the following items need to be checked:

- The Chairman's previous two or three Statements

- The Interim Statement

- Any press releases and comments made at Annual or other Meetings

- Any interviews or observations made by the Chairman

- The results and developments of the business and any strategy adopted by the Board

- Any press or other comment made on the company and/or its products (in case criticism can be answered and/or the record corrected).

Qui s'excuse, s'accuse

There is little doubt that some statements made by chairmen to those who have invested in their companies are less than strictly accurate – and might perhaps more appropriately be entered for the Booker prize for fiction. In November 2005 the Times published a number of the 'most preposterous' excuses for poor results. These included:

- a ban on the import of Indian prawns (which was very odd since when the same ban was lifted, 'market instability' was blamed for a continuing decline)

- (collectively) high interest rates, a hot summer, a deadline for self-assessment tax forms, flooding at Easter and the 'Diana' effect (i.e. a downturn in sales following Princess Diana's death)

- the Islamic month of Ramadan (because super-rich Muslims deserted the tables of 'our casinos') – completely ignoring the fact that Ramadan is celebrated annually

- the fall of Saddam Hussein (for a 50% reduction in sales of motor caravans!)

- the football World Cup (potential purchasers were supposed to be glued to their TV sets rather than buying sports strips).

Presumably the authors thought their shareholders would be gullible enough to believe these 'reasons' which are really little more than pie in the sky. The companies might have won more plaudits had they simply said – 'trading conditions have been poor' and then explained what they were trying to do to rectify the situation. (Contrast this kind of confidence trickery with the approach of Lee Iacocca recounted in Chapter 15 and with welcome comments from some companies on directors' accountability. For example, in Diageo PLC's annual report a statement regarding terminating directorships includes the words 'If the board determines that the executive has failed to perform his duties competently, the remuneration committee may exercise its discretion to reduce the termination payment on the grounds of poor performance.)'

Directors' Review

From 1st January 2005 listed PLCs and other large companies were to be required to publish an Operating and Financial Review (OFR) which was intended to extend the scope of information to be made available to interested parties and to give a discursive and balanced overview of the company's trading and financial position.

In November 2005 this requirement was scrapped – although some of the data originally required (see following checklist) is required to be included within a 'Directors' Review' (DR).

Directors' review content checklist

- Information on the nature of the business, its markets, the regulatory environment, and its objectives and strategies

- Information on the development and performance of the company over the past financial period and in the future

- Details of resources together with risks and uncertainties possibly affecting long-term prospects and value

- Data re capital structure, policies re treasury matters and liquidity

- Details of environmental matters (including the impact the company activities have on the environment)

- Relationships essential to the business including employment data

- Financial analysis and performance indicators

- Receipts from and returns to the members

- Any other matters considered by the directors to be relevant.

Corporate social responsibility

Employers also create one of the most important requirements of society – employment and wealth without which none of the public services could be funded. Increasingly larger/higher profile companies provide a public statement (usually published within their Annual Report) of their attitude to, and means of attaining, some level of Social Responsibility. This is a trend which is likely to continue, not only for such companies but also for far more employers since it will come to be expected not least by the 'good employees' – those who progressive employers should wish to recruit.

In a competitive employment market, those applicants who we can refer to as the 'above average' employees who many employers will wish to attract will want to know:

- what the organisation stands for (Will we trade in tobacco, alcohol, armaments, gambling, etc?)

- how it wishes to trade (attitude on safety, value, quality etc) (Will we become involved in organisations experimenting with animals and any other potentially damaging activities?)

- how it interacts (i.e. with society as a whole, as well as with suppliers, customers, employees, shareholders etc), and so on.

Companies that fail to address this need may find they lose their cutting edge. This is not meant to imply that a few words in an Annual Report is all that is needed – any paper commitment must be evidenced in practice. The first essential of such a programme is a willingness to commit to the principle of having a duty to trade in a way that enhances society, uses materials in as 'non-wasteful' a way as possible, treats all-comers with respect and so on. NOP conducted a survey for the Institute of Directors and discovered that:

- in roughly 50% of the 500 organisations contacted, the Board discussed social responsibility (66% of large companies)

- 60% discussed environmental issues (66% in large companies and 85% of those engaged in manufacturing)

- 36% had a Board member whose responsibilities included social issues

- 48% had a Board member whose responsibilities included environmental issues.

Employers operate within society and since they use resources, create scarcity by such consumption. There is a growing expectation (very widespread in these 'environmentally-friendly' days) that such resources should be used wisely and efficiently. Many processes also create by-products (and emissions) which may harm the environment.

Increasingly operations and operators (companies and their Boards of directors) are required to take account of environmental matters and the potential and detrimental effect their activities can have on the environment. The EU's report *'Promoting a European Framework for Corporate Social Responsibility'* as well as addressing CSR, echoes previous appeals to businesses to adopt and promote:

- lifelong learning for employees to maximise talents (see below)

- improved work organisation

- equality of opportunities for everyone

- social inclusion and

- sustainable development.

Employers are expected not only to adopt such guidelines but also to use them as a base and to go beyond them to develop their employment and social responsibility in the widest sense of those words. The aim is to make the EU *'the most competitive and dynamic knowledge-based economy in the world, capable of sustainable economic growth and with more and better jobs and greater social cohesion'.* The current aim is to move the principle underlying that statement ahead by:

- promoting social responsibility of corporations and employers within the EU and world-wide

- using existing (best) practices and encouraging their adoption on a universal basis

- encouraging the development of innovative policies for the future

- promoting the concept of transparency of the concept and their adoption of policies and practices to develop the concept

- evaluating the impact of the policies.

In the UK we are already experiencing a skills shortage which can only become more acute as we move more and more to a service-based nation. The greater the proportion of the workforce that is skilled – the greater pressure there will be on employers to demonstrate their credentials regarding 'what they stand for', the employment package, and attitudes to social responsibility, the environment, waste control and so on.

In January 2007 when announcing the proposal to increase the school leaving age to 18, the Government pointed out that there would progressively be fewer and fewer unskilled jobs, whilst the major demand would be for those with proven skills – either academic or vocational. Gordon Brown addressing the Microsoft Government Leaders Forum at the Scottish Parliament stated that it was vital for Britain to move from being an over-average economy to one that was at all times 'world class'. He went on:

'Of 3.4 million unskilled jobs (in 2007) by 2020 we will only need 600,000. So unless you have skills you are at risk of being unemployed. High skilled jobs must and will replace lower-skilled jobs. The 9 million highly skilled graduate jobs today will become 14 million by 2020.'

Board activity

There are recommendations published by the Association and British Insurers (Disclosure Guidelines on Social Responsibility) which encourage institutional investors to require their companies to answer questions such as the following in their companies Annual Reports.

- Does the Board regularly review Social, Ethical and Environmental (SEE) matters?

- Has the Board reviewed both short and longer term risks arising from SEE matters?

- Has the Board adequate information for this purpose and train directors and managers in SEE matters?

A plea for realism

The challenge with a commitment to CSR, is surely that it must be rolled out – and down – to every level in the company, otherwise the statements are purely an opportunity for wordsmiths to exercise highflown hyperbole.

- Tesco PLC is a rightly admired leading UK company whose Annual Report features over a page plus on its CSR commitment. In the Sunday Times 'Companies that count' survey (which seeks to rank companies in terms of continually improving the impact that they have on society) the company scored the highest ranking of 'Platinum'. Neither initiative prevented the company selling a 'pole dancing kit' aimed at 8 year old girls for a Christmas present. Immediately senior management's attention was drawn to it, the 'toy' was withdrawn. The question begged of course is 'where was the intelligence of the buyer representing a leading company'? CSR is a far wider commitment than saving energy and the environment.

- Sony, the electronics giant, launched its 'God of War II' game for its PlayStation 2 console with a video that featured the corpse of a freshly slaughtered goat, into whose entrails guests at the launch were invited to reach. When challenged, Sony immediately issued an apology and recalled the print run. But why should it be necessary for a challenge to be made before consideration of the effect of such an obscene act on the corporate reputation?

- Sony also annoyed the Christian church by setting one of its mass assassinations in a violent 'game' in a replica of Manchester Cathedral without any input from the Church. When challenged however, no apology was forthcoming this time. The company replied that had it needed permission it would have applied. Regardless of wondering whether they would have dared to use a replica of a Mosque to stage such a bloody massacre, one must wonder whether these are the actions of responsible management in the 21st Century?

Examining the issues

The following areas might be worth examining as a precursor to formulating a CSR policy:

Macro level issues

- what are ethical investments or activities – e.g. are alcohol, tobacco, military arms, gambling businesses unacceptable etc

- does a small dependence on such items require examination and explanation

- is there experimentation on animals

- do we need to explain to or be responsive to pressure groups from the shareholders, customers, investing bodies, campaigning groups, society etc.

Micro level issues

- how concerned are we with the welfare of our customers and our suppliers (are our goods or raw materials supplied from exploited markets)

- how concerned are we with the health and safety and welfare of our workforce

- should these opinions be taken into account and at what level.

The Association of British Insurers published 'Disclosure Guidelines on Social Responsibility', through which it suggests companies should disclose their policies concerning Social, Ethical and Environmental matters. These could include stating whether the Board:

- regularly review the above items

- has reviewed short and long term risks arising from the subject

- has sufficient information for the purpose and provides coaching in the area

The Annual report could include:

- Information on the matters covered

- Details of provisions in place to bring the requirements about

- Reporting on the compliance with the policies and the verification of progress.

Example

Centrica plc's Annual Report includes a whole page on Corporate responsibility including headings such as 'Living our values in the workplace', 'Improving service in the marketplace', 'Reducing impact on the environment', and 'Working with the wider community' – and commentary on how the company approaches those concepts.

Human Capital Management

The introduction of reporting under this heading was noted in Chapter 11. Some time ago the UK government through the Department for Trade and Industry set up a Task Force to examine the manner in which UK employers could and should take a strategic approach to the development of their human assets in order to maximise their performance (and through their performance, their employer's performance) and ways in which this could be reported on to their owners. Historically directors of companies have been required to report to their shareholders mainly on financial figures. However that emphasis has been changing over the last decade.

Whilst Boards of Directors have the ultimate responsibility to manage and direct, their aims can only ever be achieved via the actions of their employees. As former chief executive of ICI, Sir John Harvey Jones stated in 'Making it happen' (his best-selling management book) *'with the best will in the world and the best board in the world and the best strate-gic direction in the world nothing will happen unless everyone down the line understands what they are trying to achieve and gives of their best'.*

The benefits that flow from employers:

- attempting where possible to deal with an organisation's human resources in a mature and adult way by a process of real and pro-active communication (which has already been described as a 'communicaction' principle that is 'communication in action'; trying to focus attention on the essential dynamism of the process)

- recognition that those employees have other strong pressures in our modern society which may require the employer's preferences to be sublimated at times (the flexibility principle)

- acceptance that most employees are rational thinking human beings with ideas and opinions of their own which can be of considerable mutual benefit to both employer and employee (the 'consultabil-ity' principle)

can be considerable.

Other documentation

Summary Financial Statement

In place of the full Annual Report, companies may send to their share-holders a summary statement. A Summary Financial Statement (SFS) must be consistent with the full accounts and the auditors are required to certify that this is so. The SFS must state whether the Auditors Report on the full accounts was qualified or not.

Required content of SFS checklist

- Key section of the directors report:
    - business review
    - post balance sheet events
    - future developments
    - directors details

- Summary profit and loss account containing:
  - pre-tax profit/loss for financial period
  - tax and post-tax profit
  - extraordinary and exceptional items
  - dividends paid and proposed
  - Directors payments
- Summary Balance Sheet showing:
  - issued share capital
  - reserves
  - provisions
  - liabilities and assets
  - contingent liabilities
- Auditors report.

To discover whether shareholders would prefer to have the SFS, companies must first either:

- Send both summary statement and full report to their shareholders with a reply paid card, stating that unless the shareholder indicates, he will in future only be sent the summary version, or

- Canvas their shareholders in advance to discover who wishes to receive the summary version.

The interim report

Listed PLCs are required to produce an interim report – usually as at a date 6 months into their financial period although some companies produce quarterly interims (and there is a current suggestion that, in order to improve and speed up the publication of results that this should become the norm). Either such a report must be sent out or the company can advertise its results in 2 national newspapers. In either case the information must be supplied not later than 4 months after the end of the period. Interim statements do not have to be audited but most Auditors may wish to at least review the figures (particularly in view of the recent criticism of their profession).

The preliminary announcement

As soon as the results for the full year are known a listed PLC company is required to publish a Preliminary Announcement giving the salient details. This tends to be published around 3 months after the year end, with the Annual Report published up to a month later. Any price reactions of the shares will tend to be made in response to the information contained in the Preliminary and strict confidentiality must surround its production and dissemination.

Employee Reports

There is no legal requirement to produce an Employee report but around 200 listed PLCs do produce employees reports as do a larger number of other organisations. The best of such reports tend to be successful because they are relatively unconstrained by legal requirements, although there is a requirement, often ignored, for such reports to contain a statement that the figures are an extract from the full Report and Accounts which have been lodged with the Registrar of Companies.

Unfettered by legal requirements, employee reports can provide a clear and instant guide to the overall trend of the business and, for this reason, private shareholders, in particular, value the best of such reports. Research has shown that where such reports are sent to shareholders, often much of the information retained by the shareholders has been derived from reading the employee report rather than the annual report. The following checklist of contents should be used as a guide from which perhaps a majority of the items should be selected for inclusion. The need is to produce a report which explains the salient features and significance of the results.

Suggested content for Employee Report checklist

a)   Statements of the aims of the business and of the report

b)   Specially composed statement (i.e. not a reprint of the statement in the Annual Report) by the Chairman or Managing Director in ordinary English which avoids jargon

c)   Highlights of the year (i.e. clearly indicating progress – or lack of same)

d)   Balance sheet (with an explanation of the terms used)

e)   Simplified Profit & Loss a/c or Added Value statement

f)   Statement of sales and profit, particularly expressed on a per employee and/or a localised or divisional basis. (If inflation is high it may help show real growth by adjusting for inflation.)

g)   General information regarding products or services, employees, share schemes, environmental and community matters, etc.

h)   Organisation charts

i)   Comment on future plans or developments.

j)   Graphics and illustrations supporting and complementing the above items.

NOTE: Since most readers 'minds' eyes' can capture trends and proportions far more easily if expressed in graphic form than in a line or list of figures/text, the use of clear uncomplicated graphics should help achieve better reader comprehension. (from *'Financial Reporting to Employees – a practical guide'* David Martin)

Letter of welcome

An increasing number of listed PLCs write to new shareholders welcoming their investment and setting out the financial calendar of the company. There is no requirement to issue such a letter but it can create a rapport between new shareholder and company. There may be other matters that the Board would like to indicate to the shareholder – urging them to attend the AGM, details of any discount scheme, payment of dividends by direct transfer rather than by warrant and so on.

Letter of invitation to the AGM (and other General Meetings)

The notice of General Meetings tends to be included in the Annual Report and as such, often because space is limited, may be fairly formal. Some companies have amplified the formal notice with such a letter from the Chairman, particularly if there are matters other than the routine business to be considered at the Meeting. The letter can explain the reasons behind proposals which could, for example, have the result of gaining support where none might otherwise have been forthcoming.

Admission card

Companies with large numbers of shareholders tend to issue admission cards bearing their name, the number of shares etc. If a shareholder attends the meeting without such a card they cannot be barred from entering but the production of the card simply aids the admission formalities.

Summary checklist

- The person responsible for the compilation of the Annual Report must consider the requirements of the target audience and write the report accordingly (i.e. as clearly as possible) if it is to gain the attention it deserves and be understood.

- The dates by which filing the accounts must be filed with the Registrar are now policed strictly

- The editor must include items required by law but, to make it interesting, should consider adding a variety of additional information, presented in a way that can be easily comprehended by the target audience.

- Careful consideration must be given to the content of the Chairman's statement ensuring that items included in previous statements are not contradicted without explanation etc.

- The preparation of a summary financial statement and/or an employee report etc. may aid to the easy comprehension of the results by the target audiences.

Chapter fifteen

No such thing as bad publicity?

The public image

Who do we serve?

Devising and using media releases

Media interviews

Communication aspects of crisis reaction

Summary checklist

Who do we serve?

Regularly certain parts of the media make great play that the number of people employed by the State (essentially the wealth consuming part of the economy) in parts of the UK is around 25 per cent of all employed persons. Whether the expenditure on such activities is cost-effective is debatable and no doubt will be subject to further debate. Unfortunately justified criticism of the waste perpetrated by the wealth consuming entities is tempered as far as wealth-creating entities are concerned by the several scandals and failures of such entities in recent times. Despite their own spectacular lack of control over their own activities (it has been estimated that the Government wastes around 30 per cent of its income) the Government's answer is further legislation and control of those in control of companies – even though it is probable that those intent on defrauding investors and customers will pay as little attention to new requirements as they did to the old. One area where there is pressure for greater input concerns the use of non-executive directors. To no small extent this is a two-pronged attack:

a) from the EU which in one of its draft company law directives wants PLCs to have a majority of non-executive directors on such company's Boards (although where such numbers of quality directors can be sourced is difficult to identify) and

b) from the recommendations of a UK investigation into the effectiveness of non-executives (The Higgs Report).

The Higgs recommendations include:

• the promotion of Boardroom meritocracy by an open, fair and rigorous appointment processes

• redefining the description of the non-executive director for inclusion in the Combined Code on Corporate Governance

• separating the roles of Chairman and Chief Executive

• defining the word 'independence' for inclusion in the Combined Code to try to ensure that non-executives can and will speak out when they have concerns regarding compliance etc. It is suggested that at least half the Board should be 'independent' or capable of independent thought

• identifying a senior 'independent' director so that shareholders could approach that person if their concerns have not been satisfactorily answered by the Chairman and/or Chief Executive

- the provision of and requirement for structured induction and personal development for directors

- provision of a process of annual evaluation of directors individually and the Board collectively

- clarification of the liabilities of non-executive directors

- the Chairman and the Company Secretary should regularly assess what information is required by non-executives

- that the Company Secretary should be secretary to all Board committees and that person should be accountable to the Board via the Chairman on all corporate governance matters

- the appointment and/or removal of the Company Secretary should be a collective Board responsibility.

Generally there is a move towards Society raising its expectations of the level of probity and compliance at Board level which it is suggested is best done by monitoring the activities of companies at Board level by those who do not depend on their position in order to meet the obligations – that is their financial independence of the Company can encourage them to be entirely objective.

The customer is always right

The above developments seek to do in terms of the management of the Board, what the market place does for the sales of the products or services of a company operating in other than a monopolistic manner. This is so even though the requirements placed upon Boards of wealth-creating companies are such that it may be all too easy for Directors concerned to look after the interests of society, shareholders, employees, the environment and the safety of visitors to overlook the fact that at the end of the day their companies can only survive if they remember to satisfy their customers – a party whose interests it is interesting to note were recognised in the consultative document which preceded the draft of the new Companies Act – and whose interests must always be considered under the Competition and Enterprise Acts.

Case study: Impossible delegation

A customer was experiencing a series of problems with an account with one of the UK's largest banks and was so disillusioned with their performance that he wrote to the Managing Director. Back came a letter from the 'Manager, Customer Relations' who commenced her letter 'I have been asked to reply as we have overall responsibility in this department for the level of service provided by the Bank.' What arrant nonsense – the only people who have 'responsibility' for the level of service provided for their customers are the Board of Directors – and such responsibility can be delegated only at the peril of the business of the company. Such an attitude may explain why the financial services sector in general, and traditional banks in particular, are so poorly regarded by their customers.

Wealth-creating companies exist for one purpose only – to make a profit – an aim they can only achieve if they please and continue to please their customers. The company that fails its customers will ultimately fail itself. One of the top priorities for all Directors is therefore ensuring the satisfaction of their customers – and more of them.

A customer's perception of a company is derived from a number of sources – personal experience, quality of product and/or service, estimates of value for money, how they are treated if they have a problem with a company's product or service, and, increasingly from the reported perception of others notably those in the media. For the Board, hand in hand with the responsibility to their customers must go the responsibility for the protection and preservation of company product, name and reputation. The operations and activities of organisations (particularly those which have a high consumer profile) and the individuals that control or direct them are increasingly subject to the attention of 'the media' and through them the public. The range of such interest – like the scope of the laws that govern companies and their operations – is ever-increasing. Indeed it is the development of the laws and a company's compliance (or more likely non-compliance) with them which tend to generate much media interest. For example the extension of employment law has led directly to media interest in and scrutiny of Employment Tribunal hearings of occurrences and disputes which would formerly have been regarded as purely internal matters, not warranting any interest from third parties. Thus the interface with the public, and the continuing effect on the public perception of the company can alter on a daily basis. Without awareness and control, a positive image can be converted to the opposite very swiftly – with potentially disastrous effect on customers, demand and thus the business.

A protection policy

Reputation and public awareness may be indefinable and incapable of quantification, nevertheless their value can be considerable. A reputation can take years to build – and just seconds to lose – as witness the events following Gerald Ratner's presentation to the Institute of Directors when following him comparing to 'crap' some of the products sold by his company's shops, the company bearing his name almost failed, its name had to be changed and 200 shops had to be sold. In addition Ratner's own career was rudely interrupted as he was forced to resign firstly as Chairman of the company and then as a Director. Protecting the reputation of the company (and its products/services) from all-comers should be high on the list of priorities of every Board – provided of course that such protection is not blind to real and serious failings where rectification is in everyone's interests. What is required is a proactive rather than reactive approach.

Public relations commitment checklist

- The Company recognises the natural interest that will be evinced by the media 'on behalf of the public' as well as the public itself in its operations and will make all information, other than that which is regarded as confidential, regularly available primarily to accredited sources.

  NOTE: Such sources would include named journalists, a list of journals, newsletters, radio and TV outlets (as well as any Internet Web site) etc., and be included on a mailing list of those who would automatically be sent all literature produced for external use as a matter of course. In this way dependable information would be available to such sources which may be result in facts being substituted for supposition which may be used if such information is not available.

- [Name and deputy] will act as company spokesperson and will be briefed continually by [Directors/executives as applicable] responsible for each [division, product, etc.]

- In the event of other employees being contacted by representatives of the media, they will be referred to the spokesperson

- In interfacing with the media, the spokesperson will endeavour to be truthful at all times, and to ensure that all information is correctly presented and correctly reported – endeavouring to correct the record where this is not the case.

- Contacts with each branch of the media will be made and such contacts will be regularly briefed so that they have background knowledge of the organisation, which is then updated continuously

- In the event of a serious occurrence the senior manager responsible must brief the spokesperson as quickly as possible.

- On no occasion regardless of the circumstances should the products, services or reputation of the organisation or of any person working in it or of any third party connected with it be called into doubt or questioned in any way whatever without the knowledge of [name].

Devising and using media releases

Capturing attention

From time to time (and only when there is a real piece of news to impart) a media release can be issued. The media receive such a mass of information that only the most newsworthy will capture their attention. Strict parameters should be observed.

Media release checklist

1. The subject matter must be really newsworthy – not to the organisation but to the target readers/listeners/viewers of the media targeted.

2. Newsworthy subject matter must be made attention-worthy. Thus the release should both capture initial attention and provide all the relevant information in an easy to read (and use) form. If the first paragraph does not grab the reader's attention, no matter how good the rest of the document, it is unlikely to be read. If the release is written in a way whereby the editor can use it (or more likely a part of it) without much editing, re-writing or recourse to the contact named (see below) then it stands a better chance of being used.

3. The release should be as brief as possible commensurate with the subject matter. Further the language used should be simple, straightforward and should avoid jargon. Trying to 'pad out' a short release with extraneous information may mean the whole thing is discarded.

4. A release is not the place to build a climax. The most important point should be featured first or prominently. Everything else should support or explain this 'headline' material.

5. A release is not the correct conduit for organisation promotion – if attempted, it will fail. The purpose of a release is to provide information that it is believed will be of interest to the readers/listeners /viewers as a news item – not as promotional puff.

6. A quote from the Managing Director, or better still from a household name customer or equivalent may add interest.

7. If the release features a product and it is feasible to do so, include a sample with it. As a (poor) substitute, a photograph might be used. If a number of photographs are available, reference to this in the release and a crib of what is available might generate interest providing obtaining the photo is made easy and in a form capable of being used by the editor.

   NOTE: If samples are sent, the greatest care should be taken to send the best quality items.

8. If providing advance information about a forthcoming event ensure that the information is 'in advance'. Giving less than a week's notification is unlikely to generate an interest.

9. Keep a careful note of the correct names, positions and addresses of all those on the mailing lists – and keep all the details updated. Addressing releases to the wrong person, or the right person with the wrong title, or to either at the wrong address reflects poorly on the organisation.

10. Always incorporate a contact name and telephone number and ensure that the contact is available on that number at the times stated after the release has been issued.

Golden rules – the four 'ONLYs'

1. Only issue a release when something of interest to the target audience is to be featured

2. Only issue a release if it passes the 'blind man's test'. This comprises reading the release once only to someone who knows nothing of the subject matter and will have no chance to re-read it and asking them to state the story. Unless they can repeat the salient facts the release needs to be re-written – and probably shortened.

3. Only issue a release to the particular part of the media who are likely to be interested in the item.

4. Only issue the release if there is someone always on call ready and prepared to answer questions and provide additional data should the target media channel require this.

Media interviews

The policy statement covers the area of media/public interest in very general terms and needs developing to address individual circumstances. As far as the spokesperson is concerned however they will need to have access to a range of data and to be in command of the latest developments at all times. No media briefing or interview will be successful unless adequate preparation and research has been carried out. Thus the items set out in the following checklist should be addressed. Inevitably the media will often try to obtain statements or comments from the Chairman or Chief Executive. Unless such persons have received training in communicating with the media, it may be preferable for a more junior but trained or experienced person to act as spokesman. Good Chairmen do not always make good spokespersons. Whoever is chosen, they must be able to keep calm under pressure, to think swiftly, to appreciate that some answers may be double-edged (i.e. that either response may be self-critical) and to try to avoid this effect, and, above all, to show their knowledge is sound.

Interviews checklist

General research

- Identify the areas of operation in which the media/public could be interested

- Identify the target audiences and the information they will require

- Identify the nature of the interest of each part of the target audience and what information will be required

- Establish who is to deal with the ongoing enquiry and how they are to be briefed and updated concerning progress and all related aspects

- Encourage the spokesperson to create links with representatives of all media (establishing names, positions, main interests or 'angles', deadlines, potential bias etc.)

- Examine all features, stories and reports concerning the company to ensure the (correct/required/positive) image is being created

- Continually develop questions (and, more importantly, answers thereto) that the company least wants asked and become conversant with both (updated as necessary)

- Prepare and update a summary of all the recent successes of the company so that good news is available which may leaven the bad.

Particular preparation

- Before agreeing to the interview, discover as much as possible about the circumstances (name of interviewer, programme, general purpose, scope of enquiry, whether live or recorded, scope for restricting/controlling questions, length of item to be used and likely use date, etc.)

- As comprehensive and complete brief as possible must be prepared on the subject matter and supporting items – company data, performance, products, problems, plans, etc.

- If the topic is likely to be controversial or embarrassing, appropriate responses and statements should be prepared, ideally trying to limit the 'damage' that could be caused or to develop news which offsets the effect.

- The spokesperson needs to have total control of the brief, of all facts and of prepared responses, to be able to speak knowledgeably concerning the subject matter. Any hesitation, lack of confidence or inadequate knowledge will be communicated to the listener or viewer and create doubt and/or undermine veracity.

  In this respect it may be better to admit 'I don't know' rather than trying to 'flannel' through an answer. At least saying 'I don't know' (although it should only be used once or twice in any one interview) does have the ring of truth about it and can indicate – and win plaudits for – honesty and straightforwardness.

- Three or four simple messages, or arguments that the company wishes to promote, must be developed, possibly with 'changes of direction' sentences, so that if the interviewer leads off in one direction, the spokesperson may be able to direct it to the company's preferred message. This approach needs to be controlled since a constant refusal to answer the actual questions put may lead to a more inquisitive or confrontational interview.

- There should be no assumption that the interviewer will not have full knowledge of all the facts. It is better to assume that everything is known and then prepare answers accordingly.

- The spokesperson must be ready for the 'off the cuff' and unrehearsed question deliberately introduced and designed to catch him/her unawares leading to the making of an unprepared or unwise comment or answer.

- The spokesperson must be able to keep calm under pressure and/or goading, to be able to think quickly and laterally in order to fend off or turn aggression and criticism, to retain control, and, above all, NEVER lose their temper.

- Most live media interviews last a minute or less and thus it may be possible only to put across two or three authoritative comments. The spokesperson needs to be calm, alert and interested and serious – never humorous, flustered, or flippant. To a large extent, particularly on television, the manner a message is delivered can be more effective than the content.

- They should take a little time to think about the questions – asking for them to be repeated if necessary

- False statements should not be allowed to pass unchecked – the record should be corrected, tactfully but firmly.

- Be positive not defensive. It may be better to 'own up' to a bad performance or event with a 'promise to improve' or rectify, rather than trying to defend an untenable position. The latter alternative will normally display the company in a poor light regardless of the circumstances – the impression will be 'they have learned nothing from the mistake', so nothing will change. This is particularly important when there has been loss, injury or death. In such instances it is essential that genuine sympathy is expressed and that there is an indication that steps are being taken to try to ensure there is no repetition.

Case study: Telling the truth

When Lee Iacocca, the person credited with turning car manufacturer Chrysler round in the 1980s, was in charge of the company a fault was discovered in one of the models. The company tried to conceal the matter but was caught out. Rather than simply issuing a recall notice, the company advertised the problem and Iacocca was quoted as stating 'selling cars that had been damaged went beyond dumb all the way to stupid – it was unforgivable and will not happen again'. When the story originally broke 55 per cent of the public asked thought Chrysler were 'bad boys'. After Iacocca's comments and the campaign both 'owning up' 67 per cent of those asked stated they were in favour of the company.

During an interview concerned with bad news, particularly if it reflects poorly on the company, some rapport with or positive feeling from the audience may be gained if the spokesperson can, provided the circumstances are suitable, introduce details of facts that show the company in a better light – or at least try to put the current incident in some kind of perspective.

A real apology

If the organisation has been caught doing wrong, the safest bet is to hold up one's hands and say a genuinely contrite 'sorry'. Trying to evade questions or argue one's way out of the situation only leads to more questioning and a very poor reflection on the organisation.

One of its choirmasters was uncovered by the Church of England to be a paedophile. Rather than reporting the matter to the Police, the Church required him to leave his position and 'not to work with children again' – a request which he totally ignored and continued to work with and to abuse other boys. When the matter came out many years later, rather than saying 'we are very sorry, we got it wrong' and apologising (particularly to the subsequent victims whose anguish might have been avoided had the Church taken the proper action) the spokesperson put up by the Church refused to discuss the specific matter (even though the case was over and the sentence had been handed down). All she would say was:

'These matters are always reviewed after they occur and we learn from our mistakes and our good practice is improved at all stages when these matters are looked at. Robust policies are improved through learning from the past and from following the guidance and good practice that happens now.'

In other words – a mass of weasel words supposed to be an apology. As Gerald Ratner might more pointedly (and accurately) say, 'what a load of c**p', or, as, Lee Iacocca might have said, 'failing to alert the Police went beyond dumb all the way to stupid'.

It was left to the Archbishop of Canterbury to issue a real and far more humble apology a day or so later.

Communication aspects of crisis reaction

Whilst briefing the media on the more mundane aspects of company performance may be relatively easy, dealing with such interest in the aftermath of a calamity or disaster, poses considerable problems capable of being tackled only if based on contingency planning, i.e. anticipating the disaster and making advance plans for dealing with the effects. The advantage of 'planning for disaster' is that lengthy and calm thought can be given to alternative tactics and reactions, without the considerable time pressure for reaction that the incidence of disaster can cause. In addition, consideration of alternative actions in the event of disaster, may suggest beneficial changes in current operations. Obviously if it is to be of value such planning must be both comprehensive and regularly updated. Accordingly it will be an expensive operation albeit one that should be regarded as an investment – certainly trying to cope with the innumerable requirements for action and comments following a disaster without at least a little planning will be virtually impossible.

Increasingly, as a means of determining appropriate cover for insurance purposes insureds are encouraged to consider first a process of risk management. Many of the 'disasters' that could generate media interest would be included in the process of risk management and linking these twin approaches could be beneficial. In any event, included in any 'insurance-generated' disaster plan should be consideration of the requirement to deal with the media.

Crisis communication checklist

1. Initial contact will usually be by telephone. A person should be nominated (possibly the Company Secretary, though there should always be one or two back up personnel) to handle all initial queries

2. Listen carefully to what the enquirer is asking

3. Make notes of (or tape record) the call content, time, the caller's name, position and media represented, the caller's telephone number and location

4. Do not respond to questions, comments, observations – simply make notes as set out in 3 above and state that by a (stated) time someone will respond either in a news release or by telephone, e-mail, etc.

5. Do not be flustered by indications of deadlines. Those are the caller's problems not yours. Attempted insistence on immediate response, outrageous accusations, innuendoes etc. should also be noted but not commented upon.

6. By the time promised (not less than an hour) ensure someone does ring the caller back with comments

7. Keep responses, press statements etc., short. Embroidery can both offset the punch effect and provide angles from which the reporter can come back at the author.

8. Provide a contact name/number

9. Should such contact be used – the above guidelines should be applied – if necessary with the spokesperson ringing back after time for thought

Event impact

When Harold Macmillan was Prime Minister and the Conservative Party was riding high, someone commented that it was difficult to see what could impact their position – 'Events, dear boy, just events' Macmillan is reported to have replied. Despite the best planning and preparation in the world, reputation and prospects can be damaged by events over which the company may feel it has little control. This is reality – even if unfair!

Case study

The fire at the Buncefield oil depot near Hemel Hempstead in December 2005, was probably the largest peacetime disaster to hit the UK. It affected not only the oil depot and stocks, but also hundreds of businesses and houses. 3Coms' headquarters were destroyed by the fire yet only 48 hours later, the company was back in business. 3Com is US owned and the parent company had a detailed disaster recovery plan. Temporary offices were in use by the Wednesday after the fire and the company claims to have lost no revenue or employees as a result. Indeed many said the effect was to improve communication no end as everyone pulled together and talked to one another. The HR director commented that he met and talked to more people in the three months after the fire than he had in the three years he had been there!

Part of the responsibility of directors could be to 'expect the unexpected' and plan accordingly. Not that costs may only be incurred by such spectacular disasters.

The ramifications of employment law are such that many employers need to appear in an Employment Tribunal to defend their actions. Such is the complexity of the law that even organisations which are correctly regarded as 'models of good employment principles and practice' have needed to defend tribunal actions and several have lost such cases. The problem for the employer is that the fact of appearing can be taken as adverse by many employees whilst the circumstances of the case, since the vast majority of such cases are open to the public and many are reported in the local and national media, are available for all to review and consider.

Case study: Hypocritical?

a) A leading company known for its positive and progressive employment practices was found to have unfairly dismissed an employee who was injured (and eventually unable to resume her normal job) whilst trying to protect her employer's goods from a thief. Would it not have been more positive to have tried to find her an alternative job when she was unable to resume her original duties because of permanent injuries?

b) A company refused to pay Statutory Sick Pay to an employee who injured her back whilst working for them. Their point was that she was employed on a daily contract and thus did not accrue the three months service then necessary to enable her to claim SSP. The Court of Appeal held her 8 months service on single day contracts was 'continuous' and thus she was entitled to be paid. The costs of fighting such a case all the way to the Court of Appeal must have far outweighed the cost of the SSP the Company was trying to avoid paying. If it is a matter of 'principle' litigants should remember that 'principles tend to be expensive'.

c) An employer refused to allow a woman the holiday to which she was entitled because it had accrued during the time she was on maternity leave. The legislation states that a woman is entitled to all 'non-monetary' benefits at such a time. Her claim was upheld.

Does this create the impression of a responsible employer in the eyes of potential employees – let alone the other employees?

The exact circumstances of these cases will not concern most of those who will read or hear about the decisions at the time as they will tend to judge on the effect as reported rather than the evidence and the reasons. What is important is that in each case the employers (leading UK companies – one wonders where their 'social responsibility' was in such cases). could be regarded by many as 'doing the wrong thing' which sends messages to all onlookers – not least the other employees in the company without whose efforts the Board will be unable to achieve its aims. It would be hardly surprising if the reaction to such cases was negative, and as a result morale and commitment to the companies were impaired. Were these the kind of messages the organisations wished to send not just to their employees but also to all others doing business with them? If not, should not the Board have been able to avoid the messages being conveyed?

Reserve the decision

It may of course be that there were precedents which needed to be protected, or principles to be maintained which led to the above cases being fought. If so, and the decisions were taken at the tops of the organisations then hopefully the effect of losing was taken into account and the cases were thought to be worth the cost of resisting if not, then perhaps responsibility has been delegated too far. In the generation of such messages, the Board needs to be in control, to be seen to be in control and to be adopting the positions that it wants, not as may be suspected here defending positions foisted upon them by more junior managers. Although it has been stated that there is no such thing as bad publicity, the Board will never know whether it lost sales as a result of some onlookers feeling dissatisfied at the company's approach.

Of course it is not only in the field of employee relations that such 'messages' can be publicised. A company which has a reputation for not paying its accounts promptly, or for always dealing harshly with those with whom it does business (whether buying or selling), or which refuses to support local charitable activities can swiftly build a reputation at variance to, but possibly more accurate than, that it which it may strive to give. It may be preferable to adopt as policy: 'All decisions which may result in legal action and/or generate publicity and public attention should only be taken:

a) At a senior level in the organisation [by name/position], and

b) After a full assessment has been made of the financial effect of the decision, the precedent involved and the effect of the result of the action on both internal and external audiences.'

Failure to retain such control to the Board and/or to require that everyone seeks to maintain reputation or adheres to corporate style, may lead to a situation where employees who need to represent the organisation – or give or interpret its rules externally – have to operate by devising their own guidelines and style guide. This can only lead to inconsistencies and mean that decisions related to the appearance and promotion of the entity are not being taken in a cohesive and considered way, but rather executed in a piecemeal and fragmented manner not at all reflective of the way the company sees itself and wishes others to see it.

Corporate style/approach guidelines checklist

1. The organisation as a responsible operator and employer will endeavour to communicate to all interested parties those details regarding its activities which may be of interest to them.

2. The areas of information that will be constantly reported upon are – future plans, new products (once any confidential aspects are removed), competitive position, details regarding employment and benefits and social responsibility programme.

3. Information will be provided usually in written form under the authority of a [Director] to ensure compliance with these guidelines.

4. This company has developed a reputation for [honest dealing, good value products, quality service and responsible employment] over the years and wishes these characteristics to guide all connected with it in their work and their relationships with external audiences at all times. No exceptions to these guidelines are acceptable. Failure to adhere to these precepts will be regarded very seriously.

5. Interviews can be granted with advance notice and an indication of the range of topics likely to be covered. Those interviewed will be required to comment only on items indicated in advance as being the subject matter. If questions outside this area are posed, the spokesperson will be required to answer 'policy requires that I do not answer questions on those subjects since I have not been briefed upon them'. Directors asked such questions may comment in general terms without committing the organisation.

6. All newsworthy information about the organisation will be published in Media Releases and in all cases a contact will be provided so that additional information can be obtained.

Summary checklist

- Consider improving Board effectiveness by using non-executive and truly independent directors

- Retain responsibility for dealing with customers and customer care (in the widest sense of the words) to the Board so that those who have the ultimate responsibility know at first hand the opinions and attitudes of customers

- Devise and adhere to a public relations policy and brief those required to interface with the media. Issue media releases only when subject is really newsworthy to those not otherwise involved with the company

- Coach and brief all those required to give interviews and research reason for interview before agreeing to participate

- Be prepared to provide information to media following a crisis and reflect this need in all disaster planning

- Control events likely to generate attention directed in public arena resulting in adverse comment and potential reputation damage

Chapter sixteen

'A personal viewpoint'

Employment considerations

The 4 key employment 'abilities' for the 21st Century

Pro-active recruitment

The 'family friendly' regime

Public duties

Avoiding Age discrimination

The challenge of retirement – post October 2006

Summary checklist

The 4 key employment 'abilities' for the 21st Century

As recently as the 1970s, employment was still regarded as the relationship between 'master and servant'. The rapid development of Trade Unions and increased employment protection did much to break this outdated and patronising description. Society itself and even the Courts have also been instrumental in changing attitudes to this kind of relationship. Thus in the Horkulak v Cantor Fitgerald case, the judge stated *'the notion of an employment contract giving rise to a 'master and servant' relationship is now obsolete'*.

The judge went on to state *'an employee's participation in the business cannot simply be regarded as the work of a servant for the benefit of an employer, but must be recognised as one of the most important things in an employee's life. It gives not only a livelihood, but an occupation, an identity and a sense of esteem'*.

The power of Trade Unions during the 1960s and 1970s was considerable and was often successful, as much as a result of managerial default as from Union campaigning. In many cases management was weak and seemingly unable to communicate effectively with their workforce. Not for nothing was the phrase – 'he who communicates leads' coined by Jack Jones, the then General Secretary of the Transport & General Workers Trade Union. If directors and managers were not communicating with their employees, trades unions were certainly communicating with their members and it was the unions who came to be regarded as workforce leaders. The power of the Unions – often then used less than wisely – was curbed not only by increasing legal restrictions enacted during the Thatcher government years, but also since many of the rights for which Unions fought began to be prescribed by law. This led to an environment which generated an employment relationship more akin to one of partnership for mutual gain with an increasing understanding – at least in the private sector – that wealth must be created before it can be spent. The UK membership of the European Union has also resulted in much domestic legislation being required to reflect continental attitudes. The culmination of these various factors has resulted in a widely adopted different attitude to using people in the workplace. I would suggest that there are a number of key employment 'abilities' for successfully operating in this field in the 21st Century – for example: 'flexibility', 'comparability', 'consultability' and 'retention-ability'.

Flexibility

Increasingly there are legislative enactments which require employers to provide a flexible approach as part of the work:life balance (or work:leisure balance which may be a more accurate description since to many employees work is a pleasure, an integral part of their life and even provides a substantial part of their social life). A DTI study in early 2004 disclosed that 80% of employees want to spend more time with their family and friends, and that more flexible work practices would allow people to take up interests such as sport and learning a foreign language (or at least that is what the respondents stated). Presumably flexibility in this context meant a re-arrangement rather than a reduction of hours, so that income was maintained. Already those with parental responsibilities for children aged up to 6 (18 if the child is disabled) have the right to lodge a request to work flexible hours, and it has been announced that this right may be extended to those who have caring responsibilities for aged relatives. In addition, many of those not otherwise entitled are pressing to be given such a right. The challenge for employers is that although it may be relatively easy to grant the first (or first few) of such request(s), this may become progressively harder as more requests are lodged.

Comparability

Legislation already requires part-timers and fixed term workers who perform jobs that are comparable to full-timers and permanent employees respectively, to be given the same rights and benefits as them. In two further instances – homeworkers and agency staff – similar requirements are to be introduced shortly.

NOTE: The EU is considering establishing a new '3 way' employment relationship for agency staff or 'temps' recognizing that the interaction of agency, client and person is not always clear cut. This echoes other moves within the EU to address the rights of the 40% of workers within the EU that are now working either on 'non-standard' contracts or are self-employed. The EU wishes to try to provide a proposed 'floor of rights' which would apply to all workers regardless of the manner or form of their contract.

The EU Commission has published a consultation document addressing 'flexicurity' entitled 'Modernising labour law to meet the challenges of the 21st Century'. The latest abandonment of any revision of the existing opt out provisions of the working time directive is at least indicative of the awareness of some of the EU membership that flexibility is essential if EU employers – and their employees – are not to lose out to the emerging economies of China and India.

Consultability

There is an increasing number of instances where employers must consult with their employees and, if requested by their employees, need to regularise this via the introduction of works councils. One of the themes running through this book is that 'communication is essential' – the 'communicaction principle'. This may be obvious yet it is often misunderstood. It is very sad that as the means of passing information improves, real communication often worsens. Technology can actually impede the process.

Retention ability

In the UK we have a shrinking working population and a growing skills shortage. Employers need to retain the best skills – good performers – rather than having to replace them. Foundation Degrees published a survey in early 2004 which indicated that 28% of employees planned to leave their jobs. 47% of employees between the ages of 20 and 65 said they 'drifted' into their jobs and 26% said their current job was 'just a way to pay the bills'. Quite apart from the cost of replacing leavers (and the wastage of time it entails) sourcing and then retaining the better employees is essential for those that wish to move their organisation forward. A computer model for the Brookings Institute in Washington demonstrated that 'the most successful organisations are not those that set high profit margins but those that attract and retain the most productive staff'. Employee retention is not just 'good man-management' as an end – it is the means to better financial performance. As Rhiannon Chapman, human resources expert commented recently:

There is a close link between staff retention and customer retention… and repeat business is six to eight times more profitable than new business.'

As a management tool, trying to retain the better employees may require a change of attitude on the part of some people and a conscious effort to lead the workforce rather than manage them – '*you manage processes but you lead people*'. It is relatively easy to ensure that terms and conditions are conducive to employee retention but the challenge is encapsulated in the need to adopt positively what is required by the previous three key words. The greatest managerial skill needed for the 21st Century is to be ready, willing and able to adjust to changing expectations – failing to do so can only mean problems with recruiting and retaining the best employees, thereby stultifying the business.

Pro-active recruitment

It is relatively easy to recruit an employee, less easy to ensure one recruits the most appropriate person, and far less easy to dispense with their services fairly and without generating a tribunal case which might cost the employer many thousands of pounds – win or lose. Trying to be extremely selective to achieve the most appropriate appointment whilst it may delay an offer, could be a sound investment if it avoids subsequent disciplinary and dismissal proceedings. Generating an updated job and person description, requiring completion of a comprehensive application form, structuring the interview and short-listing process, checking background and qualifications and taking up references can all assist in this aim.

There are an increasing number of legal restrictions before employment can be offered. Since May 2004 employers have been required to check before employment commences that ALL applicants are entitled to work in the UK by asking for documentary evidence. Under the Immigration (Restrictions on Employment) Order 2003 the appropriate documentation is limited to one of:

*   passports with correct certification (right to work);

*   EEA identity cards ;

*   UK residence permits issued to EEA nationals; and

*   Home Office issued residence permits.

If none of the foregoing is available applicants must provide two of the following:

- A full (not short form) UK birth certificate. The short form birth certificate is provided free on first registration. If the long certificate which, as well as name, sex, and date and place of birth, provides details of parents, is required this costs £3.50 on first registration but up to £8.50 later and £11 if the general register office number is unknown.

- Certificate of registration or naturalisation or letters from the Home Office.

- Approval documents issued by Work Permits UK

- Evidence of the national insurance number (e.g. P45 or P60).

Employing a person with no right to work is currently subject to a £5,000 fine which is being considered for considerable increase.

It may also be prudent to make all job offers subject to:

a) the new recruit being subject to a probationary period during which their employment can be terminated by a week's notice;

b) receipt of references satisfactory to the prospective employer;

c) receipt of a 'basic' (standard or enhanced certificates are required for those working with children or vulnerable adults) certificate from the Criminal Records Bureau. Applications from those who refuse to grant permission for the generation of such a certificate may be best discarded and

d) the recruit signing a contract. (The point of this is that if the contract is explained to them and they sign it, should they be dismissed it will be difficult for them to claim subsequently 'I didn't know').

During the probationary period (and possibly for some months after it) a full 'familiarisation' programme (see 'consultability') should be undertaken with support, coaching, mentoring etc. aimed at encouraging the employee to both to 'feel a part of the team', to perform and to remain.

The 'family friendly' regime

Maternity

The first of an increasing range of leaves and benefits for those with family responsibilities, statutory maternity pay and leave were introduced in the 1970s. There have been many improvements and changes over the years and further improvements continue to be considered.

Procedure

A woman must produce form MATB1 to her employer. This form is available from the 20th week before her 'expected week of childbirth' (EWC). A woman wishing to exercise her entitlements must notify her employer in or by the 15th week before her EWC, giving the employer a copy of the MATB1 if the employer requires this. She must also state to her employer when she wishes her maternity leave (and her Maternity Pay – if she is eligible – see below) to commence. She must give 28 days notice of the leave/pay start date.

Within a further 28 days her employer must confirm to her, in writing, her rights to:

i) pay;

ii) preservation of contract; and

iii) return (see below).

If the baby is born before the expiry of the woman's 28 day notice period the leave (and pay if applicable) commences at the date of birth.

The mother's rights

1. Leave. All new mothers are entitled to 26 weeks Ordinary Maternity Leave (OML) plus 26 weeks Additional Maternity Leave (AML).

2. Pay. Provided a woman has 26 weeks service as at the 15th week before her EWC and has earned above the Lower Earnings Level for at least 8 weeks, she is also entitled to be paid Statutory Maternity Pay (SMP) by her employer.

3. SMP is paid for 26 weeks OML plus 13 weeks AML. A woman is entitled to 6 weeks of this 39 week period at 90% of her pay (averaged over the 8 weeks prior to the 15th week before her EWC). The other 33 weeks are paid at the lower of the above figure or the annually reviewed amount of SMP. (An employee who is not eligible for SMP

may be entitled to Statutory Maternity Allowance paid direct by the State.) Any increase agreed during the whole of her maternity leave must be reflected back to the calculation of her SMP and any short-fall made good.

For the first 6 weeks of her OML she is entitled to 90% of her earn-ings averaged over the 8 week period before the 15th week before her EWC. If there is a subsequent backdated pay increase her '90%' payment must be adjusted accordingly (*Alabaster v Woolwich plc.*)

Case study: Maternity pay problems

In *Alabaster v Woolwich Building Society*, the ECJ stated that all rises during the whole of a woman's Maternity Leave had to be applied from the start of a woman's maternity leave. This means that amounts already paid need to be recalculated and any shortfall paid. The decision seems to lack all logic since the effect not only means that the '90% for the first 6 weeks' calculation needs to be adjusted but also that women who were not previously eligible for SMP (since their 'average week's pay' was below the lower earnings level) may eligible for payment leading to a complete adjustment to their benefits (i.e. taking account of any Maternity Allowance already paid).

In addition, one effect is that a woman on maternity leave could receive the benefit of a pay rise before her colleagues. Given that a woman's maternity leave can last a year this could also have an effect on earn-ings in prior years.

Payment recovery

92% of the Statutory Maternity payments made to a women during her maternity leave are recoverable by 'large' employers by deduction from their NI contributions. A 'large' employer is regarded as any employer whose total National Insurance liability for the previous tax year was above an annually reviewed figure. Other, 'small', employers can reclaim the whole amount plus a 4.5% 'admin' charge. If a small employer would find it difficult to fund the SMP they can apply for an advance. (This concession is expected to be phased out by 2008.)

Return to work

A woman must give 56 days notice of the date that she wishes her maternity leave to start. Her employer must (within 28 days of that notification) state the latest date by which she must return to work. If she changes (which she may) the leave 'start date', then within 28 days of the notification of the change, the employer must advise a new 'return date'.

The employer will always KNOW her required date of return since:

- If the woman only takes OML, her 'return date' is 26 weeks after she starts her leave

- If the woman takes AML her 'return date' is 52 weeks after she starts her leave.

The employer can therefore state the 'return date' with certainty – although if the baby is born before the notified start, obviously this will bring the end of the OML and, if applicable, any AML, forward.

There is NO right for the employer to ask the employee if and when she wishes to return. If she wishes to return BEFORE her 'return date' she must give her employer 56 days notice, although her employer can postpone her return for any period but not to a date later than her return date. Otherwise the woman can simply arrive for work on her return date – she does not have to give any notification, although in practical terms this would be advisable.

Keeping in touch

A woman is allowed to work for her employer during her maternity leave for a maximum of 10 'in touch' days. There are no restrictions on when she can do this – although she cannot work within 2 weeks (4 if she works in a factory) of having given birth. It may be logical for her to work such days during the unpaid period of her maternity leave. It is for the parties to agree the rate per day although it might be sensible to suggest a rate which brings SMP (if any) to the normal rate of pay.

Contract of employment

A woman's contract continues during maternity leave and thus any rights other than pay (e.g. holiday) continue to accrue. Thus, a woman on maternity leave for 52 weeks could have a full year's holiday entitlement (including Public Holidays) which she should take (and be paid for) during that leave.

During her OML and the whole of any Additional Maternity Leave (AML) she needs either to be paid for her statutory leave (plus any contractual holiday or for all the holidays) to be added to the end of her AML. Since the last 13 weeks of her AML is unpaid (at least at present) she might decide to take the last part of such unpaid leave as paid holiday.

Job on return

A woman taking only OML has a right to return to the job she was doing before her leave, but a woman taking OML and AML has a right to return to a similar job (on no less favourable terms) but not necessarily the job she left.

Some women may wish to work part-time etc. on return and mothers (and fathers) with children up to age 6 (18 if the child is disabled) will be entitled to request their employer to consider a request to work flexibly – and to have such a request considered objectively (see below).

Failure to return

If a woman fails to return on the due date, this should be carefully investigated before any action is taken. If she is sick she should be treated in exactly the same way as any other sick employee (that is asked for certification etc.). If she is not sick then the matter may need to be dealt with under the employer's disciplinary procedure.

Other aspects of the right

i)   It is possible for a woman to claim maternity pay from one employer whilst continuing to work for another (but not within 2 weeks (4 if working in a factory) of her having given birth). However, she cannot claim payment from any work for the same employer whilst claiming SMP.

ii) If a woman leaves employment (irrespective of reason) after her qualifying week (15 weeks before her EWC) she is still entitled to be paid her SMP.

iii) If the woman becomes pregnant during her additional leave she is entitled to a further 26 weeks ordinary leave but NOT any additional leave (because she had not returned to work after the first birth). If she has returned to work and then finds she is pregnant then the whole process is repeated.

iv) Provided an employee has the required service (and has earned at the required rate) she is entitled to these rights irrespective of hours worked, casual status etc.

Case studies: Unwitting discrimination

In *Visa International Service Assn v Paul* it was held that it was discriminatory for an employer not to inform a woman of a job opportunity whilst she was on maternity leave – even though she would have probably been unsuitable for the job.

Failing to allow a pregnant woman to attend a training course for which she had been selected previously and which could have led to her promotion was held to be discrimination in *Ministry of Defence v Williams*.

Director on maternity leave

The number of female Directors is increasing – too slowly – but the trend is in the right direction. (It was recorded recently that only 10.5% of directors of the FTSE 100 companies were women and 22 such companies had no female director at all.) Inevitably some will become pregnant and the rights set out above apply to them as much as any other woman. However, there is an added dimension as far as those with directorships are concerned.

As we have seen in earlier chapters, Directors retain a duty of care whether or not they attend Board meetings at which decisions are taken. Thus the 'sleeping directors' in the Dorchester case (see Chapter 1) were held personally liable because they had not exercised their duty of care.

The current levels of maternity leave mean that a new mother could be away from work for up to a year. Female Directors wishing to take such leave should consider their position carefully vis-a-vis this duty.

Although she could (and should) insist on being sent all the papers given to the Board during her absence, it may be impossible for her to attend Board meetings and thus be party to discussions and decisions etc, although she could be held jointly responsible for such collective decisions. One solution might be (subject to there being authority under the Company's Articles) for her to appoint an alternate Director who could attend Board meetings in her place and report back to her.

Alternatively, it would seem the only other (perhaps somewhat drastic) option would be for the Director to resign for the period of her leave. If a combined service/employment contract has been used to evidence the twin relationship (i.e. officer and employee) that executive Directors have with the company, it may be that a clause could be incorporated allowing a Director in such circumstances to 'resign' her directorship for the period of leave whilst preserving her employment status. This should avoid the 'resignation' being taken as being final and absolute.

NOTE: Since April 2007, during her maternity leave, a woman has been allowed to work for (and be paid by) her employer for up 10 'in touch' days, which might cover the above point.

Risk assessment

Under the Management of Health and Safety at Work (Amendment) Regulations 1994 employers are required in anticipation of a woman of child-bearing age entering their employ to carry out a pregnancy risk assessment.

Case study

In *Day v T. Pickles Farms Ltd* the EAT stated that if an employer fails to assess the risks to a pregnant woman in the workplace (or even fails to carry out such an assessment in the anticipation of a woman of child bearing age entering their employ) this amounts to a detriment within the meaning of the Sex Discrimination Act 1975 and thus the employer could become liable for discrimination penalties.

The risk assessment process (which covers those who have recently given birth and are breastfeeding as well as pregnant women) requires employers:

a) to assess all risks to which such employees might be exposed

b) to ensure they are not exposed to those risks, and

c) if a risk remains despite preventative and other actions, terms of work (hours, place, etc.), to offer such employees alternative work or grant them paid leave if this is not available.

Detailed guidance can be found in the Health & Safety Executive's guidance booklet 'New and Expectant Mothers at Work: A Guide for Employers' ('New mothers' are defined as women who have given birth within the last 6 months.)

The HSE identify 5 general risks that there are to pregnant women in the workplace but these should be taken as guidance only since each risk assessment of each workplace will inevitably be different. In addition each employer should identify the particular risks related to their own operation

1. Working with unhealthy substances

Perhaps the most widely encountered substance with which a pregnant woman and new mother might come into contact is lead. Any use of lead should be identified and women of child bearing age prohibited form working anywhere near its use or handling products which have been in contact with lead. (Similar restrictions apply to a range of other substances – e.g. radio-active material.)

(NOTE: Under the Control of Asbestos at Work Regulations, those who occupy buildings as well as those who own them have an obligation to identify, record, monitor and assess the risks from asbestos in their building.)

2. Violent or stressful environments

What some people find acceptable, other may find stressful – e.g. some people can stand loud music, others cannot. The environments within which people work should be assessed and those working in areas felt to be potentially stressful should be specially advised and if and when a woman states she is pregnant she should be asked if she wishes to transfer elsewhere.

The situation of a pregnant or new mother working within an environment which is 'rough' or 'tough' or in any way violent, needs to be assessed very carefully with specific guidance depending on individual problems and risks.

3. Lifting

Employees are generally prohibited from lifting loads heavier than around 55lbs without manual or mechanical assistance. However applying this weight restriction could be unwise for many pregnant women and a more realistic maximum load is perhaps 4 kilos or 10lb. The volume of a package is also important since a light weight but bulky object might pose considerably greater danger than a small but heavier item.

4. Confined working space

The simple increase in body size due to pregnancy, can create problems of its own if the working environment is at all confined or small, or there is a restricted access etc. Such items should be identified. If it is impossible to change them, the possibility of the woman working elsewhere should be considered.

5. Using an unsuitable workstation

Where the woman is using a visual display unit, the ergonomic arrangement of such equipment may often leave much to be desired. Whilst this may be acceptable in the ordinary course, there may be specific dangers to a pregnant woman whose condition requires attention to posture etc. Those using VDUs should have:

*   a comfortable, adjustable chair with good back support

*   a desk surface which allows them to position the VDU at least 10 inches from their head and provides sufficient space for other working papers

*   a monitor which is not situated so that it creates a reflection or glare, and generates minimal radiation

*   the capacity to keep the screen clean and be able to adjust brightness and contrast to create a good working light

- the right to take regular rests (not necessarily from work but from the VDU work) and to allow the eyes to refocus on a more distant subject than the VDU screen

- a working environment so that their wrists are parallel with the keyboard, 'float above it', and can rest on a support regularly

- a raked footstool to remove strain from the back. Thighs should be parallel with the floor.

- a position where they face any window (or else natural light should be capable of being filtered with blinds or curtains).

Procedure

1. Accompanied by a pregnant woman (or a woman who has given birth) tour the whole area where a pregnant woman/new mother might work – identify all risks.

2. Consider whether any risks can be removed or minimised – and, if so, implement changes to effect this.

3. List risks which cannot be removed and/or minimised on a written risk assessment.

4. Immediately a woman indicates she is pregnant, give her a copy of the risk assessment (possibly walking round and identifying the risks with her).

5. Invite the woman to advise the employer if she notes any additional risks so that the risk assessment can be updated.

6. Regularly review and update the risk assessment.

Action

If there are serious risks, during the time she continues working, a pregnant woman has a right:

a) to have the risks removed from her normal place of work. If this is impossible then she can

b) carry out her work elsewhere where there are no risks. If this is impossible then she can be asked

c) to work on other tasks (without any detriment regarding salient features of her contract – hours, pay, benefits etc.). If there is no work she can undertake she has the right

d) to be suspended on full pay until such time as her maternity leave commences.

Case study

In *Hardman v Mallon (t/a) Orchard Lodge Nursing Home*, Mrs Hardman was a care assistant – a job which required a certain amount of patient lifting or supporting. When she became pregnant and informed her employer of that fact, she attended a meeting which discussed the need for a risk assessment although one was not carried out. Her employer's only action was to offer her alternative work as a cleaner. She refused and obtained certification that she should refrain from heavy lifting. Another meeting ensued where the employer again offered the cleaning job – which she again refused. She complained of sex discrimination and the EAT found that because:

- she had suffered less favourable treatment the cause of which was her pregnancy

- the employer had breached the law by not conducting a risk assessment as set out in *Day v T Pickles Farms Ltd* which was a detriment on her, Mrs Hardman had suffered sex discrimination (for which of course there is no upper limit on compensation).

Paternity

Fathers (meaning those who have responsibility for a child) are entitled to Statutory Paternity Pay and leave. To claim Paternity pay and leave, a man has to have worked for his employer for 40 weeks by the EWC and to have earned at the rate of at least the Lower Earnings Level (LEL).

Payment and leave

Statutory Paternity Pay is paid at the rate of 90% of the fathers average earnings for the 8 weeks ending at the 15th week before the mother's EWC or the annually reviewed rate of SPP whichever is LESS.

Statutory Paternity Leave lasts one or two weeks and must be taken within 8 weeks of the birth. For a multiple birth the father is only entitled to one term of leave and payment.

Proof of entitlement

An employer has NO right to ask for proof that the baby is expected or has been born. However before there can be any payment, a father needs to complete and sign a Declaration (SC3 available from the Inland Revenue) which includes:

i) the expected date of birth;

ii) the date he wishes the leave and pay to start;

iii) that he is in an enduring family relationship with the mother; and/or

iv) that he will be responsible for the child's/children's upbringing; and

v) that he will be taking the leave to support the mother/care for the child

The form requires the father's national insurance number.

Other employment

Other than the fact that the father is required to declare that he is taking leave to support the mother/child, there does not seem to be anything to prevent him from working for another employer – though he cannot work for the employer who is paying the SPP.

Recovery

92% of the Statutory Paternity payments are recoverable by 'large' employers by deduction from their NI contributions. 'Small' employers can reclaim the whole amount plus a 4.5% 'admin' charge. If a small employer would find it difficult to fund the SPP they can apply for an advance. (This concession is expected to be phased out by 2008.)

NOTE: The Work and Families Act 2006 stipulates that paternity leave is to rise to 27 or 28 weeks, i.e. an additional 26 weeks on top of the existing amount. This change is not due to be implemented before April 2009. It is proposed that this additional paternity leave would be allowed where their partner has returned to work and has not used the whole of her maternity leave.

Assuming in April 2009 the current 39 weeks paid maternity leave is extended to 52 weeks (which is the Government's intention), if a woman wished to return to work at the 39th week, she would have 13 weeks which she could transfer to her partner. The problem is that (other than those instances where both partners work for the same employer) two disrelated employers are involved. It is proposed (to avoid a cumbersome exchange of information between the employers of the parents) that the parents self-certify (i.e. that both mother and father certify to the father's employer).

Obviously this lends itself to fraud. The Government is saying that provided an employer has 'carried out checks on an employee's entitlement' any losses as a result of a fraudulent claim being made will be borne by the State – not by individual employers. Employers would need to complete a standard checklist which must be kept for at least 3 years. Obviously employers will have an additional administrative obligation. These proposals were subject to consultation which had not been completed as this edition was being published.

Adoptive parents

Couples who adopt are entitled to adoption leave and adoption pay. An adoption takes effect on a date notified by a registered Adoption Agency and is confirmed on a 'Matching Certificate' (MC).

The week that adoption takes place is called the 'Matching Week' (MW). Adoptive parents are termed either 'main' parent or 'other' parent (both can be of either sex). Ordinary adoption leave (OAL) is the first 26 weeks leave. Additional adoption leave (AAL) is a second period of 26 weeks leave.

Procedure

Adopting employees need to have worked for their employer for 26 weeks by the end of the Matching Week to qualify for these rights. The main parent must give their employer 28 days notice of the date on which (s)he wishes his/her adoption leave to commence – and this must be within 7 days of the issue of the MC.

The other parent must give their employer 15 weeks notice of their wish to take their leave entitlement which is the equivalent of Statutory Paternity Leave (SPL). The other parent will usually (but need not) be the 'father' who must sign a Declaration (SC4 available from the Inland Revenue) which includes:

i)   the expected date of adoption;

ii) the date (s)he wishes the adoption leave and pay to start;

iii) that (s)he is in an enduring family relationship with the main parent; and/or

iv) that (s)he will be responsible for the child's upbringing; and

v) that (s) he will be taking the leave to care for the child.

The form requires the claimant's national insurance number. Only those who have earnings over an 8 week average that at least match the LEL will be entitled to pay during the leave. Neither parent must be in prison. Adoptive leave is available only on a single basis – if two or more children are adopted, only one set of leaves/pay is available for each parent.

Leave and pay

The 'main' parent is entitled to both OAL and AAL – making a total absence of 52 weeks. If (s)he wishes to return before the end of either leave, 28 days notice must be given. The 'other' parent is entitled to up to 2 weeks leave (which must be taken either as a one or two week period and must be taken within 56 days of the adoption).

Payment is available to both parents:

- For the main parent the pay mirrors that for new mothers except that the first 6 weeks is at the normal rate of SMP (not the 90% of pay unlimited)

- For the other parent, the pay mirrors paternity pay.

Return and recovery

Once the main parent has notified their Matching Week, the employer must confirm the date of leave and the date of return.

92% of adoptive leave payments (AP) are recoverable by 'large' employers by deduction from their NI contributions.

'Small' employers can reclaim the whole amount plus a 4.5% 'admin' charge. If a small employer would find it difficult to fund the AP they can apply for an advance. (This concession is expected to be phased out by 2008.) Presumably since the leave/pay rights parallel those of maternity and paternity, these will be increased in line with those extensions.

Parental leave

Subject to an employee having one year's service this entitlement applies to all employee parents of able-bodied children. They each have the right to 13 weeks unpaid leave until the child's 5th birthday. A maximum of 4 weeks can be taken in any one year. Even if only a day is required the employer can insist a week is taken.

Those who adopt have the right to 13 weeks unpaid leave for 5 years from adoption or an adopted child's 18th birthday (whichever occurs sooner). A maximum of 4 weeks can be taken in any one year. Even if only a day is required the employer can insist a week is taken..

Parents of a child who has a disability, have the right to 18 weeks unpaid leave until the child's 18th birthday. A maximum of 4 weeks can be taken in any one year, with sole days being counted singly.

Procedure

Those wishing to take the leave must give at least 3 weeks notice. The employer has the right to postpone the leave (for no more than 6 months) if business needs so require, but fathers who give three weeks notice of the expected week of confinement of their baby will be able to take leave immediately after the baby is born, and this leave cannot be postponed by the employer.

NOTES:

a)   Leave is per child and per parent.

b)   The Government has stated that employers do not need to keep records but this is naïve. Unless records are kept, how are employers to know how much leave has been taken (leading to disputes)? In addition, employers might want to know how much leave has already been taken whilst working for a previous employer.

Family emergency leave

Regardless of the amount of service they have, all employees are entitled to take a 'reasonable' amount of unpaid leave to deal with 'family emergencies' – that is for the following purposes:

• To help when a dependent is ill, gives birth, or is injured or assaulted.

• To arrange for an ill or injured dependent to be cared for.

- Because a dependents' care arrangements are unexpectedly changed.

- As a result of the death of a dependent.

- To deal with an incident involving a child which occurs unexpectedly in school time.

'Dependent' is defined as a spouse or cohabitee, child, parent and for the purposes of the first 3 items above anyone who relies on the employee for help or to make arrangements. For this reason this leave has been called 'the carer's leave'.

Case studies: Defining the right

In *Qua v John Ford Morrison*, an employee's son was taken ill and she took emergency leave to take him to the doctor. This scenario was repeated but this time the doctor diagnosed a recurrent problem. When it re-occurred her employer would not let her take 'emergency leave' (since she knew there was a recurring problem).

The Employment Appeal Tribunal stated:

'*Whilst we recognise that no limit has been set on the number of times when an employee can exercise this right, an employee… is not entitled to unlimited amounts of time off work… even if in each case s/he complies with notice requirements. The legislation contemplates a reasonable period of time off to enable an employee to deal with a child who has fallen ill unexpectedly. Once it is known that the particular child is suffering from an underlying medical condition which is likely to cause him to suffer regular relapses, such a situation no longer falls within the scope (of this leave). **The right is essentially a right to time off to deal with the unexpected**.*'

This leave is intended to cover emergencies in the 5 categories set out on the previous page only. Although it entitles employees to leave to make arrangements following a dependant's death it is not meant to cover 'bereavement leave'.

In *Forster v Cartwright Black Solicitors* the EAT held that the purpose of the provision (of emergency leave) was not to introduce a right to compassionate leave but to give time to make arrangements following a bereavement. Ms Forster had taken time off following the death of her mother – such time being covered by sick notes which her employer rejected (since she was not sick) and dismissed her. (Ms Forster in a period of under a year had taken 42 days leave for a variety of reasons and she was dismissed for having a poor absence record; having less than a year's service she could not claim Unfair Dismissal.)

Flexible working

Those who have a minimum of 26 weeks service with an employer and who:

- have parental responsibilities for a child up to the age of 6 (18 if the child is disabled) OR

- have caring responsibilities

have the right to lodge a formal request to work flexibly. Such requests must be in writing and must set out the hours/days etc the employee(s) would like to work. Any change is permanent. An employee can ask once a year (if their request is rejected). A 'carer' is defined as someone who is, or expects to be caring for an adult to whom they are married or with whom they have a civil partnership, or that person is a close relative or lives with the employee.

Procedure

- The employer must make a practical business assessment of the request (and its impact) – it would be best if this were in writing.

- Within 4 weeks of the request a meeting between employer and employee must be held to discuss the request and its implications. At such a meeting the employee has the right to be accompanied by a workplace colleague.

Failure to allow representation is a breach of a statutory right for which the penalty is 2 weeks pay (at a rate reviewed each February).

- Within 2 weeks of the meeting the employer must write to the employee setting out, either:

  i) any required action on which the decision to agree the flexibility is to be based and setting a date for commencement. (This date is suggested should be at least two months later to allow arrangements to be set up.), OR

ii) any compromise offer (which should include a date by which a response is expected), OR

iii) a rejection of the request giving explanations of the business reasons for such decision AND setting out the appeal procedure.

- Suggested business reasons for rejecting the request could include:
  - The burden of costs on the employer
  - Problems meeting customer demand
  - An inability to reorganise the work
  - Problems meeting quality levels required
  - Problems meeting performance output
  - Any inability to find other employees to cover the hours not now to be worked
  - Other reasons specific to the employer.

- Employees can appeal an adverse decision (using the Appeals procedure outlined in the Employment Act 2002).

- If (and only if) all internal procedures have been used, employees have the right of access to an Employment Tribunal which can award up to 8 weeks pay (at a rate reviewed each February). A Tribunal will have to examine the procedural aspects of the case (referring it back to the employer if these are faulty) or facts claimed have been found to be incorrect.

Case study: Cost is no defence

One of the legitimate reasons set out above for an employer rejecting a request to work flexibly is that they will incur 'additional cost'. However, in both *Steinicke v Bundesanstalt fur Arbeit* and *Kutz-Bauer v Freie und Hansestadt Hamburg*, the European Court of Justice held that the fact that part-time working might increase an employer's costs could not justify discrimination against such workers.

NOTE: The right under this legislation is merely to have a request to work flexibly considered objectively. However a refusal to consider part time working for a female employee with parental responsibility could be held to be discriminating on a sexual basis.

At the very least a trial period should be allowed.

Case study

In *Dillon v Rentokil Initial UK Ltd*, on returning from maternity leave, Ms Dillon proposed a trial period working her normal hours when her husband was at home (looking after the baby) and shorter hours when he was working (although on these days she could make herself available for assistance at the end of a telephone line at home).

Her proposal was rejected out of hand by her employer who stated that she either worked her normal hours or none. Dillon resigned and successfully claimed unfair constructive dismissal and sex discrimination. The tribunal stated that any reasonable employer would have allowed her to work the proposals on a trial period.

'The writing on the wall'

In Spring 2007 the Government floated the concept of all employees being able to make such a request. Given that research indicates a growing backlash from employees who do not fit into the above categories since they would like the same right to request flexible hours, it is quite possible that this right could well be a matter for parliamentary consideration – or possibly something forming part of a manifesto at the next Election.

An earlier DTI survey disclosed that 80% of employees want more time with their family and friends and that more flexible work practices would allow people to take up interests such as sport and learning a foreign language. Presumably flexibility in this context meant a re-arrangement rather than a reduction of hours, so that income was maintained. This could be compared to the Chartered Institute of Personnel and Development's survey which contained the important statistic that 47% of those asked stated that staff not entitled to make the request for flexible hours 'resent those who are'. This could well be storing up trouble in the future. Almost certainly the right to request flexible hours will some time in the future (because of the pressure of society) be extended to all employees.

(In running seminars throughout the UK, I ask delegates to choose between an extra £1,000 salary, a company car or the ability to choose their own hours of work – invariably over 80% [often 100%] choose flexible hours and I refer to this as 'the writing on the wall' – i.e. being indicative of a preference likely to be favoured by an increasing number of employees. The organisation that wishes to attract and retain the 'best' employees will need to offer an attractive package, and these days flexible hours seem to be more attractive to many employees than is extra cash.)

A 'PAPP' proposal?

Creating a working situation that will allow flexibility is perhaps the greatest current challenge for employers. Whereas in the 1970s and 1980s the preference of most employees was for increased pay rather than anything else, the DTI survey referred to above, as well as more recent research in 2005 and 2006, indicates that many employees would prefer to have more time off rather than more money.

At the other end of the average workforce are those who until recently would have been forcibly retired at 60 or 65 but who will increasingly have rights to work on (or be forced to do so by economic pressures). It is highly likely that as these employees age, they will be more likely to prefer to work other than full time.

It is not impossible to imagine a situation where a larger and enlightened employer could introduce what I call a *Parents And Pensioners Preference scheme* so that older employees working part time could cover the working hours that those with parental responsibilities wish to give up.

Like them or hate them, both the 'family friendly' regime and working older employees are here to stay. Marrying their preferences may well be the way forward for the creative employer embracing the flexibility preference.

Public duties

Employees have the right to take reasonable time off to undertake public duties. Such duties include serving as a magistrate (justice of the peace) or tribunal member, for military leave, as a local councillor, governor of a state school, or member of various public authorities, and jury service. With jury service, it would be contempt of court if the employer did not allow the employee the amount of time off as set out in the paperwork calling the employee to attend court for this purpose. In other instances the operative word is 'reasonable' which is open to some degree of interpretation.

Where an employee wishes to serve as a magistrate the right is specifically granted under legislation, namely the Employment Rights Act 1996. That Act sets out the reasonableness test but also requires employers to take into account any leave already given for Trade Union activities, and the effect on the employer's business of the employee taking the amount of leave they wish.

Case study: Policy could provide defence

In *Riley-Williams v Argos Ltd*, Ms Riley-Williams worked in an administrative position which could only be covered by one other person. She was appointed a magistrate and applied for 13 days (unpaid) leave for her duties as a magistrate (there is a requirement from the Lord Chancellor's dept that magistrates should sit for a minimum of 26 half days each year).

Argos had no public leave policy and instead used its 'compassionate leave' policy as a criteria. Under this policy an employee could have 5 days unpaid leave for compassionate purposes. Argos stated they would allow her a similar amount of unpaid leave and the other 8 days she would need to take as part of her holiday entitlement (which would of course be paid).

Ms Riley-Williams felt this was unacceptable and resigned claiming unfair constructive dismissal. At the Employment Tribunal her claim failed as the ET found that it was not unreasonable for the employer to require her to take 8 days of the commitment as holiday.

She appealed to the Employment Appeal Tribunal who amongst other comments stated that the ET should have taken into account (as the statute requires) whether she was also taking time off for Trade Union activities. Since they did not, but accepted the employer's referral to the amount of 'compassionate leave' (which is not something required to be taken into account under the statute), the decision that it was not an unfair decision was overturned. The matter was referred to a different tribunal to re-hear the whole case.

However, some of the comments made by the EAT regarding the calculation of a reasonable amount of time off are pertinent:

a) Some employers pay for such leave.

b) Some employers allow the whole of such leave either as paid, unpaid or as a combination of the two.

c) The *'absence of any policy by [Argos] to deal with applications for time off under the statute [for this purpose] has caused this litigation to be conducted. We would urge employers … to put in place policies for time off for public duties.'*

NOTE: The Lord Chancellor has announced that he is to advise the Government to introduce legislation clarifying employers' obligations regarding granting time off to their employees to serve as Justices of the Peace.

Example: Public duties policy

1. This organisation supports those employees who wish to undertake public duties

2. Reasonable amounts of time off will be allowed to undertake such duties

3. In calculating what is a reasonable amount the needs of the business must be taken into account particularly whether the duties undertaken by the person requesting the leave can be undertaken by at least one other person whilst the public duties are undertaken and whether the person is already taking leave for other such purposes

4. In order to support persons undertaking such duties the organisation will make payment for [50% of the time taken] and expect the remainder to be taken either as unpaid leave of absence or as paid holiday from the employees' annual entitlement.

5. Alternatively, if the person taking public leave wishes credit could be given for additional hours worked at other times which could be regarded as 'paying' for any unpaid amount of time off.

6. Application for public duty leave should be made to [specify name] who will review the position in the light of the forgoing and decide whether there are any extenuating circumstances that might justify additional unpaid leave.

7. If a person is unhappy with the decision they have the right to exercise a right of appeal using the Grievance procedure.

NOTE: The 50% contribution in clause 4 is included purely for example.

Avoiding age discrimination

Anti-ageism discrimination came into effect in the UK in October 2006. Unlike other anti-discrimination legislation this affects every employer and every employee and its implications are far-ranging as the following checklist seeks to demonstrate. Directors must manage the practical effects of these new requirements to avoid expensive compensation payments.

Checklist: Potential areas for discrimination on an age basis

a) Recruitment

Only where the demands of the job can objectively justify stipulating ages (e.g. 'young' actors to play Romeo and Juliet; an 'older' actor to play King Lear etc.,) will it be acceptable to specify age limits. Otherwise any reference to age, or using words that give an impression of age, will almost certainly be a breach of the legislation.

Traditionally, copy for advertisements has included phrases such as 'young and dynamic', 'energetic', 'graduate', 'needs youthful outlook', 'mature', 'wanted to join a young (or, perhaps less likely, older) team', 'vigorous/vibrant', 'young at heart' etc. But these must no longer be used. Even the fact that an environment is perceived to be 'youthful' (e.g. IT, pop records, fashion orientated, etc) must not be used to 'justify' trying to exclude 'older' applicants.

Phrases and descriptions that are 'age-neutral' should be used or subjective descriptions should be avoided and the description should concentrate on the essentials of the job and the challenge. Age-neutral phrases could include, for example, 'able to deal with pressure', 'self-starter', 'educated to tertiary level', 'experience of [detail] for at least X years' (provided that level of experience can be shown objectively to be required), and so on.

Action required: Review wording of all job adverts., and instructions to agencies, headhunters etc. Remove any words that indicate or could be perceived to be age-related. Stipulating a level of fitness for a sedentary job could also be held to be discriminatory since it is likely that it would exclude older applicants.

b) Person descriptions (PDs) and/or Job descriptions (JDs)

Very often PDs (which often form the basis for job advertisements) actually generate the language and phrases such as those referred to above which are likely to be in breach of the legislation. By their nature JDs should not be age specific (other than reflecting any legal requirements) and thus may be less likely to require alteration.

Action required: All wording should be reviewed ensuring that it is, unless the reverse can be objectively justified, in accordance with the new requirements.

c) Appointment – Contract terms / Handbook content

Terms may also be used in both contracts and handbooks which are age discriminatory. Any benefit, or disbenefit, which is linked to the attainment or non-attainment of a particular age should be checked and if necessary revised to become age-neutral. However benefits related to (for example) years of service (i.e. loyalty related benefits) may not offend this legislation unless they are manifestly unfair, because only those of a particular age could qualify.

Action required: Review all wording ensuring that it is, unless the reverse can be objectively justified, in accordance with the new requirements.

d) Appraisal, training and promotion

When completing 'appraisal' or 'performance review' documentation, managers should be trained to ensure they avoid any reference to age or phrases that generate the concept of a required, preferred or 'not preferred' age. It should be acceptable to state:'I think you need x months training' whereas 'we won't be able to promote you until you are 25' is almost certainly discriminatory. If Appraisal is linked to Training no age limits should be applied to either aspect (unless legally stipulated or objectively justified).

Almost inevitably when considering training personnel, the question of how long a person is likely to remain with the organisation – and thus for how long they will benefit from the training and the sponsoring organisation will obtain a return on its investment – is likely to be raised. Older employees have widely and traditionally suffered from this attitude, not least since it is understood 'they will be retiring soon'. Apart from the fact that this comment is, under the new rules, discriminatory, the argument may soon become unreliable as more and more people wish (and/or may be forced due to financial pressures) to work past their 'normal' retirement date.

The test for promotion should be reduced to the simple assessment 'is this person – with the skill and experience they have – appropriate to perform the collection of duties which together comprise this job'. In this regard it might be acceptable to stipulate that, say, '3 years experience' was essential before a person could be considered provided this was an objective requirement. Moving to a variable retirement age (see below) the challenge of succession planning becomes more acute. No assumptions should be made either in discussion or, even more importantly, in written format that anyone will retire on a set date.

Action required: Train all involved in appraising and assessing employees with a view to promoting them to ensure 'age' or age related considerations play no part. Check that, irrespective of age, all those who should have been considered have been considered. The wording of any training plan and the procedure for implementation should be checked to ensure that there is (particularly) no 'upper cut off' for training.

e) Benefits

Whilst additional benefits will usually be able to be given where these are related to 'length of service' (e.g. an extra day's holiday) anything which relates the benefit to the age of the employee (e.g. insurance) must not be discontinued simply because of advancing age. Where an employee wishes and has been allowed to work past a stipulated retirement age, employment benefits must be maintained since obviously removing or reducing such benefits would disadvantage an older person and could be discriminatory.

Action required*: Revise any policy or procedure which cuts across these requirements. All documentation may need to be checked.*

f) Bullying, victimisation and harassment

Whilst employers should have become used to ensuring that such practices do not occur based on sex, race and disability, and, more recently, religion, religious belief and sexual orientation, they now have to appreciate that such practices could be occurring on an age basis. Words and phrases such as 'grey haired', 'wrinklies', 'long in the tooth', 'grand-dad', 'you coasting to the pension, then?', 'baby-faced', 'young 'un', 'immature', 'why aren't you retired' etc., are all arguably age discriminatory. Unfortunately it is very likely where employees continue working past their traditional retirement ages thereby occupying jobs that could have facilitated promotion of younger personnel that there could be a backlash from those employees.

Action required*: Review Equal Opportunities or Dignity at Work policy taking account of the above, and re-issue it (preferably through face to face coaching sessions) to all employees emphasizing the need to avoid 'age-related' comments, to be positive about older workers working past traditional retirement dates, and not to patronise younger employees.*

g) Working environment

Increasingly employers will have to plan for the implications of people working longer than has been customary. Not only will this impact on promotion prospects for younger employees, but also ultimately there could be a number of instances where an employee wishes to work past the time when their employer thinks they are ceasing to perform adequately. This could result in capability investigation/disputes. Since these could involve longer service employees this could be particularly unfortunate.

Action required*: Ensure there is a capability procedure and that this is geared to dealing with these particular problems.*

The challenge of retirement – post October 2006

This is possibly the area likely to cause directors the greatest challenge since it can no longer be assumed that an employee will retire at a set date. Indeed why should it? There are some employees perfectly capable of performing well past the traditional (and discriminatory!) State pensionable date for the sexes.

Other than where objective criteria (e.g. safety considerations) require it, realistically there is no need in most situations for there to be a fixed retirement age. Indeed there could be positive benefits in abandoning a fixed retirement age and encouraging employees to work longer – until they no longer wish to work - or the employer feels they are no longer capable of performing the requirements of the job.

Many people facing retirement may wish to continue working (for companionship, a sense of fulfilment, to offset financial pressures, etc) but not necessarily on a full time basis. Allowing such personnel to continue working (on a part time basis) could help create a reservoir of skills and experience available to cover the hours no longer being worked by those using 'family friendly' initiatives (i.e. those wanting to work flexibly whilst they are responsible for young children), as well as retaining a reservoir of experience.

Providing an employer adheres to the procedure, forcing an employee to retire at 65 should be a fair dismissal. Breaching the procedure renders a potentially fair reason for dismissal automatically unfair (and thus subject to the compensation payments).

Requiring an employer to retire at a lower age than 65 may be unfair unless the lower age can be objectively justified.

Suggested procedure

1. Identify the birthdays of all employees attaining 65 on a rolling 12 month forecast basis. (Note: For ALL recruits post 1st May 2004, since the employer must require evidence of their right to work in the UK, the employer should have access to these dates as the date of birth is shown on such items of evidence.)

2. Not more than 12 months and not less than 6 months before the 65th birthday, the employee must be given a dated notice stating that the employer wishes them to retire when they become 65. The note must also state that the employee has the right to request that

they be allowed to work past that date but that any such request must be made not earlier than 6 months – and not later than 3 months – before their 65th birthday. It would be best if the service of this notice was witnessed so that the employee cannot later state that they were not given it.

(If the employer misses the 6 month prior to the 65th birthday deadline but still wishes the employee to retire, it may be wise to give the full 6 months notice and then follow the rest of the procedure, i.e. not terminating the employee until the end of the 6 month period. This could still create unfair dismissal but such actions might reduce some liability. Failing to give the required notice generates a potential penalty at tribunal of up to 8 weeks pay to the annually reviewed weekly maximum.)

. . . .

TO (EMPLOYEE)   [Date]

As you are aware you attain the age of 65 on [date at least 6 months ahead of date above] and we wish you to retire on that date.

You have the right to request that you be allowed to work beyond this date and if you do you must let us know not later than [date at least 3 months prior to 65th birthday].

We will then set up a meeting to discuss the matter. You have the right to be accompanied at such a meeting by a workplace colleague.

After the meeting we will consider what you had to say and give you a decision within a reasonable time.

If the decision is that we still wish you to retire you have the right of appeal against that decision.

This form is provided in duplicate – please sign and return one copy.

. . . .

3. It may be prudent (and avoid later dispute) if the employer actually gives employees forms allowing them to apply 'to work on'. The regulations state that such a request must refer to the legal authority. Very few employees (unless advised) are likely to know this and, unless and until, the Courts can, if they wish, dilute this rather absurd requirement (breach of which could invalidate the request) a set

format may be best used. (It may, in any event, be unwise for an employer to dismiss a request which is not strictly in accordance with the law.)

. . . .

Dear

[Date] *(being not more than 6 nor less than 3 months prior to 65th birthday)*

I acknowledge receipt of your request that I retire on [date] being my 65th birthday. I hereby give notice in accordance with paragraph 5 of Schedule 6 of the Employment Equality (Age) Regulations 2006, that I do not wish to retire on [65th birthday] but would prefer to extend my employment to

EITHER [a stated date] OR [indefinitely]

Please arrange a meeting at which we can discuss my request.

Yours etc.

. . . .

4. It the employer wishes to resist the request a meeting must be set up a 'reasonable time' later. The employee has the right to be accompanied by a workplace colleague at the meeting. The employer should listen to the request and then within a reasonable time give a decision – in writing and dated. Witnessing the delivery of the decision may be advisable.

5. If the employer agrees the request (or possibly a compromise) then any extension should be set out in the note. If the employer does NOT agree (and no reason has to be given) then the note should state that the original date stands, BUT that the employee has a right of appeal. (This actually gives the employee a problem since if no reason is given, it is difficult to base the appeal on anything other than 'could you think again').

6. If the employee appeals, the same rules as for the original meeting apply. A decision must be given within a reasonable time. It would be prudent not to enforce retirement until the appeal process is exhausted.

A final thought

The existing ages for drawing State Pension (60 and 65) were set many years ago. During the period since 1940, age expectancy in most parts of the UK has increased by 2 years per decade. Thus, in the six decades since 1948 age expectancy has increased by 12 years. Logically if 60/65 were appropriate ages then, 72/77 would be appropriate in 2008.

The Government has recently announced that the school leaving age is to be increased to 18. The 'legal age at which retirement can be enforced' (now 65) is to be reviewed in 3 years time and will most certainly be increased to 68 (possibly even 70).

It is not impossible to forsee (say by 2020) a normal working life lasting from 18 to 80 with perhaps a greater use of part-time contracts – and even a situation where a person might work for a number of employers on such a basis. This would pose challenges for both employees and employers. A flexible approach will be essential – as will a readiness to invest in training and retraining.

Summary checklist

- Ensure guidelines regarding recruitment attempt to find the most appropriate applicants for vacancies.

- Encompass the result of a growing preference for employees to work hours more suitable to their lifestyle.

- Ensure latest rules regarding employee-parents rights are known and applied.

- Detail amount and dates of all leaves (paid and unpaid) in case of later dissent regarding amount taken.

- Deal positively with the growing demand for flexible hours.

- Provide guidelines regarding the amount of time allowed for public duties.

- Be pro-active in seeking compliance with anti age discrimination legislation.

Chapter seventeen

'Comparability and consultation'

Comparability

Part-time employees

Fixed term contract personnel

Temporary personnel

Homeworking

Transferring employees

Consultability

Retention ability

Summary checklist

Comparability

The 'comparability principle' requires employers in four areas (see below) to ensure that a person working under non-standard arrangements and performing tasks that are broadly similar or comparable to full-time, permanent etc. employees is provided with the same benefits and rights as such comparable employees. However, if there are no comparable personnel then the pay and benefits can be individually tailored and the comparability principle can be ignored.

Part-time employees

Under The Part Time Employees (Prevention of less favourable treatment) Regulations 2000 it is illegal for employers to apply less favourable treatment to those whose only difference from their colleagues is that they work fewer than full-time hours (a figure which will vary according to individual employers).

Part-time employees (including homeworkers) should (for example) be advised of vacancies (as are full-time employees) and to receive similar benefits to their full-time colleagues (doing similar work) – e.g. training, mentoring, long service awards.

It is customary for overtime to be paid at a premium rate although this may be restricted to time in excess of a minimum over and above the contract hours. For example, if the normal full-time hours are 35 hours a week, an overtime clause for a full timer might state that although payment will be made for all hours in excess of 35, only hours in excess of (say) 40 will be paid at (say) time plus 50%. A part-time employee will have to work the full-time hours plus (as in this example) 5 before any premium was due.

Fixed term contract personnel

Under the Fixed Term Employees (prevention of less favourable treatment) Regulations (unless any differences can be objectively justified) those working on a fixed term basis:

a) generally must not be treated less favourably than a permanent employee doing comparable work (thus must, for example, be given similar occupational holidays, sickness benefits etc.)

b) must be advised of permanent vacancies in case they wish to apply to transfer to permanent status

c) have a right to receive an explanatory statement if they believe they have been subjected to less favourable treatment

d) are protected from sanction if they try to enforce the rights given them by the Regulations

e) have the right to convert to permanent employment once they have worked under a fixed term contract(s) for 4 years

f) cannot waive their redundancy rights even if such a clause is inserted in their contract(s).

WARNING: Bringing a fixed term contract to an end is subject to the new 'reasonable notice of a disciplinary hearing' requirement. A note such as the following might be used:

. . . .

TERMINATION FORM   [Date]

To [fixed term employee]

As you are aware your fixed term contract of [period] expires on [date]. We would like to discuss the expiry of your contract on [date, time, place]. Please attend this meeting at which you may (if you wish) be accompanied by another colleague or Union representative. If the termination date is confirmed you will have the right to appeal to [name] within [e.g. 5] working days.

Please sign, date and return the attached copy of this note.

(At such a meeting the possibility of alternative work might be discussed but if this is not available this too could usefully be stated.)

. . . .

Temporary personnel

Great care needs to be taken not to unwittingly create an employment relationship with a person, for example, supplied by an employment agency.

At no time should the client organisation ever discipline the 'temp'. This should be left to the Agency. Applying discipline means exercising control over a person which could create an employment relationship even though none is wanted.

In several cases the point has been made that the test is one of 'mutuality' – i.e. is there an obligation on the part of the worker to perform work for the client and for the client to give work to the worker. If there is, then mutuality is present and probably the worker is an employee. If not, then there is almost certainly no employment relationship.

Case study

In *James v Greenwich Council*, the EAT stated that what needed to be reviewed where a person was supplied by an Agency to a Client was:

- whether there was an implied contract of employment with the user (for example if the client insisted on the agency supplying a particular person this could create such a contract),

- where there is a routine agency:client contract it is rare there will be evidence entitling a tribunal to imply an employment relationship between the person and the client, and

- that mere passage of time does not justify the implication that the person was an employee of the client.

NOTE: The EU had proposed that those working on certain 'non-standard' contracts performing work which is comparable to those working on 'standard' contracts (the *COMPARABILITY* principle) to receive the same rights and benefits unless it can be objectively justified otherwise. There is a proposal that this should apply to 'temps' supplied by employment agencies if the 'temp' is retained for more than 6 weeks. Currently this proposal has been shelved as part of an abandonment of 'unnecessary' directives.'

Homeworking

The rapid advancement of 'family friendly' policies such as those set out previously has tended to provide an impetus to employers to use domestic premises for work – i.e. promoting homeworking for a variety of tasks. There are estimated to be around 3.5 million people working from home now – a number expected to double by 2010. Due to the technological revolution even some of the most senior jobs can be conducted remotely from the traditional workplace. Employers need to be ready to consider requests to work in this way, not least since there are advantages to both parties as set out below:

Advantages (and disadvantages) of homeworking

Advantages for the individual:

- avoidance of the stress and fatigue of travelling

- being fresh when starting

- avoidance of travelling costs

- flexibility to carry out domestic obligations whilst still working the required hours

- avoidance of normal workplace distractions (noise, irrelevant conversation, phone bells and conversations, other interruptions etc.)

- contribution to domestic living costs if a dedicated room is made available and 'rent' is paid.

For the employer:

- ultimately less office and/or other space (which, almost certainly, will be more expensive than domestic space)

- lower rates of pay and costs (particularly for city commuters) as no allowance needs to be made for travel costs (and even clothing, food etc.)

- lower overheads (e.g. reduced catering, car parking and other ancillary space, lower security costs, lower incidence of staff theft etc.).

Disadvantages for the individual:

- homeworking can be a somewhat lonely occupation and this aspect needs to be addressed in terms of supervision and contact

- the normal flow of information through which workplace-based employees acquire knowledge can be lacking

- the homeworker may find it less easy to gain answers to problems or assistance with difficulties being remote from supervision

- the social aspects of working are largely absent

- some workplace-based employees may have a patronising approach to those who do not share their experiences.

For the employer:

- the flexibility of working hours can pose supervision/control problems (although this can be overcome using e-mail and/or answerphone systems)

- higher communication costs (telephone, postage, e-mail etc.)

- higher propensity for mistakes to be made and for delay to occur in correcting these

- lack of feeling of being fully in control, although a requirement for strict adherence to procedures may compensate in part

- increased demand for supervision time – with consequent increase in costs.

Gaining control

The fact that the arrangement is itself flexible has tended to encourage some employers to deal with the arrangements casually and somewhat haphazardly. In fact there is a need for greater delineation of expectations and arrangements than is needed with a workplace-based employee. The following need to be addressed:

Guidance. At the workplace much of this is carried out informally through personal contact – almost without either party being aware of it. This effect is largely absent with homeworkers. There needs to be some substitute for the lack of direct supervision – e.g. regular contact arrangements, regular exchange visits to the workplace by the homeworker and to the office at the premises (the homebase) by supervision, etc., accepted measurement of work quantity and quality, and so on.

Standards of quality and output may be easy to set where (say) a number of products are generated, but where the work is administrative or creative, output may be difficult to assess.

Location extension, access etc. Despite the employee using their own home as their place of work, that location becomes an extension of the employer's place of work and needs to be treated as such. Supervisory access, control of the employee, insurance of property and liabilities, travelling arrangements to the base office etc., all need to be clarified.

Equipment funding. Normally the homeworker, where there is a dedicated room for the employer's business, will expect to receive payment for such use. The equipment they need may be provided by the employer but questions of liability, insurance, recovery etc. must be addressed.

Contractual matters. The employee is entitled to a contract of employment but, in addition, there are unique contractual arrangements regarding the homeworking which need either to amend or to sit alongside the employment contract.

Productivity

Research indicates that, properly introduced, there may be substantial benefits to be obtained from flexible working including the ability to work from home.

- Xerox (UK) estimates that it has saved over £1 million over the last 5 years through reduced labour turnover achieved via better leisure:work balance policies.

- HSBC Bank used to lose 70% of their maternity leavers before they introduced their Childcare Programme. Now in the scheme's 13th year they have an 85% retention rate. (Lloyds TSB estimate it costs around £50,000 to replace a senior female employee.)

- BT claim that flexible working arrangements reduce absenteeism by between 20% and 40% with productivity boosted by similar figures.

- The AA claim that working from home boosts productivity by up to 30%.

Boosts for homeworking

1. An allowance was included in the 2003 budget which enables employers to make a non-taxable payment of £2 per week to those working from home as a contribution to their additional household costs. The contribution is also exempt from NI. Amounts in excess of £2 per week can be paid subject to proof of the additional costs the payment is intended to cover.

2. Ms Tully (who works for the Inland Revenue) recently won a case against that employer, the dual effect of which is that:

   • no business rates will be charged against people using part of their houses to work at home, provided they do not employ people to work at the house on their business and the house does not lose its 'domestic character', and

   • capital gains tax will not be sought on any 'profit' (made on selling the house) related to the proportion used as a business.

Transferring employees

If employees are to be transferred, care should be taken to protect their positions and also to try and protect the organisation from sanctions as a result of such actions.

Where employees are wholly engaged in work which constitutes an *'organised grouping of persons and assets facilitating the exercise of an economic entity which pursues a specific objective'* and such work is transferred to another ownership, the principles of the EU Acquired Rights (AR) directive may apply. The underlying principle of the directive is that if the work (in an economic entity) is transferred then the employment rights of those undertaking such work is protected. The affected employees can either

• transfer to a job with the replacement employer on terms (which cannot be changed by reason of the transfer) which they enjoyed with the original employer, or

• resign (without compensation) although they may have a case of unfair dismissal against their original employer (see *Boor* and *Wilson* cases below).

The UK implemented the requirements of the AR directive by the Transfer of Undertakings (Protection of Employment) Regulations 1981 ('TUPE'). Not only were the UK regulations a somewhat diluted interpretation of the original directive, but also over the 24 years since TUPE was enacted there have been changes of interpretation of the meaning of the AR directive by the European Court of Justice.

The difficult practical problems associated with this principle and the changes of interpretation have led to a very unclear situation where those transferring employees away from or into their organisation can be forgiven for not appreciating their obligations. Whether there is a TUPE (and thus protected transfer) can be difficult to determine and in the *RCO Support Systems v Unison* case, the Court of Appeal stated that every factor should be taken into account – what it termed a 'multifactorial test'.

Although the ECJ in the Daddy's Dance Hall case stated that any change to an employee's contract as a result of the transfer breaches the directive, this has to some extent been offset by a more recent case. In *Boor v Ministre de la Fonction Publique et de la Reforme Administration*, (where an employee was given a lower salary when she was transferred from a private to a public employer), the ECJ stated that there was nothing to stop the new employer reducing the salary to comply with public pay scales BUT **if the reduction was material she would be able to resign and claim constructive unfair dismissal.** To some extent this has been the case in the UK for some time. In *Wilson v St Helens Borough Council* the House of Lords held that a dismissal arising from a transfer of an undertaking was effective. This would mean that the transferring employer could face a claim for unfair dismissal/redundancy.

In *Viggosdottir v Islandspostur (Iceland Post Ltd)* a manager who was transferred under the protection of the AR directive, but given a reduced salary, was made redundant. She claimed her redundancy settlement had to be calculated on the basis of her 'pre-transfer' contract which had superior terms to those she was now working under. The court said that employees can never waive rights conferred on them by the directive by agreeing changes to their contracts if the reason for the variation is the transfer itself.

In *Martin v South Bank University* the ECJ held that benefits conditional on agreement of the employer also had to be preserved and provided on the same basis by the purchaser. The employees could not waive these rights – which echoes the comments in the *Viggosdottir* case above. Thus when employees who were members of Sainsbury's share scheme under which they could take either shares or cash were transferred from Sainsbury's to an offshoot of Pitney Bowes under a TUPE transfer, the employees claimed that they should still be allocated the appropriate number of Sainsbury shares each year (which they argued their new employer should buy in the stock market). A tribunal agreed but on appeal the EAT held that this was not necessary as it gave rise to an absurd interpretation of the law but that 'they would expect an equivalent scheme to be negotiated with the employees or their representatives.'

Changes to a transferred contract can however be made where there are 'economic, technical or organisational reasons' (ETO).

The range of benefits under a TUPE transferred employees contract that must be preserved by the new employer is wide. In *Beckman v Dynamco Whicheloe Macfarlane Ltd* the ECJ held that early retirement benefits had to be preserved and thus the purchaser retained liability for these benefits. The Pensions Act 2004 provides that employees who are members of a Pension scheme and who are transferred under TUPE arrangements (unless following the insolvency of their original employer) have the right to have a certain level of pension provided by their new employer.

Where there is a TUPE transfer both employers must consult with their employees or elected representatives about the matter. If there are no elected representatives either the employer should encourage employees to elect them or there must be consultation with the individual employees.

In *Howard v Millrise Ltd (in liquidation) and anor*, the EAT held an employer had a duty, where a TUPE transfer is in prospect, no Trade Union is recognised and there are no employee representatives, to initiate an election for representatives (and then consult them) or to inform and consult individuals.

The latest revisions

The original principle (that employees working for an economic entity have the right to transfer to the new ownership of that entity on their existing terms and conditions) remains. The aims of TUPE 2006 are to:

- extend coverage of the principle to 'service provision changes'

- require the transferring employer to provide employment details of transferring employees

- clarify the situation re transfer-related dismissals and changes to terms and conditions of transferring employees

- provide greater flexibility where the transferring employer is insolvent.

A. Service provision changes: These occur when an acquiring employer brings into their organisation, work previously performed by a third party on their behalf, or where they contract such work out to a third party.

In these cases there will be a transfer if:

a) there is an economic entity (an organised grouping of employees/ resources) of a business (or part thereof) that immediately before the transfer was situated in the UK

and/or

b) there is a change to the provision of such services – i.e. a transfer in or out of the organisation.

NOTE: One-off contracts (and contracts for supply of goods) are not covered.

B. Information and consultation: The prospective new employer must be provided with full and accurate information (identity, age, contract terms, details of disciplinary and grievances in the previous two years and actual or potential legal action being brought by the employees) concerning those employees involved in the transferring entity. Both transferring and 'receiving' employers must consult with those affected.

Note: Failure to disclose information could mean the new employer could sue the other and, if successful, obtain an award of at least £500 for each transferred employee where full disclosure was not given. Failure to consult could mean either or both employers being held liable for up to 13 weeks pay per employee.

C. Transferring employees' rights. A transferred employee has a right to transfer on terms and conditions which cannot be changed as a result of the transfer, and to resign (and claim unfair constructive dismissal) if the transfer involves a substantial change in his or her working conditions to their material detriment.

An employee who does not wish to transfer is not obliged to but (assuming there was to be no material change to their working conditions) they will be deemed to have resigned.

Any employee dismissed prior to the transfer for a reason connected with it, will nevertheless transfer to the new employer.

Notes: A 'substantial change' could include a major relocation of the work.

Where a transferring employee lacks the necessary skills to perform their duties since these are to be carried out in a different way, it is suggested that the employees should be retrained or made redundant.

D. Harmonisation of terms. Inevitably there will be instances where the terms of the transferred 'in' employees are not the same as the existing employees and the employer wishes to harmonise such terms. In 1995 the Court of Appeal stated that the only 'safe' way to achieve harmonization was to undertake a wholesale reorganization involving the work of the (combined) workforce which might lead to changes of numbers, job functions etc.

Where there are 'Economic, Technical or Organisational' (ETO) changes to the workforce it may be possible to negate the transfer requirements – or make changes legitimately. Using this method is fraught with danger since if there is a challenge and the changes are not regarded as genuine ETOs, those affected could claim unfair dismissal.

E. Insolvency. Where an employer is insolvent the rights of transferring employees under these regulations can be largely negated. This relaxation is available to try to preserve employment. Prospective purchasers would otherwise be deterred from taking on employees with potentially expensive rights.

NOTE: TUPE transfers are fraught with danger – legal advice should be taken.

Consultability

American management guru Professor Chris Argyris says 'I ask managers how long it would take them to learn to play (from scratch) a moderate game of tennis. They say 'oh about two years'. Well then, how come they don't have that sort of commitment to developing people's learning?'. At no time in an employee's career is there a greater need for informal and formal communication, and a structured and comprehensive guidance to familiarising a newcomer to both the organisation and their own responsibilities than when they have just joined. The successful implementation of a familiarisation procedure – which is more dynamic and comprehensive than the old 'induction' process – is a combination of user-friendly documentation, verbal briefings and genuine interest from both departmental and personnel functions.

Recruitment is expensive, whilst labour losses tend to be highest in the first year of employment. Recently, retailer W H Smith estimated that it cost over £3,000 to recruit and train a shop assistant, whilst LloydsTSB estimated the cost of recruiting and training a junior clerk at £10,000. In launching the family friendly changes in April 2003, the DTI quoted a figure of around £3,500 for recruitment of the average employee.

Yet a recent survey by totaljobs.com indicated that:

- 10% of starters leave after a single day's work;

- a further 14% leave within the first week; and

- a further 17% leave within the first month.

If 40% of those an organisation recruits are likely to leave within a month, familiarisation/induction is vitally important.

The process of 'employer/employee and job familiarisation' can be divided into three periods:

1. An 'introduction period' covering the time from the conclusion of the final interview, the period of offer and acceptance, and up to and including arrival.

   Whilst care must be taken not to overload the appointee, if information can be given to them prior to the start date the process of assimilation can start that much earlier.

2. An 'induction period' covering the time from arrival to, say, the end of the second month of employment, when a great deal of information must be absorbed so that the recruit can actually begin to work and to work effectively.

The advantage of this period is that it ends at the time by which employers must provide new employees with a contract of employment. If an 8-week probationary period is used, all three aspects can be tied into one process.

3. An 'instruction period' covering the time from, say, the beginning of the third month to the end of the first year of employment. The aim during this time is to enable the new employee to become completely at ease in their environment, increasingly productive and to lead up to their first appraisal which may identify further training needs.

During each of the periods various items need to be explained and the recruit's comprehension checked. To ensure a reasonable degree of comprehension certain items can be duplicated at the second and third stages, with the mentor or supervisor/manager checking the employee's knowledge on these occasions. This kind of structured approach should not only ensure that nothing is missed, but also provides an opportunity for dialogue with the newcomer which can be used to check knowledge, attitude and approach.

Induction course

Recruits should also be required to attend an induction course 6/8 weeks after they join – which could be linked to the end – or approaching end – of the induction period mentioned above. Running a well-structured induction course gives the employer an opportunity to address all newcomers, each newcomer to hear questions from those facing similar challenges and problems to their own, and an opportunity to generate an informal dialogue.

Mentoring

An additional method of making it easier for a recruit to learn about the organisation and to be assimilated by it, is to set up a system of mentoring. The concept of a mentor is somewhat akin to an 'eminence gris' – a powerful guiding force which remains in the background, although it has also been described as a 'mother hen' process, and perhaps the true description lies somewhere between the two. The essential need is for someone to watch over the recruit, to be on hand to answer their questions or concerns and to guide them with both information and advice on 'the way things are done around here' on an informal basis.

Whilst the aim of the mentoring process is to assist the newcomer to settle down – and to avoid the high wastage of newcomers experienced by many employers, it is the first opportunity that the employer has to assess how well the employee copes with the new challenges, how likely it is that they will be successful in their current tasks and whether there is any likelihood of the newcomer being able to progress.

Formal consultation

Employers are required to consult an elected representatives of their workforce in a variety of situations:

- with recognised trades unions for collective bargaining

- if making employees redundant or transferring them under a Transfer of Undertakings Protection of Employment (TUPE) arrangement

- on matters affecting their safety in the workplace

- with employee representatives on the Board of Trustees of an occupational pension scheme

- to vary the legal requirements of the working time regulations regarding breaks, night working etc.

- when attempting to make reasonable adjustments to enable a person covered under the Disability Discrimination Act to work and, if eligible and required

- with elected representatives of a works council.

Under existing regulations, employers with 1,000 employees and 150 in more than one EU country must set up means by which they can consult with their employees elected representatives. Commencing 2005 the 'number of employees' threshold has been drastically reduced so that employers must set up a works council (if 10% of the employees want this to happen – and they must be told that they have this right) by April 2008 if they have 50 or more employees.

In the constitution it might be prudent to stipulate that whoever are elected to the Works Council are automatically the persons to be consulted under the requirements for redundancy, TUPE transfer, safety, pension matters and working time regulation variations.

The required subjects for discussion at Works Councils include:

a) information about the business's economic situation – the recent and foreseeable development of the business and its financial situation;

b) information and consultation about employment prospects; and

c) information and consultation about decisions likely to lead to substantial changes in work organisation, contract terms, redundancies etc.

Failure to set up an Information and Consultation forum when requested can attract a £75,000 fine.

Discipline and dismissal

Consultation is also essential when disciplining employees, and under the Employment Act 2002 there are new rules requiring greater consultation and a more transparent system when calling employees to account for breaches which could lead to dismissal. Employers who fail to abide by these rules (which override Contracts of Employment) may find they create an unfair dismissal. Before any hearing of an alleged offence which, if proven, could result in a formal warning or more severe sanction, the employee must be given a written summary of the complaint(s). A form such as the following example, may be appropriate.

g

Complaint form

To [Name] _____ Department _____

Details of alleged incident (time place etc)

[Note: this could include:

- a reference to rule being broken

- evidence that the employee was aware of the rule

- previous warnings in relation to breaches of the rule

with dates, written notes, statements whether the employee was given copies of such notes, comments made by employee etc.

- full details of the current breach]

1. The above summary outlines details of a complaint made against you. In addition, set out below are brief particulars of statements (if any) made by witnesses.

2. This information is being provided so that you may consider your position and prepare your version of the events and/or any defence to, and/or mitigation of the allegations.

3. An examination of the incident will be made on [date / time / place of hearing] by [name] who will act as hearing chairman and adjudicator. It is obviously in your interest to attend that hearing, at which you have the right to be accompanied by a representative of your choice – that is another employee or union representative.

4. At the hearing you will be able to question [the organisations] witnesses, to call your own witnesses and to present any other data relevant to the complaint.

5. If you wish to refer to documents or written data (including statements made by your witnesses) you should bring six copies of every item so that all involved can have an individual copy. Please ask [name] to provide you with copying facilities.

   Similarly, during the hearing, you will be given copies of every written item being referred to by the employer.

6. If you are found to be responsible for the alleged incident /complaint this could lead to the issue of a formal warning (and/or in serious cases to dismissal), so you should prepare your version of events carefully. You might also wish to identify any points in your

favour or in mitigation that you think should be taken into account should the hearing chairman need to consider a penalty.

Your version of the events and any points you wish to be considered may be entered in the section of the form provided for this purpose below. This will enable the adjudicator to review both versions of the events and prepare appropriate questions for both parties.

However, there is no need for you to do this if you prefer not to disclose your version of the events until the hearing itself. In that case simply sign and return the spare copy of this form to evidence the fact that you are aware of the hearing.

7. If there is anything you do not understand about this form please ask [nominated employee] for impartial and confidential advice, before signing and returning the copy.

8. [Specific rules regarding disciplinary hearings applicable to the organisation.]

9. In the event of a penalty being imposed in respect of this alleged offence, you have the right to lodge an appeal in accordance with the guidelines set out in the Grievance procedure, a further copy of which will be provided at the time.

Please return this form by _____ [date]

Signed (Manager/Supervisor) _____

Date _____

Summary of witness statements/supporting evidence

_____

_____

_____

[Employee name]:YOU ARE REQUIRED TO SIGN EITHER A OR B BELOW

AND TO RETURN THIS FORM TO _____ [NAME] BY
_____ [DATE]

A: To [the employer]

Re: incident [details]

I acknowledge receipt of a form of which this is a copy and will attend the disciplinary hearing on [date] at [time].

Employee's statement:

_____

_____

Witness statements/supporting evidence:

_____

_____

Factors to be taken into account:

_____

Signed _____ Date _____

B: To the employer

I acknowledge receipt of a form of which this is a copy and will attend the disciplinary hearing on [date] at [time].

I will/will not* require assistance taking copies.

I will/will not* require assistance obtaining witness statement(s)

Signed _____ Date _____

*Delete as applicable

NOTES:

1. The advantage of such a form is that it not only sets out the complaint (and may force reconsideration of the exact offence complained of and the rule being breached) but also the procedure so that the employee knows both what has been alleged and what (s)he has to do as a result and, perhaps more importantly, cannot claim 'I didn't know' or 'I didn't know what to do'.

2. The form should be handed to the employee personally, preferably witnessed by an independent third party.

3. Requiring the case to be set out in writing, particularly if the copy for the hearing chairman or adjudicator is given to them before the copy is given to the employee, allows time for second thoughts before the employer is committed to the course of action.

4. If a warning or other sanction is given as a result of the disciplinary hearing, this must state that there is a right of appeal. This may be best set out as:

   'If you do not agree with this decision or with the severity of the sanction you have the right of appeal to [specify]. You can use the form attached to this sheet. An appeal must be lodged with [name/position] within [5] working days. If you have any difficulty framing or lodging an appeal please refer to [name/position] for assistance.'

5. A similar procedure (written notification, hearing, appeal) is required for Grievances.

WARNINGS:

1. Since employment is 'brought to an end' by reason of redundancy, and the expiry of a fixed and/or short term contract (possibly even including a probationary period), when enforcing retirement, etc., a similar process should be undertaken to avoid the dismissal being judged unfair.

2. Failure to adhere to this procedure makes the dismissal automatically unfair (regardless of the circumstances). It was stated, when the procedure was introduced, that the main reason for it was to try and reduce tribunal claims and simplify the process. However, ignorance being no defence, many smaller employers unaware of the requirement have been caught as a result of the 'automatically unfair' aspect. Not only is compensation payable but in addition an uplift

of between 10% and 50% is applied to any compensation because the statutory process was not used. A recent report indicates that this new procedure has made the challenge of dismissal more complex with the result that the burden of cases on the tribunal system has increased, totally negating the original reason for its introduction. Even the Government which legislated for the concept admits that it is not achieving its aims – making it easier for small organisations to dismiss fairly and reducing tribunal claims. Accordingly the procedure is to be revised.

Retention ability

A Board of Director's employment challenge can be defined as 'how to source (and maintain) the appropriate skills (and mix of skills) in the right jobs at the right time – and to have back-up skills resources available in case anything goes wrong with those performing their current functions'. In many areas there is a shortage of skills and thus, the more that the best people can be retained the smaller should be the problem of finding those with appropriate skills. With the requirement to address a potentially increasing number of requests for flexible working, retaining the best employees may become one of the major challenges facing Boards in at least the first part of this century.

Since change is endemic (indeed, one could say the only constant is change) there is also a widespread expectation that an increasing number of employees will want their employers to invest in them – that is to provide them with on-going training so that they in turn can cope with the rapidly changing working environment. However, a recent survey conducted by opinion polsters MORI revealed that 58% of employees asked felt their training was ineffective.

Other research (by the Hay Group – 'The Retention Dilemma') indicates that:

a) employee turnover increased by 25% in the previous 5 years

b) the main causes for employees leaving are lack of a career path – and lack of strong leadership

c) the cost of labour turnover can be as much as 40% of annual profit

Many personnel practitioners assert that 50% of UK personnel are capable of operating at a level one higher than that at which they do operate. The Chartered Institute of Personnel and Development's (CIPD) 'Annual Labour Turnover Survey' discloses that over 50% of all recruits leave within 2 years and 75% leave within 6 years of joining.

Each time an employee leaves, an accumulation of knowledge is lost. Whilst in some cases the amount may be small – particularly with those employees who have only been in a post for a short time – in many cases this 'accrued knowledge' can be considerable. In the same way that the 'easiest way to make more money is to stop losing it', the 'easiest way to ensure there is a well-trained workforce is to stop losing those with accumulated knowledge'.

Employee retention

- Ensure managers consult with (and create) their teams, and motivate them by involvement and stretching (without straining) their capabilities.

- Outlaw demotivational forces such as unfairness, discrimination, harassment, favouritism, verbal and physical violence, bullying and perceptions of personal worthlessness, etc.

- Construct a reward package that is fair, in accord with market forces (or is perhaps slightly more favourable) to attract/retain the better candidates, to reward initiative and endeavour, and to motivate the workforce.

- Have due regard for the personal lives and responsibilities of employees, creating flexible and positive policies that demonstrate such commitment.

- Identify areas of high labour turnover and, by constructive and open exit interviews and advance surveying of attitudes, investigate the real reasons for labour turnover, identifying strategies to avoid this loss.

- Ensure policies and procedures are applied fairly and that the views of employees are encouraged to be stated, and then are listened to objectively.

- Reward loyalty – (i.e. encouraging motivation) e.g. by giving additional days holiday after, say, 5 and/ or 10 years service, etc.

- Involve all employees at all levels in the organisation. Employees who feel their views are listened to and taken account of, are less likely to leave than those who are ignored.

Continuous development

Since most organisations are now changing at a rate much faster and more comprehensively than at any time previously, this places an obligation on employees to change their approach and attitudes and, indeed, to learn new skills and procedures. In its statement Continuous Development – People and Work, the CIPD makes the point that training needs to be integrated with the needs of the work and to reflect the organisation's operational plan, with an impetus coming from the Chief Executive regarding commitment to continuous development as being as important as capital investment, research, etc. To this end it would be helpful if every employee had and retained throughout their career (that is taking it with them when they change employers), a record of the training they have undergone.

Nearly all professional bodies now require, as a condition of membership, that their members undertake regular updating and training with required levels of time to be spent each year on such activities. Learning and Skills Council (LSC) Chairman, Bryan Sanderson, stated recently that research demonstrated that businesses that invest an extra £50 per week in training see their profits grow nearly twice as fast as those that do not.

The Council's study demonstrated that companies that increased their training budget saw their profits increase by 11.4% whilst those that did not grew only by 6.3%. Simply retaining 50% of those that would otherwise leave and thus avoiding their recruitment costs, could add substantially to profit. Motorola estimates that every $1 spent on corporate learning translates into $30 of productivity gains within three years, whilst Sony claims that a $300,000 investment in training packages reaped $500,000 savings virtually immediately.

Summary checklist

- Ensure that where there is comparability those on non-standard contracts are given similar rights and benefits.

- Consider use of homeworking to reduce occupation costs and allow further alternatives of flexible working.

- Be pro-active in sourcing the best people and making sure that they are well-treated when starting, given adequate and tactful support whilst they are newcomers and training to enable them to cope with their required duties.

- Ensure full details of alleged offences are given to employees prior to holding any hearing that could lead to the termination of the employment.

- Recognise that the skills shortage could be a brake on expansion and progress, and ensure as few as possible of the best employees are lost unnecessarily.

- In motivating people – 'invest to get their best'.

Chapter eighteen

'Directing now'

The combined code

As previously noted, during the last 20 years there have been a number of committees considering the role and duties of directors. The original Cadbury Committee was followed by committees headed by Greenbury, Hampel, Higgs, Smith and Turnbull.

The reports and recommendations of these committees have now been reconstituted into a Combined Code of Corporate Governance to which all listed PLCs must now subscribe.

Included as one of the principles in the combined code was the requirement that there should be sound controls to safeguard the company's assets and to protect the shareholders' interests. Virtually simultaneously the Law Commission recommended that it should be made easier for shareholders to take action against directors who do not act in their best interests. A claim of 'failure to act in shareholders interests' could occur if a board failed to protect the assets of the business.

The following checklist (taken from the author's special report 'Corporate Governance' for Thorogood's Professional Insights series) was developed to act as a guide for listed PLCs. However many aspects can be used by all boards seeking to measure or check on their performance, transparency and accountability. (The boxes are incorporated so that it can be used as a checklist.)

Corporate Governance – a checklist for boards

A1 The Board

A1.1 Every company must be headed by an effective board whose members are collectively responsible for the success of the company.

Boards should provide entrepreneurial leadership with prudent and effective controls. Strategic aims and risk should be assessed and managed. Financial and human resources should be put in place with regular reviews of managerial performance. Boards should set values and standards and should ensure the shareholders obligations are understood and met. (It has been suggested that shareholders should be urged to vote and make their views known.) Decisions should be made in the interests of the company as a whole. ☐

Non-executive directors should be ready to challenge constructively and to help develop strategy. They should scrutinise
management performance against goals and objectives as well
as satisfying themselves on financial information and its integrity.

☐

Non-executives should also ensure there is adequate and
robust risk management, be responsible for setting appropriate
levels of reward for their executive colleagues and play a prime
role in hiring and firing them. They should also ensure there is
adequate succession planning.

☐

A1.2 The board should meet sufficiently regularly to meet these
requirements and a statement should appear in the Annual Report
about how the board operates, how many times it meets, the
attendance record of each director, where it delegates responsibility, and where it does not.

☐

A1.3 The Annual Report should identify the Chairman, Deputy
Chairman (if any), Chief Executive, senior non-executive and chairpersons on the nomination, audit and remuneration committees.

☐

A1.4 The Chairman should hold regular meetings with non-executives (without the executive directors) to discuss performance.
The non-executives should meet regularly to discuss the Chairman's performance.

☐

A1.5 Any director's concern about the running of the company should
be recorded in the board minutes. If a non-executive director
resigns (s)he should provide a written statement of any concerns
for distribution to the board.

☐

*(Note: The concept here is that of the 'noisy exit'. Directors
perpetrating wrongdoing might be constrained by the possibility of one of their number resigning and making his
reasons public.)*

A2 Chairman and Chief Executive

A2.1 There should be a clear division at the top of the company for
the running of the board and the running of the business. No
one person should have unfettered powers. The chairman is

responsible for the running of the board and for leadership. The chairman must ensure there is receipt of accurate, timely and clear information and should facilitate effective non-executive director contribution, constructive executive/non-executive relations, and effective shareholder information. ☐

A2.2   The Chairman and chief executive officer roles should be split. The division of these responsibilities should be clear, written and have board acceptance. ☐

A2.3   The Chairman should meet the independence criteria set out at A3.2 below. CEO should not become chairman of same company unless (exceptionally) with explanation to and acceptance by major shareholders and a declaration in the next following Annual Report. ☐

A3 Board balance and independence

A3.1   The board should contain a balance of executives and independent non-executives so that no individual group can dominate. ☐

(Note: Under draft EU requirements listed PLCs would be required to have a majority of non-executives.)

The Board should not be so large to be unwieldy but should contain sufficient skills and experience that there would be no disruption to its efficient operation in event of board changes. Committee membership should reflect the need to refresh membership without placing undue reliance upon individuals. ☐

A3.2   The board should identify in the Annual Report those non-executives that it considers to be independent. In reaching its conclusion it should have regard to independence of character, judgement and real or apparent conflict of interests. If any of the following apply to an independent non-exec, the company must state its reasons for ignoring these requirements:

• has been a company or group employee within the previous 5 years

• has had a material business relationship with the business in the previous 3 years

- receives remuneration or benefits from the company apart from directors fees

- has close family ties with any adviser, director or senior staff

- has cross-directorships or other links with other directors through other bodies

- represents a significant shareholder

- has served on the board for more than 9 years ☐

A3.3 Other than 'smaller' listed PLCs (that is those below the FTSE 350 throughout the year before the reporting year), at least half the board (excluding the Chairman) should be independent non-executive directors. 'Smaller' companies should have at least two independent non-executive directors. ☐

A3.4 The board should appoint one of the independent non-executive directors to be the senior non-executive who should be available to shareholders for concerns that they have not been able to resolve with the Chairman, CEO, or finance director. ☐

A4 Board appointments

A4.1 There should be a formal, rigorous and transparent procedure for appointing new directors, on merit and against objective criteria. It should be checked that directors – especially the chairman – will have enough time for their duties. There should be adequate plans for orderly succession, maintaining appropriate balance and representation of skills and experience. ☐

A4.2 Compliance with A4.1 is the responsibility of the nomination committee on which there should be a majority of non-executives. The Chairman should however preside over the selection of his/her successor. The terms of reference of such a committee must be available to shareholders etc. ☐

A4.3 The committee should evaluate the balance of skills, knowledge and experience on the board against that required, and assess job and person descriptions accordingly. ☐

A4.4 The committee should prepare a job specification for the Chairman – including an assessment of the time commitment –

especially in times of crisis. The prospective chairman's other commitments should be reported to the Board before appointment and included in the Annual Report. Changes to such commitments should be reported to the Board as they occur, and to the members in the next Annual Report. No individual should be chairman of more than one FTSE 100 company.

A4.5   The terms and conditions of appointment of non-executive directors should be made available for inspection by any member of the public at the company's registered office during business hours and from 15 minutes before to the conclusion of the AGM. Non-executive directors must confirm they have sufficient time to meet their obligations. Their other commitments (and any changes thereto) must be advised to the board.

A4.6   A full-time executive director should not take on more than one non-executive directorship or chairmanship of a FTSE 100 company.

A4.7   There should be a section in the Annual Report that describes the work and methods of the nomination committee and explains if neither open advertising nor a search consultancy has been used in appointing a chairman or non-executive director.

Case study

The idea of limiting the number of Boards on which a person can serve is to ensure the individual pays enough attention to each. Several years ago a director was disqualified from acting after it was discovered that he was on the boards of 1400 companies and it was stated that there was no way in which he could perform his obligations to so many companies. Living on the Channel Island, Sark, he was purely a 'front man' for the operators of those companies. Other residents of Sark performed a similar function. Generally it was known as the 'Sark lark'.

A5 Information and professional development

A5.1   The board should be presented with timely information in a form and of the quality necessary for it to do its job. All directors should receive induction upon appointment and should regularly update and refresh their skills and knowledge. ☐

A5.2   This is the responsibility of the chairman. Directors should seek clarification and/or additional data if necessary from management which must provide it. The company should provide the necessary resources for developing directors' knowledge and capabilities. Under the Chairman's direction, the Company Secretary has the responsibility for ensuring good information flow within the board, its committees, between executive and non-executive directors as well as facilitating induction etc. The Company Secretary should be responsible through the Chairman for advising the board of all CG matters. ☐

A5.3   All directors should have access to professional advice at company expense where they judge it necessary. Committees should have access to sufficient resources for them to do their job. ☐

A5.4   All directors should have access to the Company Secretary for advice and services. The Secretary is responsible for ensuring that board procedures are carried out. The appointment (and removal) of the Company Secretary should be a matter for the whole board. ☐

A6 Performance evaluation

A6.1   The board should annually review its own performance and that of its committees and individual directors formally and rigorously. Checks should be made that each director is contributing effectively and providing enough time for board and committee commitments. The chairman should take action where there are shortcomings disclosed as a result of the performance reviews. ☐

A6.2   The manner in which this review is conducted must be stated in the Annual Report. Non-executive directors, led by the senior non-executive, are responsible for evaluation of the Chairman. ☐

A7 Re-election

A7.1   All directors should be submitted for re-election at regular inter-
        vals, subject to satisfactory performance. The board should ensure
        planned and progressive refreshment of its composition (i.e.
        proper succession planning). ☐

A7.2   All directors must retire at the next following AGM after appoint-
        ment and thereafter regularly at not more than 3 yearly
        intervals. Sufficient personal details must be provided to share-
        holders for them to make informed decisions thereon. ☐

A7.3   Non-executive directors should be appointed for specified terms
        subject to re-election and to legal obligations regarding removal.
        The board should give reasons for re-election to the sharehold-
        ers. The Chairman should confirm to shareholders whether
        performance evaluations are satisfactory. Non-executive direc-
        tors serving more than nine years should be subject to annual
        re-election. ☐

B. Remuneration

B1   Remuneration should be sufficient to attract, retain and moti-
        vate directors of the right quality and should be aligned with
        shareholders interests. A significant proportion of the package
        should be related to corporate and personal performance. The
        remuneration committee should judge where and how to draw
        comparisons with other like companies and should be sensi-
        tive to pay and conditions elsewhere in the group, particularly
        when reviewing salaries. ☐

B1.1   Share options should not be issued at a discount greater than
        that allowed under the UK Listing Rules. ☐

B1.2   Non-executive pay should reflect time commitment and respon-
        sibilities but should not normally include share options (since
        this could preclude their independence). If, exceptionally,
        share options are granted this should only be with the share-
        holders prior approval and should be held for a year after (s)he
        has left the board. ☐

B1.3   Where an executive director is released to serve elsewhere as a non-executive the Remuneration Report should state whether the director will retain the earnings from that work and, if so, what they are.   ☐

B1.4   The remuneration committee should consider carefully what total commitments the company could have in the event of early termination of each director's service. Where this results from poor performance, this should be a robust review and take account of a director's obligation to mitigate loss.   ☐

B1.5   Notice periods under contracts for directors should be for one year or less. On initial appointment a longer period could be allowed but ultimately this must revert to one year.   ☐

B2 Remuneration review

B2.1   There must be a formal transparent procedure for developing a policy on executive pay and benefits and for fixing the amounts for individual directors. No director should fix their own remuneration. Contact with principal shareholders must be maintained in this regard.   ☐

The remuneration committee should consult the Chairman and/or the CEO about their proposals for remuneration of other executive directors. The committee should be responsible for sourcing and appointing external advisers on the subject. Conflicts of interest should be recognised and allowed for.   ☐

B2.2   The Remuneration Committee should comprise at least 3 non-executive directors (for smaller companies 2 independent non-executives). The committee's terms of reference should be made available delineating its authority. If consultants are retained, any connection with the company should be explained.   ☐

B2.3   The committee should be responsible for setting all remuneration including pension rights for all executives including the Chairman. The committee should monitor remuneration of all senior management as defined by the board (including the level immediately below the board).   ☐

B2.4   The Board, or where required by the Company's Articles of Association, the shareholders, should decide the remuneration of non-executive directors. If permitted by the Articles, the board may delegate this authority to a committee which could include the CEO. ☐

B2.5   Shareholders should be invited to approve all new long-term incentives as defined in the Listing Rules, including significant changes to existing schemes. ☐

C1 Accountability and Audit

C.1   The Board should present a balanced and understandable assessment of the Company's position and prospects. This covers interim and other price-sensitive announcements and reports to regulators. ☐

C1.1   The Annual Report should explain the directors' responsibility for the preparation of the accounts together with a statement of the Auditors' responsibilities. ☐

C1.2   The directors should report whether the business is a going concern with supporting assumptions or qualifications. ☐

C2 Internal control

C2.1   The Board should maintain a sound system of internal control to safeguard shareholders' investments and the company's assets. ☐

C2.2   At least annually the Board should review the effectiveness of internal controls and report to the shareholders that this has been done. The review should cover all material controls including risk management systems. ☐

C3 Audit committee and Auditors

C3.1   The Board should establish formal and transparent arrangements for considering how they shall apply the financial and internal control principles and for maintaining appropriate auditor relations. ☐

C3.2   The Board should establish an Audit Committee of at least 3 (2 for smaller companies) independent non-executive directors, at least one of whom, the Board must ensure, has relevant and recent financial experience. ☐

C3.3   The committee should have the following written terms of reference:

- monitoring the integrity of financial statements, formal financial statements and reviewing the judgements contained therein

- reviewing the company's internal financial controls, internal controls and risk management systems, unless this has been delegated to a risk committee set up under similar provisions or by the board

- monitoring and reviewing the effectiveness of internal audit

- recommending to the Board (and thence to the shareholders) the appointment, re-appointment and removal of external auditors

- reviewing and monitoring the external auditor's independence and objectivity; as well as the audit process itself, taking account of relevant professional and regulatory practice

- developing and implementing a policy on the engagement of external auditors on non-audit work, taking account of appropriate ethical practice

- reporting to the board when it considers action or improvement is needed and suggesting appropriate action ☐

C3.4   The terms of reference of the Audit Committee and its role and delegated authority should be made available generally. The Annual Report should contain a statement of its activities. ☐

C3.5   The committee should review 'whistleblowing' arrangements so that employees are aware and can raise concerns in confidence (and without sanction) and these can be investigated appropriately and follow-up action implemented. ☐

C3.6   The committee should monitor and review internal audit activities. If there is no internal audit facility its absence should be kept under review, any recommendations should be advised to the Board who should explain the absence of such a facility in the Annual Report. ☐

C3.7   The committee should have primary responsibility for recommendations on appointment, re-appointment or removal of external auditors. If the board does not accept such recommendations this fact should be reported on in the Annual Report. ☐

C3.8   If the external auditor provides non-audit services, this fact must be reported in the Annual Report, explaining how the auditor retains objectivity. ☐

D. Shareholder relations

D.1   The Board has a duty to ensure that a satisfactory dialogue takes place with shareholders, based on a mutual understanding of objectives. The Board should ensure that there is sufficient shareholder contact so that they understand the shareholders issues and concerns. ☐

D1.1   The Chairman should discuss governance issues with major shareholders and ensure that shareholders concerns are communicated to the whole board. Non-executive directors should attend meetings with major shareholders and should expect to be asked to attend if shareholders request this. The senior non-executive director should attend a sufficient number of meetings with major shareholders to develop a balanced view of their issues and concerns. The board should explain in the Annual Report how this shareholder:board communication is effected. ☐

D2 The Annual General Meeting

D2.1   The AGM should be used to communicate with investors and to encourage their participation. ☐

D2.2   The company should ensure that all votes are properly received and recorded. Proxies should be counted and (if no poll is called for) after a show of hands, those for, against and abstaining should be announced. ☐

D2.3   Separate resolutions should be tabled for all substantially separate issues, including any related to the Report and Accounts ☐

D2.4   The chairpersons of the Remuneration, Audit and Nominations committees should attend the AGM and be ready to answer questions. ☐

D2.5   The AGM notice and supporting papers should be sent to shareholders at least 20 working days in advance of the meeting. ☐

E1 Institutional shareholders

Such shareholders should enter into a dialogue with companies based on a mutual understanding of objectives. They should follow the principles set out in the Institutional Shareholders' Committee's *'Responsibilities of Institutional Shareholders and Agents – Statement of Principles.'*

E2 Governance disclosures

Institutional investors should carefully consider any reasons for the company departing from the Corporate Governance Code and make reasoned judgements in each case. These should be explained to the company and expect to enter into a dialogue if they do not accept the company's position. The size of the company should be borne in mind in making judgements.

E3 Shareholder voting

Institutional shareholders have a duty to make considered use of their votes and should ensure that their voting intentions are acted on. On request they should tell their clients how they voted. Where practical they should attend AGMs and companies and registrars should make this easy.

Good Governance Code

The EU has put forward proposals for a new framework directive. It echoes the US Sarbanes-Oxley legislation introduced as a result of the several corporate scandals in America, and would require:

- the setting up of supervisory boards to oversee the accountancy profession

- all publicly quoted companies (and public corporations) appointing independent audit committees

- the group auditor taking full responsibility for group consolidated accounts

- any conflicts of interests being revealed by auditors

- lead auditor being rotated after 5 years and whole audit firm after 7 years

- international accounting standards being introduced throughout the EU.

WARNING: Insurers have advised their clients that should they fail to comply with new accounting and corporate governance requirements they may find that their liability insurance cover is withdrawn. Compliance with the requirements of the International Financial Reporting Standards, Corporate Governance, Social Responsibility, and Operating and Financial Review will rapidly become a necessity as well as a listing requirement. Multinational companies will also have to comply with the Sarbane-Oxley Act if they are to retain liability cover in America.

Corporate governance in the 21st Century

The scope of anticipated changes

As has been referred to several times, a new Companies Act is being introduced and will be fully implemented by October 2008. The Act that it replaces was drafted in 1980 when only 10% of UK companies had a computer; there was no Internet; faxing was in its infancy; there was virtually no legal right for employees to have time off (even for holidays), there were no mobile phones and so on. Less than 25 years later we have a totally different environment and must respond accordingly.

Change is endemic – it has become the only constant. It is not only fitting, in the early years of the 21st Century, that there should be a revision of such 'old' law but also, in view of these fundamental changes, a necessity. Ironically the fact that time, an entirely man-made device, indicates that the century has changed, should not really have any effect. Realistically, however, the first few years of a new Millennium, like the start of a new year, do encourage the contemplation of change. Being ultimately responsible to their shareholders for the preservation, protection and growth of the company, Directors must be ready to face – even embrace – these changes. Areas where quite fundamental changes can be expected include:

- Liability

- Veracity

- Creativity

- Transparency

- Accountability

- Flexibility

- Comparability

- Jollity.

Liability

Reference has been made throughout this book to the increasing liabilities placed on those that direct companies. The extent and severity of such liabilities seems destined to continue to grow. Within the immediate future there is expected to be enacted a strengthening of the law (and penalties) against employers who bring about (or are in some way responsible for) the deaths of or cause injuries to their employees and/or others. This proposal, to enhance the existing – and less than effective – corporate manslaughter legislation has had a chequered career over the past years. The latest proposal, re 'Corporate killing'. '**Corporate killing**' is the title of a new bill which seeks to hold organisations responsible for the manslaughter of employees or others. It is expected that once enacted there would be an increased number of successful prosecutions in this area.

Veracity

Mainly because of well-publicised scandals and the collapse of large corporations on both sides of the Atlantic, as well as a widespread suspicion that the prime task of some of those at the top of some of the UK's companies seems to be to feather their own nests, the regard with which many of those in control are held by society in general is at a pretty low ebb. Increasingly it is likely that what will be demanded is more akin to partnerships with suppliers (as is already the case with several leading companies), employees (see below) and even customers. These developments can only occur if there is a firmer belief and confidence in the integrity of those at the top. Unfortunately business life abounds with lies such as:

- 'The cheque is in the post' (there is new legislation from both the UK and the EU legislation which tightens the obligation to pay promptly and to declare the company's policy in this regard).

- 'The customer is king' (in which case why does research indicate that many top managements place little priority on communicating with or satisfying existing customers, yet considerable importance on attaining new business. Since it is five times as expensive to source a new customer than to retain an old one, it would appear some Boards have odd priorities and an even less understandable appreciation of economics or plain common sense).

Most organisations find that the majority of their profits are derived from a small proportion of their turnover – termed the 'pareto' effect. Vilfredo Pareto was an Italian economist who proposed the '80:20 rule' (i.e. that 80% of profit is derived from 20% of sales).

Case study: Misunderstanding Pareto

Following British Airways extending their executive class at the expense of space for customers paying lower prices for other tickets (to improve profitability by adopting the Pareto rule) a former customer wrote to the *Financial Times* complaining that because of BA's arrogant attitude to their customers he (having flown with them for 14 years and spent in excess of £250,000 with the company) would fly with them no longer.

Whilst cutting costs to improve profits is laudable, alienating customers may cut sales and thus profits. In any event, cutting the number of lower priced tickets (unless overheads are similarly cut), will in turn make the other tickets less profitable. Further any downturn in executive travel (such as occurred post 9/11) will immediately pose problems for a company deciding to concentrate on the lucrative business traveller. The customer may not always be right but he and she must never be taken for granted.

(Perhaps what was overlooked was that Pareto also stated that despite all attempts to change it, income distribution actually remains the same!)

- 'Our staff are our most valuable asset' (which is certainly the case, although few companies seem to treat their employees in the way that one would think the 'most valuable asset' would be treated – see below).

- 'We value our customers' (in which case why does a customer with a problem have to wait in a telephone queue whilst an insufficient number of operators try to cope with the weight of calls).

- 'We create value for our shareholders' (which may sit oddly with some records which show that in years when performance is poor, and/or employees pay increases are restricted or numbers are reduced by redundancy, directoral rewards have been high).

If Directors and Boards are to gain (or simply preserve) a valued reputation and maintain any integrity with suppliers, customers, employees and shareholders, such corporate lies (the seeds of which are sown by a widespread managerial arrogance) need to be shown for what they are – nonsense – and outlawed, unless they can be objectively justified.

Creativity

From which source are most Directors appointed? The answer is from the ranks of senior managers. However, the job of Director is vastly different from the function of manager. Managers have a range of duties – usually within a pre-determined area of operation. Such duties tend to be clear cut and often with definite levels of performance as criteria. This is not true of Directors. The scope of their operation is not simply over the whole company irrespective of functional responsibilities, they also have the major task of driving the company forward, of planning for the future, of creating the products or services that will be in demand – not next month, but next year and in 5 years time. To do this requires:

- a creative approach;

- an ability to spend time in thought in preference to action;

- being able to prioritise (often instinctively and usually quickly); and

- the ability to marshal the various assets at their command.

One could almost summarise their respective responsibilities as:

- for managers

  'the ability to deal with pre-determined issues in a hands on manner' (after all the origin of the word 'manager' is the Latin 'manus' = hand), and

- for Directors

  'the ability to 'dream' (or at least think without limitation) and innovate'.

Few Directors feel they have sufficient time to think, create and plan – not least due to the impact of the rapid increase in legislative requirements which each year over-proliferate. Yet time to think and innovate is essential if the company is not to stagnate. The products and services we market and sell today are the result of long since past initiatives, whereas, hopefully, in the more recent past we have initiated products for tomorrow. But the successful Board is one that is already considering and designing the products or services that they believe will be wanted by the consumer of next year, or the next decade. To quote management guru Peter Drucker '*the enterprise that does not innovate inevitably ages and declines and in a period of rapid change such as the present, an entrepreneurial period, the decline will be fast*'. As already noted the rate of change is likely to increase still further as the 21st Century ages – placing more pressure on Boards to invest in creativity and flexible responses.

Case study: Who dares wins

Boards are appointed by shareholders not simply to guard the existing assets but also to take the business forward, bearing in mind that companies do not stand still – they either expand and survive, or contract and ultimately go out of business. Richard Branson was identified as one businessman in whom supervisors, surveyed in over 100 recent seminars throughout the UK, had perceived confidence as both Director and leader. Reflecting his entrepreneurial style, his company, Virgin, has invested in several ventures far removed from the original record label which was the foundation of his fortune. In some instances the gambit has not been successful and the response in many circles, including some of the media, has been to criticise – even ridicule – the idea. Such a reaction is completely nonsensical. Directors of companies are expected to take risks – 'nothing ventured is nothing gained'. Inevitably some risks will turn out to have not been worth taking – that may be unfortunate. But the important factor, as far as the corporate body is concerned, is that the new venture was tried – and useful experience can often be drawn with perhaps more from failure than success.

Attempting to diversify may be risky – but sticking only with what is tried and tested can only ultimately lead to the demise of the company, as tastes and preferences change and 'me-too' competitors proliferate. One of the challenges for Directors is to learn from failure and to use such experience in future endeavours.

The Egyptian pyramid

Perhaps Directors should visualise themselves sitting on top of a pyramid which represents their company. They may be tempted to regard the lines of the pyramid and its bulk, and to take pride in its existence. It might be better to raise their eyes and look around – not least at the environment which ultimately will destroy the structure. Boards must look outwards at other pyramids – not inwards. Companies do not exist as islands immune from their environment. Sometimes the environment can destroy the company. The number of household-name companies – some being market-leaders – that no longer exist is legion. Under Lord Weinstock, GEC was a revered and powerful brand and leading UK company. Within a few years of him retiring, the company (by then renamed Marconi) virtually failed – saved only by support from its creditors (who now own over 99% of the shares).

Only 32 companies that were in the UK's top 100 industrial companies in 1965 remain there now. In the USA virtually half the 'Fortune 500' fell out of that category during the 1980s. Of the 100 largest US companies in 1900 only 16 still exist.

Perhaps Boards may have spent too much time admiring the sides of their own pyramid – and not the building of others. (Those with their eyes firmly focussed internally might also like to consider that the top of the pyramid only remains in place because of its base and what lies between the two – at least this might dent managerial arrogance which seems all too commonplace and encourage meaningful dialogue (communication or, better still, 'communicaction') with those at the base of (and those at other levels in) the pyramid.)

Transparency

In terms of corporate governance, at least as far as listed PLCs are concerned, change is endemic and already taking place, not least due to the recommendations of the Cadbury, Greenbury and Hampel committees already referred to and now encompassed by the Combined Code. The inception and deliberations of these committees reflected widespread concerns (replicated in countries such as the USA, Japan, France, Germany, Australia etc.) regarding control of and the increasing power of corporate bodies – particularly resulting from the globalisation of markets and businesses. Already there are over 50 corporations out of the top 100 wealthiest entities in the world that are bigger than some third world countries and with the incidence of international mergers there exists an imminent prospect of the creation of a few mega-corporations rivalling the size, power and influence of larger countries. For example, the sales of Wal-Mart exceed the national output of Sweden. Politicians in western democracies are, at least in theory, subject to control by the ballot box. No such control exists over corporations, the Boards of which can be largely self-perpetuating. It is partly for this reason that in recent years there have been several initiatives aimed at encouraging those who own companies (particularly corporate investors) to become more aware of the activities of those who direct them and to provide or exercise guidance and controls over them. There have in past years been a number of initiatives and consultation documents concerning shareholder reporting and interfacing, and a number of institutional shareholders have gone on record requiring actions (e.g. restricting service contracts length to one or two years) aimed at curbing the opportunity for boards or individual members to abuse their powers, and there are currently proposals to:

- extend the number, scope and power of non-executive Directors (under the Higgs recommendations); and

- limit termination payments to Directors who have not performed.

These initiatives have so far been aimed at PLCs, but there is an inevitable overspill into the whole corporate arena. Basically what PLCs are required to do today, may well be required of all companies tomorrow. Generally Directors need to anticipate being required to provide greater and more detailed explanations of their activities, strategies and attitudes – and to give proper account when things go wrong.

In a recent survey of professional development issues the Institute of Directors (which offers an examination course leading to the qualification 'Chartered Director') commented that a Director must be able:

- to think strategically ('dream');

- to provide his company with vision ('innovate');

- to stand back from the everyday problems and look at the company's situation today and tomorrow;

- to provide leadership; and

- to communicate strategy and vision to all employees.

This is broadly the same list of aims that is set out in the Institute's own 'Standards for the Board'.

Accountability

Directly leading on from Transparency is the need for Directors to be accountable.

Accountability is required to a number of interested parties:

- Shareholders

- Customers

- Employees

- Society, and so on.

Currently company law requires Directors to produce each year a report of their company's activities – the Annual Report. As previously noted, most of these are couched in language, format and presentation that neither entices the reader to study them, nor provides information in a readily accessible fashion. A recent survey of over 100 leading companies indicated that although 75% of those asked felt the annual report was an important way of communicating with the target audiences, 60% actually produced it with only the 'City of London audience' in mind.

This can hardly be said to be evidence of a genuine wish to report meaningfully and give account to those who own the company, let alone with other interested parties. The most recent UK recession left many consumers far more aware of price and value, more conservative about their expenditure – and demanding improved levels of delivery, service and quality. Retail demand in the UK is not expected to regain the level it reached at the height of its boom in the middle 1980s until around 2007 (and current uncertainty is likely to further delay regaining that level), whilst many producers of goods and providers of services are being forced to operate in markets smaller than hitherto, and unlikely to grow rapidly – if at all.

Demand is thus under pressure and customer retention rather than new customer acquisition is key. In conducting a survey, P Four (a marketing consultancy), discovered that although 70% of the top management representatives who were asked felt that customer focus was a first or second priority, less than 25% felt that time spent with customers was important. Far too many boards are remote from customers (on whom they depend for the continuation for their business) and display what can be termed corporate arrogance to both customers and shareholders (and probably their employees). Both categories (as well as employees) are likely to be far more demanding and vocal in the 21st Century.

Whilst not ideal for the purpose, the Annual Report provides an opportunity to 'market' the company and its products or services in an advantageous light – yet only 30% of those in the above survey saw the report as serving this need. The document is required to be produced in any event – why not make it work and use it to market the organisation to all with whom it interfaces?

Perhaps before this new century ages too much, we can hope that there will be a trend for the report to become what a few companies already do, which is to produce two reports – one concentrating on financial aspects and one which endeavours not only to provide a meaningful commentary but also attempts to place the activities of the operation within the framework of the society in which it operates.

Flexibility

Change challenges what is known and trusted, forcing humans (essentially creatures of habit) to face what is new, unknown, and perhaps risky. The temptation may be to avoid the latter and stick with the former. However, Directors are paid to drive the company forward, which must entail a willingness to embrace the new and the risky. Directors are paid (often highly) in part to take risks (albeit having first analysed the opportunities and the dangers fully), since only if they do are the rewards for the company likely to be high. Legal changes are often unwelcome, and whilst such a reaction may be understandable, those who persist in 'opposing' the trend may do their companies a disservice. Such changes cannot be resisted and it might be more beneficial (and economic) to accept the new requirements and to assess whether there are any ways in which the company can use them to its own advantage.

Legal compliance – and the social climate

Directors may be excused for antipathy towards legislation – and railing against it with the lawmakers may assist changes being made – but refusing to work within it is foolish and costly, as well as being a breach of the duty they owe to their shareholders. As the 21st Century progresses, we are likely to see the 'sexual glass ceiling' shattered as more and more women occupy more and more senior positions. Once again this development will require fresh approaches not least in the area of personal and employment relationships. However, not all approaches may be beneficial. There is little doubt that faced with the extensive rights of women to both leave and pay) when they are pregnant and new mothers, that some employers (as already happens) will not employ women of childbearing age. Whilst this is illegal if the woman is the best person for the job, (since it would be sex discrimination) there is no doubt it occurs. Indeed, whilst giving seminars throughout the UK, I have been told on several occasions (sometimes even by women and with approval) that this is their company's attitude! Legislation – particularly in social engineering – can have the opposite effect to that intended. Conversely the company that embraces diversity may find benefits.

Case studies: Accepting the challenge

a) It was reported in the Sunday Times in January 2003 that there is a company in Chesterfield which has 35 employees – and 35 different shifts. The employer has managed to create a situation where every individual's preference regarding hours worked can be met. Over the 5 years that the scheme has been working, productivity has doubled.

b) Farrelly Engineering and Facilities in the West Midlands were suffering from high labour turnover. They felt the main cause was the long hours employees worked and reduced the working week, allowing employees flexibility for family and domestic commitments. Their sales figures have doubled. Mr Farrelly stated 'We don't compete on price – we compete on people – to do this we had to change the traditional working methods. People aren't as stressed, … they're more refreshed and turnover has been dramatically reduced. That's helped the customers, too, so everyone wins'.

c) At the opposite end of the 'number of employees' spectrum Tony
DeNunzio, Chief Executive of Asda, claims that that company's flexible working practices had contributed greatly to a £4 million
reduction in absence costs, act as a key retention tool and are a significant inducement in attracting recruits. Asda employees can swap
'shifts' for family or domestic reasons, 'swap stores' where students
work in one shop and in holidays return to their main home and
even have 'grandparents leave' for older workers. De Nunzio claims
that the success of the process is simply due to the fact that it is
'based on what colleagues want and need'.

It may be easier to arrange such flexibility in a small company although
it must be said that with larger numbers, particularly where jobs are
replicated, such flexibility may actually be easier to achieve. The essential ingredient is not size at all but the will to make the system work.

WARNING: One can only hope that the practices of Asda's American
parent – Wal-Mart – do not spread to the UK. Wal-Mart (largest retailer
in the world and largest employer in the USA) is introducing a new
type of contract for its 1.3 million employees whose work patterns
will be determined by the number of customers in a store.

Wal-Mart's employees will be on call on an unpaid basis until the
company needs additional labour in which case employee(s) will be
called in – and only then will they be paid. The scheme is called the
'optimiser' and whilst it may benefit the employer, it is difficult to see
how it benefits the employees many of whom will have no idea from
week to week how long they will have to work – and how much they
are likely to earn. The scheme also allows the company to ensure that
no part-timer ever works such hours that would enable them to claim
'full-time status' which under US law entitles them to better employment protection etc.

It is unlikely that this scheme could operate legally in the UK. In
Landeshaupstadt Kiel v Jaeger, the Court stated that being on call on
site counts as working time. Wal-Mart's 'optimiser' arrangement, of course,
would be 'on call' off site. However, under the Working Time Directive,
these hours could be held to count towards the number of hours
'worked' in a week. If an employee is on-call for (say) 20 hours but not
used (and paid for) for more than (say) 10, the effective rate of pay is

halved which could mean the national minimum wage rate is breached – which is potentially a criminal offence.

(One would have thought that being the world 'No. 1' Wal-Mart would like to demonstrate that it was a 'good' employer rather than indulging in practices unused by even the most oppressive mill-owners during the Industrial Revolution.)

Comparability

Until the 1960s there was very little employment law and the relationship between employer and employed was very much one of 'master and servant'. Since then there have been introduced a plethora of law and protections for employees. The reaction whether conscious or not of some employers, has been to reduce the number of people they 'employ' and to use 'workers' to do tasks formerly done by employees. Thus, some of the impact (and associated costs) of the employment protection and rights legislation has been negated.

Over the past few years there has been a deliberate move initiated by the EU to rectify this situation by granting the same rights enjoyed by employees to such 'non-employees'. This is the 'comparability principle' which states that where a person is performing duties that are broadly the same as an employee, then regardless of their status they are entitled to the same rights and benefits enjoyed by the employee, unless this can be objectively justified. Thus, legislation effecting this principle is already in being as far as part time staff and fixed term employees are concerned, and is proposed regarding agency staff and homeworkers.

In effect the trend to move workers 'off the employment establishment' is to a large extent negated by this. Further, the administrative challenge of making sure that the requirements are complied with could be so complicated (and prone to mistake) that it may be safer to reverse the trend and take more workers back in real 'employment'.

Jollity

Most people spend half their waking life at work. Work has become a social activity for many, even though it is also an economic necessity. A majority of lasting friendships, partnerships and even marriages are formed through workplace encounters. Indeed, so important a part of life can the working environment become that, let alone financial consideration, many are unable to cope with redundancy, simply because as well as the stigma of 'not being wanted' they have to face the loss of the social interaction that working provides. (This is a very important consideration that those that implement redundancies often entirely overlook.) For many, a recent reports states, 'home is a place of oppression whilst work is a place of liberation'. Half those asked in that survey, stated they liked their job and would carry on working even if they had enough money not to need to.

Since the workplace is where a considerable amount of time is spent, ideally the environment should be as convivial as possible. Perhaps 'jollity' pushes the point too far, but many well-regarded leaders endeavour to create a situation where at least work is enjoyable. An environment that is enjoyable is likely to be one in which employees can be motivated to produce their best work, to work together as a team and be encouraged to make suggestions for the improvement of existing and development of new products or services. It is likely that costly labour turnover can be reduced (retention of quality staff being currently recognised by many leading organisations as of vital importance) – whilst the reputation of such an employer creating such an environment may aid the recruitment of the 'best' people.

That this should be so can be argued by considering the opposite type of environment. It would hardly be surprising if employers known or regarded as 'poor' experienced difficulty in recruiting decent calibre personnel.

NOTE: A survey from the Work Foundation (formerly the Industrial Society) found that gossiping at work (within time limits presumably) improved productivity. One in three said that work was the most important part of their life and for some it can mean so much that they feel like they have been divorced if they are fired.

The report criticised assumptions that home is a preferable environment to work and went on to state that employers should give their staff more room to enjoy their work. Instead of seeing sociability at work as the antithesis to efficiency and productivity, the report suggests employers should see it as being crucial to the bottom line. Gossip is the cement which holds organisations together; indeed it allows employees to share information, knowledge, and build relations that benefit both company and employee.

In his guide to how he tries to do business, '*Screw it – lets do it*', Sir Richard Branson repeatedly makes the point that he tries to make doing business 'fun'. Inevitably this cannot be other than an aim and at times it may be anything but. However, unless it is an aim, business never will be fun. One advantage of the full employment enjoyed by the UK is that it should be possible for many of those in jobs that they do not enjoy, to find alternatives. Increasingly employers are needing to change their stereotyped hours and to offer flexibility to suit the pressure of employees anxious to achieve a better 'work:leisure' balance. This move will not 'go away', it is here to stay – realistically employers better start to 'enjoy' it!

Relationships

Inherent in the duties of a Director is an obligation to interface with a variety of people – suppliers, customers, shareholders, regulatory authorities and last, but certainly not least, employees, only through whom can they achieve their companies' aims. The days when the relationship could be regarded as between 'master and servant' have long since gone. Increasingly this relationship should be regarded as akin to a partnership – and one where the employer acknowledges and appreciates that at times employees priorities lie outside their employment. To some extent, at least for public corporation bodies (those that are 'emanations of the State') the impact of the European Convention on Human Rights through its UK enactment the Human Rights Act (which, inter alia, grants to everyone the right to be accorded respect for their private and family life), is likely to be felt increasingly.

With the current thinking of the European Union it is difficult to envisage any change in this climate – at least for the next 15 years or so. Rightly or wrongly, such circumstances, aided by:

• a widening of popular share ownership enabling many more people to acquire at least a little capital and/or to understand the need for investment and profits to create new jobs (or simply maintain the old ones); a boost to which movement is continually given by tax advantages for Share Incentive Plans and the like.

- a growing awareness that the days of confrontation may actually have achieved relatively little in the long-term (as the late management guru Peter Drucker once warned '*adversarial management is fine as long as you don't have to see or work with the bastards again*')

- the current UK government being more pragmatic regarding industrial relations, and particularly

- as a result of the UK's membership of a 'socially committed' European Union, a re-assessment of the employment relationship seems warranted.

Mutual respect and trust between capital and labour may be the only way in which an improved and sustainable level of productivity and profitability can be achieved. That this may be a considerable challenge for some managements is inevitable. The report 'Impact of People Management Practices on Business Performance', concludes, 'The results suggest that if managers wish to influence the performance of their companies, the most important area they should emphasise is the management of people. This is ironic given that our research has also demonstrated that emphasis on human resource management is one of the most neglected areas of managerial practice within organisations.'

Moving towards an employment partnership is not simply 'a good idea' or the latest fad, it is based on economic reality and advantage. In a report 'Benchmarking the Partnership Company' the Involvement and Participation Association concluded of a number of companies committed to partnership that 'partnership pays off – organisations have a better psychological contract, there is greater trust between employees and employers and performance is higher'.

Employers' challenge

The initiators of this new relationship must be Directors, in which regard the report of the Hampel Committee on Corporate Governance provides guidance:

'*Business prosperity cannot be commanded. People, teamwork, leadership, enterprise and skills are what really produce prosperity ... an effective board... should lead and control the company*.' The report does not use the word 'management' at all – the operative term is the more positive and dynamic term 'leadership' whereby people are motivated to perform as a team and thus achieve a greater output than the sum of the parts.

NOTE: In this regard it is perhaps worth stressing that there are two motivational forces:

a)   the basic requirement to earn a living for self and dependents; and

b)   the motivation to perform well which depends for its existence and cultivation on the environment and treatment experienced in the workplace.

Unfortunately, in the UK the number of managers able to motivate their employees in the workplace is relatively few – over 66% admitted in a recent survey by recruitment specialists Robert Half, that they possess only limited motivational skills. Unfortunately the national media may do little to change this situation. There have been a number of TV programmes – for example, The Weakest Link, Hell's Kitchen etc.,- where despite the 'aim' being to create teams and in the latter case additionally to teach the uninitiated, the attitude of those in authority is diametrically opposed to the best method of achieving such aims. It may make fascinating television but it is neither good leadership and team-building (other than by binding in adversity) or training – and these are appalling examples to set as a perceived standard.

Research indicates that the majority of employees want good management/leadership and to be treated with fairness and respect; unfortunately it seems that only a minority actually receive either – but if partnership is required, leadership by one of the partners is essential. Indeed, it is arguable that because management did not lead in the 1950s and 1960s, that vacuum was filled by trades unions, a situation which led directly to their growth of power and influence. If management perform effectively and properly – i.e. communicate and lead as is both their right and their responsibility – there will be less opportunity for others to fill this vacuum; a telling comment given the recent changes in legislation that make it easier for there to be pressure for wider Union recognition.

Working time/ personal time balance

The various protections and rights granted by employment legislation, particularly that emanating from the European Union, has not only created a requirement for all employers (since there is no exception made for small employers in the UK) to have a 'family friendly' environment, but also, particularly from those aged 18 – 35 (whose views will obviously increasingly become the norm) an expectation that this is not only a right but also that it is right.

Employers who wish to obtain and retain the best employees will increasingly be those that embrace this movement positively. The actual details are relatively unimportant – the overriding requirement however, is to treat employees and their views with respect, which requires those in charge of companies to listen to their employees which is not only good practice but is also a legal requirement in many instances. This will increasingly be the case.

A sting in the tail?

The challenges for the 21st Century are for Directors to be able to respond (and respond swiftly) to changing demands of a fast changing society. This may be difficult for some to deal with. As Gary Hamel (co-author of 'Competing for the future') stated recently '*Where are you likely to find people with least diversity of experience, the largest investment in the past and the greatest reverence for industry dogma? – At the top*'. Yet it is from people at the top (and only from that source) that can come the preparedness and willingness to face the challenges of tomorrow:

• the ability to provide creativity, drive and vision; and, above all,

• leadership (bearing in mind as previously quoted)

'management is about doing things right but leadership is doing the right thing'

and

'management without leadership is like arranging the deckchairs on the Titanic'

Case study: Sauce for the goose?

On the same day I was asked to start revising and updating this book for this new edition, British Airways was facing a damaging and very costly strike of its cabin crews objecting to the tightening of controls over the number of days sickness they were 'entitled' to each year.

There is little wrong in a company tightening such rules and few onlookers – other than those wishing to fly on the dates of the anticipated strike – would have much sympathy for employees who on average were taking around four times the number of days' sickness as the national average. So far so good.

However at exactly the same time BA's 'left hand' was undergoing some very tough negotiating to tighten or restrict employees' employment terms, BA's 'right hand' was proposing that directors and their families should not only have unlimited first class travel on BA, but also that if they wished to travel, other paying customers could be 'bumped off' so that seats could be made available for them.

What kind of an example is that to the employees – and indeed the customers who pay all their wages? Where was common sense – or commercial 'nous'? Where indeed was any vestige of leadership?

Never mind – presumably the deckchairs had been well-arranged.

If there is one expertise UK corporate activity cries out for it is for Directors to lead – get that right and everything else simply falls into place.

One easy task for directors is to try and put themselves in the 'other seat'. That is to try to imagine they are sitting on the other side of their desk when seeking to move matters forward and asking themselves 'if this was being done to me rather than by me, would I think what is being done is fair and just etc?'. If so go ahead – if not: think again. This is the very simple – but it seems rarely used – 'doasyouwouldbedoneby' principle, the adoption of which principle could probably avoid 10-15% of employment tribunal claims!

Appendices

Appendix I:
Bibliography

Chartered Secretary – monthly journal of the Institute of Chartered Secretaries and Administrators (ICSA Tel: 0207 580 4741)

Company Law Reform – Modern Company Law for a competitive economy (DTI 1998 Tel: 0207 215 5000)

Financial Reporting to Employees – a practical guide (Gee 1997 Tel: 0207 393 7400) David M Martin (Tel: 01202 420 248)

Committee on Corporate Governance (Hampel Final Report) (Committee on Corporate Governance/Gee 1998 Tel: 0207 393 7400)

Impact of People Management Practices on Business Performance (CIPD 1998 Tel: 0207 263 3434) Patterson, West, Lawthom and Nickell

Manipulating Meetings, Tough Talking, How to be a great communicator, (Pitman/Institute of Management Tel: 01202 420 248) David M Martin

Making corporate reports valuable (The Institute of Chartered Accountants of Scotland/Kogan Page 1988)

Making it happen (Collins 1988) Sir John Harvey Jones

One Stop Company Secretary, (5th edition 2007) (ICSA Tel: 01202 420 248) David M Martin

Screw it, let's do it (Virgin Books 2007) Sir Richard Branson

Summary Financial Statements – The way forward – a report by the Institute of Chartered Accountants (Butterworths 1996) Professor R Hussey (Tel: 0117 965 6261)

Takeovers (Pan 1988) Fallon and Srodes

The A-Z of Employment Practice (Thorogood 2006) David Martin

References

Registrar of Companies, Companies House, Crown Way, Maindy, Cardiff CF4 3UZ (www.companieshouse.gov.uk)

Appendix II:
Who is liable

In Chapter 4 we posed the above question in reference to Board members involved in the ultimate failure of a company.

In the scenario outlined the Court could well differentiate between the liability of the members of the Board holding some more culpable than others because they would be deemed to have (or should have) knowledge of the correct approach in such a situation.

1. Prime position would probably go to the Finance Director ranked either slightly ahead or in joint first place with the Chairman.

2. If the Finance Director holds first place the Chairman must hold second.

3. The remaining executive directors would probably be next in line although there might be some differentiations amongst them. Thus a Personnel or Production director might be held less liable than, say, a Commercial director, since their skills are in non-financial areas. It might be unwise to rely on this as many Courts will expect all directors to know their responsibilities.

4. Finally the non-executive directors might be held liable unless they could show they had tried to exercise their rights to find out the position (as in this instance) and were foiled by a deliberate process of evasion and even lies. It is in this situation that the Minutes (demonstrating what was – and, more importantly, what was not – brought to the Board and what was concealed).

(Readers feeling that this is highly coloured and fictional, might like to know that it is based on a real life company and situation.)

Appendix III: Companies Act 2006 Implementation timetable

January 2007

1. Electronic communications overhauled, and companies were required to add certain information to such communications. Thus a company must display the same statutory data on websites, order forms and e-mails as it should have been displaying on its letterheads, statements, bills of exchange etc since at least 1985, namely:

   - name
   - place and number of registration
   - registered office

   and, where a customer can place an order, the VAT number must be shown.

   Companies are allowed to communicate electronically with their shareholders however they will have to first submit a resolution to their members (having checked that there is nothing to prohibit the use of electronic mail in their Articles. Once the resolution is passed they should write to their shareholders stating that they have the option of continuing with hard copy or opting for the electronic version. They must be advised that if they do not reply within 28 days they will be deemed to have opted for the electronic option. However even if they do not reply (or do not give an electronic address) they must still be sent a hard copy notification of a meeting with reference to the company website carrying full information re the meeting. They would not be sent (for example) the report and accounts – the shareholder would need to request these. Those who do not opt for electronic communication can be re-invited to do so once a year.

2. Statutory liability provisions were introduced which have the effect of allowing an investor to claim compensation against a listed PLC where that person has suffered loss as a result of a misleading or untrue statement in, or omission from, published reports (including the preliminary statement).

3. Required evidence of ownership of shares. A listed PLC has been able to require a shareholder to disclose ultimate ownership of shares held in their name by issuing a '212 notice' that is a request to disclose under section 212 of CA1985. This has been replaced by section 793 of CA2006.

April 2007

Abolition of the bar on directors aged 70 or over being directors of PLCs or their subsidiaries unless the shareholders voted in favour.

October 2007

Members rights (to be sent notices and resolutions, require convening of General Meetings, receive notice of meetings, to appoint proxy, received accounts and reports etc)

All aspects of directorship (EXCEPT conflicts of interest, residential addresses protection, controls on underage and/or corporate directors, which will be introduced in October 2008):

- Derivative actions brought by shareholders/members
- New requirements re meetings and resolutions
- Control of political donations
- Business review and content of directors report
- Fraudulent trading (alterations re sanctions).

April 2008

- Alterations to company secretaries status for LTDs
- Changes to accounts, reports and audit
- Debentures
- LTDs (prohibition against offering shares) and PLCs (minimum capital)
- Certification and transfer of securities
- Distributions, arrangement and reconstructions
- Mergers and divisions of PLCs
- Auditors and their liabilities

October 2008

- Company formation and changes to constitution
- Capacity, name, registered office
- Re-registration

- Members and directors – (conflicts of interest, residential addresses protection, controls on underage and/or corporate directors)

- Share capital, acquisition of own shares

- Annual Return

- Charges

- Dissolution and removal from and reinstatement to the Register

- Provisions re companies formed outside the Companies Act

- Registrar of Companies provisions

- Business names

During implementation

All the secondary legislation (referred to in the Act) which will give detailed requirements on a number of issues is subject to commencement orders (or laid before Parliament if necessary) during 2007/8. These will include transitional arrangements which will obviously be of considerable interest to existing companies.

Appendix IV: Possible additional clauses for LTD's Articles

Although they provide very useful guidance regarding the way the directors should operate, the published draft set of Articles for an LTD are short on detail regarding (or altogether ignore) a number of key areas. Using Table A of CA85, we can highlight some items which companies might wish to add if using the new draft as a base.

a) Granting the right to the company to have a lien over shares where the shareholder has not paid in full for the amount due (1985 Companies Act, Table A Reg 8). Alternatively consideration could be given to reserving the right to disenfranchise shares where calls made have not been paid.

b) The administration by which the board can make calls on shares issued partly paid (Reg 12).

c) How shares are to be transferred (Reg 23 and 25-31). The invaluable right reserved to the board of a private LTD to be able to refuse to register a transfer of shares to a person they do not wish to have as a shareholder – contained in Reg 24 of Table A – is retained in the new draft.

d) If an LTD wishes to continue to use AGMs the provisions concerning such meetings need to be added (Regs 36- 63).

e) If an LTD wishes to continue to operate with a Company Secretary it might be as well to make this clear (Reg 99).

f) If required, granting the board rights to waive the bans on voting etc. when they have an interest in the subject matter being considered.

g) Since the 'objects clause' in the Memorandum will in future form part of the Articles, consideration should be given to how much (if anything) of the clause, should be retained – or whether these 'old objects' should be revised.

Whilst the Articles of many private LTDs use Table A (Table B for a Guarantee company) a substantial number have 'customised Articles' in addition. That is they have incorporated additional Articles to reflect their own position. Consideration should be given to whether these specific Articles should be repeated if adopting the new draft.

Cases

Alabaster v Woolwich Building Society (ECJ 30.3.04, C-147/02)

Beckman v Dynamco Whicheloe Macfarlane Ltd
(2002 ECR1 4893 ECJ)

BMK Holdings Ltd v Logue (1993 ICR 601 EAT)

*Boor v Ministre de la Fonction Publique et de la Reforme
Administration* (11.11.04 C-425/02)

Bryans v Northumberland College of Arts & Technology
(1995 People Management 10/95)

Buchan v Secretary of State for Employment (1997 IRLR 80)

Cobley v Forward Technology Industires plc (Court of Appeal,
15.5.03)

Contex Drouzhba Ltd v Wiseman and anor.(2006 All ER (D)40Nov)

Cureton v Mark Insulations Ltd (2006 EWHC 2279 QB)

Dacas v Brook Street Bureau (UK) Ltd (2004 ICR 1437)

Day v T. Pickles Farms Ltd (1999 IRLR 217)

Denco v Joinson (1991 ICR 172 EAT)

Dentmaster (UK) Ltd v Kent (IDS 601, 11/97)

Dillon v Rentokil Initial UK Ltd

D'Jan of London Ltd (Copp v D'Jan) (1BCLC 561 1994)

Dorchester Finance Co Ltd & Anor. v Stebbing and ors
(1989 BLLC 498)

Dunedin Independent plc v Welsh (Scottish Court of Session)

Enterprise Glass Co Ltd v Miles (1990 EAT 538/89)

Fleming v Secretary of State for Trade & Industry (1997 IRLR 682)

*Fiorentino Comm Guiseppe Srl v Farnest and anor (Directors of
Portofino Collections (London) Ltd)* (2005 All ER(D) 176)

*Forengingen of Arbejdsledere I Danmark v Daddy's Dance Hall
A/S* (1988 IRLR 315)

Forster v Cartwright Black Solicitors (UKEAT/0179/04/DM)

Fox Gregory (FG) v Spinks and anor (2006 EWCA Civ 1544)

Gwyer & Assocs and anor, v London Wharf (Limehouse) Ltd & ors (Times 24.1.03)

Hardman v Mallon (t/a Orchard Lodge Nursing Home) (2002 IRLR 516 EAT)

Haringey Council v Al-Azzawi (2002 IDS 703)

Heffer v Secretary of State for Trade and Industry (25.9.96 EAT 355/96)

Helmet Integrated Systems Ltd v Tunnard & ors (2006 EWCA Civ 1735)

Horkulak v Cantor Fitzgerald (HC 31.1.2003)

Howard v Millrise Ltd (in liquidation) and anor (UKEAT /0658/04/LA)

Item Software (UK) Ltd v Fassihi & ors (Ch.Div. 5.12.02)

Ivey v Secretary of State for Employment (1997 IRLR 80)

James v Greenwich Council (EAT 21.12.06 0006/06)

Jones v Tower Boot case the Court of Appeal (1997 ICR 254 CA)

Landeshaupstadt Kiel v Jaeger (2003 IRLR 804 ECJ)

Martin v South Bank University (C-4/01, 11/2003 ECJ)

McLean v Secretary of State for Employment (1992 (S) EAT 672/91)

National Rivers Authority v Alfred McAlpine Homes East Ltd

R v Carl Rigby (IoD Directors Handbook)

R v Ian Leaf (Times 13.10.05)

Re Mea Corporation, Secretary of State for Trade & Industry v Aviss [2006 All ER (D) 291(Jul)]

RCO Support Systems v Unison (2002 IRLR 401)

Secretary of State for Trade & Industry v Bottrill (1998 IRLR 120)

Secretary of State for Trade & Industry v Holler (2006 All ER 232)

Smith v Henniker-Major (High Court, 17.10.01)

Tesco Stores Ltd v Pook (2004 IRLB 618 EAT)

Trojan Developments (Times 16.1.04)

UK Safety Group v Hearne (1998)

Viggosdottir v Islandspostur (Iceland Post Ltd) (EFTA court 22.3.02)

Williams and anor v Natural Life Health Foods Ltd and anor (Times 9.1.97)

Wilson v St Helens Borough Council (1999 IRLR 706)

Other titles from Thorogood

THE A-Z OF EMPLOYMENT PRACTICE (2nd Edition)

David Martin
£19.99 paperback, £42.00 hardback

This book provides comprehensive, practical guidance on personnel law and practice at a time when employers are faced with a maze of legislation, obligations and potential penalties. It provides detailed and practical advice on what to do and how to do it.

The A to Z format ensures that sections appear under individual headings for instant ease of reference. The emphasis is not so much on the law as on its implications; the advice is expert, clear and practical, with a minimum of legal references. Checklists, procedures and examples are all given as well as warnings on specific pitfalls.

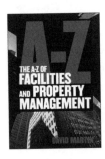

THE A-Z OF FACILITIES AND PROPERTY MANAGEMENT

David Martin
£19.99 paperback, £49.99 ring-bound

Inefficient control of property assets is costing industry £18 billion every year, according to the Royal Institution of Chartered Surveyors. Every organisation which either owns or leases its building is 'in property' but few seem to tackle the subject in a professional manner.

This valuable new reference provides detailed and expert guidance in an accessible A-Z format which enables the user to search quickly and to focus on each particular topic rather than the subject being buried in a longer chapter. Case studies add helpful further background and the book includes valuable checklists and sample forms throughout.

Like all of David Martin's books, this is clear, concise and concentrates on what needs to be done in practice. It covers every aspect of Facilities Administration, Budgetary and Expenditure Control and Property Administration from Accommodation planning, Acquisition, Building works and Condition survey through Dilapidations, Environmental considerations, Health and safety and insurance to Maintenance, Outsourcing, Privity of contract, Rating, Underletting, VAT, Waste and Zoning.

THE COMPANY SECRETARY'S DESKTOP GUIDE

Roger Mason

£16.99 paperback

Written in a clear, jargon-free style, this is a comprehensive guide to the complex legislation and procedures governing all aspects of the company secretary's work. The Company Secretary's role becomes more demanding with every change to the law and practice. The author's considerable experience as both Company Secretary and lecturer and author has ensured a manual that is expert, practical and easy to access.

THE CREDIT CONTROLLER'S DESKTOP GUIDE
Proven procedures and techniques for getting paid on time and preserving cash

Roger Mason

£16.99 paperback

Clear and jargon-free, this is an expert and practical guide to the techniques of effective credit control. This book takes account of all the recent changes to the law and practice, including: winding up, bankruptcy, receivership and administration, following implementation of The Enterprise Act 2002; statutory interest; obtaining judgment for unpaid debts; the abolition of Crown Preference and the effect on ordinary creditors; new rules concerning the recovery of VAT when there is a bad debt; what is available from Companies House; the latest thinking on retention of title clauses in conditions of sale.

DEVELOPING AND MANAGING TALENT

How to match talent to the role and convert it to a strength

Sultan Kermally

£12.99 paperback, £24.99 hardback

Effective talent management is crucial to business development and profitability. Talent management is no soft option; on the contrary, it is critical to long-term survival.

This book offers strategies and practical guidance for finding, developing and above all keeping talented individuals. After explaining what developing talent actually means to the organisation, he explores the e-dimension and the global dimension. He summarises what the 'gurus' have to say on the development of leadership talent. Included are valuable case studies drawn from Hilton, Volkswagen, Unilever, Microsoft and others.

EXIT RIGHT

Achieving a golden goodbye by realising the maximum value for your business

Barrie Pearson

£16.99 paperback, £35.00 hardback

This book offers comprehensive, streetwise and practical 'how to' help for every step involved in selling or floating your business. Various exit routes are considered, as he explains all the steps required to maximise the profit from your sale: deciding on the route and timing, how to choose advisers, grooming your business for disposal, valuing the business, finding prospective purchasers, negotiating the sale, steering safely to completion and how to eliminate losses before selling. This book is a goldmine of expert advice, written by a highly skilled professional who later employed his own advice to achieve spectacular success.

HIGH-PERFORMANCE CONSULTING SKILLS
The internal consultant's guide to value-added performance

Mark Thomas

£14.99 paperback, £24.99 hardback

This book provides a practical understanding of the skills required to become a high-performance internal consultant, whatever ones own area of expertise. It will help you to: market your services and build powerful internal networks; secure greater internal client commitment to initiatives and change projects; enhance your own worth and value to the organisation; develop stronger more productive working relationships with internal clients.

THE COMPLETE GUIDE TO INTERNATIONAL FINANCIAL REPORTING STANDARDS
Including IAS and interpretation

Ralph Tiffin

£18.99 paperback, £29.99 hardback

This book is not a re-write of the standards but rather summarises the issues which give rise to the standard practice, explaining the accounting and disclosure requirements and practical problems of compliance. The accounting ideas behind them and the effect on financial statements of each of the Standards, is explained.

SUCCESSFUL BUSINESS PLANNING

Norton Paley

£14.99 paperback, £29.99 hardback

"Growth firms with a written business plan have increased their revenues 69 per cent faster over the past five years than those without a written plan."

FROM A SURVEY BY PRICEWATERHOUSECOOPERS

We know the value of planning – in theory. But either we fail to spend the time required to go through the thinking process properly, or we fail to use the plan effectively. Paley uses examples from real companies to turn theory into practice.

THE SHORTER MBA

A practical approach to the key business skills

Barrie Pearson and Neil Thomas

£35.00 Hardback

A succinct distillation of the skills that you need to be successful in business. Most people can't afford to give up two years to study for an MBA. This pithy, practical book presents all the essential theory, practiced and techniques taught to MBA students – ideal for the busy practising executive. It is divided into three parts:

- Personal development
- Management skills
- Business development

Thorogood also has an extensive range of reports and special briefings which are written specifically for professionals wanting expert information.

For a full listing of all Thorogood publications, or to order any title, please call Thorogood Customer Services on 020 7749 4748 or fax on 020 7729 6110. Alternatively view our website at www.thorogoodpublishing.co.uk.

BUSINESS SEMINARS

Focused on developing your potential

Falconbury, the sister company to Thorogood publishing, brings together the leading experts from all areas of management and strategic development to provide you with a comprehensive portfolio of action-centred training and learning.

We understand everything managers and leaders need to be, know and do to succeed in today's commercial environment. Each product addresses a different technical or personal development need that will encourage growth and increase your potential for success.

- Practical public training programmes

- Tailored in-company training

- Coaching

- Mentoring

- Topical business seminars

- Trainer bureau/bank

- Adair Leadership Foundation

The most valuable resource in any organisation is its people; it is essential that you invest in the development of your management and leadership skills to ensure your team fulfil their potential. Investment into both personal and professional development has been proven to provide an outstanding ROI through increased productivity in both you and your team. Ultimately leading to a dramatic impact on the bottom line.

With this in mind Falconbury have developed a comprehensive portfolio of training programmes to enable managers of all levels to develop their skills in leadership, communications, finance, people management, change management and all areas vital to achieving success in today's commercial environment.

What Falconbury can offer you?

- Practical applied methodology with a proven results

- Extensive bank of experienced trainers

- Limited attendees to ensure one-to-one guidance

- Up to the minute thinking on management and leadership techniques

- Interactive training

- Balanced mix of theoretical and practical learning

- Learner-centred training

- Excellent cost/quality ratio

Falconbury In-Company Training

Falconbury are aware that a public programme may not be the solution to leadership and management issues arising in your firm. Involving only attendees from your organisation and tailoring the programme to focus on the current challenges you face individually and as a business may be more appropriate. With this in mind we have brought together our most motivated and forward thinking trainers to deliver tailored in-company programmes developed specifically around the needs within your organisation.

All our trainers have a practical commercial background and highly refined people skills. During the course of the programme they act as facilitator, trainer and mentor, adapting their style to ensure that each individual benefits equally from their knowledge to develop new skills.

Falconbury works with each organisation to develop a programme of training that fits your needs.

Mentoring and coaching

Developing and achieving your personal objectives in the workplace is becoming increasingly difficult in today's constantly changing environment. Additionally, as a manager or leader, you are responsible for guiding colleagues towards the realisation of their goals. Sometimes it is easy to lose focus on your short and long-term aims.

Falconbury's one-to-one coaching draws out individual potential by raising self-awareness and understanding, facilitating the learning and performance development that creates excellent managers and leaders. It builds renewed self-confidence and a strong sense of 'can-do' competence, contributing significant benefit to the organisation. Enabling you to focus your energy on developing your potential and that of your colleagues.

Mentoring involves formulating winning strategies, setting goals, monitoring achievements and motivating the whole team whilst achieving a much improved work life balance.

Falconbury – Business Legal Seminars

Falconbury Business Legal Seminars specialises in the provision of high quality training for legal professionals from both in-house and private practice internationally.

The focus of these events is to provide comprehensive and practical training on current international legal thinking and practice in a clear and informative format.

Event subjects include, drafting commercial agreements, employment law, competition law, intellectual property, managing an in-house legal department and international acquisitions.

For more information on all our services please contact Falconbury on +44 (0) 20 7729 6677 or visit the website at: www.falconbury.co.uk.